LIFE INSURANCE, ANNUITIES AND PENSIONS

ARTHUR PEDOE FIA, FSA, FCIA, now retired, was for many years life manager and actuary for Canada with the Prudential Assurance Company of England.

COLIN E. JACK FCIA, FSA, succeeded Mr. Pedoe at the Prudential. He is now a consulting actuary and a director of the National Reinsurance Company of Canada.

Although Canada has made outstanding contributions to the theory and practice of life insurance and pensions, this book, originally published in 1964, remains unique as a text designed specifically for Canadian use. This revised and updated edition follows the format of the original, dealing with the fundamentals of life insurance from its first actuarial principles, with notes on historical origins, and special references to present Canadian conditions.

An invaluable text for students, the book is also a fundamental reference for professionals in life insurance and organizations serving the fields of life insurance, annuities, and pensions.

'Mr. Pedoe's book proffers an excellent survey of the functional field of Canadian life insurance, reflecting the author's long years of practical experience in the industry.' *The Canadian Chartered Accountant*

LIFE INSURANCE, ANNUITIES & PENSIONS

A Canadian Text

THIRD EDITION

Arthur Pedoe, FIA, FSA, FCIA

Colin E. Jack, FCIA, FSA

UNIVERSITY OF TORONTO PRESS
Toronto Buffalo London

Toronto Buffalo London
Printed in Canada
Reprinted in 2018

Canadian Cataloguing in Publication Data

Pedoe, Arthur, 1897–
Life insurance, annuities & pensions

Includes index.
ISBN 0-8020-2316-9
ISBN 978-1-4875-8730-7 (paper)
1. Insurance, Life – Canada. 2. Annuities – Canada. 3. Pensions – Canada. I. Jack, Colin E. II. Title.

HG9010.P4 1978 368.3′00971 C78-001074-4

Preface to the Third Edition

The first and second editions of this book (as well as previous editions in mimeographed form) were the work of Arthur Pedoe, one of Canada's best known actuaries who contributed many papers to professional journals, and who is still, in his eightieth year, a keen student of life insurance and finance.

The book is available to all persons interested in life insurance but has been used mainly as a text for the courses of the Life Underwriters Association of Canada. When the question of a new edition arose, Arthur Pedoe did not wish to undertake the labour involved. The Association invited me to undertake the revision, with his consent. He has given me complete freedom to revise the text; I thank him for his confidence and take the opportunity of recording in print the great debt which I owe to him for what I learned in twenty-three years as his junior.

It is no easy task to revise the work of another; each of us has his own modes of expression, his attitudes, and his prejudices. I have tried to avoid petty changes made simply to display mine. The main problem is to decide when to patch and when to rewrite. I have undoubtedly patched in many cases where I ought to have rewritten and *vice versa*, rather like the judge who said he had in his day convicted many innocent persons and acquitted many guilty ones, but hoped that, on average, justice had been done.

It may seem strange that the most complete rewriting has been in the material concerning the Family Income Plan, a subject on which Arthur Pedoe was an authority, and the development of which was undoubtedly furthered by his writings. As explained in the text, the Family Income Plan as such has largely disappeared, but it was the forerunner of 'decreasing term,' which now plays a very important part either as a separate policy or a rider in a large proportion of insurance programmes.

Other extensive rewriting may be found in chapters on pensions; on financial statements, largely to reflect the increasing importance therein of segregated funds; and on inflation, made necessary by changes in attitude due to the performance of the stock market since the last edition was published; it should be mentioned that the possibility of this happening was not unforeseen in the previous text.

Several references to British and U.S. practice have been deleted, particularly as regards pensions; legislation in that field differs so widely between countries that comparisons are of little value. The final chapter on Social Insurance has been omitted, as not being altogether relevant; moreover, information on the Canada Pension Plan and the Quebec Pension Plan is available elsewhere. Some government legislation of 1977 was not, unfortunately, enacted in time to be treated in this edition.

It would be impossible to mention all of the people who have helped me in one way or another with my work. To the National Reinsurance Company of Canada are due thanks for office space and stationery, and my friends there for typing, photocopying and other little kindnesses. Many of my former colleagues at the Prudential of England and friends at the Sun Life of Canada helped me out when I needed information. Special thanks are due to the ladies in the Sun Life Library and the staff at the office of the Department of Insurance in Montreal.

Individual acknowledgments ought to be recorded for the assistance given by those who read and suggested revisions to whole chapters or to important sections, namely: Archie MacCracken and Charlie Black on Term Riders and Special Plans, Ian Leznoff on Disability Benefits, George Chalmers and Ron Till on Accident Benefits, Alan Keltie on Selection, Frank Morewood on Group Insurance, Jean Grégoire on Pensions, Bill Wilson on Statements, Doug Parkin on Investments, John Galbraith on Inflation, Claire Sheehan on the history of CREF, Donald Maier and Alex Sweeton on Industrial Insurance, and Sam Eckler on Fraternals. I should make it clear that what has finally appeared is not necessarily exactly what they proposed. I must accept responsibility for what appears in print.

Finally thanks to Louise, for typing, proof-reading, and putting up with me.

COLIN E. JACK

Montreal, Canada
July 1977

Contents

Introduction

The object of this book is to provide a comprehensive narrative of the history, development, status, and practice of life insurance, annuities, and pensions in Canada.

Canada has occupied a leading position in life insurance for many years. At the present time the people of Canada lead the world in the ratio of voluntarily purchased life insurance to national income. Life insurance was one of the first Canadian "exports": as long ago as the 1880's, when Canada was practically unknown internationally, Canadian life insurance companies were operating in several countries abroad. By the late 1920's they were operating in fifty countries throughout the world. Further, the record of Canadian government supervision of life insurance companies is unsurpassed by any other country.

It was a curious phenomenon that professional men and others entering the service of, or conducting business with, Canadian life insurance companies and seeking a text to assist them in their understanding of the business as conducted in Canada, would have had to depend on an American text which in most cases would be entirely confined to the law and practice in the United States. There has been no Canadian text available to the public and the present book seeks to remedy this.

This book is addressed primarily to employees and officials of life insurance companies engaged in the specialized work of administration, accounting, law, medicine, finance and investment, and sales. Although it is a complete text in itself it should prove of value to those who would wish to continue further with their specialties. Care has been taken to indicate the various professional bodies and their proceedings which cater to these specialized fields. To the actuary this text should prove a satisfactory inclusive introduction.

No preliminary knowledge is assumed. This text should prove a splendid training for a college student, indicating the necessary compromise between theory and practice in adapting actuarial science to a major economic need. However, there has been no deliberate writing down to the reader or avoidance of any difficult point. A sincere effort has been made to explain matters as simply as possible.

CHAPTER ONE

Some Early History and Background

THE CONCEPT OF LIFE INSURANCE

In 1757 a petition was presented to the British Parliament with the following purpose:

> That great numbers of His Majesty's subjects, whose subsistence principally depends on the salaries, stipends, and other incomes payable to them, during their natural lives, or on the profits arising from several trades, occupation, labour, and industry, are very desirous of entering into a society for insuring the lives of each other, in order to extend after their decease the benefits of their present incomes to their families and relations, who may otherwise be reduced to extreme poverty and distress, by the premature death of their several husbands, fathers, and friends, which humane intention the petitioners humbly apprehend cannot be effectually carried into execution without His Majesty's royal authority to incorporate them for that purpose.

This was to lead to the founding of the first life insurance company as we understand the term today. No better statement than the above could be made of the purpose of life insurance: the replacement of earning power on death for the protection of dependents.

As an indication of the extent of this protection, the amount of life insurance in force with life insurance companies and fraternal associations at the end of 1974 was in Canada $190,000 millions ($190 billion) and in the United States $1,900,000 millions ($1,900 billion). This means that in these countries contracts have been entered into voluntarily for these amounts to be paid during the period covered by the present generation. The amounts stated are in each case about two and a half times what they were ten years earlier.

The provision for a pension to a man in his declining years is "protection" as much as the provision for widows and orphans. Life insurance companies have always dealt in providing such pensions for retirement, but the growth of such business in recent years, as will be indicated, has been extraordinary. The inclusion in life insurance contracts of benefits payable on total disability has been a modern development of life insurance as has been the provision of additional amounts payable on accidental death.

VERY MODERN YET VERY OLD

Although co-operation to provide amounts payable on death and to provide income to the aged has been one of man's earliest social endeavours, the life insurance and pension business is still in the development stage. New forms of life insurance have been evolved in recent years which pre-suppose entirely new concepts of the business; these will be examined later. As for pensions, the business may be described as very much in a state of flux due to recent developments.

Well over four thousand years ago the merchants of Mesopotamia had already a highly developed technique in business affairs. They made contracts and bought and sold all kinds of wares in far-off countries—wools, spices, silver, and slaves, traversing the then-known world in their caravans and ships. The caravan and the ship represented an accumulation of wealth subject to many hazards and the concept of "sharing the risk" first developed in connection with marine hazards. With marine insurance, the idea of paying a sum on the loss of the master of the ship would normally follow.

Among the ancient Egyptians, Greeks, and Romans, the merchants were treated as a subordinate class and trading was considered dishonourable. Our western civilization has its origin in the Mediterranean basin and the struggle for power there may be looked upon as between trader and warrior, ending when warrior Rome levelled to the ground the great trading city of Carthage in 146 B.C.[1] Our western civilization has its origin in the Roman and Greek traditions. As most of what we know of ancient times has come to us from the writings of these earlier civilizations, it may explain the fragmentary nature of our knowledge of early insurance practices.

There is no intention to trace here the many ways by which, in the early development of towns, efforts were made to mitigate the hardships arising from the death of the breadwinner. This became necessary when the lives of people were first divorced from direct dependency on the soil and its fruits. The church and philanthropy played their part and the

[1] Miriam Beard, *A History of the Business Man* (New York, 1938).

association of men in guilds—whether fraternities or by trades—logically developed into the payment of benefits to those in need whether due to fire, sickness, or death. In those days opportunities for investment were limited and contributions would be sought mainly as the need arose. There was also the primitive desire—almost as old as man himself—for proper burial, and funds to provide this were among the earliest co-operative efforts of civilized man.

TERMINOLOGY

Insurance may be described as the undertaking of the liability to pay a sum of money on the happening of a certain event. In *life insurance* one party called the *insurer* undertakes to pay a specified sum called the *sum insured* upon the death of a specified person called the *life insured* in consideration of payment to the insurer of a specified sum or sums called the *premiums*. The document evidencing the arrangement is called the *policy*. The party effecting the contract is known as the *insured*. The party to whom the sum insured is to be payable is known as the *beneficiary*. The phrase sum insured is also used when a specified sum is payable on the survival of a party to the end of a specified period.

The insured, life insured, and beneficiary can be one and the same person as when a sum insured is payable on the survival to the end of a specified period of the person who effected the insurance on his own life and is payable to that person. Most often the insured and the life insured are the same person. In cases where one person (the insured) effects insurance to be payable on the death of another person (the life insured) it is referred to as a *third-party policy*.

When the policy states that specified sums are to be paid on the survival of a named party over various consecutive periods it is called a *life annuity*.

A life insurance policy and a life annuity policy are closely connected as both relate to amounts expressed to be payable as dependent on human life. The statements made in this section are not intended to be definitions but first explanations of terms to be used. In life insurance, phrases have been used quite loosely for many years so that a strict definition may not always be possible. There are legal requisites for a life insurance contract which will be dealt with later.

Insurance or Assurance? It will be noted that except in quotations we have used the word *insurance*, instead of *assurance*. In the early days the word assurance was generally used for life insurance but not for other forms of insurance as marine, fire, etc. Some well-known life insurance companies adopted the word assurance in naming their companies when they were formed following the early use of the word but such distinctions have ceased to be of any practical significance. As there is no purpose in using two words which currently have identical meanings so far as our subject is concerned, we will use the word insurance throughout this text irrespective of the class of insurance under discussion.

THE FIRST LIFE INSURANCE POLICY

The first life insurance policy which we would recognize as such was written in the reign of Queen Elizabeth I, in 1583 in London, England, and comes to our attention because the claim was disputed and so noted in the legal records of the time.

Richard Martin, a citizen and alderman of London took out insurance on the life of William Gybbons. The policy was for a period of twelve months and the rate of premium was 8 per cent. Gybbons died within the period of a calendar year and the dispute arose from the contention that twelve lunar months (28 days each) was meant. The underwriters to whom the premium was paid were merchants of the city of London and they lost their case.

The wording of the policy[2] indicates that it was not the first of its kind and has such a familiar ring that we note with surprise it was written almost four hundred years ago. However, nowadays, we do not begin our policies with the words: "In the name of God, Amen" or end them with the prayer: "God send the said William Gybbons health and long life." A point of interest is the occurrence of the phrase, "the underwriting hereof by the assurers hereafter subscribed" and the insurers severally signed the bond, namely the sixteen underwriters with the various amounts they each accepted, the largest being £50 for a total of just over £383.

It will be noted that the policy on the life of William Gybbons was for one year only and almost another one hundred and eighty years were to pass before insurances for the duration of life were commercially obtainable. This long delay was due to the lack of knowledge about death rates and their commercial use; this knowledge grew to become the science of life contingencies. The development of life insurance bogged down in the morass of gambling and wagering which culminated in the

[2]The complete wording is given in *Journal of the Institute of Actuaries*, vol. 25 (1885), p. 119.

bursting of the South Sea Bubble of 1720 and Law's Mississippi Scheme[3] and their aftermath.

The century following the year 1700 has been called "the Gambling Century": to drink deep and wager high were the hallmarks of the "young bloods" of that day. The gullibility of the public and the rage for "get rich quick" schemes are not just a modern phenomenon; they ran full riot in that century.

The sale of government annuities, giving the same rate to both old and young and the raising of funds by "tontine" schemes[4] and state lotteries were the desperate means of raising money used by governments of that day and all tended to bring discredit on legitimate attempts to develop life insurance. However it was during this century that the three main branches of insurance: marine, fire, and life (and in that order) became established and led the way to the sound development of the great institutions of the present day.

PLAGUES OR PESTILENCES

Another reason for the long delay in the successful establishment of life insurance was the repeated recurrence of plagues or pestilences. It was only when they devastated a country or a city that they are mentioned in history books. In the cities, where it would be expected that life insurance would originate, living conditions were extremely hazardous until after 1750. This was due to the appalling lack of standards of cleanliness, the lack of systems of sewage disposal and the ignorance of the cause of disease generally. The bubonic plague (swelling of the glands) originating in the East was just one of the pestilences which periodically spread to Western Europe and England. This was the cause of the Black Death which in some areas of Europe, including Britain, killed two-thirds of the population in the middle of the fourteenth century. It was also the cause of the Great Plague of London, England in 1665. For some reason this plague disappeared, at least as far as England was concerned, after the Great Plague of 1665 and outbreaks in Europe were localized after that date. It seems that about 1750 the death rate became relatively stable in Western Europe and Britain, and in more recent years there has been a definite trend downwards in death rates. Disturbances over certain years have arisen due to two world wars and the influenza epidemic of 1918, but the long-term trends have not been affected.

[3]See notes at end of this chapter.

[4]Tontine: where benefits are shared among survivors only. See Index for various references throughout the text.

THE OLD EQUITABLE

This chapter was introduced by the preamble of a petition presented in 1757 to form a life insurance corporation. It was refused as were other attempts to obtain a charter; the law officers of the Crown giving as one of their reasons that it had no share capital. However, yielding to the persistence of the promoters they did suggest that the object desired could be attained by forming a "voluntary partnership." On September 7, 1762, the deed was signed forming the "Old Equitable," as it is generally known, which is not to be confused with life insurance companies bearing a similar name in Canada or the United States.

The full name of the society was "The Society for Equitable Assurances on Lives and Survivorships." The "practical experiment" (as the law officers of the Crown described it) in which it was to engage was to grant insurances for the whole of life on payment of level annual premiums varying with age at entry. The word "Equitable" in the title related to the variation of the premium with the age at entry. Further the Society proposed to make provision for a reserve fund which, as will be demonstrated in Chapter 7, is essential for a level annual premium plan.

The Society provided that in the case of some epidemic, described in the policy as a "time of public calamity," substantial reductions in the sums payable at death could be made temporarily and if necessary to one quarter of the sum insured. Further, if the premiums proved inadequate, members could be called upon for additional payments. Any such claims either withheld or additional premiums paid were to accrue at 3 per cent interest per annum for the benefit of the policyholder or his estate. Fortunately these precautions proved unnecessary and although progress was slow at first the society grew steadily until by the year 1800 the Old Equitable had 5,129 policies in force for a total of almost £4 million sums insured. What was even greater evidence of its success was that it had accumulated an insurance fund of one million sterling, which was a substantial sum in those days. Further, it was granting substantial "dividends" to its members in the form of additional amounts of paid-up life insurance.[5]

Thus by the year 1800 scientific life insurance can be said to have been successfully inaugurated. The next fifty years, that is, the first half of the nineteenth century, were fruitful as evidenced by the establishment of a number of English companies, seven United States companies, and one Canadian company, all devoted to the business of life insurance. Among

[5]See notes at end of this chapter.

them were some of the world's outstanding companies of the present time. If we consider the long history of human endeavour—many tens of thousands of years—we note the short period during which scientific life insurance has been operating—just two hundred years.

GAMBLING VERSUS INSURANCE

We referred to the seventeen hundreds as the Gambling Century and stated that the prevalent gambling or wagering ("betting" as one would call it today) delayed the development of life insurance. The words "insurance" and "assurance" were freely used by the betting establishments then in vogue. One pernicious practice was to bet on the recovery or death of any well-known personage as soon as a paragraph appeared in the newspapers of the day announcing that he was ill. The odds offered fluctuated wildly as rumours circulated one way or another. The persons participating had no interest, financial or otherwise, in the death of the party other than the bet being won or lost.

Economic life is impossible without hazard or the taking of risk. It is the prudent thing to enter into an arrangement whereby on the happening of a certain event which would result in financial loss, the loss thereby suffered is covered. The social benefit of the arrangement is obvious. Insurance is the reverse of gambling which is the deliberate risk of gain or loss without any social benefit. The purpose of insurance is to replace loss. Gambling arises when no benefit accrues to the participants in the taking of the hazard; the mere exchange of money is not a benefit in itself.

It was a landmark in legal history when the Life Assurance Act 1774 was enacted by the British Parliament outlawing gambling so far as life insurance was concerned. It was entitled *An Act for regulating Insurances upon Lives, and for prohibiting all such Insurances, except in Cases where the Persons insuring shall have an Interest in the Life or Death of the Persons insured.* It established the principle that policies of life insurance were only valid in law when the insured had an *insurable interest* in the life insured. This doctrine has been developed out of a regard for public welfare rather than the protection of the insurance company.

This legal principle will be referred to again in Chapter 16 but to illustrate its importance the following Quebec case should be of interest. The application in May, 1894, was for life insurance by one Antoine Pettigrew, aged 66, and was for $2,000; the insurance was made payable to one J. N. Anctil. In reply to the question of relationship the answer (translated) was "My protector if at any time I am in need." The policy became a claim within two years. The company after investigation refused payment on the grounds that it was a wagering policy and as no insurable interest existed, it was invalid in accordance with the Civil Code of Lower Canada. Although the occupation of Pettigrew was given as "farmer," he had no occupation or means but was given odd jobs around Anctil's hotel. Here he had access at all times to plenty of liquor, which hastened his death. The court upheld the company both in the original jury trial, the Appeal Court, the Supreme Court, and the Privy Council.

A great responsibility devolves on the officials of life insurance companies to ensure that the beneficent operations of life insurance are not abused or any life endangered thereby. The relative insignificance of the claim compared with the cost of fighting this case through to the highest court illustrates that in this case such responsibility was realized. The company involved was the Manufacturers Life Insurance Company.

PRESBYTERIAN MINISTERS' FUND

It is important to note that the first life insurance benefits granted on the North American continent were by a church organization incorporated in 1759 which under the name "Presbyterian Ministers' Fund" is still in operation with assets of some $150 million. The original name was "The Corporation for Relief of Poor and Distressed Presbyterian Ministers, and of the Poor and Distressed Widows and Children of Presbyterian Ministers." It started in 1717 as a fund for pious uses and developed into an organization in the hands of trustees who undertook to pay certain pensions for which definite specified contributions had to be made.[6] It was located in Philadelphia and at that time the United States was under the British flag.

Ten years later in 1769 a similar organization entitled "Corporation for the Relief of the Widows and Children of Clergymen in the Communion of the Church of England in America" was set up to operate in a similar fashion. Both these organizations were assisted in their early days by voluntary donations by non-members and hence could not strictly, at the time of their organization, be considered life insurance companies as we understand the term today.

Among the obstacles which the early life insurance companies had to overcome, particularly in Canada and the United States, was the prej-

[6] A copy of one of the early policies dated in 1761 is given in *Transactions*, Actuarial Society of America, vol. 1 (1890), p. 13.

udice that to insure one's life was working against "divine providence." That the first corporations set up in North America to provide life insurance were by ministers of the Gospel should counter any religious prejudices which may still exist. An appropriate quotation from the Bible is I Timothy 5, v. 8: "But if any provide not for his own, and specially for those of his own house, he hath denied the faith, and is worse than an infidel."

THE ACTUARY

The actuary with his special duties occupies a prominent position in the field of life insurance, pensions, and annuities. The choice of the title "actuary" for the chief executive officer of the Old Equitable was probably an antiquarian whimsy of Edward Rowe Mores who drew up the deed of co-partnership on which it was established.[7] The name originated from the title given to the official recording the proceedings of the Senate under the Roman Empire. The use of the title "actuary" by the Old Equitable gave the name to the profession.[8]

The actuary's main work in life insurance is the calculation of premium rates and of the reserves or funds which have to be held to fulfil the future obligations of the life insurance company under its policies. From this the surplus earnings of the company are obtained. The actuary is concerned with the allotment of dividend to policies, that is, the share of surplus earnings to be apportioned to individual policies when these have the right to share in surplus earnings. A special task of the actuary is keeping the records of the mortality experienced. Apart from the duties stated the actuary's work may extend to the selection of risks, drafting policy forms, and the preparation of the government returns. In recent years the scope of actuarial practice has widened to include the fields of government social insurance, medical care, and social security generally. The actuary's work in pension funds corresponds to that outlined regarding life insurance with the significant difference that an important part of the pension field operates outside the life insurance industry and government schemes.

Under various laws in Canada, both federal and provincial, dealing with life insurance and pension plans, an actuary is required to be qualified as a Fellow of the Canadian Institute of Actuaries (FCIA).

[7] The Institute of Actuaries, *Year Book 1961–1962*.

[8] William Morgan, F.R.S., held the post of Actuary to the "Old Equitable" from 1775 to 1830. His son succeeded him in the post which they together occupied for a total of ninety-five years. Alec and the late Evelyn Waugh, the well-known novelists, are direct descendants of the Morgans.

This institute was incorporated in 1965 by an Act of the Parliament of Canada. It is the successor to the Canadian Association of Actuaries which in 1946 replaced the Actuaries Club of Toronto, founded in 1907, incorporating at the same time the Actuaries Club of Winnipeg.

The first formal organization of actuaries to be established was the Institute of Actuaries, founded in London, England, in 1848; in Scotland, the Faculty of Actuaries was formed in 1856; both are still flourishing. In the United States, the Actuarial Society of America was formed in 1889 and the American Institute of Actuaries in 1909; they combined in 1949 under the name of the Society of Actuaries.

Examinations of the Canadian Institute of Actuaries are held jointly with those of the Society, the examinations being identical in those parts dealing with theory but differing to some extent in those dealing with practice, reflecting differences in legislation between Canada and the United States.

Fellows of the Society, of the Institute of Great Britain, and of the Faculty may obtain the degree of FCIA after passing a special examination to demonstrate their familiarity with Canadian practice.

Canada occupies a special place in actuarial education. Courses in mathematics and actuarial science covering the early parts of the actuarial examinations are given by several Canadian universities. The actuarial courses given by the University of Toronto were the first ever given in any university throughout the world. The Actuaries Club was a pioneer in actuarial education as regards the later and more technical examinations and this work has been carried on by the succeeding bodies.[9]

Another actuarial organization in the United States is the Conference of Actuaries in Public Practice founded in 1950 and operating from Chicago. Its main object is to unite the profession of public practising actuaries. Its published *Proceedings* emphasize this interest by dealing with pensions, employees benefits, social security matters, and consulting actuaries problems.

NOTES

SOUTH SEA BUBBLE

This was the name given to a series of financial projects which originated with the incorporation of the South Sea Company in London, England, in 1711. The

[9]The origin of this pioneering educational work is given in a paper by the author, "The Actuary in Canada," *Record*, American Institute of Actuaries, vol. 24 (1935). Some early history of the Actuaries Club or, as it was commonly known, the Actuaries Club of Toronto, is given in the paper mentioned.

idea was that the state should sell certain trading monopolies to the company in return for a sum of money to be advanced in reduction of the British national debt. As the national debt consisted of annuities sold by the state, that is cash sums paid as a fixed income for life, the project was to exchange these government annuities for South Sea Company shares which were to be issued at a high premium. From $128^1/_2$ at the beginning of the year 1720, the price of the shares rose to 1,000 in July. The success of the South Sea scheme encouraged a host of imitators and the result was a wild orgy of speculation of such extremes as to be almost unbelievable. The result was inevitable and by November the price of South Sea shares had fallen to 135. The collapse of the Bubble ruined thousands and the plight of those who had exchanged their government annuities for the shadow of a dividend on South Sea shares was serious.

JOHN LAW (1671–1729)

Scottish economist and originator of the Mississippi scheme. Born in Edinburgh, he obtained the confidence of the Regent of France following the death of Louis XIV. Louisiana was then a French possession and a company was founded to exploit the resources of the Mississippi Valley and, in return for various monopolies granted by the French state, it undertook payment of the French national debt. Speculation reached an unparalleled height by December 1719 when the sum which would be needed to pay a five per cent dividend on the market value of the shares would have required eight times the current income. The result was inevitable.

THE OLD EQUITABLE

A history of the Old Equitable (M. E. Ogborn, *Equitable Assurances*, London, 1962) adds much to our knowledge of the part played by that company in establishing the principles of life insurance. Its subsequent history is also illuminating. It was a mutual company and in 1816 the policyholders voted to restrict all dividend payments to the five thousand oldest policies in the society. Thus a new policyholder would not receive any dividends until his policy had been many years in force.

As a result the society entered a period of stagnation which all but terminated its proud history. Its total assets which had risen to a peak of £11 million declined to less than £5 million by 1869 during a period when the life insurance business was growing substantially. It was not until 1892 after the last of the members entitled to vested rights under the resolution of 1816 had died that any change was made.

The revitalization of the Old Equitable was mainly due to Sir William Elderton who served the Society from 1913 until his death in 1962, filling, in succession, the offices of Actuary and Manager, President, and finally Chairman of the Board. Elderton was the outstanding actuary of his day with a worldwide reputation.

CHAPTER TWO

Life Insurance in Canada

THE BEGINNINGS OF LIFE INSURANCE IN CANADA

Very little is known of the early history of life insurance in Canada, and the following extract from Walford's *Insurance Cyclopaedia*, published in England in 1871, is worth recording:

> Prior to 1847 but little life insurance business had been transacted in Canada. The National Loan Fund of England was almost the only company in the field. In 1847 the Canada Life was founded at Hamilton. In the same year the Colonial of Edinburgh founded a branch in Canada. For several years the two last-named offices transacted nearly all the business of this class in the province; but the total was very small. ... Year by year new competitors entered the field, chiefly British offices; and by means of continuous competition, they in the end made the advantages of life insurance understood. About 1866, several of the American offices commenced operations in the province; and they infused into the business an amount of enterprise which it had never before experienced.

The records indicate that the Standard of Edinburgh had an agency in Quebec City in 1833 but the development of that company's early business in Canada was through the Colonial Life founded in Edinburgh in 1846 with the specific intention of developing life business abroad. The Colonial had very close associations with the Standard and later was absorbed by it.

THE FOUNDING OF THE CANADA LIFE, 1847

The reputed circumstances of the founding of Canada's first life insurance company, the Canada Life Assurance Company, should be of interest. According to a manuscript history in their library:

> A young man of Hamilton, Ontario, being desirous of obtaining life assurance, was compelled to travel to New York to comply with the requirements of a British company. That young man was Hugh C. Baker the founder and afterwards the President, Actuary and Manager of the Canada Life Assurance

Company. He was then local Manager of the Bank of Montreal and on his return to his home after this journey of 1,000 miles, by stage-coach, saddle and stream, he determined that his own countrymen should have an opportunity to obtain assurance protection without the necessity of travelling so far afield.

Other versions of this journey have appeared. One states[1] that it was an American company that sent Hugh C. Baker to New York for, presumably, his medical examination. It is rather puzzling why a British company should require an applicant to go to New York which at that time was a week's journey away and only reached with the greatest difficulty. As to the other version, there is no record of an American life insurance company doing business in Canada prior to 1850. Anyone planning to establish a life insurance company at the time of the journey, 1846, would undoubtedly visit either Britain or New York. It would appear from his personal medical history that Baker was a substandard life, possibly uninsurable by the standards of that day and this may have been a factor in his interest in the life insurance business. He was under thirty at the time of the journey and died in 1859 at the age of forty-two.

When Hugh C. Baker went to New York in 1846 the life insurance companies there had only been established a matter of months. The oldest, the Mutual of New York, opened for business on February 1, 1843,[2] and the New York Life in 1845. Canada's first life insurance company was thus among the first established on the continent of North America and originated in a small town in a sparsely populated area.

The original plan was to form a "mutual assurance society" like the Old Equitable and those recently organized in New York. However, the Legislative Council refused to grant a charter unless there was a share capital. Thus the Canada Life Assurance Company was incorporated with a capital of £50,000 in 500 shares of £100 each of which £1 per share was to be paid in.

The first policy issued by the Canada Life was dated November 9, 1847, and was for £500 on the life of Hugh C. Baker, the President. Baker's policy was expressed in sterling because the official currency of Canada at that time was sterling although everyday business was carried on in dollars. It was 1858 before this dual currency system was ended. The incident of Baker's journey does emphasize the remoteness and isolation of that part of Canada at that time. Hamilton then had a population of about 11,000 and the neighbouring city of Toronto some

[1]George H. Harris, *The President's Book* (Montreal: Sun Life, 1928).

[2]A tablet at 56 Wall Street, New York City, bears in part this inscription: "To the memory of Morris Robinson, a Canadian, born in Nova Scotia ... who as first president of the Mutual Life Insurance Company of New York, established on this spot the business of modern life insurance on the American Continent..."

25,000, about half of them new arrivals. The Canadian metropolis of that day was Montreal, with a population of less than 50,000, and the second city was Quebec with less than 40,000 population.

Baker was a self-taught mathematician and actuary and undoubtedly had more than a touch of genius. Many of his ideas were well ahead of his time. "To him may fairly be awarded the honor of being the first Canadian actuary."[3] He was succeeded on his death in 1859 by A. G. Ramsay who had been trained at the head office of one of the Scottish life offices. Ramsay was an actuary by training and a man of exceptional ability.

PIONEER DAYS

The difficulties which faced the new company cannot be exaggerated. Apart from the prejudice against life insurance, ready cash was scarce. Capital was even scarcer and attracted quite high rates of interest. Some of the early investments of the Canada Life were mortgages shown as yielding 12 per cent per annum "free of expense to the Company." The great majority of the people in Canada still lived close to the soil on which they depended for their livelihood.

The country was still struggling for self-government and the union of Upper and Lower Canada (the provinces of Ontario and Quebec) in 1841 was not functioning well. In 1846 the Corn Laws were repealed in England and the paralysis of the grain trade in Canada brought ruin to many. The burning of the Legislative Assembly in Montreal in 1849, during a riot, illustrates the unsettled political conditions of the time.

The dreaded cholera which had ravished Quebec City and Montreal in 1832 and 1834 reappeared in Canada, brought by Irish immigrants, and the scenes in the ports at entry, Quebec City and Montreal, were some of the unhappiest in Canadian history. It reached Toronto in 1849 and appeared again in 1854 with increased severity. These outbreaks were a cause of much concern to the young company.

The bright spot was that in the 1850's began the railway era with a large influx of English capital. While in 1850 Canada had only sixty-six miles of railway, by 1860 she had two thousand.[4] By Canada, here, is meant mainly Ontario and Quebec for Canada west of Ontario was still unknown country.

[3]T. B. Macaulay, *Proceedings*, International Congress of Actuaries (Paris, 1900).
[4]George M. Wrong, *The Canadians* (Toronto, 1938), p. 338.

THE CONFEDERATION ERA

The confederation of the four provinces of Ontario, Quebec, New Brunswick, and Nova Scotia, each with its own provincial government forming the Dominion of Canada, took place in 1867. It acted as a spur to the formation of life insurance companies, for the Canada Life was still the only one. The four which commenced business in the 1870's were: Mutual Life (1870), Sun Life (1871), Confederation Life (1871), and London Life (1874). Some details of these companies are given later in this chapter.

By 1871 the population of Canada had increased to 3,500,000 apart from about 100,000 in that vast territory from Ontario westward to the Coast, including British Columbia; there was no rail connection between the Maritimes and Central Canada.

The 1870's were difficult years economically, not only in Canada but in the United States and Britain. That the Canadian life insurance companies organized in that period survived is a tribute to the type of management and the effect of the supervision emanating from Ottawa. The earliest figures of life insurance in force in Canada are for the year 1867, indicating a total in force of $20 millions. By 1871, a space of four years, this had doubled, but it was not until 1879 that business in force doubled again to $86 millions. Illustrating the trials of the 1870's are the figures given in Table 2.1 of the number of companies and business in force in the State of New York.

TABLE 2.1

Year	No. of companies	Amount of life insurance in force
1859	14	$ 141 millions
1870	71	2,023 "
1879	29	1,439 "

CANADIAN COMPANIES ESTABLISHED IN THE 1870's

Mutual Life of Canada. It was twenty-three years after the founding of the Canada Life that the next Canadian life insurance company was formed and curiously it was also in what might be called a "backwoods hamlet," as Waterloo was in 1870. The local business men and farmers had already organized successfully a mutual fire insurance company. Apparently there was no difficulty in obtaining a provincial charter, although the proposed company was without any share capital and it was named the Ontario Mutual Life Assurance Company. The charter required the acceptance of 500 applications for at least $500,000 before any policies could be issued and it is recorded that these were mainly placed by the local member of the provincial legislature. The first president was Isaac E. Bowman, "M.P. of the United Canadas." The first general manager was William Hendry, who served from 1870 to 1897; he was a Scot by birth, brought up on a pioneer farm and a self-taught actuary. In the founding of the company Elizur Wright, a well-known actuary from Boston, Mass., was consulted by him. The company was reincorporated in 1878 with a Dominion charter and assumed its present name in 1900.

Sun Life of Canada. When in 1868 the new Parliament of the "United Canadas" passed a law requiring registration and deposits by insurance companies, the consequent withdrawal of one of the American companies led to the organization of the Sun Life by the Canadian representative of that New York company, M. Hamilton Gault. It commenced business in 1871 under the name of the Sun Mutual Life Insurance Company of Montreal, changed later to its present name. The dominating personalities responsible for the growth of the Sun Life were Robertson Macaulay who had been an official of the Canada Life for sixteen years and his son T. B. Macaulay. The latter may be ranked as one of Canada's outstanding actuaries and life insurance executives. Both father and son served as presidents of the Sun Life.

Confederation Life. The founder of the Confederation Life came to Canada as a boy from Scotland. He was intended to enter the Presbyterian ministry, but became prominent in business and finance. He was J. K. Macdonald, who was thirty-four when he founded the company in 1871 and was at that time (and for some years thereafter) treasurer of Peel County near Toronto. He had associated with him many of the leading citizens of the day and the first president of the Association was Sir Francis Hincks, who had occupied many prominent positions in the government and in financial circles and had been prime minister of Canada in 1851. Several members of the Macdonald family have served the Confederation as actuaries and senior executives, the last such member—a grandson of the founder—having been president.

In 1868 the new federal government of Canada passed its first Insurance Act to regulate the business of insurance and it was not long before the Minister of Finance felt the need for a deputy in insurance matters. In 1875 an insurance department was established at Ottawa, and Professor J. B. Cherriman of the University of Toronto, an outstanding mathematician and an actuary, was appointed to be the first Superintendent of Insurance. Professor Cherriman had played a prominent part in the founding of the Confederation Life, being its first actuary and a director at the time of his appointment. The prestige attaching to the position of Superintendent of Insurance has meant much in the history of life insurance in Canada both as to the type of civil servant appointed to the position and his influence with the chief executives of the companies under his jurisdiction.

London Life. In 1871 London, Ontario, was referred to as the "westernmost city in Canada" and had a population of 20,000. The company was founded in 1874 by Joseph Jeffery, manager of the local branch of Molson's Bank, with whom were associated a number of the business men of the city. Its early growth was painfully slow and again one must ascribe the foundation for its later success to another self-taught actuary, then aged twenty-eight, who was appointed manager in 1883—J. G. Richter. He rectified an impairment of capital by a call on the shareholders and among other changes he began in 1887 to issue *industrial life insurance*, i.e., insurance where the sums insured are for small amounts and the premiums are payable weekly (and sometimes monthly) and are collected at the homes of the insured. The latter is a particularly difficult kind of business to organize successfully and Richter's success may have been due to concentrating on this class of business until success was assured. Associated with Richter for many years and succeeding him was E. E. Reid, another brilliant "actuary executive," who did much to develop life insurance in Canada. Of all the Canadian companies organized prior to the turn of the century, only the London Life continued to transact industrial business although it had been tried by others.

OTHER CANADIAN COMPANIES ORGANIZED BEFORE 1900

In the 1880's the following Canadian life insurance companies commenced business: North American Life in 1881, with its president Alexander Mackenzie, the second prime minister of the Dominion of Canada; Manufacturers Life commenced business in 1887 with its president, Sir John A. Macdonald, the first prime minister of the Dominion of Canada and the master mind and spirit behind Confederation. The gentlemen mentioned had been the leaders of the Liberal and Conservative parties in Canada respectively. In the 1890's: the Excelsior Life commenced business in 1890, the Great-West Life (with its head office in Winnipeg) in 1892, both the Imperial Life and the Northern Life in 1897, and the Continental Life in 1899 (name changed to Zurich Life in 1965).

ECONOMY OF OPERATION OF THE EARLY COMPANIES

One of the striking aspects of the organization of the early Canadian life insurance companies was their economy of operation. According to the histories of several of the companies the costs of organization were trivial and no difficulty seems to have been encountered in the early years in meeting costs of operation, organization, commissions, and overhead, out of the premiums paid without touching the capital (where they had share capital). The founders and directors gave their services gratuitously until the company was established and even then their remuneration was on a minor or nominal scale. There appeared to be a sincere realization that life insurance was a special kind of business, almost religious in character, in the service of which satisfaction could be obtained outside of pecuniary gain alone.

THE ARMSTRONG-HUGHES INVESTIGATION

We now refer to a New York State investigation which, although primarily based on conditions in that state, had a strong reaction throughout both the United States and Canada. Its importance cannot be exaggerated so far as life insurance is concerned, but its influence extended far beyond the life insurance industry.

It has been said that life insurance practice on the North American Continent is B.A. or A.A., i.e., before or after the Armstrong-Hughes Investigation. It was set up by the government of the state of New York in 1905 to investigate the life insurance companies operating in that state. Although Senator Armstrong was the chairman of the committee, the counsel who directed the greater part of the inquiry, who wrote the subsequent report and drafted the ensuing legislation was Charles Evans Hughes, later Chief Justice of the Supreme Court of the United States.

The inquiry must be viewed as part of the social and economic history of the U.S. at the turn of the century. It was the culmination of the doctrine of laissez-faire in economic matters: that in business and manufacturing the law of the jungle should prevail and by the survival of the fittest, true progress would be achieved. Government regulation was an evil to be abhorred.

The reorganization of industry just prior to the turn of the century and the exploitation of the resources of a continent made the need for capital very pressing and the funds of the large life insurance companies of New York and adjoining states were a major source of such capital. The overflowing supplies of cheap labour due to unrestricted immigration from Europe contributed to a tremendous growth in the wealth of the country and the evils of the Industrial Age became only too apparent. "The nation was fabulously rich but its wealth was gravitating rapidly into the hands of a very small portion of the population."[5]

In mentioning the name of any company, it is as well to state that those responsible ceased to be connected with the companies following the investigation which took place over half a century ago. At the turn of the century the U.S. public had been regaled by lurid accounts of the evils existing in American business and industry through books, novels, newspapers, and magazine articles. This was the background when a quarrel arose between the president and vice-president of the Equitable Life Assurance Society of the U.S. with accusations and counter-accusations duly aired in the press. The son of the founder had inherited the majority of the share capital which gave control of the company. Although in his twenties, within five years of leaving college his salary as vice-president had been increased to that of the president ($100,000 a year), and he was drawing as well some $25,000 as salary from two controlled companies. By 1905 he had become a director of forty-eight companies, mostly banks, trust companies, and railroads. The Equitable of the U.S. was one of the largest life insurance companies of the world transacting business in many countries and had assets at that time exceeding $400 millions.

The investigation was mainly confined to the "Big Three" life insurance companies: Equitable of the U.S., Mutual of New York, and New York Life. It disclosed that the funds of these U.S. life companies were, at that time, being exploited for the personal advantage of the officers and directors and that nepotism was rampant. The introduction of "tontine dividends," where the policyholders' dividends were pooled and shared among the survivors, contributed to the popularity of life insurance but the large accumulations of funds brought a mania for size and consequent extravagance of operations. The optimistic estimates of future results of policyholders' dividends and the actual results, due partly to the low interest yields current at the turn of the century, was another major source of criticism.

The ensuing legislation in 1906 was revolutionary in its restrictions

[5]S. E. Morrison and H. S. Commager, *The Growth of the American Republic* (New York, 1942), vol. 2.

imposed on life insurance companies and some of it bore evidence of the haste with which it had been introduced. However, although modified later, the New York insurance law, in many of its aspects, became a model for other states in the U.S.; it will be referred to repeatedly in this text. One serious charge was of the gross inefficiency of state supervision of life insurance companies generally in the U.S. and in New York State in particular.[6]

The Armstrong-Hughes Investigation might well be regarded as marking an epoch in U.S. economic history. Although some of the worst aspects of American business were disclosed, U.S. public opinion made it clear in no uncertain terms that such would not be tolerated in the life insurance business. Grover Cleveland, former President of the United States, who became a trustee of the Equitable during its reorganization put it thus: "... Life insurance has to do with the most sacred things that stir the human affections; and that its management involves a higher duty and more constant devotion than we associate with a mere business enterprise."[7]

The Mutual of New York and the New York Life were mutual companies. The Equitable was mutualized later, i.e., its funds were used to purchase its own share capital. As an indication that the new life insurance legislation was ahead of its time, it should be mentioned that, although New York State passed legislation to make mutualization possible, the courts supported any odd shareholder who refused to sell his shares. It was not until 1925, i.e., almost twenty years later, that all the share capital was acquired.

ROYAL COMMISSION ON LIFE INSURANCE, 1906

It would be expected that the impact of the Armstrong Investigation would be felt in Canada. Following accusations made by one newspaper against Canadian life insurance companies, a Royal Commission was appointed by the Dominion government. Its *Report* published in 1907 helped to clear the air. Considering the business practices of the time, the frequently recurring financial crises, and the difficulties inherent in the development of life insurance companies in their early years, the disclosures were relatively minor.

One matter mentioned in the *Report* has continued to be raised repeatedly in criticism, i.e., the "concentration of economic power"

[6]B. M. Anderson, "The Armstrong Investigation in Retrospect," *Proceedings*, Association of Life Insurance Counsel, 1952.

[7]R. C. Buley, *The Equitable Life Assurance Society of the United States, 1859–1959* (New York, 1959).

and the illustration there given is of interest. Senator George A. Cox was the outstanding business personality of his day. Starting as the local agent of the Canada Life in Peterborough, Ontario, in 1862, the limits of his agency were gradually enlarged to include most of eastern Ontario and Michigan. He became president of the Canadian Bank of Commerce, founder and sole owner of the Central Canada Loan and Savings Company, which was connected with and in control of the Toronto Savings Company and through which he organized and controlled the Imperial Life and Dominion Securities. He was appointed to the Board of the Canada Life, and, not without opposition of the other directors, became president in 1900. His other interests included control of the British America and Western Fire Assurance Companies and a major interest in the National Trust Company.

Considering the limited financial resources of Canada in the period just described, this close association of banks, bond houses, insurance, and trust companies mainly under one man's control would invite criticism. The important point at issue is whether the policyholders of the Canada Life benefited by this interlocking of interests. The Royal Commission stated in its *Report* (p. 14) regarding Senator Cox: "He says he has always made the interests of the Canada Life Assurance Company his first and chief concern, but many of the investments made by or on behalf of that company have been made to serve other interests as well. The dual position and conflicting interests of Mr. Cox in many of these transactions have been most clearly defined."

A draft bill accompanied the *Report* with revolutionary restrictions along the lines of the Armstrong-Hughes legislation. Fortunately, wiser counsel prevailed, for had the original proposals been carried out a death blow might well have been given to Canada's budding life insurance industry. After much study and discussion, the original draft bill was radically revised and the new legislation, passed in 1910, has formed the foundation of Canadian life insurance development. It suffices to state here that the intervening half century has fully justified the legislation adopted.

NUMBER OF COMPANIES

In 1910 there were 43 companies licensed by the federal government to transact life insurance business in Canada: 25 Canadian, 7 British, and 11 American. In 1975 there were 166 active life insurance companies operating in Canada: 84 Canadian, 66 American, 9 British, and 7 European. Of the Canadian companies 26 operated under provincial licences. In addition there were a number of fraternal benefit societies, both

Canadian and originating in the U.S. Canada is certainly one of the most competitive fields for life insurance in the world today, and the British and U.S. companies represent some of the largest life insurance companies in the world.

VENTURING INTO FOREIGN FIELDS

Canada in the early days of life insurance provided a limited field for business due to its widely scattered population, many of whom were newcomers, not firmly established. This was particularly so after 1870 when there were a number of Canadian companies to share the field apart from the British and American companies. Thus by 1880 the Sun Life already had branches established outside Canada. T. B. Macaulay of that company at the International Congress of Actuaries, in Paris, in 1900, stated "... Five of the leading offices (of Canada) now transact business abroad,... In almost every portion of the British Empire, in the United States, in France, in Belgium, in Chile, in the open ports of China and elsewhere, some one or more of our companies are represented ..."

In recent years conditions have changed and "the continued operation of business on the wide geographical scale of former years is impossible and impracticable because of compulsory reinsurance, complete take-overs and currency devaluation,"[8] and as a result Canadian companies have withdrawn from active business in a number of countries. Illustrating this, the Manufacturers and Sun Life show business in force in forty different currencies but new business in only fourteen. However, several Canadian companies do a considerable business outside Canada, particularly in the U.S. Thus eight of the largest Canadian companies doing an international business and with total liabilities exceeding twelve billion dollars, at the end of 1974 show liabilities in U.S. dollars of 31 per cent, £ sterling of 9 per cent, and Canadian dollars of 57 per cent, with the balance of 3 per cent in other currencies.

THE EXPANSION OF LIFE INSURANCE IN CANADA

Figures 1 and 2 which follow show the remarkable expansion of the life insurance business in Canada in the past fifty years, and indicate the trends. These figures show the outstanding position of life insurance as one of the largest businesses in the country. Relative to its size, Canada

[8]Alistair M. Campbell, "International Business of Canadian Life Insurance Companies," *Proceedings*, Canadian Life Insurance Officers Association, Annual Meeting, 1963.

is a country of the first rank in the life insurance world today. Most of the following statistics are taken directly from the official reports of the Superintendent of Insurance at Ottawa, and cover only the companies registered by Ottawa referred to as "federally registered" companies. There are provincially incorporated companies operating under provincial licenses, i.e., without federal registration, whose figures are not included. They represent less than 10 per cent of the total business and there is no significant distortion by their omission. They are referred to as "provincial" companies.

In these figures certain terms are used which have not yet been explained:

Ordinary: This is used to distinguish regular business from group and industrial business. It is applied to both life insurance and annuities. Both group and industrial business were introduced as particular forms of business many years after life insurance and annuities were established, hence the implication of the word "ordinary." Industrial business has already been defined.

Group: This may apply to either life insurance or annuities where one contract (the master contract) covers a group of people. In the great majority of cases they are effected by an employer for the benefit of his employees. In group life insurance there is, generally, no individual selection; the participants come in as members of a class, determined by employment, salary or wages.

Segregated Funds: These refer to contracts the policy-reserves of which vary with the market value of a specified group of assets. Canadian companies began to issue such contracts in 1961. The introduction of segregated funds has proven to be a most significant development in Canadian life insurance. In 1974 there was a total of $430 millions paid into such funds on behalf of policyholders and $102 millions paid out to policyholders and beneficiaries. The funds amounted to $1,751 millions at the end of 1974. Figures in respect of segregated fund policies have been included with those for fixed-dollar policies in each category in Figures 1 and 2 except for the period 1961–69 inclusive. Because of a change made in the Superintendent's report in 1970 direct comparisions cannot be made between figures for 1970 and later and those of 1961–69.

TOTAL PREMIUMS PAID: FIGURE 1

The total amount of premiums for life insurance and annuities paid to the federally registered life insurance companies in Canada in 1974 amounted to $2,899 millions—nearly three billion dollars. The corre-

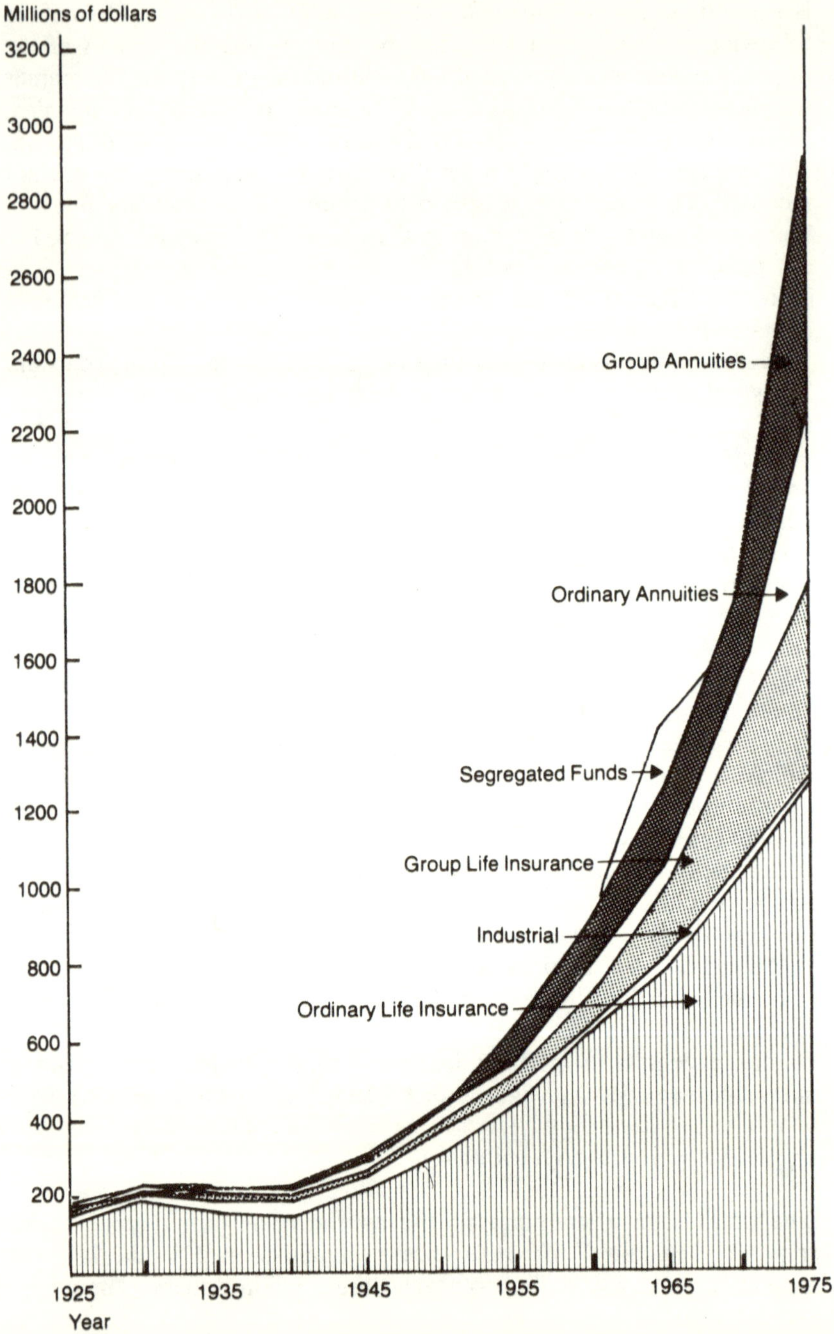
Millions of dollars
3200
3000
2800
2600
2400
2200
2000
1800
1600
1400
1200
1000
800
600
400
200
Group Annuities
Ordinary Annuities
Segregated Funds
Group Life Insurance
Industrial
Ordinary Life Insurance
1925
1935
1945
1955
1965
1975
Year

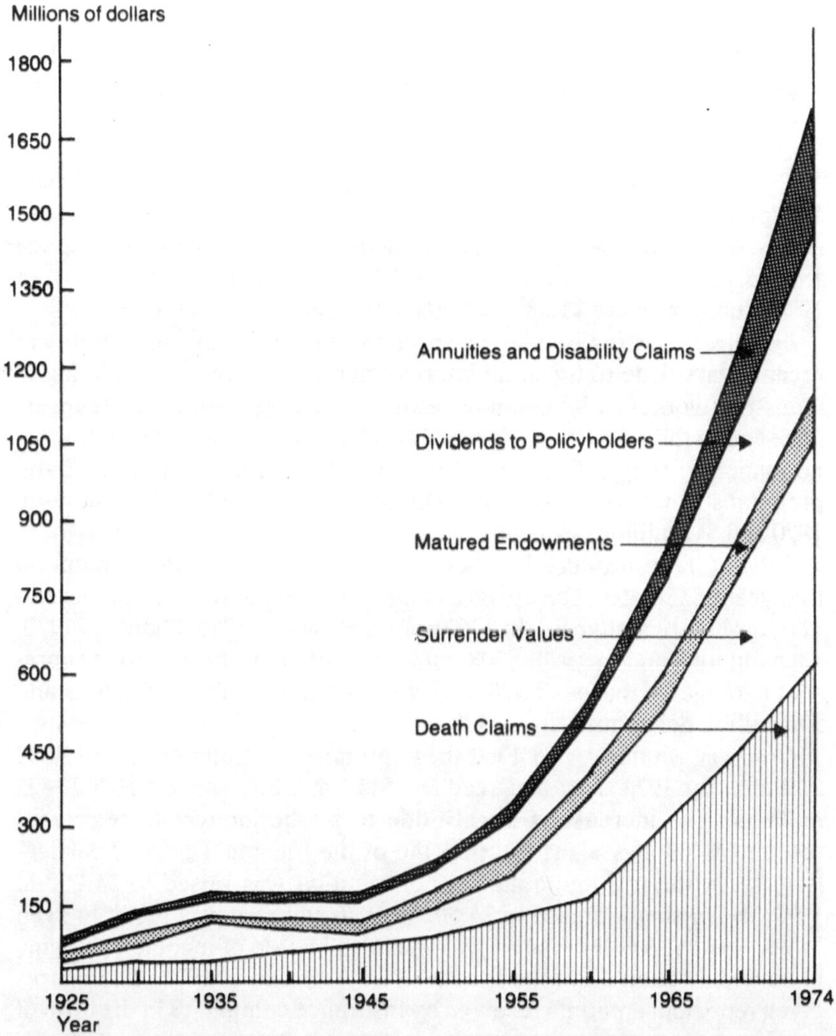

FIGURE 2. Total Benefit Payments to Policyholders in Canada by Federally Registered Life Insurance Companies, 1925 to 1974

FIGURE 1. Premiums paid in Canada to federally registered life insurance companies, 1925 to 1974
Source: Report of the Superintendent of Insurance for Canada

sponding amount for 1960 was $907 millions and for 1970, $1,765 millions. In 1925 the total was only $147 millions. The figure shows a break in the upward trend which followed the stock market crash of 1929. It is important to observe that this break did not occur until 1932 and that the lost ground was not recovered until 1942—well into the Second World War.

Ordinary Life Insurance: Although the premium income has not risen as rapidly as that for annuities or for group policies, a rate of growth of nearly 6 per cent per annum compounded has been maintained since 1960 (5.7 per cent from 1960 to 1970; 5.9 per cent from 1970 to 1974). In 1974 premiums were $1,285 millions, or 44 per cent of the total.

Industrial Life Insurance: The premiums have fallen considerably in recent years. Due to the great improvement in the standard of living of industrial workers who can now afford to purchase ordinary life insurance and to the expansion of group life insurance, industrial insurance is no longer written in Canada. The business in force is running off and premiums which were $39 millions in 1960 had dropped to $22 millions in 1970 and $15 millions in 1974.

Group Life Insurance: This began in Canada in 1919 with premiums in that year of $20,469. The upward climb has been almost continuous and very rapid in recent years. In 1960 premiums were $106 millions; in 1970, $308 millions and in 1974, $508 millions. Note that these figures represent average increases of $20 millions per annum through the 60's and $50 million per annum since 1970.

Ordinary Annuities: In 1960 these premiums amounted to only $32 millions; by 1970 they had reached $117 millions and by 1974, $495 millions. The increase is largely due to public interest in registered retirement savings plans (section 146 of the Income Tax Act) particularly since the maximum annual contribution was raised to $4,000 in 1972; the further increase to $5,500 in 1976 will no doubt result in even larger figures. Another factor was the introduction of income averaging annuities (section 61 of the Income Tax Act) also in 1972. The figures given represent amounts received by insurance companies in the form of regular savings as well as those paid in single amounts from funds accumulated elsewhere.

Group Annuities: A premium item first appeared under this heading in 1928 when the figure was $1,139. Although the increase was continuous the premium income did not attain one million dollars until 1934 or ten millions until 1945. For 1960, the total was $146 millions. In spite of a short-lived break in the upward trend in 1966 due to the introduction of the Canada and Quebec pension plans, the total for 1970 was $299 millions and for 1974, $596 millions.

TOTAL BENEFITS PAID: FIGURE 2

In 1974, the federally registered companies operating in Canada paid to their policyholders in Canada under their life insurance and annuity contracts a total of $1,683 millions; in 1960, the total was $543 millions and in 1970, $1,248 millions.

The subdivision into the various items such as death claims, surrender values, etc. is shown in Figure 2 for the period 1925 to 1974. For the period 1961–69 payments under segregated fund policies were included with annuities and disability claims; for 1970 on, they are included in the appropriate category. As they had reached a maximum of only $7 millions per annum in 1969, the change in method of recording is not apparent in the scale used in the graph.

Note in Figure 2 the peak of payments to policyholders for the year 1933, due to the large amount paid out in cash surrender values to policyholders cashing in their policies due to the depression. The actual surrender values paid in that year amounted to $92 millions. This compares with $94 millions in 1956, some twenty-three years later. Also note dividends to policyholders were at a peak in 1931: $42 millions, which they did not exceed until 1951, some twenty years later.

It is not always possible to classify a "surrender value" accurately. When a policyholder takes the cash value of his policy at a pension age, or after the policy has been in force for many years and served its original purpose, it is treated as a surrender value in the life insurance company's accounts. Economically it is actually the same as the maturity of an endowment. Note the rapid rise of death claims as compared with the slow increase in matured endowments indicating that Canadians do not favour endowment insurances, particularly those of short duration.

Particularly noticeable in recent years has been an increase in annuity and disability payments from $34 millions in 1960 to $121 millions in 1970 and to $231 millions in 1974. This has been due mainly to the expansion of registered retirement savings plans and group pension plans to which reference has already been made; disability payments increased from $6 millions to $21 millions in the 14-year period but annuity payments from $28 millions to $210 millions.

As will be noted from Figure 2, payments to living policyholders amount to nearly twice as much as death benefit payments to beneficiaries; in 1974, the figures were $1,069 millions to living policyholders and $614 millions to beneficiaries on death.

CHAPTER THREE

The Place of Life Insurance in a Modern Society

THE MAGNITUDE OF LIFE INSURANCE OPERATIONS IN CANADA

As shown by Figure 1 the premiums paid in Canada for life insurance and annuities has been increasing rapidly and for 1974 for federally registered companies exceeded $1,800 millions. The same rapid growth is indicated in the benefits paid to policyholders and beneficiaries in Figure 2: in the same year these companies paid out the sum of over $1,600 millions. The funds of life insurance companies operating in Canada represent the amounts they require to fulfil their obligations under the policies they have issued in Canada and amounted at the end of 1974 to $21,656 millions. If included were the funds held by Canadian life insurance companies to fulfil their world-wide obligations the total would be over $27,000 millions.

The amount of new life insurance effected by federally registered companies in 1974 in Canada was $25,488 millions and at the end of that year their total life insurance in force in Canada as shown in Table 3.1 was $177,000 millions. If provincial companies and fraternal associations are included, the amount of life insurance in force in Canada is $190,000 millions.

TABLE 3.1

	New		In force	
	Amount	Average policy or certificate	Amount	Average policy or certificate
Ordinary	$13,927 millions	$17,960	$80,965 millions	$8,844
Industrial	—	—	—	—
Group	11,561 "	not available	96,155 "	4,686
Total	$25,488 millions		$177,120 millions	

In the annuity field federally registered companies issued in 1974 in Canada over 133,000 policies and certificates on individual lives involving future annuity payments by the companies of over $206 millions a year and this business in force at the end of 1974 amounted to over 974,000 policies and certificates for an annual future payment of $1,397 millions.

THE NEED FOR AND USES OF LIFE INSURANCE

At the head of Chapter 1 the basic need for life insurance was given in a statement made over two hundred years ago and a summary of the needs met by life insurance in present-day society should be of interest. It may be stated that this book deals with the theoretical basis and the procedures by which these needs are met in practice. A summary of these needs follows:

Death and Burial Fund. This is generally referred to as a Clean-up Fund. The death of a member of a family creates new obligations such as the expenses of the last illness and burial. In the case of the head of the family there are debts, current bills, instalment payments, and the like, to be paid. For a man of means there are death duties and outstanding income tax payments or property taxes. Death duties can be very substantial and unless ready cash is available it may force the sale of property or securities at a disadvantageous time with serious losses to the beneficiaries. Life insurance not only provides the cash, but it can be bought and paid for by annual or more frequent payments and the full amount provided for at the outset is available immediately on death whether death occurs early or late.

Replacement of Income to Family. The changes in social attitudes of the past two or three decades have caused a reassessment of the role played by life insurance in replacing family income. When few married women, and even fewer widows, were employed outside the house, the typical insurance programme on the life of the husband was based on:

1. an income for a readjustment period of two or three years;
2. an adequate income for a period extending until children would have completed education;
3. a smaller income for life for the widow after children were educated.

Now that many married women work outside the home, even when children are quite small, insurance needs are somewhat different. It must be recognized that the death of either partner will result in a considerable decrease in the family income and provision should be made for it. Thus the amount of insurance bought on the lives of married women has increased considerably. On the other hand, the needs of widows are not so acute because most of them can obtain an income on the labour market, although usually much less than enough to maintain the accustomed standard of living.

Income on Retirement. In Canada, age 65 is generally considered the usual age for retirement; the universal old age pension in Canada commenced at age 70 when originated but this has been successively reduced to age 65. The minimum amount of income required may, generally, be considered as from 50 to 60 per cent of that earned during the last few years of active working life. According to the latest figures for Canada,[1] a man at age 65 should, on the average, have another 13.7 years to live; a woman, another 17.5 years. Modern life insurance has been built on the need to provide not only for amounts payable following death but also an amount or equivalent income payable following retirement.

Desirable Additions. We have dealt with the essential needs covered by life insurance companies: death and burial fund, income to family in readjustment period, income to family to provide for children, income for the widow, and income on retirement. Other desirable needs to be covered would include a *mortgage redemption fund* to pay off any mortgage existing on the family home. House-ownership has increased greatly since the Second World War and retaining the family home for as long a period as possible is a great consolation. Another would be an *education fund* to ensure that the benefits of a college education are obtained should the father or mother die prematurely. Under this type of policy the amounts required would be payable on a specific date or dates, but the premiums would cease to be payable on the previous death of the parent. Other policies available to cover special needs are an income to a *dependent parent* should the life insured die before the parent; the premiums here cease to be payable on the first death. The needs of a *handicapped child* can be provided for by arranging for the income on a lump sum to be paid to the child on surviving the life insured.

There are also *special occasion funds* as an amount payable to a child on his or her twenty-first birthday or marriage. In this class would be

[1]*Canadian Life Tables, 1970–72* (Ottawa: Queen's Printer, 1974). See also Table 4.2 of this text.

bequests either continuing donations to a church, college, or charity after death or a lump sum as an endowment for a specific purpose. Through settlement options, as will be outlined in a later chapter, any lump sum falling due under a life insurance policy can be paid as an annuity throughout the lifetime of a specified person or in instalments, however required, to meet the particular circumstances.

Business Insurance. Life insurance has important uses in business. Just as the loss of earnings of husband or wife can seriously affect the family finances, so the financial stability of a business enterprise can be threatened by the death of a key member of the management, sales, or research staff. The vast majority of firms in Canada are small, the owners being entirely dependent on the business as a source of revenue. Where there is a partnership it is dissolved on the death of one of the partners; insurance on the life of a deceased partner can enable the surviving partner or partners to buy the deceased's share of the asset so as to keep the business going. Should it be a sole proprietorship it is desirable, if feasible, for a key employee to purchase the business on the decease of the owner and this can be arranged through life insurance. If it is a limited company the sale of interest to an outsider on the death of a principal shareholder might introduce a serious situation for surviving shareholders.

We have above referred to, most briefly, the main types of business ownership to indicate the problems arising in business on death and to indicate the place of life insurance in solving them.

ESTATE PLANNING AND PROGRAMMING

From the previous section it is clear that the life insurance needs of individuals vary considerably and in business insurance or where people of substantial means are involved the matter can become one of some complexity. The analysis of a man's existing estate—business, investments, real estate and life insurance—and their evaluation in the circumstances of death, provision for death duties and other shrinkages, the effect of taxation, the status of the beneficiaries, and the conservation of the estate: the consideration of these is called *estate planning.* The other aspect is to determine the needs following death as outlined in an earlier part of this chapter and advising how life insurance or additional life insurance can meet these needs: this is called *programming.*

It can be seen that in many cases special advice will have to be sought. The life insurance expert whose advice is necessary and whose training fits him to take charge or at least to play a major role in this planning is the Chartered Life Underwriter and his role and training will be referred to when the head office and sales organization of a life insurance company are covered in Chapter 10. In particular the Chartered Life Underwriter's experience should be helpful to recognize special problems requiring the advice of a lawyer or a chartered accountant.

HUMAN LIFE VALUES

We have referred to the monetary needs of a family on the death of husband/father. By a simple calculation we can place a value on these monetary needs. Let us assume a parent aged thirty-five and that the monetary needs of his family, excluding his own, are $1,000 a month, i.e., to provide food, rent, clothes, education, health and recreation. Such a person might be earning about $1,500 a month and the deductions from gross income would be savings, personal insurance, income tax and pension and other deductions at source, daily travel, and personal needs. Assuming a retirement age of sixty-five, such a person would have thirty more years of earning power.

The present value or discounted value of one dollar a month payable for thirty years, assuming interest of 6 per cent per annum is $169.67. Thus the present value of $1,000 a month would be $169,670. This is the capital value of the man's future earning power to his family and if this amount were invested, placed in a bank or left with the life insurance company at interest of 6 per cent per annum and was drawn upon month by month for 30 years the capital and interest would provide the family with exactly $1,000 a month. The present value and income are exactly proportionate so that if the family required only $500 a month the monetary value would be $84,835; for $100 a month the equivalent present value would be $16,967.[2]

We noted above that the average ordinary life policy in force in Canada is about $8,400 and current purchases indicate an average of about $18,000, so that the inadequacy of life insurance purchases by the public is apparent when related to what is desirable. We should allow for persons holding more than one policy and undoubtedly the average policy per husband/father exceeds that of all policyholders. On the other hand there are still families who do not own any life insurance.

[2]These discounted values are based on a rate of interest of 6 per cent per annum. Corresponding to $16,967 for $100 a month payable for 30 years are the following values for other rates of interest: 4% p.a. $21,128; 8% p.a. $13,998.

How Much Life Insurance? The question as to how much life insurance should be carried is dependent on individual circumstances: the amount of other property and investments and the number of dependents and their circumstances. An old rule was three times the annual income of the husband/father, but one would consider this as a minimum on the North American continent and more likely to apply to wage earners whose margins for savings are limited.

What Proportion of Income to be Spent? The question of the proportion of income which should be devoted to life insurance also varies with the individual; it cannot be separated from other personal savings. A total of 15 per cent of earnings to cover both life insurance and pension should be satisfactory for one in the employee category. For the self-employed this should be greater for the employer's contribution to pension would have to be added to get a corresponding figure. However the self-employed may offset against this the value of his business or the income which would be received on a part-time or absentee basis following the usual retirement age. This compares with the 7.20 per cent of disposable personal income (personal income less taxes) which represents the total personal savings of Canadians, including life insurance, in the four years 1970–73 inclusive.

THE PROBABILITIES OF DEATH AND TOTAL DISABILITY

According to the latest population mortality statistics published in Canada (Canadian Life Table 1970–72), of a group of men aged 35 less than 3 per cent will die before age 45; however 25.5 per cent or more than one in four will die before age 65. This is the hazard faced by the average Canadian man aged 35 in considering the support of his family after his death.

At age 35 the probability of a man suffering from a long-term total disability (lasting three months or more) and occurring before age 65 is 33 per cent. The average length of the disability will exceed five years and nearly 30 per cent of the cases will prove to be permanent, i.e., total disability continuing until death or what would normally be called a retirement age. These figures are derived from life insurance statistics.[3] Total disability has been called the "living death" and its integration

[3]Society of Actuaries, *1952 Report*. (See B. J. Helphand, "The Role of Disability Income Insurance," *Journal*, American Society of Chartered Life Underwriters, vol. VIII (1953), no. 1.)

with "insurance payable on death" called life insurance, is a development since the 1920's. This will be dealt with in Chapter 19.

CONSIDERABLE ROOM FOR EXPANSION

It must be agreed from what has been stated in this chapter that the life insurance companies are providing for important major social needs in the economic and social life of Canada. We must be impressed by the magnitude of the total amounts involved: over one and one-half billion dollars a year in benefit payments, over twenty-one billion dollars in assets, nearly two hundred billion dollars in life insurance sums insured and provision made for the payment of well over one billion dollars a year in annuities and pensions. Yet we must acknowledge that the needs are so great that when these amounts are evaluated on a per-person basis they indicate there is considerable room for expansion.

LIFE INSURANCE AND SAVINGS

Until required to pay benefits, dollars received from policyholders in Canada for life insurance protection and provision for retirement are put to work for the good of Canada. In a relatively young country like Canada with huge areas almost unexplored, certainly undeveloped, the need for capital is great, and what is not provided by its own people from their savings must be obtained from abroad. This foreign capital introduces complications when it involves the ownership of the means of production, industrial plants, mines, and oil wells. Without discussing the political aspect of these matters, it will be agreed that the more Canadians save, within reason, the better off for them and for the future of Canada.

Part played in the Financial System. The $21,656 millions of assets play a major part in the Canadian financial system. Since 1950, the mortgage and real estate investments of life companies have financed more than a million homes for Canadians. As at the end of 1974 life insurance funds had financed 18 per cent of all mortgages in Canada distributed 29% on single-family dwellings, 38% on multiple-family dwellings, and 33% on non residential buildings. Also at the end of 1974 life insurance funds had financed approximately 33 per cent of Canadian corporate bonds outstanding, 18 per cent of municipal bonds, 10% of provincial bonds, and 5 per cent of Government of Canada market securities.[4]

[4]*Canadian Life Insurance Facts*, 1975 ed. (Toronto: Canadian Life Insurance Association).

TABLE 3.2

Mortgage loans	$ 8,705 millions
Bonds and debentures	7,817 "
Preferred and common stocks	2,052 "
Real estate	1,215 "
Policy loans	1,114 "
Other assets	753 "
Total	$21,656 millions

The assets in Canada of the federally licensed and provincial life insurance companies at the end of 1974 were distributed as shown in Table 3.2.

PRIVATE INSURANCE VERSUS SOCIAL INSURANCE

Objections may be raised to the heading of this section. The words "private insurance" are used to describe insurance purchased voluntarily by individuals and employers for their employees. There is also some objection to the use of the word "insurance" when applied to many schemes of social welfare where the existence of the "insurance principle," that is, the sharing of risk, may be questioned. Further the large annual volumes of reports issued by the Superintendent of Insurance at Ottawa giving every detail of the operations of the life insurance companies provide little privacy for the business.

Private Insurance. The basic difference between benefits provided by life insurance companies and those under government social insurance plans is this. In private insurance plans the lives insured are graded as far as possible in accordance with the degree of risk involved and each class is required to pay for the cost of the benefits received. Also each insured decides in accordance with his resources and needs the amount of benefit he wishes to purchase and pays the corresponding premium accordingly. This equivalence between premium payments and benefits is the essential element in private insurance.

Where, as will be demonstrated later, in private insurance a level premium is paid for an increasing risk, a policy-reserve has to be accumulated, and it is these accumulations which are represented by the $21 billions of assets referred to above. Even if the company ceased accepting new business, the policy-reserves together with the future premiums payable should be adequate to pay all benefits under every policy issued until the last death or the last contract matures for payment. To ensure that this will be so is the aim and object of the actuary's calculations.

Social Insurance. In social insurance there is, generally, no equivalence between benefits received and contributions made by the party receiving the benefits. Unfortunately, under government schemes where, at the outset, some equivalence is attempted, political considerations arise, only too soon, to destroy the equivalence by increasing benefits and sometimes reducing contributions at the same time! The amounts required to achieve the equivalence are, of course, paid from the public purse: the taxing power of the government.

The comments in the above paragraph are not made to decry the social considerations which have inaugurated social security plans throughout the world or their social justice, but only to underline an essential point material to the present text. With good reason the word "insurance" should not be used for social security plans, but the word has become so common in public use that it must be accepted. Another important difference is that the accumulation of funds and their investment is an essential part of the solvency of private insurance plans whereas in social insurance the contributions are, as a rule, treated by the government as part of its revenue and the claims of the contributors are on the taxing power of the government.

CHAPTER FOUR

Age and Mortality

THE THREE "MYSTERIES" OF LIFE INSURANCE

In 1883 when a young man was formally apprenticed to a life insurance company, the articles of indenture obligated the company to teach him "the Art, Trade and Mystery of the General Office business of Life Insurance."[1] One of the objects of this book is to explain away the so called "mystery" of life insurance. The three variable factors in the accurate measurement and forecasting on which so much depends are mortality, interest, and expenses. They may well be called the three mysteries of life insurance and this chapter deals with the first: mortality.

AN ESSENTIAL CONDITION FOR LIFE INSURANCE

It has already been stated that until the death rate became stabilized about the year 1750, permanent life insurance, as a commercial product, had little possibility of success. The word "permanent" is used to distinguish it from "temporary" life insurance for we have already mentioned that life insurances covering a period of one year were already in commercial use some two hundred years before 1750. What is the position regarding mortality at the present time? Table 4.1 gives the death rate in Canada of the adult male population according to age, for each of five successive years, taking selected age groups to reduce the bulk of the table.[2] In the year 1974, in Canada, out of 651,400 males aged

[1]The young man was Thomas Bradshaw and the company the North American Life of Toronto. Bradshaw was later Secretary and Actuary and, later still, Managing Director of the Imperial Life. He had an outstanding career in business and finance and later returned to become President of the North American Life and was instrumental in mutualizing that company in 1931. He was the first president (1907) of the Actuaries Club of Toronto, the first Canadian actuarial organization, now the Canadian Institute of Actuaries.

[2]*Canada, Vital Statistics 1974* (Ottawa: Queen's Printer, 1976).

TABLE 4.1

Canada, Death Rates per 1,000 Population, Males

Calendar year	Ages 30–34	40–44	50–54	60–64	70–74	80–84
1930	3.7	5.8	10.8	23.2	58.0	141.3
1940	2.8	4.9	10.6	24.7	59.3	147.5
1950	1.9	4.0	10.0	25.1	54.9	132.2
1960	1.6	3.3	9.3	24.0	54.3	128.5
1970	1.6	3.5	9.3	23.7	53.3	119.7
1974	1.5	3.5	9.2	22.7	53.1	121.5

40–44, 2,283 died in that year: this is a death rate of 3.5 per 1,000 as shown in the table.

Two facts of importance should be noted: firstly that the rate of mortality increases with age and, secondly, that the rate may fluctuate from year to year but such fluctuations, in normal times, are within quite narrow limits, as indicated in Table 4.1. A third factor which has influenced life insurance practice is that at the younger adult ages, say below age 55, the trend of the rate of mortality has been definitely downwards. Thus the death rate per 1,000 in the age group 30–34 in the year 1930 was 3.7, in the year 1940, it was 2.8 and in the year 1950 it was 1.9 as compared with 1.5 in the year 1974 as shown in Table 4.1. This downward trend has been a great factor in recent years in the liberalization of benefits, reduction in rates, and broadening of the scope of life insurance.

When considering death rates we are dealing with people in the aggregate. The death rate of an individual can have no meaning; the individual must be considered as one of a class. As stated above, the Canadian population death rate of 3.5 per 1,000 for ages 40–44 for the year 1974 was based on 651,400 male lives. Life insurance can be operated with far smaller classes than this, but the principle does apply, namely, that the larger the class the less should be the fluctuation in the death rate experienced from year to year.

HOW MORTALITY VARIES

The rate of mortality is the starting point of all the actuary's calculations of premium rates and the amounts which must be accumulated to meet future obligations. There are innumerable tables showing the rates of mortality of diverse peoples at various times over the past two hundred years and more. Mortality varies:

1. By age and sex. Had the corresponding rates to Table 4.1 for female lives been shown they would have indicated that, for each age group and for each calendar year, the rates of mortality for female lives were substantially lower than for male lives;

2. By country of residence and even in different parts of the same country;

3. By occupation and socio-economic class, which is due partly to actual occupational hazards and partly due to environment, education, standards of health, and availability of medical services;

4. As between the general population and those selected by life insurance companies as standard risks;

5. As between those recently selected for life insurance and those of the same age who had been selected some years earlier;

6. As between lives under life insurance policies and those under immediate annuity policies.

Thus, almost the first thing to ask about a mortality table is: "What does it represent?"

AGE AND MORTALITY

The symbols defined in this section appear in all published mortality tables. Let us assume that we had a large number of people of exactly the same age and we followed their record from birthday to birthday, recording the numbers dying between birthdays and hence the number surviving from one birthday to the next. The index x can represent any age from birth when x is 0 to the end of the mortality table. Define

l_x as the number living on their birthday at exact age x,

d_x as the number dying from birthday x to birthday $x + 1$,

q_x is the rate of mortality at age x,

then $q_x = d_x/l_x$, i.e., the rate of mortality at age x is equal to the number dying in the year following attainment of age x divided by the number living at age x.

Although the first life insurance companies, like the Old Equitable, had to base their premium rates on the mortality of the general population, it was not many years before they had their own experience from which to determine q_x, and life insurance companies for many years have been doing this. However, the first conceptions of rates of mortality were obtained from population figures.

Canadian Census. Quinquennially since 1951, and at decennial periods previous thereto, the government of Canada conducted a census and recorded every person living in Canada showing their ages last birthday, their sex, and other details for national record purposes. The deaths registered in Canada were then tabulated by age last birthday and sex, for the year of census, for the year preceding the year of census and the year following the year of census. The average of the number of deaths in these three years was used in order to take into account any abnormality which might affect the deaths in any one year. It is from such statistics that the rates of mortality for the population of Canada are obtained.

The calculation of the rates of mortality at individual ages from population statistics or the experience of life insurance companies is a technical operation forming a special branch of actuarial science.

A CANADIAN POPULATION MORTALITY TABLE

In Figure 3 the rates of mortality are shown for the population of Canada for the three years 1970–72 centring on the census year 1971. It shows the rates of mortality for male and female lives separately from birth to age 70. The tables were cut off at age 105.[3] They were the latest Canadian population mortality tables available when this book was being prepared.

THE LIFE TABLE

When the rates of mortality have been calculated they are used to construct a life table. In Table 4.2 we show the life table corresponding to Figure 3. For economy of space we show the first ten years and the figures from age 95 on, with quinquennial values for the remainder. The complete figures are given in the government publication.

The method of construction of the male table is as follows. Assume that 100,000 male children are born and experience through life the mortality indicated by Canadian Life Table 1970–72. The rate of mortality in the first year of life is 20.02 per 1,000 so that the number dying in the first year is 2,002 and thus 97,998 are alive on their first birthday. The rate of mortality in the second year of life is 1.28 per 1,000 so that the number dying in the second year of life 97,998 × 1.28 ÷ 1,000 or 125, leaving 97,873 alive at exactly age 2 and so on.

[3]*Canadian Life Tables: 1970–1972* (Ottawa: Queen's Printer, 1974).

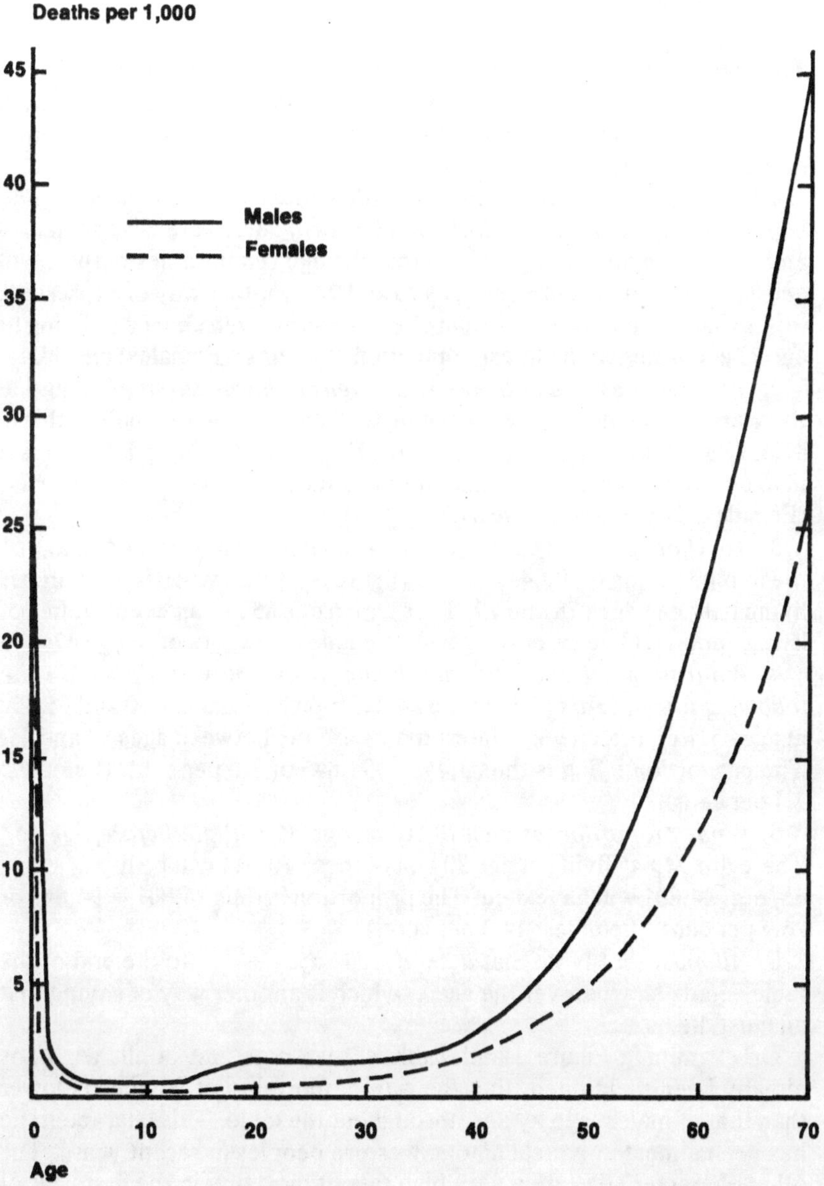

FIGURE 3. Canadian Population Rate of Mortality 1970–1972, $1000q$

SOME STATISTICS DERIVED FROM CANADIAN (POPULATION) LIFE TABLE 1970–1972

The following figures are obtained from Table 4.2 for male lives. In parentheses the corresponding figures are given for female lives. There is no limit to the number of questions which can be answered as regards mortality and vitality by this table.

1. *At what age is the number of male children born reduced to one half?* According to Table 4.2 of 100,000 born, 58,575 are alive at age 70 and 44,788 are alive at age 75, so that the age required lies between 70 and 75. It is actually between ages 73 and 74. Another way of expressing this is that any male child born in Canada has an even chance of living to age 73 according to the latest population statistics. (Females: age 80)

2. *To what age has a man age 30 an even chance to survive?* At age 30 there are 94,845 men living according to Table 4.2 and one-half of this is 47,422. The number living falls to this between ages 74 and 75. Thus a man age 30 has an even chance of living another 44 years or to age 74. (Females: 51 years or to age 81.)

3. *To what age has a man age 65 an even chance to survive?* At age 65 the number living is 70,044; half this figure is 35,022 which is the number living between ages 78 and 79. Thus a man age 65 has an even chance of living another 13 years or to age 78. (Females: 17 years or to age 82.)

4. *What proportion of the men living at age 30 will die within the following fifteen years?* There are 94,845 men living at age 30 and 91,390 at age 45, i.e., fifteen years later; thus 3,455 die between ages 30 and 45. The proportion dying is thus 3,455 ÷ 94,845 or 3.6 per cent. (Females: 2.1 per cent.)

5. *What proportion of men living at age 30 will die before age 65?* There are 94,845 living at age 30 and of these 70,044 will be living at age 65, i.e., 24,801 will have died. The proportion is thus 24,801 ÷ 94,845 or 26.1 per cent. (Females: 14.3 per cent.)

6. *All must die!* Note that $d_x + d_{x+1} + d_{x+2} + \ldots$ to the end of the table equals l_x, whatever the age x, which is another way of saying that all must die.

On examining Figure 3 and Table 4.2 we note first of all, what has already been mentioned, that the rate of mortality of females is lower than that of males, age by age, throughout the table. This characteristic has been almost universal among western peoples in recent years. The other characteristics are a very high rate of mortality in the first year of life, falling precipitously to that at age 1 and then a gradual fall to age 9 or 10. From then on the rate increases but for males the increase is so

TABLE 4.2
Canadian Population Life Tables 1970–72

Males				
Age x	Number living l_x	Number dying d_x	Rate of mortality q_x	Complete expectation of life $\mathring{e}_x$
0	100,000	2,002	.02002	69.34
1	97,998	126	.00128	69.76
2	97,872	92	.00094	68.85
3	97,780	83	.00084	67.91
4	97,697	69	.00071	66.97
5	97,628	59	.00061	66.02
6	97,569	51	.00052	65.06
7	97,518	45	.00045	64.09
8	97,473	39	.00041	63.12
9	97,434	38	.00038	62.14
10	97,396	38	.00039	61.17
15	97,129	102	.00106	56.33
20	96,447	172	.00178	51.71
25	95,575	157	.00164	47.16
30	94,845	144	.00152	42.50
35	94,072	176	.00188	37.83
40	93,035	271	.00291	33.22
45	91,390	423	.00464	28.77
50	88,821	676	.00761	24.52
55	84,761	1,028	.01213	20.57
60	78,719	1,509	.01918	16.95
65	70,044	2,073	.02961	13.72
70	58,575	2,598	.04436	10.90
75	44,788	2,934	.06552	8.47
80	29,976	2,908	.09701	6.41
85	16,332	2,345	.14355	4.74
90	6,491	1,362	.20977	3.43
95	1,600	481	.30027	2.45
96	1,119	360	.32166	2.28
97	759	261	.34435	2.13
98	498	183	.36827	1.98
99	315	124	.39334	1.84
100	191	80	.41969	1.71
101	111	50	.44741	1.59
102	61	29	.47662	1.48
103	32	16	.50724	1.37
104	16	9	.53921	1.26
105	7	4	.57263	1.15

Note: Quinquennial Values only are given from age 10 to age 95.

TABLE 4.2 (*continued*)

Females				
Age x	Number living l_x	Number dying d_x	Rate of mortality q_x	Complete expectation of life $\mathring{e}_x$
0	100,000	1,544	.01544	76.36
1	98,456	113	.00114	76.56
2	98,343	72	.00073	75.64
3	98,271	60	.00061	74.70
4	98,211	56	.00057	73.74
5	98,155	49	.00050	72.79
6	98,106	40	.00041	71.82
7	98,066	33	.00034	70.85
8	98,033	29	.00030	69.87
9	98,004	28	.00028	68.90
10	97,976	28	.00028	67.91
15	97,819	45	.00046	63.02
20	97,557	55	.00057	58.18
25	97,278	58	.00060	53.34
30	96,963	74	.00077	48.51
35	96,530	108	.00112	43.71
40	95,886	166	.00173	38.99
45	94,898	247	.00260	34.37
50	93,433	376	.00403	29.86
55	91,197	564	.00618	25.53
60	87,896	819	.00931	21.39
65	83,092	1,204	.01449	17.47
70	75,995	1,776	.02337	13.85
75	65,624	2,543	.03876	10.63
80	51,237	3,337	.06514	7.88
85	33,628	3,620	.10766	5.67
90	16,620	2,848	.17137	3.99
95	5,262	1,375	.26132	2.76
96	3,887	1,099	.28286	2.56
97	2,788	853	.30581	2.37
98	1,935	639	.33010	2.20
99	1,296	461	.35564	2.04
100	835	319	.38255	1.89
101	516	212	.41096	1.74
102	304	134	.44098	1.61
103	170	80	.47253	1.49
104	90	46	.50554	1.37
105	44	24	.54013	1.26

Note: Quinquennial Values only are given from age 10 to age 95.

sharp, near age 20, as to create a slight "hump" in the rate of mortality in the early twenties. The flattening out of the curves to age 30 should be noted after which the rate begins to climb, the rate of climb increasing with age to the end of life.

EXPECTATION OF LIFE

The *complete expectation of life* is referred to so often and is given in tables of vital statistics in this book and elsewhere that its meaning should be clarified. It is designated by the symbol $\mathring{e}_x$, x being the age. It is also called the "average after lifetime" which explains what it represents.

Let us calculate an actual example from Table 4.2, taking a male aged 100 to reduce the arithmetic but the same process applies to any other age. Of the 191 men living at age 100 the total complete number of years they will live is 80 in the first year, 50 in the next, and so on to the cut-off at age 105. Also, on the average, each one who dies will live half a year in the year death occurs. Thus the average number of years lived by the 191 men, or, the complete expectation of life at age 100:[4]

$$\frac{1}{2} + \frac{111 + 61 + 32 + 16 + 7}{191} = \frac{1}{2} + \frac{227}{191} = 1.69$$

Contrary to its wide public use, the complete expectation of life, $\mathring{e}_x$, is rarely used in actuarial computations. It gives the "average after lifetime" so that at birth it lumps together all the probabilities of death from the first year to the hundredth year of age, and even beyond, which indicates little about any one period of life in which we may be interested. As a matter of interest, in Canada the complete expectation of life $\mathring{e}_x$, at birth for males and females as given by the life tables for the census years 1931, 1941, 1951, 1961, and 1971 are given in Table 4.3.

TABLE 4.3

Males					Females				
1931	1941	1951	1961	1971	1931	1941	1951	1961	1971
60.00	62.96	66.33	68.35	69.34	62.10	66.30	70.83	74.17	76.36

These figures indicate (i) the advantage of female lives over males in regard to longevity which has already been noted, (ii) the continued improvement in longevity in recent years, and (iii) the greater improvement of female than male lives.

[4]As shown in Table 4.2 the value of the Complete Expectation of Life at age 100, males, is 1.71. The small difference is due to the cut-off in the published table.

MORTALITY TABLE OF INSURED LIVES

The year from one policy anniversary to the next is called a *policy year*. As previously mentioned, life insurance companies now use their own mortality experience to compute their premium rates and actuarial liabilities. When dealing with the records of insured lives one essential difference may be noted. In population statistics we cannot follow individual lives. People enter and leave a country and the deaths counted may not be related to the actual individuals counted at the census. In a life insurance company mortality investigation, we can trace the experience of each life and we have records of when each life insured entered or left or whether it existed at the end of the period. The investigation is generally confined to a definite period of time, usually from the policy anniversary in one calendar year to the policy anniversary in a later year, and we follow each life during that period from entry until the actual date of death, lapse, surrender, or other mode of termination.

In such an investigation the rate of mortality at age x is the number of lives dying in one year out of the number of lives of exact age x exposed to the risk of death for one year. We take age nearest birthday at entry as the equivalent of the exact age at entry, and so get the exact age on each policy anniversary.

We allow for withdrawals during a policy year, due to lapse, expiry or surrender of the insurance (but not death) by taking the withdrawals to the nearest policy anniversary. We know the age on the anniversary when the risk begins and the age on the policy anniversary when the risk ceases. In this way all entrants and withdrawals (except death) are summarized as occurring on actual policy anniversaries, and we have recorded their exact ages at that particular anniversary.

It is thus a method of counting and sorting to get the "exposed to risk of death" at attained age x and the number of deaths in the policy year from attained age x to attained age $x + 1$. Thus,

Rate of mortality at attained age x

$$= \frac{\text{Number of deaths in policy year from attained ages } x \text{ to } x + 1}{\text{Number exposed to risk of death at beginning of policy year where attained age is } x.}$$

Note that for lives we can substitute policies or the amount of insurance of the policy. By using amounts of insurance we get the financial effect of the claims on the insurance company issuing the policy.

Tables constructed in this manner, in which all the lives, or the policies, or the amounts of insurance corresponding to the same attained age are grouped together for the purpose of ascertaining their mortality experience, are known as *aggregate tables*.

SELECT MORTALITY TABLES

In practice, lives insured for individual life insurance are selected at entry. That is, they have to satisfy the company by medical examination or otherwise that they are acceptable at regular rates for insurance and are called *select lives* from that point of view. As would be expected the rate of mortality among such selected lives is less than among a more general body of lives, at least for some time after entry. Tables of mortality showing this selectivity at entry are known as *select mortality tables*.

As would be expected, the effects of selection diminish in time and in our investigations in Canada we have found that there is little advantage in continuing to segregate lives beyond the fifth policy year from entry. This enables us to aggregate all lives after the fifth policy year according to their attained age, which is of considerable practical advantage. The table aggregating the experience after the select period is called the *ultimate table*.

Table 4.4 gives part of a select table of mortality (from age 50 on to age 55 at entry) showing the aggregation by policy years from entry. It is the *Canadian Men Table*. Note how moving to the right you get the mortality according to the first, second, . . . to the fifth policy year, and then you get the ultimate rate of mortality for that age which is five years older than the age of entry. Note how much less the mortality is at age 55 at

TABLE 4.4
Canadian Men Table
(1900–1915)
Part of Select Mortality Table
Rate of Mortality q

Age at entry	Year of insurance 1	2	3	4	5	More than 5	Attained age
50	.00674	.00809	.00931	.01098	.01289	.01471	55
51	.00728	.00871	.01006	.01189	.01399	.01599	56
52	.00788	.00937	.01087	.01289	.01521	.01741	57
53	.00856	.01013	.01177	.01400	.01654	.01897	58
54	.00928	.01096	.01276	.01522	.01802	.02069	59
55	.01011	.01186	.01386	.01657	.01964	.02258	60

TABLE 4.5

Canadian Men Mortality 1900–1915
(Ultimate) Life Table
CM(5)

Age x	Number living l_x	Number dying d_x	Rate of mortality q_x	Complete expectation of life $\mathring{e}_x$
15	100,000	343	.00343	51.20
16	99,657	355	.00356	50.38
17	99,302	367	.00370	49.56
18	98,935	379	.00383	48.74
19	98,556	391	.00397	47.92
20	98,165	404	.00412	47.11
21	97,761	414	.00423	46.31
22	97,347	421	.00432	45.50
23	96,926	424	.00437	44.70
24	96,502	425	.00440	43.89
25	96,077	423	.00440	43.08
26	95,654	420	.00439	42.27
27	95,234	415	.00436	41.46
28	94,819	410	.00432	40.63
29	94,409	406	.00430	39.81
30	94,003	402	.00428	38.98
31	93,601	398	.00425	38.14
32	93,203	397	.00426	37.30
33	92,806	398	.00429	36.46
34	92,408	402	.00435	35.62
35	92,006	409	.00445	34.77
36	91,597	419	.00457	33.92
37	91,178	431	.00473	33.08
38	90,747	445	.00490	32.23
39	90,302	461	.00511	31.39
40	89,841	479	.00533	30.55
41	89,362	499	.00558	29.71
42	88,863	522	.00587	28.87
43	88,341	548	.00620	28.04
44	87,793	577	.00657	27.21
45	87,216	609	.00698	26.39
46	86,607	645	.00745	25.57
47	85,962	684	.00796	24.76
48	85,278	728	.00854	23.95
49	84,550	775	.00917	23.15
50	83,775	827	.00987	22.36
51	82,948	884	.01066	21.58
52	82,064	964	.01153	20.81
53	81,118	1,013	.01249	20.05
54	80,105	1,085	.01354	19.29
55	79,020	1,162	.01471	18.55
56	77,858	1,245	.01599	17.82

TABLE 4.5 (*continued*)

Age x	Number living l_x	Number dying d_x	Rate of mortality q_x	Complete expectation of life $\mathring{e}_x$
57	76,613	1,334	.01741	17.10
58	75,279	1,428	.01897	16.40
59	73,851	1,528	.02069	15.70
60	72,323	1,633	.02258	15.02
61	70,690	1,742	.02464	14.36
62	68,948	1,856	.02692	13.71
63	67,092	1,974	.02942	13.08
64	65,118	2,095	.03217	12.46
65	63,023	2,217	.03518	11.85
66	60,806	2,339	.03847	11.27
67	58,467	2,460	.04208	10.70
68	56,007	2,578	.04603	10.15
69	53,429	2,690	.05035	9.61
70	50,739	2,794	.05507	9.10
71	47,945	2,888	.06024	8.60
72	45,057	2,968	.06587	8.12
73	42,089	3,031	.07201	7.65
74	39,058	3,074	.07870	7.21
75	35,984	3,095	.08601	6.78
76	32,889	3,090	.09395	6.37
77	29,799	3,057	.10259	5.98
78	26,742	2,995	.11200	5.61
79	23,747	2,901	.12216	5.25
80	20,846	2,771	.13322	4.91
81	18,069	2,623	.14517	4.59
82	15,446	2,442	.15810	4.29
83	13,004	2,238	.17210	4.00
84	10,766	2,014	.18707	3.73
85	8,752	1,779	.20327	3.47
86	6,973	1,539	.22071	3.22
87	5,434	1,301	.23942	3.00
88	4,133	1,072	.25938	2.78
89	3,061	859	.28063	2.58
90	2,202	668	.30336	2.39
91	1,534	502	.32725	2.22
92	1,032	364	.35271	2.06
93	668	253	.37874	1.90
94	415	169	.40723	1.76
95	246	107	.43496	1.62
96	139	65	.46763	1.49
97	74	37	.50000	1.35
98	37	20	.54054	1.20
99	17	10	.58824	1.03
100	7	5	.71429	.79
101	2	2	1.00000	.50

entry, which is 10.11 deaths per 1,000 exposed, than for attained age 55 which is 14.71 deaths per 1,000 exposed.

The q_x column of Table 4.5 gives the ultimate rates of mortality corresponding to the select rates in Table 4.4 and from age 15 upwards, being the range of the mortality investigated in the Canadian Men experience to which both Tables 4.4 and 4.5 relate.

A CANADIAN MORTALITY TABLE OF INSURED LIVES, CM(5)

We are basing our illustrations of the principles of the calculation of actuarial functions on the *Canadian Men Ultimate Table* which is given in Table 4.5. It was published in 1918 and was the first investigation into the joint experience of life insurance companies operating in Canada. The Canada Life had, several years earlier, published its own experience. In the Canadian Men Table the period of the "exposed to risk" was all years of issue from 1900 up to 1914, traced to the policy anniversary in 1915. Where the policy was issued prior to 1900 it was traced from the anniversary in 1900. The experience was based on sums insured, but in order to minimize the effect of any one or more large policies on the experience, where policies were issued at the same age on any one life for more than $100,000 it was considered throughout the experience as $100,000. The designation CM(5) indicates that it is the ultimate experience after the first five years from entry.[5]

The Canadian Men Ultimate Life Table is constructed along the same lines as indicated for Table 4.2. Let us assume 100,000 lives insured, all exact age 15 and all of them having been insured for five years at least. They are exposed to a death rate of 3.43 per 1,000 so that 343 die in the year with 99,657 survivors at age 16. In the year of age following 16 the rate of mortality is 3.56 per 1,000 so that the number of deaths is 99,657 × .00356 or 355 with 99,302 survivors to age 17 and so on. As will be illustrated later a life table such as this is the basis of all the functions used in life insurance calculations.

The Canadian Men Table dealing with the period 1900 to 1915 may be said to be sixty years out of date as a measure of mortality, if one wishes to say so, and it is not dealt with here as an indication of current life insurance mortality. This will be shown later (see Table 8.1). In fact, life insurance mortality has been falling for many years and the latest table would give the lowest mortality possibly ever experienced. As the

[5]Actuarial tables are designated throughout the text according to typographical convenience. The alternatives to the official actuarial symbols are those used in the *Reports* of the Superintendent of Insurance, Ottawa.

reader will note in the next few pages the calculation of premium rates and actuarial liabilities from first principles is very tedious and for illustration purposes only, the Canadian Men Ultimate Table may as well be used as any other. Further it has this major advantage, that extensive tables have been calculated and published based on it giving almost every conceivable actuarial function at various rates of interest.

CHAPTER FIVE

The Three Basic Plans: Term, Straight Life, and Endowment Insurance

We call these three the basic plans because most life insurance plans consist of one of these in its simplest form or a combination of them.

TERM INSURANCE PLAN

Term insurance may be defined as life insurance under which a fixed sum is payable on the death of the life insured, should death occur within a specified period. Another name for it is *temporary insurance* which describes it best.

The contractual obligation to pay a sum on the death of an insured life within a short period was the earliest form of life insurance of which we have any record. We have already referred to the case of William Gybbons and the legal action which arose from it. That was in the days of Elizabeth I and the period of insurance was for a term of twelve months.

There is a wide variety of term plans now available. We describe here the plans available with most companies apart from which there are plans peculiar to individual companies.

The simplest term plans are for a short period, such as 5 or 10 years, with level premiums payable throughout the term period. Longer periods are available up to 15 or 20 years or to a possible retirement age of 60, 65, or 70 with level premiums payable throughout the term of the policy.

Term insurance can also be purchased where the premium paid in any year covers the risk of death in that year. This is called *one-year renewable term insurance*. The important fact has already been noted that the rate of mortality increases as age increases, and beyond age 35 the rate of such increase also increases. Hence, under one year renewable term insurance or similar plans, there are limiting ages as 60 or 65 beyond which the renewable feature is not continued, as the cost becomes prohibitive. Also at the higher ages *selection against the company* becomes important. In practice the policy may be continued above the limiting age only on the basis of conversion to a permanent plan of insurance at the corresponding premium for the attained age. This conversion privilege is referred to below.

The sales aspect of life insurance must always be kept in view for it is a voluntary undertaking. Thus, (1) the low rate of premium is an essential feature of term insurance; (2) people do not relish plans where substantial increases in the premium occur year after year.

The matter of selection against the company also requires explanation. The option to renew a term insurance policy or to convert it into a permanent form of insurance is largely an individual choice and should a high rate of premium require to be paid under the new policy, only those highly impaired in health, say, would renew or convert. As a result the claims would be relatively high on the renewed term policy or the new class of policies changed from the term plan and allowance for this or, the cost of the option, as it may be described, must be included in the term insurance rate. This could make the plan unattractive to a potential purchaser. Hence to reduce the cost, the option to renew or convert is restricted to a range of ages within which a number of renewals or conversions could be expected without obviously selecting against the company, that is by those who would in the normal course continue the insurance.

Conversion Privilege. Term insurance plans generally contain a conversion privilege under which the insured can convert the term policy to a permanent plan of insurance without evidence of health or insurability. For practical purposes, as explained in the previous paragraph, conversion is not permitted beyond age 60 or 65. For similar reasons the exercise of the conversion privilege is generally required to be made some time before the expiry date of the term policy.

The Importance of Term Insurance. In recent years term insurance has increased enormously in volume and importance particularly as an additional benefit to other basic forms of life insurance. This development may be said to have introduced a new phase into life insurance in recent years and is one of the factors in the huge increase in life insurance sold as already noted. These developments and other aspects of term insurance will be discussed in Chapters 8 and 12.

THE STRAIGHT LIFE PLAN

Where a fixed sum is payable on the death of the life insured whenever it may occur and the premiums are level amounts payable periodically until the death of the life insured, the plan of life insurance is called the *straight life plan.*

This plan is also called "ordinary life," "whole life," "whole life—continuous premiums," or just "life." The term "whole life" is incomplete for technically it means that the sum insured is payable on death whenever it may occur and makes no reference to the period for which premiums are payable. Objections to the use of the expression "ordinary" life are that "ordinary" insurance has a special meaning to distinguish it from "industrial" insurance and "group" insurance.

An All-Purpose Policy. The importance of the straight life plan is that it has the lowest rate of premium for level premium permanent life insurance and further it can provide:

(i) *Insurance to the end of life*, whenever death may occur;

(ii) *A savings fund for emergencies.* The cash surrender value which increases every year can be withdrawn at any time after the end of the first two or three policy years;

(iii) *A retirement fund* consisting of the amount of guaranteed cash surrender value and (if policy is participating in profits and the dividends are left to accumulate) accumulated dividends which may be withdrawn at any age, say at retirement;

(iv) *A pension policy* obtained by using the retirement fund to purchase a pension at a rate guaranteed at the time the policy was originally purchased;

(v) *A paid-up policy* for a reduced amount on which no further premiums are payable. This can be used for estate taxes or other obligations on death. If the policy is with participation in profits, the amount of the reduced paid-up insurance plus the amount of accumulated dividends may possibly exceed the original face amount of the policy.

Omitting the references to policies participating in profits, it will be noted that most of the benefits are available to a straight life policy which does not participate in profits and which is available at a lower rate of premium.

From the above the popularity of the straight life plan will be apparent. It is an "all-purpose" plan, particularly when it has added to it various term benefits to increase the amount payable on death in the early years of a policy when such protection may be needed most. In many companies the sale of the straight life plan exceeds by far all the other plans put together. In the last statement we include all the various plans which are in effect straight life plans with term insurance added. These plans will be discussed in a later chapter.

ENDOWMENT INSURANCE PLAN

Where a fixed sum is payable at the end of a specified period if the life insured is then living or on his or her previous death, the plan of life insurance is called an *endowment insurance*.

The specified periods for which rates are quoted are usually ten, fifteen, or twenty years and longer periods; also periods to the usual retirement ages such as 60, 65, or 70. In the simplest form the premiums are level amounts payable periodically until the end of the specified period or until the previous death of the life insured.

The advantages of a long-term endowment insurance are all those outlined for the straight life plan with added emphasis on the investment element; the shorter the endowment period the greater is the investment element and the higher is the rate of premium. The use of the shorter-term endowment in providing a fund for the education of a child is apparent. For many people the appeal of the long-term endowment insurance plan is as follows. Their life insurance purchased may represent their entire planned savings, combining protection and savings to meet their needs and financial circumstances. Thus the statement in the policy of the latest date on which the face amount will be paid is an attractive feature.

RELATIONSHIP BETWEEN BASIC PLANS

We show in Table 5.1 the net annual premiums on the Canadian Men Ultimate 3 per cent basis for these basic plans at representative ages at entry and the calculation of these premiums will be demonstrated in the next chapter. We assume the mortality of the lives insured will follow the CM(5) Table (Table 4.5) and that the premiums will be paid annually in advance and invested to earn a net rate of interest of 3 per cent per annum. The phrase net annual premium will occur very often. *Net premium* means that in the calculation of the premium we have ignored overhead, commission, taxes and all other expenses; we have also ignored margins for contingencies and profits; only mortality and interest are taken into account. Further, no allowance is made for options of conversion and renewal under term plans. The premiums charged by

TABLE 5.1

Net Annual Premiums per $1,000 Sum Insured
CM(5) 3%

Entry age	1-year term	5-year term	10-year term	20-year term	Term to age 65	Term to age 90
25	$ 4.27	$ 4.23	$ 4.20	$ 4.58	$ 7.57	$12.80
35	4.32	4.60	5.11	6.83	9.78	17.69
45	6.78	7.75	9.31	13.87	13.87	26.25
55	14.28	16.91	20.92	30.94	20.92	41.42

Entry age	Straight life	Endowment insurance				
		5 years	10 years	20 years	To age 65	To age 90
25	$12.92	$184.68	$86.81	$38.64	$16.81	$12.94
35	17.88	184.76	87.08	39.44	25.08	17.91
45	26.56	185.97	88.83	42.54	42.54	26.62
55	41.99	189.55	93.99	51.19	93.99	42.13

the life insurance companies are called *gross premiums* and include allowances for expenses, margins for contingencies, and allowances for any options such as those mentioned and which may be contained in the policy.

The premiums quoted in Table 5.1 are for illustration only but they do indicate the following points, just as actual premium rates calculated and quoted by life insurance companies would do for the basic plans which have been considered above:

1. All premium rates, for the same plan and payable for the same number of years, increase with age at entry.
2. From age 31 the mortality increases with age and as the period of the term policy increases the rate of premium increases. In the extreme case where the period is long enough the rate of premium on the term plan increases to approach that of the straight life plan for the same age at entry.
3. As the period of the endowment insurance increases the rate of premium decreases until in the extreme case where the period is long enough it approaches that of the straight life plan for the same age at entry.

The net premium rates for term to age 90 and endowment insurance to age 90 illustrate how the basic plans merge into each other. One should compare them with the straight life net premium rates for the same age at entry to illustrate what has been stated above.

CHAPTER SIX

The Calculation of Net Premiums

This chapter and the next are of particular importance. Much of the difficulty experienced in understanding the theory of life insurance is resolved by a clear understanding of rate-making and the calculation of policy-reserves covered in these two chapters. Much misguided criticism of the practice of life insurance is due to the lack of recognition of the principles on which it is based.

It is strongly suggested that the arithmetic be followed, line by line, with pencil and pad. The insight which will be obtained will repay the extra effort.

COMPOUND INTEREST[1]

Interest is the reward or price paid by one party for the use or loan of something owned by another party. The interest does not necessarily have to be in money; it could, for example, be a share of a crop harvested by the use of borrowed equipment. However, in this text, units of money are always meant, both where the principal (the thing loaned) or the interest is concerned. When we deal with annuities in Chapter 13 some reference to the historical aspects of interest will be made.

When we use the phrase *compound interest* we indicate that money is never left idle and interest as soon as received or credited is immediately invested to earn additional interest. In practice interest is payable or accrues only at stated intervals, but the idea is that money, loaned at compound interest, is increasing continuously; at the stated intervals the increase is paid as interest or allowed to accumulate at the same rate as the principal.

[1]Only those elements essential to the demonstration are given here. A comprehensive text book at college level is N. E. Sheppard and D. C. Baillie, *Compound Interest* (Toronto, 1960).

It is customary to refer to the *rate of interest* as the amount payable on a principal of $100 in the course of a year. Thus on a loan of $100 when it is stated that the rate of interest is 3 per cent per annum, the amount of the interest each year is $3.00 whether that amount is payable in one sum at the end of the year; in half-yearly instalments of $1.50 each; in quarterly instalments of 75¢ each or in monthly instalments of 25¢ each. In such a case the 3 per cent is called the *nominal* rate of interest. It is obvious that the more frequently the instalments of interest are payable the greater is the actual annual yield in interest. Thus the corresponding *effective* annual rates of interest corresponding to these interest payments are 3 per cent (annual), 3.022 per cent (half-yearly), 3.034 per cent (quarterly), and 3.042 per cent (monthly). Throughout this text we mean the *annual effective rate* when we refer to any rate of interest and in this chapter when using 3 per cent per annum as interest we mean that on each $100 principal, interest of $3.00 is due at the end of the year.

Accumulation of One Dollar. At 3 per cent per annum $100 would increase to $103.00 at the end of one year. If the total amount were left to accumulate for another year the interest earned would be $3.09 (3 per cent of $103.00) and the accumulated amount at the end of the second year would be $106.09. For a third year the interest would be $3.1827 and the accumulation at the end of the year would be $109.2727 and so on. These amounts are the accumulation of $100 so that the accumulation of $1 would be one hundredth of these amounts, namely: at the end of the first year $1.03, end of second year $1.0609, end of the third year $1.092727 and so on. In column (*a*) of Table 6.1 these amounts are shown, the results being given there to five places of decimals for the accumulation of $1 at 3 per cent per annum up to five years. Interest tables are readily available giving corresponding figures for longer periods and at various rates of interest. For convenience the figures for quinquennial periods from ten to thirty years have been added to the table.

Present Value of One Dollar. If $1 will accumulate to $1.03 at the end of one year at 3 per cent per annum interest, then $1 is the *present value* of $1.03 payable at the end of one year. Similarly $1 is the present value of $1.0609 payable at the end of two years and of $1.092727 payable at the end of three years and so on. If we want to express these amounts in terms of $1 payable at the *end* of the period, we would get the present value of $1 payable at the end of one year as 1.00 ÷ 1.03 or .97087 of a dollar and if the one dollar was payable at the end of two years the

TABLE 6.1

Compound Interest Table
3 per cent per annum

Number of years	Accumulated amount of one dollar to end of year (*a*)	Present value of one dollar due at end of year (*b*)	Present value one dollar per annum payable in advance (*c*)
	$	$	$
1	1.03000	.97087	1.00000
2	1.06090	.94260	1.97087
3	1.09273	.91514	2.91347
4	1.12551	.88849	3.82861
5	1.15927	.86261	4.71710
10	1.34392	.74409	8.78611
15	1.55797	.64186	12.29607
20	1.80611	.55368	15.32380
25	2.09378	.47761	17.93554
30	2.42726	.41199	20.18845

present value would be 1.00/1.0609 or .9426 of a dollar and so on. These present values are given in column (*b*) of Table 6.1.

Amounts Payable Yearly in Advance. A contract does not become effective until consideration is paid. In the same way the premiums under life insurance policies are payable in advance. Thus the first annual premium would be payable at the beginning of the first year, that for the second year at the beginning of the second year and so on. Thus we must get accustomed to amounts payable at the beginning of the year as is illustrated in the figures in this chapter.

Present Value of One Dollar per annum Payable in Advance. Figure 4 shows the present value of $1 payable at the beginning of the first, second, third, fourth, and fifth years respectively. When arranged in this

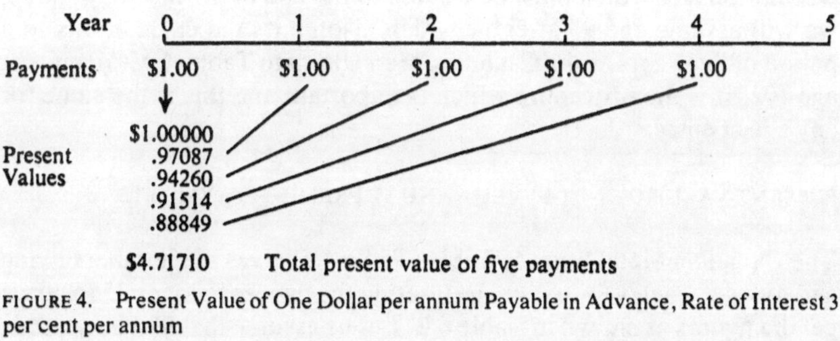

FIGURE 4. Present Value of One Dollar per annum Payable in Advance, Rate of Interest 3 per cent per annum

form it is a simple matter of addition to get the present value of any series of payments payable annually in advance. The effective rate of interest used is 3 per cent and the individual present values are taken from Column (*b*) of Table 6.1. In Figure 4 the total present value of the five yearly payments is shown. In Column (*c*) of Table 6.1 the corresponding total present values of one dollar per annum payable each year for one, two, three, . . . five, ten, . . . thirty years are given.

PRESENT VALUE OF BENEFITS EQUALS PRESENT VALUE OF NET PREMIUMS

The expression net premium has been defined in the last chapter and the values for certain ages and plans on the CM(5) 3 per cent basis were given in Table 5.1. These are the net level annual premiums which if accumulated at the rate of interest assumed (in our case, 3 per cent per annum) and the lives insured are subject to a specific mortality (we assume the Canadian Men Ultimate Table, CM(5)) the accumulated amounts will be exactly sufficient to pay the sums insured as they fall due.

What we have stated in the previous paragraph is an important principle. If the accumulation of the net premiums when due equals the benefits as they become payable then the present values of the two must be equal. Thus, at the commencement of the insurance:

Present Value of Net Premiums equals *Present Value of Benefits*

This principle will be used to calculate the net premium by equating the present values of premiums and benefits payable. To reduce the arithmetic we will confine the illustrations to the calculation of a net level annual premium for a five year term insurance and a five year endowment insurance; both for age 35 at entry. For the straight life plan the calculations for which must be carried to the end of the mortality table, we will assume age 97 at entry which also limits the calculations to a period of five years as the Canadian Men Ultimate Table, CM(5), ends at age 102. It is the procedure which is important and this is the same for any age at entry.

PRESENT VALUE OF NET LEVEL ANNUAL PREMIUM PAYMENTS

The Canadian Men Ultimate Table (Table 4.5) gives the numbers living and dying at each year of age. Extracting the figures for ages 35 to 40 we get the figures as shown in Table 6.2. Let us assume that 92,006 persons

TABLE 6.2

Age	Number living	Number dying
35	92,006	409
36	91,597	419
37	91,178	431
38	90,747	445
39	90,302	461
40	89,841	479

age 35, each purchased a life insurance policy on the same plan for \$1,000 and the net premium for which was *P* dollars. To find the present value of the premiums payable in the first five policy years we note that the total premiums payable at the beginning of the first year are \$92,006*P*. At the commencement of the second policy year there are 91,597 survivors who each pay *P* dollars and so on . . . at the beginning of the fifth policy year, that is, at age 39, there are 90,302 living and the total premiums then due are \$90,302*P*.

Figure 5 shows how the total present value (at the commencement of the insurance) of these five premium payments are calculated. The present value of the first year's premium is \$92,006*P*; that of the second year is \$91,597*P* × .97087 and so on, the discounting factors being taken from column (*b*) of Table 6.1. In Figure 5 the present values for each year are shown and the total gives the present value of the five years' payments, namely \$430,157*P*.

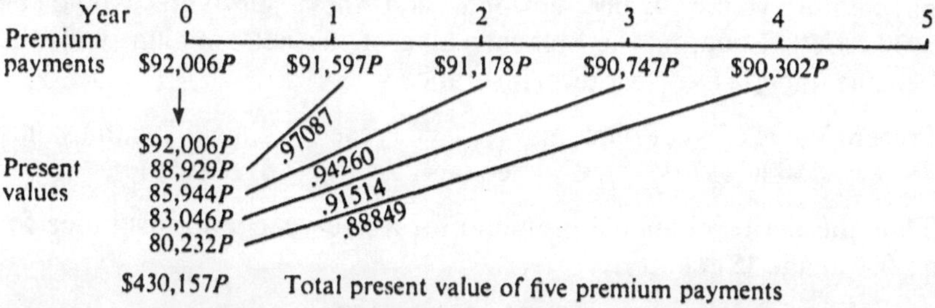

FIGURE 5. Present Value of Annual Premium of *P* Dollars Payable in Advance, Five-Year Policy, CM(5) 3% Basis, Entry Age 35

PRESENT VALUE OF BENEFITS ON A FIVE-YEAR TERM INSURANCE

For age 35 at entry consider the value of the benefits on a five-year term insurance, that is, where \$1,000 is payable on each death during the five-year period following entry. In the first year as we have noted there

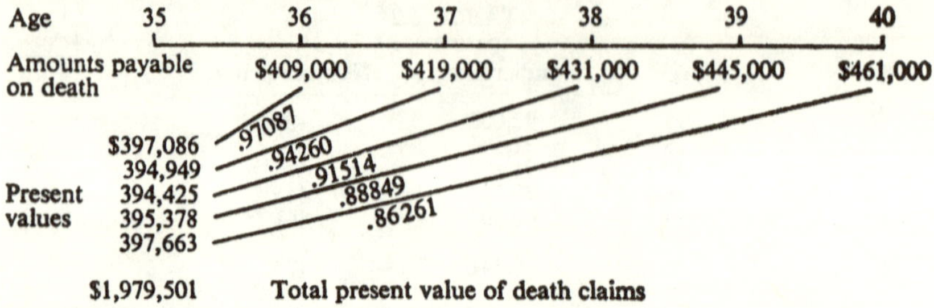

FIGURE 6. Five-Year Term Insurance Policy, Entry Age 35, CM(5) 3% Basis, Present Value of Benefits

are 409 deaths and so benefits totalling $409,000 are payable; in the second year $419,000 is payable and in the third, fourth, and fifth years $431,000, $445,000, and $461,000 respectively are payable.

On the basis that the death claims are payable at the *end* of the policy year in which death occurs Figure 6 indicates how the present value of the death claims is ascertained. The total present value at the commencement of the insurance of the death claims paid in respect of the 2,165 deaths which occurred during the five-year period on the 92,006 entrants is shown to be $1,979,501.

Net Level Annual Premium: Five-year Term Insurance. If P' is the net level premium for a $1,000 five-year term insurance for age 35 at entry it follows from Figure 5 that the total present value of the five premium payments by the 92,006 entrants and their survivors would be $430,157$P'$. Equating the present value of the net premium with the benefits under a five-year term insurance we get:

Present Value of Net Premiums		Present Value of Death Claims
$430,157 P'	equals	$1,979,501

Thus the net level annual premium for a five-year term insurance for $1,000 at age 35 at entry:

P' equals $(1,979,501/430,157) or $4.60.

THEORY AND PRACTICE IN PAYMENT OF DEATH CLAIMS

It is usual to publish net premiums on the assumption that the death claim would be payable at the end of the policy year of death, as we have assumed above. However claims are payable, as a rule, immediately following proof of death. As deaths may be assumed to be evenly distributed throughout the policy years we could assume that, in practice, on the average, the death claim would fall due for payment in the middle of the policy year, not the end, that is six months earlier than assumed in the calculation. An obvious adjustment to allow for this would be to increase the net premium as calculated above by six months' interest. In practice the actuary adjusts for this at the same time as he adjusts the net premium for expenses, contingencies etc. to obtain the gross premium, i.e., that charged for the insurance.

NET LEVEL ANNUAL PREMIUM: FIVE-YEAR ENDOWMENT INSURANCE

Present Value of Benefits. We assume age 35 at entry and a $1,000 policy for which the benefits under the endowment insurance would be $1,000 payable to each survivor at the end of the five-year period plus $1,000 payable on each death during the period. Figure 7 indicates how the

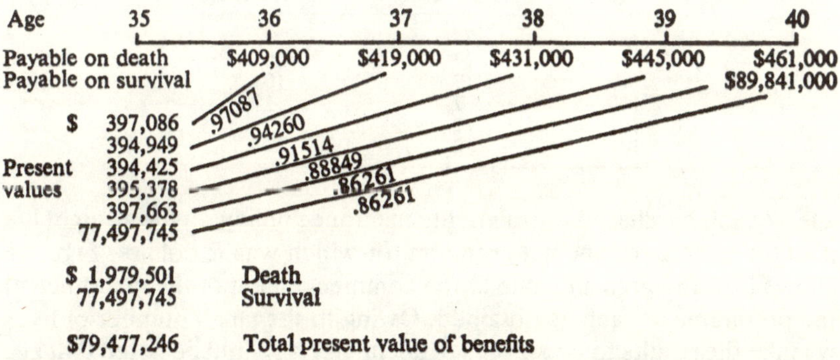

FIGURE 7. Five-Year Endowment Insurance, Entry Age 35, CM(5) 3% Basis, Present Value of Benefits

present values of these benefits are determined. It should be noted that as there are 89,841 survivors, the total payments in the fifth policy year are death claims of $461,000 payable at the end of the policy year together with the $89,841,000 payable to the survivors. The total present value is shown to be $79,477,246.

Net Level Annual Premium. It follows from Figure 5 that if P'' were the net premium for a $1,000 five-year endowment insurance at age 35 at entry that the present value at the commencement of the insurance of the premiums payable would be $430,157 P''. Equating the present value of the net premiums and benefits we get:

$$430{,}157\,P'' \text{ equals } \$79{,}477{,}246$$
$$\text{or } P'' \text{ equals } \$184.76$$

which is the net level annual premium for a five-year endowment insurance for \$1,000 at age 35 at entry.

The actuary's adjustment for immediate payment of claims on death would apply to that part of the net premium represented by the death benefit and not the endowment payable at the end of the period.

NET LEVEL ANNUAL PREMIUM FOR STRAIGHT LIFE INSURANCE

As explained above we calculate the net premium on the straight life plan for a life age 97 at entry to reduce the arithmetic involved to a period of five years. From Table 4.5 the numbers living and dying from age 97 onwards are as shown in Table 6.3. Let us assume that the 74 persons

TABLE 6.3

Age	Number living	Number dying
97	74	37
98	37	20
99	17	10
100	7	5
101	2	2
102	0	—

age 97 each purchased a straight life insurance policy on the straight life plan for \$1,000 and the net premium for which was *R* dollars. Figure 8 shows how the present value at the commencement of the insurance of the premiums payable is obtained. Owing to the small number of lives we take the results to two places of decimals. It should be noted that age 102 is the end of the CM(5) Life Table and had we demonstrated the calculation of the premium at a younger age than 97 we would have had to carry the calculation on—just as demonstrated in Figure 8 to the end

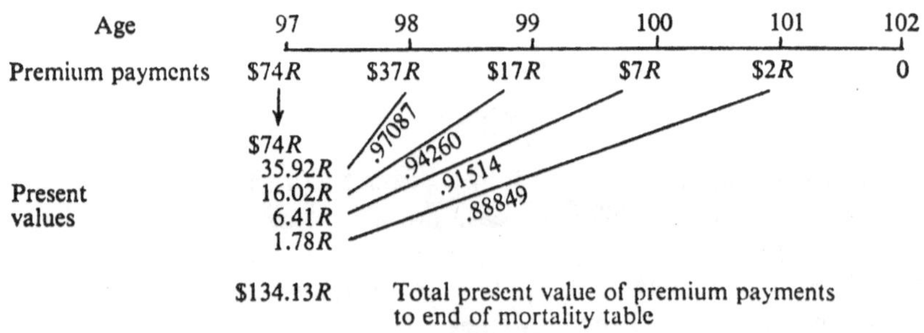

FIGURE 8. Straight Life Plan, Entry Age 97, CM(5) 3% Basis, Present Value of Annual Premiums of *R* Dollars Payable in Advance

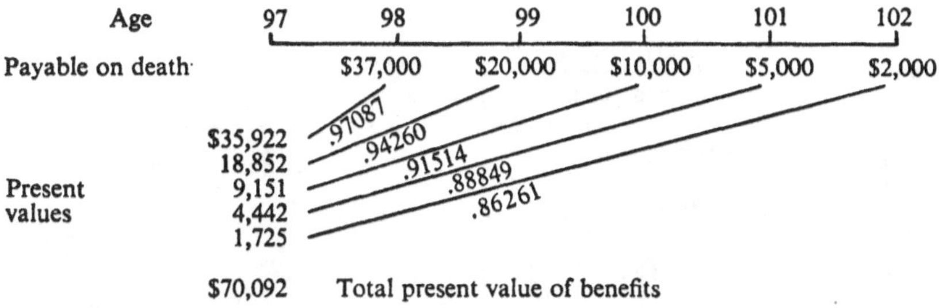

FIGURE 9. Straight Life Plan, Entry Age 97, CM(5) 3% Basis, Present Value of Benefits

of the table at age 102. In similar fashion to that demonstrated for other plans we show in Figure 9 the value of the death claims payable from age 97 to the end of the mortality table, namely age 102.

Equating the present values of the net premiums and death benefits we get:[2]

Present Value of Net Premiums (See Figure 8)		Present Value of Death Claims (See Figure 9)
$134.13 *R*	equals	$70,092
or *R*	is	$(70,092/134.13) or $522.58.

Thus $522.58 is the net level annual premium for a straight life insurance of $1,000 for a life age 97 at entry according to the CM(5) 3% Table. As will be seen from the net premiums given in Table 5.1, the corresponding net level annual premium for age 25 at entry is $12.92 and for age 35 at entry $17.88. These could be derived by similar processes to Figures 8 and 9. Actuaries have devised various processes to reduce the arithmetic involved in the calculation of net premiums without any loss in accuracy, but they are beyond the scope of this text.

ONE-YEAR TERM RATE

From Table 4.5, which is the CM(5) Life Table, the one-year term rate for any age at entry is readily calculated on the CM(5) 3% basis. At age 35, say, there are 92,006 entrants each purchasing $1,000 insurance for one year. There are 409 deaths in the year and the death claims payable at the end of the year amount to $409,000. To equate premiums payable and death claims we must take the present value at the beginning of the year of $409,000 payable at the end of the year which is done by

[2]The division gives $522.57 but if the calculations were carried out to several places of decimals the result would be $522.58 as given.

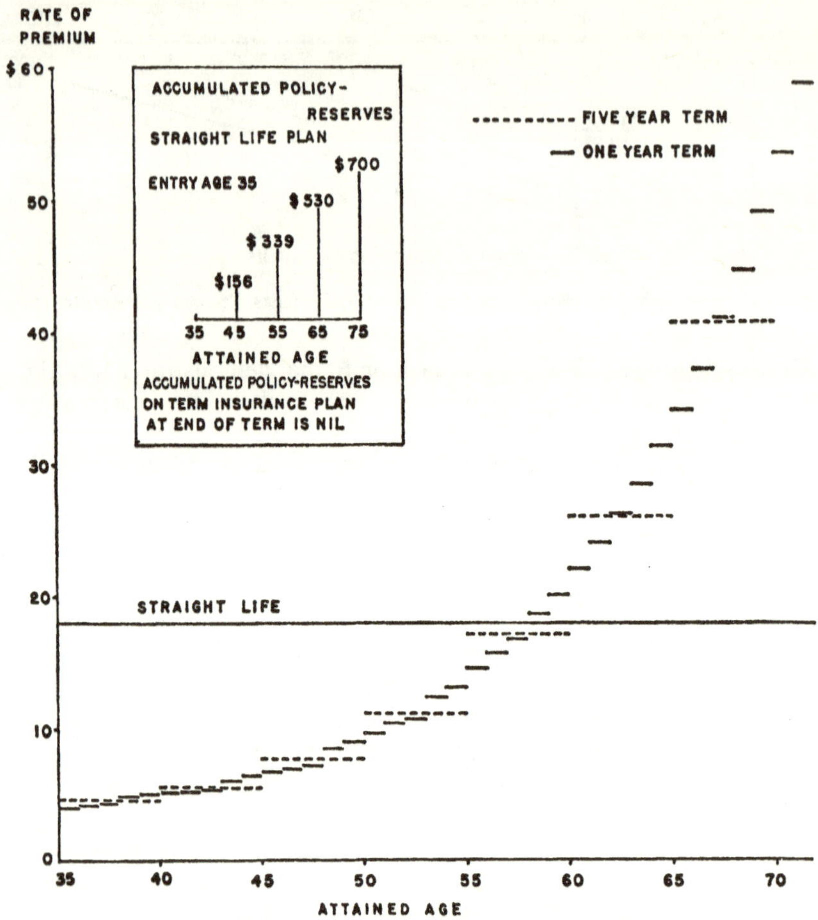

FIGURE 10. Comparison of Net Level Annual Premiums: Straight Life, Age 35 at Entry, One-Year Term, Five-Year Term, CM(5) 3% per $1,000 Sum Insured

multiplying it by .97087 giving $397,086. (The factor is given in Column (*b*) in Table 6.1.)

As the premiums paid by each of the 92,006 entrants must equal $397,086 it follows that each must pay $(397,086/92,006) or $4.32. This is the net annual premium on the CM(5) 3% basis for a one-year term insurance at age 35 at entry. In Table 5.1 we gave the rates for this and other ages at entry and in Figure 10 the rates are shown for every age from 35 to 71. Note how the rate begins to climb quite steeply after age 45. At age 55 it is more than double the rate at age 45 and at age 65 it is about two and a half times what it is at age 55.

As mentioned in Chapter 5 term insurance can be purchased on this basis, the plan being renewable year by year, paying the increased premium required each year. It is there referred to as the One-Year Renewable Term Plan.

HIGHER INTEREST, LOWER NET PREMIUM

The higher the rate of interest assumed in calculating a premium rate, the greater will be the accumulation of the premiums paid to meet payment of benefits, etc.; thus the smaller would be the net premium required to pay for any specific benefit. Hence we note the importance of interest earnings to a life insurance company.

To illustrate this we show below (Table 6.4) the net annual premiums on the CM(5) Table at interest rates of 3 and 3½ per cent per annum for a number of plans for an insurance of $1,000 and for age 35 at entry in each case. Some of these have already been given in Table 5.1. The extent of the reduction in net premium in each case should be noted.

TABLE 6.4

	One-year term	Five-year term	Straight life	Endowment Insurance 10 years	20 years	To age 65
	$	$	$	$	$	$
3%	4.32	4.60	17.88	87.08	39.44	25.08
3½%	4.30	4.58	16.64	84.77	37.53	23.48

SINGLE PREMIUMS

The premium for any life insurance benefit can be paid in one sum at the commencement of the insurance with the understanding that no part of the premium paid will be refunded in addition to the sum insured on death. In such a case the phrase *single premium* is added to the description of the plan.

We have in this chapter actually calculated the net single premiums for the various plans demonstrated. The total net single premiums to be paid by the entrants must equal the present value of the benefits. Thus it also equals the present value of the net annual premiums at the commencement of the insurance. Dealing with the plans in turn:

Five-Year Term Insurance Age 35 at Entry. The present value at the commencement of the benefits to be paid for by the 92,006 entrants according to Figure 6 is $1,979,501. Thus the net single premium to be paid by each entrant for a five-year term insurance of $1,000 is $(1,979,501/92,006) or $21.51.

Endowment Insurance, Five-Year Period, Age 35 at Entry. The present value at the commencement of the total benefits payable, according to Figure 7 is $79,477,246 and the number of entrants is 92,006. Thus the net single premium to be paid by each entrant is $(79,477,246/92,006) or $863.83.

Straight Life Insurance Age 97 at Entry. The number of entrants is 74, and the present value of the insurance of $1,000 payable on each death, whenever it occurs, according to Figure 9 is $70,092. Thus the net single premium to be paid by each entrant is $(70,092/74) or $947.19.

COMPARISON OF NET PREMIUMS

In Figure 10 the net annual premiums on the CM(5) 3% basis are shown graphically for some of the plans we have discussed. The One-Year Renewable Term Plan is shown from age 35 to age 71 at entry; note how low it is at the younger ages and how prohibitive it becomes later on; at age 80 it is double that at age 71. This also applies to the Five-Year Term Plan, which would have to be renewed every five years and the premium paid at the higher age.

Under the Straight Life Plan shown for age 35 at entry, the same level annual premium is paid year by year however long the life insured may live. Another feature of the straight life plan is that a fund called the policy-reserve is accumulated, increasing year by year which will be discussed in the next chapter. Under term plans the fund is used up by the end of the term period—in the cases illustrated, one year and five years respectively.

CHAPTER SEVEN

Policy-Reserves

ADEQUACY OF NET PREMIUMS

We have already stated that when the net premiums are calculated based on a specific mortality table and rate of interest, and such net premiums are accumulated at that specific rate of interest and claims are paid according to that mortality table, they will provide exactly for the benefits to which the net premiums relate. In the demonstrations below we actually show this to be the case for the net premiums we calculated in the previous chapter based on the Canadian Men Ultimate, CM(5) mortality table (Table 4.5) and an interest rate of 3 per cent per annum.

Five-Year Term Insurance. As shown in Table 7.1 we follow the 92,006 entrants, all age 35 and each having effected a $1,000 policy on his life on the five-year term plan, the net level premium for which we have calculated and showed to be $4.60. The net premiums received from the entrants totalled $423,394 which accumulated to the end of the year (add

TABLE 7.1

Calculation of Policy-Reserves, 5-Year Term Insurance, Sum Insured $1,000, Net Level Annual Premium $4.60, Age 35 at Entry, CM(5) 3%, Number of Entrants 92,006

Year	Premiums received	Fund beginning of year	Fund with interest	Death claims, number	Fund end of year	Number of survivors	Policy-reserve per $1,000
	$	$	$		$		$
1	423,394	423,394	436,096	409	27,096	91,597	0.30
2	421,511	448,607	462,065	419	43,065	91,178	0.47
3	419,583	462,648	476,527	431	45,527	90,747	0.50
4	417,600	463,127	477,021	445	32,021	90,302	0.35
5	415,552	447,573	461,000	461	0	89,841	0

NOTE: To reproduce the above figures exactly the net premium should be taken as $4.601804.

3 per cent interest) and death claims paid of $409,000 resulted in $27,096 being in hand at the end of the year relating to the 91,597 survivors. We proceed to the second year when each survivor pays $4.60 and the accumulation proceeds with the deduction of 419 death claims giving the fund in hand for the 91,178 survivors at the end of the second year. Note that the fund increases and then decreases to zero at the end of the five-year period when the term insurance expires. The fund decreases to zero at the end of the term period for all term insurances whatever the age at entry or period of the insurance.

At the end of each policy year we show the sum in hand per survivor or per $1,000 insurance in force; this is in the last column and is headed "Policy-reserve per $1,000." Note that for a five-year term insurance for age 35 at entry it is never more than a few cents.

Five-Year Endowment Insurance. The net premium for age 35 at entry is $184.76 per thousand and in Table 7.2 the accumulation is carried out.

TABLE 7.2

Calculation of Policy-Reserves, 5-Year Endowment Insurance, Sum Insured $1,000, Net Level Annual Premium $184.76, Age 35 at Entry, CM(5) 3%, Number of Entrants 92,006

Year	Premiums received	Fund beginning of year	Fund with interest	Death claims, number	Fund end of year	Number of survivors	Policy-reserve per $1,000
	$	$	$		$		$
1	16,999,287	16,999,287	17,509,266	409	17,100,266	91,597	187
2	16,923,719	34,023,985	35,044,705	419	34,625,705	91,178	380
3	16,846,303	51,472,008	53,016,168	431	52,585,168	90,747	579
4	16,766,671	69,351,839	71,432,394	445	70,987,394	90,302	786
5	16,684,451	87,671,845	90,302,000	461	89,841,000	89,841	1,000

NOTE: To reproduce the above figures exactly the net premium should be taken as $184.762810.

At the end of five years the amount in hand after paying all death claims arising in the five years, as they arose, is $89,841,000 which exactly provides $1,000 each for the 89,841 survivors, being the sum due to each on the maturity of his five-year endowment insurance.

Straight Life Plan for Age 97 at Entry. There are 74 entrants at age 97 (see Table 4.5) and Table 7.3 shows the accumulation of the net premium of $522.58 per thousand. Note that at the beginning of the fifth year there are only two survivors and the amount in hand is $897 ($896.64) which when increased by the net premiums then payable $1045.16 and with one year's interest at 3 per cent accumulates to $2,000 which is

TABLE 7.3

Calculation of Policy-Reserves, Straight Life Insurance, Sum Insured $1,000, Net Level Annual Premium $522.58, Age 97 at Entry, CM(5) 3%, Number of Entrants 74

Year	Premiums received	Fund beginning of year	Fund with interest	Death claims, number	Fund end of year	Number of survivors	Policy-reserve per $1,000
	$	$	$		$		$
1	38,671	38,671	39,831	37	2,831	37	77
2	19,335	22,167	22,832	20	2,832	17	167
3	8,884	11,715	12,067	10	2,067	7	295
4	3,658	5,725	5,897	5	897	2	448
5	1,045	1,942	2,000	2	0*	0*	0*

NOTE: The results were worked out to two places of decimals and inserted in the above table to the nearest integer.

*The company did have $1,000 in hand at the end of the policy year for each entrant into this policy year.

exactly the amount required to pay the two death claims arising in the year.

THE POLICY-RESERVE

In the accumulation of the net premiums in Table 7.1, 7.2, and 7.3, the sum in hand at any time is known technically as the *policy-reserve*, the *policy value*, or simply the *reserve*. In the reports of the Superintendent of Insurance for Canada they are called the "actuarial reserves." In the last column of each of Tables 7.1, 7.2, and 7.3, we give the policy-reserves at the end of each policy year per $1,000 insurance.

A great deal of misunderstanding has arisen regarding the principles of life insurance by the use of terminology which, however clear to those engaged in the business, has other meanings to the public. In an abstruse science this would be immaterial, but in a country like Canada where three out of every four families carry life insurance and the average amount owned per household at the end of 1974 was $28,200,[1] the great majority of people are personally interested and have a substantial stake in the life insurance industry.

The word *reserve*, outside life insurance circles means "something withheld as for future use; a store, a stock, an extra supply."[2] To the layman the word conveys the idea of something additional to absolute

[1]*Canadian Life Insurance Facts, 1975* (Toronto: Canadian Life Insurance Association).

[2]Webster's New International Dictionary. The Shorter Oxford Dictionary gives an almost identical meaning: "Something stored up, kept back, or relied upon for future use or advantage; a store, a stock, an extra quantity."

needs. This has led to the statement that life insurance companies accumulate enormous reserves out of the premiums paid them for the sake of the "economic power" and "profits" achieved thereby. It is a repeated criticism and misunderstanding often voiced against the institution of life insurance.

The "actuarial reserves" as given in the report of the Superintendent of Insurance as at the December 31, 1974, of the federally registered Canadian life insurance companies (business in Canada and abroad) amounted to $15,287 millions; those of British and foreign companies regarding their life business in Canada were $3,848 millions making a total of over nineteen billion dollars.

From Tables 7.1, 7.2, and 7.3 it is obvious that the sum or fund in hand arising from the accumulation of the net premiums after paying the claims as they arise which is called various names as policy values or policy-reserves or actuarial reserves is absolutely essential to enable the insurance company to carry out the conditions of the life insurance contract. It is the minimum amount which the company must have and is based on the net level premiums being accumulated at a determined rate of interest subject to death and survivorship according to a specified table of mortality; it is not something additional as the word "reserve" generally implies.

Throughout this text the hyphenated word *policy-reserve* will always be used to denote this minimum fund which the company must have in hand. When we refer to amounts additional to the policy-reserves which any going concern should have as a margin for unforeseen contingencies, etc., we will use the words *surplus* or *surplus funds*.

Although the following matter will be dealt with in some detail later it is advisable to mention it here. The main responsibility of government supervision of the life insurance industry, as determined by legislation, is to ensure that the life insurance companies hold assets to cover the policy-reserves according to the official government basis. There are, of course, other liabilities which must be covered by assets.

POLICY-RESERVE AND LEVEL NET PREMIUM

In Figure 10 (Chapter 6) compare the net level premium of the straight life plan with the rapidly increasing one-year term rate. The net one-year term rate continues to increase beyond age 71, the limit of the chart; at age 80 it is more than double that at age 71; yet the net level straight life premium continues unchanged.

Whenever a level net premium is paid, more is paid in the early years and less in the later years, than if each year's risk were paid for as it arose. This is due to the rate of mortality increasing with age. It follows that any excess paid in the early years above the net one-year term rate must be accumulated to meet the claim payments in the later years when the net premium paid does not cover the risk year by year. It may be stated in simple fashon, that this excess when accumulated gives the policy-reserve. In examining Figure 10 it should be remembered that on the straight life plan (entry age 35) the policy-reserve after ten years (attained age 45) is $156, after twenty years (attained age 55) it is $339, and after thirty years (attained age 65) it is $530, whereas for the one-year term rate the policy-reserve is nil, as it is for the five-year term plan or any other term insurance when the period of the insurance is completed.

MODIFIED POLICY-RESERVES

The policy-reserves calculated above have all been derived from a net level annual premium and should be referred to as *net level premium policy-reserves*. In practice the expenses in the first year of a policy are far greater than in subsequent years (it is not only the cost of issuing the policy and setting up the records but the remuneration of the sales force is greater in the year of acquisition than in subsequent years). To allow for this a net premium could be used which was lower in the first year and higher in subsequent years and yet the present values of which together at the commencement of the insurance was the same as the corresponding net level premium. Such net premiums are called *modified net premiums* and the policy-reserves obtained by their use are called *modified policy-reserves*.

It follows that in the early years of a policy these modified policy-reserves are lower than those based on net level premiums, the difference decreasing as the duration of the policy increases. These modified policy-reserves are permitted by law and some companies use them; they have played an important part in the development of life insurance. In Chapter 17 the subject will be discussed further.

THE BALANCING ITEM

The present value at the commencement of the insurance of the net premiums and the benefits payable must be equal. This is how the net premiums were calculated in Chapter 6. What is the position at the end of any subsequent year? Some of the premiums have fallen due and some of the claims have been paid and the sum in hand is the policy-reserve. From Tables 7.1, 7.2, and 7.3 it is obvious that the accumulation of the policy-reserve plus the accumulation of the net premiums as they fall due will exactly pay the death claims as they arise.

Thus at the end of any policy year:

> The policy-reserve *plus* the present value of future net premiums payable *equals* the present value of the future benefits to be paid.

The policy-reserve is thus the balancing item. The usual way of expressing this most important identity is:

> At the end of any policy year: the policy-reserve *equals* the present value of future benefits *less* the present value of future net premiums.

The policy-reserve can thus be derived in two different ways. Firstly, as in Tables 7.1, 7.2, and 7.3, by the accumulation of the net premiums and the deduction of the claims as they arise: this is the *retrospective* method. Secondly, as demonstrated in this section as the balancing item, it is the excess of the present value of the benefits over that of the net premiums; this is the *prospective method.*

NET AMOUNT AT RISK

On any death the loss incurred by the insurance company is not the amount payable on death but that amount less the policy-reserve held by the company for the policy. All amounts are considered as at the end of the policy year in which death occurs. The amount payable on death less the policy-reserve at the end of the policy year in which death occurs is called the *net amount at risk.* Note in Table 7.1 the five-year term plan, where the policy-reserves per policy are trivial the net amounts at risk are practically the full sum insured. Under the five-year endowment insurance (Table 7.2) where the policy-reserve rises rapidly the net amount at risk per $1,000 sum insured falls from $813 at the end of the first year to zero at the end of the last year.

In Figure 11 we show the policy-reserves for several important plans of life insurance for age 35 at entry. For term insurance we show the values for a term to age 65, i.e., a thirty-year term insurance. Note the break in the upward trend of the 10- and 20-payment life where the premiums cease to be payable i.e. the policy is paid-up but the sum insured is not payable until death occurs. Under the straight life and 10-

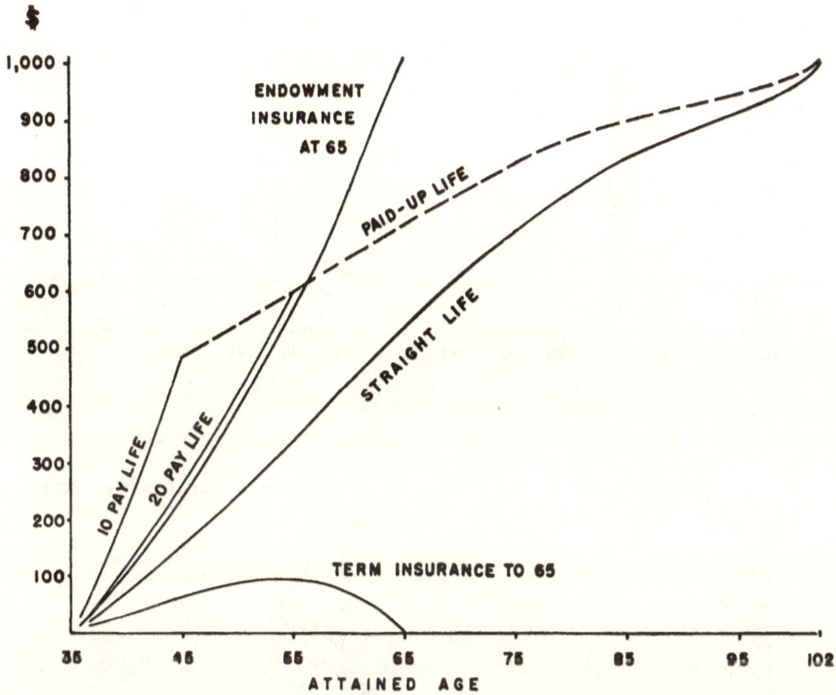

FIGURE 11. Terminal Policy-Reserves per $1,000 Sum Insured Age 35 at Entry, CM(5) 3%

and 20-payment life plans it is assumed that the policy-reserves are $1,000 per $1,000 insurance at the end of the mortality table, namely age 102 on the CM(5) Table. Should any survive to this age the company having the full sum insured in hand as the policy-reserve would pay that amount and the insurance would be terminated.[3] On the endowment insurance at age 65 (i.e., a thirty-year endowment insurance) the policy-reserve reaches $1,000 at age 65. Note how the policy-reserves of the 20-payment life are just above those of the endowment insurance at age 65 until after the twentieth year when the premiums on the former cease to be payable.

In Figure 12 the net amounts at risk for four of the plans considered above are shown.

[3]The American Experience Table (which was in almost universal use among U.S. companies until recent years) terminated at age 96 and quite a number of cases arose under straight life policies where the full sum insured was paid on attainment of that age.

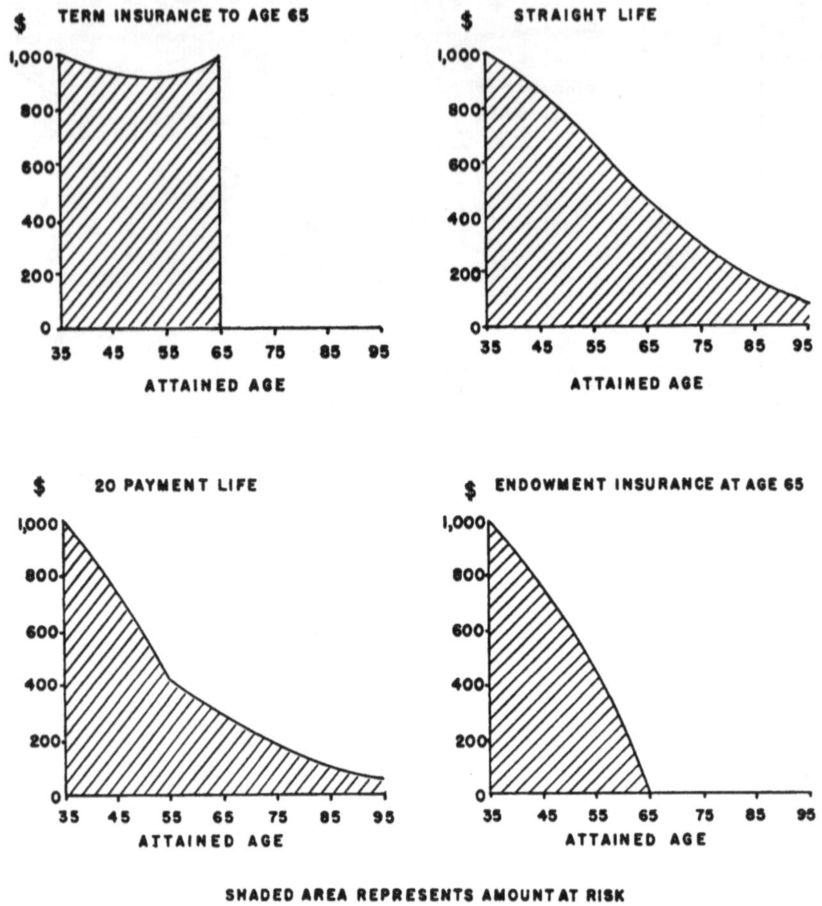

FIGURE 12. Net Amount at Risk (Sum Insured less Policy-Reserve), Age 35 at Entry, CM(5) 3%, per $1,000 Sum Insured

COST OF INSURANCE

Let us apply the procedures we used for Tables 7.1 and 7.2 for age 35 at entry to the straight life plan, the net level annual premium for which is $17.88 per thousand sum insured. There are 92,006 entrants at age 35 each paying $17.88 and we accumulate these net premiums, paying the claims as they arise, using 3 per cent per annum interest and assuming mortality according to the CM(5) table (Table 4.5). Continuing the procedure to the end of the tenth policy year let us follow the details of the eleventh policy year. The survivors entering the eleventh year number 87,216, the number of deaths in the year is 609 and the survivors at the end of the year number 86,607. The fund in hand or the policy-reserve at the end of the tenth policy year and hence the amount at the beginning of the eleventh year is $13,589,997 or $155.82 per policy. See Table 7.4. The item *xxx* in the table, the difference between $173.14 and $178.91 must be $5.77. This amount is the *cost of insurance*.

> Thus, the policy-reserve at the beginning of the year increased by the net premium due at that time and by interest on the total and decreased by the cost of insurance equals the policy-reserve at the end of the year.

TABLE 7.4

Eleventh policy year		Per $1,000 sum insured
Policy-reserve at beginning of year	$13,589,997	$155.82
87,216 enter each paying $17.88	1,559,422	17.88
Total (Initial Policy-reserve)	$15,149,419	$173.70
Add one year's interest at 3%, to give	15,603,902	178.91
Deduct 609 claims paid	609,000	*xxx*
Policy-reserve at end of year 86,607 survivors means that the policy-reserve per $1,000 in force at end of year is $173.14	$14,994,902	$173.14

This demonstration has been made for a particular plan of insurance, for a specified age at entry and a given duration; it is a general principle which applies to all plans, all ages at entry, and every duration.

Where did the $609,000 in claims come from? Note that before we deducted the claim payments we had $15,603,902 contributed by 87,216 entrants or $178.91 each. Thus each death claim contributed that amount to the fund in hand, or a total for the 609 claims of $108,956. Then each of the 86,607 survivors paid towards the death claims $5.77[4] or $500,044. These two amounts add up to $609,000 the total of the death claims paid in the year.

Above we have shown that the death claims paid in any year consist of (1) the policy-reserves of those who die in the year, and (2) the cost of insurance as contributed by the survivors to the end of the year.

[4]Using two places of decimals only, the amount would fall short of that required by a few dollars. Above we have used $5.77371 for the cost of insurance.

ANOTHER ASPECT OF THE COST OF INSURANCE

Consider the net amount at risk in the eleventh policy year, i.e., at age 45, of the 86,607 survivors and to reduce the arithmetic let us deal with each policy of \$1,000. The policy-reserve at the end of the year is \$173.14 so that the net amount at risk regarding each survivor is \$1,000 less \$173.14 or \$826.86. According to the CM(5) table of mortality (Table 4.5) the rate of mortality at age 45 is 6.98 thousand, so that for each \$1,000 exposed for one year at age 45 we could expect claims of \$6.98; thus for an exposure of \$826.86 the claims expected would be \$(6.98 × 826.86/1,000) or \$5.77 which is the cost of insurance as obtained in the previous section.[5]

The important point we make here is that each survivor must make a contribution to the death risk for each policy year he has survived, and that the death risk for which he is charged is based not on the sum insured which would be payable if he died in that year but on the net amount at risk, namely the sum insured less the policy-reserve at the end of the year.

Summarizing what we stated above:

Cost of Insurance = Rate of Mortality × Net Amount at Risk

THE STRAIGHT LIFE POLICY-RESERVE INCREASES YEAR BY YEAR

Under a straight life policy, as the period the policy has been in force increases, there are fewer premiums expected to be paid and as the age increases the death rate increases. Thus the present value of the future premiums decreases and the present value of the benefit payable increases. Thus the balancing item between these two obviously increases year by year and that is the policy-reserve. The same argument applies to every endowment insurance.

The following query may be raised by the reader. If, as we stated above when examining Figure 10, on any net level premium plan the excess of the net premium in the early years must be accumulated to meet the increasing death rate in later years when the net premium is inadequate to meet it, how can the policy-reserve increase year by year? Should it not tend to be exhausted, particularly at the longer durations of a straight life plan when the rate of mortality becomes quite high?

The answer is given by the fact that the charge in each year for the

[5]In the calculation we could have used the net one-year term rate at age 45 of \$6.78 instead of \$6.98, but \$6.78 is calculated on the basis that it is payable at the beginning of the year. \$6.78 increased by one year's interest gives the \$6.98 we used.

insurance risk, or, the cost of insurance, as we call it, is not based on the face amount of sum insured payable according to the policy but on the sum insured less the policy-reserve. Thus with increasing duration and increasing age, the mortality rate increases but the net amount at risk to which it is applied decreases year by year (See Figure 12). The cost of insurance does increase but evidently at a much slower rate than the rate of mortality. The policy-reserve plus the net premium when accumulated at interest meets the increased cost of insurance and also results in an increasing policy-reserve in hand.

POLICY-RESERVES AND RATE OF INTEREST

We have already shown in Chapter 6 that the higher the interest rate used in calculating a net premium the lower is the net premium. Table 7.5 gives specimen policy-reserves for representative plans at various durations and it is seen that the same applies there: the higher the interest rate the lower the policy-reserve. Of course, at the maturity date of an endowment insurance the policy-reserve must equal the sum insured whatever the rate of interest used.

TABLE 7.5
Terminal Policy-Reserves, Net Level Premium, Age 35 at Entry, per $1,000 Sum Insured

End of year	10-year term	20-year term	Straight life	Endowment insurance 10 years	Endowment insurance 20 years	Endowment insurance 30 years
			CM(5) 3%			
1	$1	$ 3	$ 14	$ 86	$ 36	$ 21
3	2	8	43	266	112	66
5	3	12	74	458	193	114
10	0	21	156	1000	419	244
15		20	245		683	391
20		0	339		1000	560
			CM(5) 3½%			
1	$1	$ 3	$ 13	$ 84	$ 35	$ 20
3	2	7	40	261	107	62
5	3	12	68	452	185	106
10	0	21	145	1000	407	231
15		20	230		673	375
20		0	322		1000	544

The point that higher interst rates involve lower policy-reserves and *vice versa* has considerable practical significance which will be dealt with in a later chapter. It follows from common-sense reasoning that the higher the rate of interest at which a company may expect to accumulate the funds in its hands, the lower need these funds be to meet definite future liabilities.

MORTALITY RATES AND POLICY-RESERVES

How would the downward trend of mortality rates experienced in recent years affect policy-reserves? It is obvious that lower mortality means lower net premiums and from Tables 7.1, 7.2, and 7.3 it is clear that lower net premiums and lower death claims offset each other in the accumulation which gives the policy-reserves.

The relationship between mortality and policy-reserves is not a simple one and has no direct answer. The policy-reserve is the fund to even out the increasing cost of the death benefit and thus ensure that the net premium remains constant. Its variation as between different mortality tables depends on the rate of climb or slope of the mortality curve.

The practical point is this: one does not know as a rule, what policy-reserves will be indicated by a new mortality table until they are calculated. Specimen policy-reserves under different mortality tables are shown in Table 7.6. They are given in chronological order, covering

TABLE 7.6

Net Level Annual Premiums and Terminal Policy-Reserves per $1,000 Sum Insured, Age 35 at Entry, Various Tables 3 per cent Interest

	Hm to 1863	Om(5) 1863–1893	CM(5) 1900–1915	A 1924–29 1924–1929	CSO 1958 1950–1954
		Straight life			
Net premium	$21.93	$21.56	$17.88	$16.48	$16.29
Policy-reserves end of year					
5	72	73	74	74	75
10	153	153	156	155	156
20	332	331	339	340	334
		20-payment life			
Net premium	$30.68	$30.28	$26.08	$24.45	$24.23
Policy-reserves end of year					
5	121	122	119	118	119
10	263	262	256	252	252
20	619	615	590	579	573
		20-year endowment insurance			
Net premium	$42.31	$42.06	$39.44	$38.51	$38.42
Policy-reserves end of year					
5	187	188	193	196	197
10	409	410	419	422	424
20	1000	1000	1000	1000	1000

over a century of actuarial history and all are tables which have been used and (as regards the C.S.O. 1958 table) will be used extensively in Canada in the calculation of policy-reserves; they comprise Canadian, British, and U.S. investigations.

Note from the earliest Hm to the latest table, C.S.O. 1958, the net premiums for age 35 at entry have fallen steadily. However, there is no definite trend in the policy-reserves. Taking the earliest and the latest tables shown, although there has been a considerable reduction in the net premium, the policy-reserves actually increase on the straight life and endowment insurance, taking the first twenty policy years. At the end of twenty years under the 20-payment life plan no further premiums are payable so that the value of the death benefit alone determines the amount of the policy-reserve at and after that period. This explains the fall in the policy-reserves at the end of twenty years under the 20-payment life plan from an older to a more recent mortality table with lower mortality, thus from 619 to 573 in Table 7.6

It should be appreciated that when a new mortality table is adopted and a reduced net premium is indicated, should the policy-reserves in the early policy years increase, practical problems arise of some significance. The surplus emerging in the company's operations would be disturbed as between new and older policies affecting many aspects of the business. These matters will be dealt with later on in the text.

TERMINAL, INITIAL, AND MID-YEAR POLICY-RESERVES

The policy-reserves as calculated in Tables 7.1, 7.2, and 7.3 and as given in Tables 7.5 and 7.6 are those at the *end* of the policy year shown and are known as *terminal* policy-reserves.

The policy-reserves at the beginning of the policy year immediately on payment of the premiums then due are called *initial* policy-reserves. As an example consider the eleventh policy year as analysed above for age 35 at entry under the section "Cost of Insurance." The policy-reserve at the end of the tenth year which is the same as at the beginning of the eleventh year before the net premiums are paid is $155.82. On payment of the premium the initial policy-reserve for the eleventh policy year is shown as $173.70 per $1,000 sum insured, i.e., the net premium of $17.88 is added. In the first policy year the initial policy-reserve is the net premium itself.

Mid-Year Policy-Reserves. The statement of a life insurance company has to indicate the policy-reserves of its policies as at a specified date namely that to which the statement applies, usually 31 December. It would be most impracticable to calculate the policy-reserve on policies allowing for their exact durations at the date of the statement. However, for practical purposes it may be assumed that policies are issued and the insurance commences on them evenly throughout the calendar year. Thus all policies issued in the calendar year to which the statement relates could be assumed to be exactly $1/2$ year in force; those issued in the previous calendar year $1 1/2$ years in force; in the year earlier: $2 1/2$ years in force, and so on. Such policy-reserves are called *mid-year, mean,* or *medial* policy-reserves and the "actuarial reserves" given in the government returns and in life insurance company statements are these mid-year policy-reserves.

Mid-year policy-reserves are halfway between the initial and terminal policy-reserves. Thus for $10 1/2$ years in force it would be half way between the initial policy-reserve at the beginning of the eleventh year and the terminal policy-reserve for the eleventh year. Referring to the above example of the straight life plan, age 35 at entry, the mid-year policy-reserve for duration $10 1/2$ years is $1/2$ ($173.70 plus $173.14) or $173.42. In considering the mid-year policy-reserve at any duration it should be noted that the same number of net premiums are assumed as paid both for the initial, mid-year, and terminal policy-reserves for that duration—the premiums being payable annually in advance.

SURRENDER VALUES

It is usual in Canada and the U.S., on most plans of life insurance, to guarantee in the policy the full terminal policy-reserve as a cash surrender value on the voluntary termination of the policy after it has been in force for a number of years. In the earlier years a deduction is made from the policy-reserve called a *surrender charge.* As will be demonstrated later and the point has already been mentioned, the net level premium policy-reserve which we have been calculating in this chapter does not allow for the higher expenses in the first policy year encountered in practice. Thus in the early policy years the net level premium policy-reserve of an individual policy may represent a larger amount than that which can be said to have been accumulated for the premiums paid by that individual policyholder; hence the surrender charge.

There is a close relationship between the policy-reserve and the cash surrender value of a policy. There are alternatives to the surrender of a policy consequent on the voluntary cessation of payment of premiums. This is an important subject and will be dealt with in Chapter 17.

CHAPTER EIGHT

Criticisms and Fallacies

Short of Utopia, every institution will be humanly faulty. Life insurance is good; it can be made better.

HENRY S. JACKSON[1]

CRITICISM IS VALUABLE

The goodwill of the public towards life insurance is of the greatest importance to the life insurance industry. With over twelve million individual policyholders and over twenty-one million group certificates in force (life insurance and annuities) in Canada at the end of 1975, backed by over twenty-four billion dollars of assets, life insurance is one of the greatest businesses in the country.

Because of the size of the life insurance industry and its importance to so many individuals, it is not surprising that criticism of life insurance is often heard. Despite this, the business has grown steadily, indicating that it is fundamentally healthy. In the past there were numerous publications which, either due to ignorance of the theory of life insurance, or to a desire to sell sensational books, gave a completely distorted picture of the industry.

More recent criticism has, on the whole, been more responsible, although unfortunately ignorance is still apparent. The Canadian Life Insurance Association has in the past few years taken special measures to listen to and inform the public on questions of life insurance. The Life Underwriters Association of Canada has also contributed to this work, particularly by writing to editors whose journals contain erroneous statements about life insurance.

The intention of this chapter is to mention some of the points which

[1]An eminent American actuary (1884–1955). Address to American Association of University Teachers of Insurance, "Individual Reserves and Kindred Delusions." (*Fragments*, National Life Insurance Company, Montpelier, Vermont, U.S.A., p. 76.)

have been the subject of criticism, and to set forth the pros and cons concerning them.

1. ARE OUT-OF-DATE MORTALITY TABLES BEING USED?

The answer is: "Not where it matters!" The criticism refers to the fact that companies are still calculating some of their policy-reserves on mortality tables which were introduced half a century ago and more, as the OM(5) relating to the period 1863–1893. The Canadian Men Ultimate, CM(5) table relating to the period 1900–1915 may also be said to be out of date as a measure of mortality. As already explained we used it as a basis for our demonstrations as it is the only Canadian mortality table relating to insured lives on which extensive actuarial rates, etc., are available. The principles demonstrated are unchanged whatever mortality table is used.

In the previous chapter we showed that a change in mortality table (see Table 7.6) introduced, as a rule, minor changes only in the policy-reserves.

The reader should now appreciate that, when policy-reserves are calculated on one basis, there is generally no need to change the basis even when mortality changes substantially. There is no point in undergoing the expense of extensive computer programmes (as is the case in a large life insurance company) merely to be able to say the policy-reserves are on such a table instead of another table—provided the rate of interest is unchanged.

There is also a more important reason why policy-reserve bases are not changed. It is the practice in Canada to guarantee the cash surrender values of a life insurance policy and a table of such values is printed in the policy. These guaranteed values are generally, after an initial period, the full policy-reserves. The company cannot change the policy-reserves under any policy without ensuring that on any and every policy anniversary it holds at least the amount guaranteed as a cash surrender value in that policy. Observing how the policy-reserves vary up and down as between one mortality table and another, the reasons for the present practice of companies will be readily appreciated. Unless there is a particular reason to change, once the basis of the guaranteed cash surrender value of a series of policies is decided, it determines the mortality table used in the future for policy-reserves for that series of policies.

When a company introduces a new series of policies, it may decide to base the guaranteed cash surrender values for the new series on a more recent mortality table and hence change its policy-reserve basis for the new series to the new table. It is a purely internal affair and it is a fallacy to state that the interests of the insurance-buying public are affected by the calculation of the policy-reserves on a so-called "out-of-date" mortality table.

Gross Premiums. In calculating gross premiums, that is, those actually charged by the companies, the situation is entirely different. The reductions in the rates of mortality, particularly at the younger ages in recent years, are indicated in the latest mortality tables published.

The Canadian Institute of Actuaries periodically publishes the results of a joint company investigation into the mortality of insured lives in Canada. The Society of Actuaries, to which practically all the actuaries in Canada and the U.S.A. belong, publishes annually the results of its investigations into mortality of insured lives on the North American continent. This has been going on for many years and actuaries are well aware of the trend of mortality and take it into account in calculating their premium rates and distributing surplus to participating policyholders.

The latest investigation into the mortality of insured lives in Canada for which a mortality table has been prepared is that covering the period 1958–1964, called "CA 58–64." The rates of mortality are the only figures which have been published and specimen values for quinquennial ages at entry are given as Table 8.1. Under this table the ultimate

TABLE 8.1

Canadian Assured Male Lives Table 1958–1964
Specimen Select and Ultimate Rates of Mortality per 1000 Exposed to Risk

Age at entry	Year of insurance 1	2	3	4	5	More than 5	Attained age
20	1.060	1.101	1.117	1.105	1.063	1.012	25
25	0.807	0.826	0.857	0.889	0.880	0.891	30
30	0.654	0.731	0.837	0.968	1.122	1.229	35
35	0.831	0.976	1.154	1.358	1.590	1.913	40
40	1.190	1.424	1.726	2.095	2.530	3.393	45
45	1.944	2.369	2.893	3.494	4.152	5.895	50
50	3.116	3.687	4.382	5.184	6.090	9.350	55
55	4.573	5.443	6.546	7.867	9.409	15.884	60
60	7.216	8.707	10.546	12.659	14.994	26.812	65
65	11.375	13.456	15.970	18.821	21.956	41.544	70
70	16.575	19.422	22.876	26.791	31.099	62.370	75
						94.120	80
						145.116	85
						206.364	90
						280.574	95
						480.291	100
						1000.000	105

rate of mortality (i.e., after the first five years from entry) at ages under 35 is less than 1.2 per 1,000. This table is now in general use among actuaries for the calculation of premiums for non-participating policies.

2. COMPANIES OVERCHARGE FOR THE COST OF MORTALITY

Figures are sometimes published indicating that a certain company has experienced a rate of mortality which was only, say 67 per cent of that expected. This has given rise to the criticism that policyholders are paying, say, one-third more than they should for their insurance.

If the standard on which the company calculates its death rate as "expected" is based on a mortality table fifty years out of date it is quite possible to get a rate like 67 per cent—possibly much lower! Take as an example a group of lives all age 35 and exposed to the risk of death for one year. For each 1,000 lives so exposed the number of deaths in the year would be, according to the two tables of mortality of insured lives five years or more after entry, Table 4.5 (CM(5) 1900–1915) and Table 8.1 (CA(5) 1958–1964), respectively 4.45 and 1.229 (say 1.23).

If the experience of the company was average, the number of deaths would be 1.23 per 1,000 lives age 35 exposed for one year. But if it compared its experience with what it would have been according to a table fifty years out of date and stated it "expected" 4.45 deaths then the ratio it could boast about would be (1.23/4.45) × 100 or just 28 per cent of the expected! For older ages the ratio would be higher. However the company in question is not selling life insurance in the 1960's at rates based on mortality in the period 1900–1915. Hence the use of such a ratio calculated as indicated is fallacious and the company deserves to be criticized for publishing it.

3. POLICYHOLDERS TAKING OUT DIFFERENT PLANS OF INSURANCE ARE CHARGED DIFFERENT AMOUNTS FOR THE SAME DEATH RISK

This is not so. The cost of insurance is determined by the age of the life insured and the amount at risk only, irrespective of plan. The argument is presented of three men taking out policies on three different plans, each with a face amount of $10,000: *A* buys a straight life policy at an annual premium of, say, $180; *B* buys a twenty year endowment at an annual premium of $400; *C* buys a twenty year term insurance at an annual premium of $70. The argument proceeds that if they die in the twentieth year, say, *A* has paid out two and a half times what *C* has paid whilst *B* has paid over five times that of *C*; yet the beneficiaries in each case receive the same amount, namely $10,000.

May one carry the argument one step further? Let us assume they have each survived the twentieth year. *C* gets nothing, yet he has paid \$1,400; his term policy expires and if he desires to renew it for another period it can only be done at a much higher premium than \$70.

B however gets \$10,000 cash, which is \$2,000 more than the \$8,000 he has paid and his endowment insurance policy terminates. *A* can carry on his straight life insurance at the same premium although a new straight life policy at his attained age would cost more than double. Or, he could terminate his policy and receive some \$3,000 as a cash surrender value compared with the \$3,600 he has paid in premiums.

Who appears now to have made the best bargain for himself and his beneficiaries? In fact, whether on death or survival, each has received exactly what he paid for. If people knew when death would occur, life insurance would not be feasible. If a particular individual knew he would die at an early date, he would naturally insure for the largest amount he could get on the lowest premium plan, knowing there would be no purpose in making provision for any benefits payable on survival to a later period. We have seen in the previous chapter how, in any year, the accumulated policy-reserve on those who die in that year is paid out and the balance of the claims is met by a contribution from those who survive that year.

As this goes to the root of the principle on which life insurance is based it is worth pursuing further. Referring back to Tables 7.1, 7.2, and 7.3, we note how on entry the company sets up the accumulation according to the plan chosen by the insured. Whether it is an endowment, straight life, or term plan the accumulation proceeds according to plan. To suggest that on an endowment insurance accumulation, in the event of death in any year, the amount payable should be as if a term policy had been effected, merely because it gives a larger death benefit, is not feasible; the amount is just not available.

4. WHY IS THE POLICY-RESERVE NOT ADDED TO THE SUM INSURED?

The criticism is made that, the policyholder having paid for his insurance year by year and the company having accumulated the policy-reserve out of the excess of the premiums paid over the death risk, the policy-reserve should be paid out in addition to the face amount of the policy.

Those who have followed the demonstrations in the previous chapters and illustrated as in the previous section (3) of this chapter should have no difficulty in seeing the fallacy of this argument. The policy-reserve is paid out on death as part of the benefits due on death. Any prearranged sum can be provided for to be payable on death in addition to the face amount of the policy if the appropriate premium is paid and the corresponding net premium is accumulated by the company when the policy is taken out. One plan issued by certain companies provides for the return of all gross premiums paid on death in addition to the initial face amount of the policy. The premium is, of course, greater than it would be if this additional benefit were not included.

5. DO COMPANIES OBJECT TO TERM INSURANCE. IF SO, WHY?

The figures of the life insurance industry in Canada refute this.[2] In 1925 the amount of life insurance purchased by individuals, i.e., excluding group insurance, was subdivided as follows: 71 per cent on the life plan, 24 per cent on the endowment plan, and 5 per cent on the term plan. The change in recent years has been most striking as is shown in Table 8.2.

TABLE 8.2

Year	Life	Endowment	Term and temporary additions
1974	34%	11%	55%
1968	41%	11%	48%
1962	44%	12%	44%

The increase in term insurance from a negligible proportion (5 per cent) to over 50 per cent of the new business sold is almost revolutionary and there are some life insurance officials who consider that the trend which is still continuing is to be regretted. If group life insurance were included the proportion of term and temporary additions would be increased to over 70 per cent of the total new business purchased.

The development of social security schemes by governments, the improvement in education and standards of living, have made the public better aware of the need for protection of dependents in the event of their own early death; hence the demand for substantial protection for premiums paid even at the expense of the savings element.

Yearly Renewable Term Insurance. There are definite objections to the yearly renewable term plan which permits an insured to carry on his insurance at a higher premium each year for the same amount of insur-

[2]*Canadian Life Insurance Facts, 1975* (Toronto: C.L.I.A.), p. 8. Also *Reports* of Superintendent of Insurance (Ottawa).

ance. (See Figure 10.) This can be continued to age 65 or even beyond when conversion to a permanent plan of insurance is almost prohibitive in cost. In the early years it looks most attractive. However, the increasing resentment of the insured at the increasing premium (snowballing in its effect) and the final abandonment of the policy is not relished by those who have the responsibility of deciding on the plans which will be issued for the life insurance service of the public and this includes both sales representatives and head office staff.

During his business career no one's opinions on matters relating to the public image of life insurance carried more weight than those of the late J. G. Parker.[3] In June 1950 at a meeting of the Society of Actuaries his views on term insurance are recorded as follows:

> Mr. J. G. Parker emphasized that the institution of life insurance has built up tremendous good will, largely created through the cash surrender type of insurance. He further indicated that in his many years in the insurance business practically all of the dissatisfied policyholders he had met were holders of term insurance policies. It is good for this business of life insurance that we should remember that we have created this great demand for our product, and great good will for the sale of the ordinary types of insurance which carry cash values for the later years of life.

6. THE INSURANCE AND SAVINGS ELEMENTS IN A POLICY SHOULD BE KEPT SEPARATE "BUY TERM AND INVEST THE DIFFERENCE"

The automatic regular savings provided by a life insurance policy has a great sales appeal. The critics of the life insurance business maintain that the public would be better advised to provide for their savings quite apart from their life insurance. However, where they do not, the critics insist that the two should be kept separate in the books of the insurance company. This is in line with their advocacy of the yearly renewable term plan.

In various pamphlets and books criticizing and defending the business of life insurance, the analysis of the premiums of the various life insurance plans has been carried to an extreme. It is interesting actuarially, but in the opinion of the author it has increased the misunderstandings surrounding the business. In previous chapters we have shown how the premiums for the various plans are computed. In particular we have

[3] J. G. Parker (1883–1953). Following a period on the mathematical staff of the University of Toronto he entered the service of the Imperial Life occupying various positions including Actuary, President, and Chairman of the Board. He had the unique distinction of being President of both the American Institute of Actuaries (1926–28) and the Actuarial Society of America (1934–35). His leadership was recognized by every branch of the life insurance industry.

shown the interrelationship of the net premium and policy-reserve on a level premium plan which keeps the premium on a level basis in spite of a rapidly increasing rate of mortality.

A person buying a straight life plan enters into contract whereby, whenever death occurs, certain benefits will be paid, and the premium will not be increased. The resulting policy-reserve in the hands of the life insurance company enables it to grant various benefits of which the increasing cash surrender value is one. To analyse the premium into component parts of "protection" and "savings" destroys the utility of the combination. The analogy of decomposing water into oxygen and hydrogen is appropriate—unless chemically combined into one they do not serve the needs that water does. Similarly the decomposition of a life insurance plan into parts does not serve the needs of the plan itself. The point applies to endowment insurance also.

It is often argued that it is advantageous to "buy term and invest the difference" rather than to buy a permanent policy. It is not possible to prove or disprove this conclusively for the argument must be based on assumptions concerning interest rates to be effective in future as well as mortality, policy dividends, and the effect of income tax. Calculations made on the assumption that current high interest rates will remain in effect indefinitely present buying term and investing the difference in too favourable a light. Policy dividends, based on the average yield on the fund, do not rise as quickly as interest rates in the market, but do not fall so quickly either. Thus, if interest rates in the market decline, dividends on permanent life insurance policies will not be immediately affected but estimates of the results of "buying term and investing the difference" would have to be sharply reduced.

7. LIFE INSURANCE COMPANY EXPENSES ARE TOO HIGH

Here we face an economic problem which has concerned most governments and people—the high cost of services and business operations. Life insurance companies have to compete with other firms and with governments for the service of clerks and the amenities they enjoy and pay the market rate for their services and equipment. If they did not do this, they would not get the staff or the equipment. Experts in business organizations are of the opinion that a smaller well-paid staff is less costly than a larger poorly paid one. It could be questioned whether, if life insurance companies were housed in inferior buildings, their staffs—particularly their senior officers—poorly paid, and staff amenities inferior compared with those in corresponding business in other lines of endeavour, such economics would be in the interests of policyholders.

Some detractors of the life insurance business infer that if the government ran the business it would be done at a lower cost. It still has to be shown that a government is more efficient in any operation than private industry. In any case the costs are still there. Offices have to be provided for civil servants; they have to be paid in competition with industry and, in Canada, they enjoy one of the best, i.e., costliest, pension plans in the country.

The agency system is particularly attacked as being costly. Life insurance has been available in its present form for some two hundred years and it has been demonstrated beyond argument that it must be sold and little progress would have been made if it had remained an "over-the-counter" proposition as it was, and still is, with the Old Equitable. The agent must be accepted as an integral part of the business.

There are over 160 companies active in the life insurance business in Canada today (1975). As previously stated, these include several of the largest and leading companies of the U.S.A. and Britain. This is the competition that the Canadian life insurance companies must face. A brief could be prepared arguing that this competition increases the cost of doing business. However, most authorities on business developments maintain that the public interest is best served where the competition is keen. Surely if there were any advantage to the public in adopting some special procedure or plan this competition would ensure that some companies would seek to avail themselves of that procedure or plan.

Life insurance is a highly individualistic service and so long as the public expects that type of service, its cost has to be met. Life insurance companies have been pioneers in the adaptation of automation to their work, and it is to be hoped that this may halt the upward trend in clerical costs. However, let us emphasize that in spite of a doubling of living costs in recent years, life insurance rates have decreased.

The 1947 edition of Stone and Cox's Tables[4] gave the average gross premium charged by six of the largest Canadian life companies for a ten-year term insurance policy, age 35 at entry, as $88.00 for a $10,000 policy. In the 1969 edition the average gross premium charged by the same companies for the same policy was $53.00, a reduction of over one-third. In comparing other plans, differences in cash values and current net interest earnings would have to be taken into account.

The reduction in rates shown is due mainly to reductions in mortality

[4] *Life Insurance Tables* (Toronto: Stone & Cox, Ltd.).

and partly due to a more equitable apportionment of costs between different sizes of policies brought about by the inflation in costs.

8. COMPANIES MAKE LARGE PROFITS ON LAPSES AND SURRENDERS

This is untrue. The high first-year costs in life insurance mean that early termination of policies involves the companies in serious losses. It will be agreed that lower initial expenses would enable companies to grant more generous surrender values on termination in the early policy years. A considerable amount of effort both at the head offices and branch offices of the companies is directed to reducing lapses and surrenders. Various disciplinary measures including those affecting agents' remuneration are in effect by companies seeking to reduce lapses. Life insurance companies have been criticized for these measures. This is hardly consistent with the charge that companies make large profits on lapses and surrenders.

9. ABNORMAL PROFITS ARE MADE BY STOCK LIFE INSURANCE COMPANIES

With the mutualization of several of Canada's life insurance companies in recent years, the greater part of life insurance by far is now transacted by mutual life insurance companies, that is, where there is no capital stock. However, even with the Canadian stock companies the greater part of the business is sold with the policyholder participating in profits and as will be indicated later, Canadian laws insist on at least 90 per cent of the profits on this business going to the policyholders; in some cases the proportion is higher.

10. POLICYHOLDERS HAVE LITTLE OR NO INFLUENCE ON MANAGEMENT

If any effective method could be devised where policyholders could influence the management it undoubtedly would be welcomed by the companies. The laws give policyholders of Canadian life insurance companies definite voting rights in the election of directors, but it must be agreed they are of little practical effect. The same point arises regarding the shareholders of all but the smallest stock companies in all lines of business endeavour; in the final analysis the operation of the concern must be left to the management. In the case of life insurance companies the Superintendent of Insurance at Ottawa and those of the ten provinces hold a watching brief on behalf of policyholders.

11. WITH INFLATION INEVITABLE, LIFE INSURANCE GIVES VERY DOUBTFUL VALUE

Should inflation ever be considered as inevitable by any material portion of the people of a country, the resulting reaction would have the most serious effect on the economy of the country. Life insurance is generally a long-period proposition and the payment for it is usually spread over a similarly long period. The policyholder never knows when death may occur; if early it has still been a valuable contract; if late, then the premiums paid have also been made in depreciated currency. The subject is one of great importance and Chapter 30 is devoted to it.

12. GOVERNMENT SUPERVISION SHOULD BE CLOSER AND MORE CRITICAL

Canada has been fortunate in the standard of government supervision provided by the Superintendent of Insurance at Ottawa. However, the Superintendent should not be expected to direct the policy of a company or take an active part in its management.

13. COMPANIES CHARGE TOO MUCH FOR ANNUITIES

This argument has come to the fore recently because of the popular interest in Registered Retirement Savings Plans. Under such plans, the proceeds must be used to buy a life annuity, which may have a guaranteed period or a joint and survivorship provision. Otherwise, if taken in cash, the proceeds are subject to tax as income in the year in which they are taken. If taken as an annuity, the tax is paid as annuity payments are received.

It is stated that the government forces people to pay their money into the life insurance "monopoly"—scarcely an appropriate term when 160 companies are competing. The allegation that the cost is too high is usually based on erroneous calculations.

Examples are often given purporting to show the yield on annuities payable for life, with ten years guaranteed. Sometimes, in calculating the yield, the value of an annuity certain for ten years is used, forgetting altogether that the majority of purchasers will receive payments for some years after the guaranteed period has expired.

In other cases, an annuity certain for the expectation of life is used—13.72 years for a male aged 65, according to the Canadian Life Table (population), 1971. Apparently because the expectation of life is longer than the guaranteed period of 10 years, it is not thought necessary to adjust it for the guarantee. But if we examine the method by which the expectation of life is calculated, it is apparent that an adjustment is necessary. The calculation starts with 70,044 men assumed to be living at age 65; 2,073 are assumed to die in the first year, 2,186 in the second year, and so on to the end of the table. Thus we proceed as follows:

2,073 will on average receive payments for 0.5 years—1,036.5 payments
2,186 will on average receive payments for 1.5 years—3,279.0 payments

By continuing this process and adding we obtain a total of 960,919 annual payments. Dividing by the 70,044 who started out gives an average of 13.72 payments.

If we take subtotals at the end of ten years and at the end of the table we find:

25,256 who die in the first ten years receive	133,905 payments
44,788 who survive the first ten years receive	827,014 payments
70,044	receive 960,919 payments

Now if the annuity is guaranteed ten years, we have to change this to the following:

25,256 who die in the first ten years receive	252, 560 payments
44,788 who survive ten years receive	827,014 payments
70,044	receive 1,079,574 payments

Thus the average number of payments received is not 13.72 but 15.42, an increase of nearly 12½ per cent. Moreover, the figure of 15.42 should be increased to allow for the fact that annuitants live longer than the general population.

CHAPTER NINE

Mutual and Stock Life Insurance Companies

We have indicated the important place of life insurance in the Canada of today; we have outlined some of the past history and the development of the business. The basic principles on which life insurance rates are computed have been outlined and demonstrated in the calculation of net premiums for the three basic plans: term, straight life, and endowment insurance. The fact of the increase in the rate of mortality with age has been indicated, the function of the policy-reserve when a level premium is paid has been explained, and the method of calculating policy-reserves has been demonstrated by calculating specimen values for the three basic plans.

We now reach the point, and devote this and the next chapter to it, where we deal with the actual corporation which produces, distributes, and services the product and its organization.

MUTUAL AND STOCK COMPANIES

Any incorporated company with share capital is called a stock company and is controlled by its board of directors who are elected by the shareholders. However, a *stock life insurance company* subject to the insurance laws of the federal government of Canada must have two classes of directors representing and elected by (1) shareholders and (2) participating policyholders; the latter, the policyholder directors, must number at least one-third of the total number of directors. In a *mutual life insurance company* there is no capital stock and hence no shareholders, and thus there is only one class of director, namely those elected by the policyholders. In all cases a majority of the directors in each class must be Canadian citizens, ordinarily resident in Canada. No agent is eligible to be a director of a life insurance company and there are restrictions on the number of paid officers on the board of directors.

RELATIVE ADVANTAGES OF STOCK AND MUTUAL COMPANIES

In Canada it makes very little difference to policyholders whether the company is stock or mutual. In Canada life insurace has always been considered as essentially a co-operative undertaking; this has been traditional. In the early stages of a company's history the share capital and the premium paid on it are necessary to provide initial organizing expenses and some security to policyholders. As the company develops, the premiums paid by policyholders and the interest earnings on the policy-reserves are normally adequate to cover claims and expenses and thus the share capital tends to decrease in significance and in well-established companies it becomes insignificant.

The share of profit earnings paid to shareholders in a well-established stock life insurance company is not of material significance to the policyholders. Under a non-participating policy every feature of the contract is guaranteed; the premium is fixed and cannot be increased. Under a policy participating in profits the Canadian federal insurance laws severely restrict the proportion of the profits on this class of policy which can be paid to shareholders: it varies from 2½ to 10 per cent of the distributable surplus arising from that class of business according to the size of the participating fund which, in the main, consists of the policy-reserves of this class of policy.

In the year 1955, federally registered stock life insurance companies in Canada paid out to shareholders $3,183,891; this compares with total payments to policyholders of around $290 millions plus $60 millions to the participating policyholders in dividends. The premium income of these stock companies amounted to $640 millions in that year.

The point may be made that the transfer to shareholders funds from which payments to shareholders are made rather than the actual payment to shareholders is the criterion. These transfers in 1955 amounted to $5¼ millions or less than 1 per cent of the premium income. A further item indicating the insignificance of shareholders' capital relative to the policyholders' interests is to note the total paid-up capital and shareholders' funds of Canadian stock life insurance companies which was $22 millions and compare it with the total assets of $5,500 millions of these companies. The year chosen for all these figures is 1955 being prior to the move to mutualize some of Canada's largest life insurance companies which will be referred to below.

In the U.S., although the number of stock life insurance companies far exceeds the number of mutual companies, yet 51 per cent of the life insurance in force is with mutual companies. Many of the large U.S.

mutual life insurance companies were originally stock companies such as the Prudential of America, Equitable of New York, and Metropolitan, the policyholders' funds having been used to buy out the shareholders. This has been done in Canada in recent years and has changed the relation between stock and mutual companies which had held since the first Canadian life insurance company was organized in 1847.

MUTUALIZATION OF CANADIAN STOCK LIFE INSURANCE COMPANIES

At the end of 1955 out of thirty-two Canadian life insurance companies reporting to Ottawa, twenty-five were stock companies and seven were mutual companies; but of these seven over 95 per cent of their combined assets were represented by those of the Mutual of Canada and the North American Life. Thus apart from these two companies Canadian life insurance was predominantly represented by stock companies.

In his report for 1955 the Federal Superintendent of Insurance referred to the acquisition of the share capital of two of the smaller Canadian life insurance companies by Swiss and U.S. interests and of the danger of transfer to foreign ownership of a major Canadian life insurance company. He concluded his report by emphasizing "the desirability of seeking some legislative procedure that will enable the ownership of Canadian life insurance companies to be retained in Canada."

The new law regarding the mutualization of Canadian stock life insurance companies under federal registry is Section 91 of the Canadian and British Insurance Companies Act and was passed in 1957. The procedure to be followed is outlined later in this chapter. The reports of the Superintendent of Insurance for Canada give the progress year by year of the steps taken by five Canadian stock life insurance companies to purchase their share capital, including some of the largest Canadian life insurance companies; the plan proceeded without any apparent obstacle. When all the shares were acquired and written down by the companies to their par value, the capital stock of the companies was cancelled and the companies considered as completely mutualized. The companies and the dates of their mutualization are: Canada Life and Sun Life in 1962, Equitable in 1963, Confederation and Manufacturers in 1968. Substantial sums were involved in paying off their shareholders and the companies were careful not to disturb their financial standing—measures which explain the time taken to complete their mutualization.

As has already been pointed out in Chapter 2, the Mutual Life of Canada was organized as a mutual company when it was founded in

1870. The North American Life was founded in 1881 as a stock company, but its charter anticipated its ultimate mutualization which was accomplished in 1931.

The magnitude of the change is indicated by the following figures. If in 1955 these five companies had been changed over to mutual companies the total premium income of the Canadian mutual companies would have been increased from 11 to 64 per cent of that of all Canadian federally registered companies and total assets from 12 to 67 per cent. A major change in life insurance company organization was thus accomplished.

A most important taxation concession was made by the Canadian federal government. The market value of the shares purchased exceeded by a considerable amount the share capital as shown in the balance sheets of these companies. Had the payment of this additional amount been subject to federal income tax, mutualization would have been impossible. The Canadian federal government, by making these capital payments free of income tax, made mutualization possible.

Some of the procedures of mutualization are of considerable interest and have made life insurance history; for this much credit must be given to the federal Superintendent of Insurance and his staff. Briefly they are:

1. Application for mutualization lies with the company which must have offers of not less than 25 per cent of its share capital for sale at a specified price determined by the directors which price must be approved by the Minister of Finance.

2. The company cannot apply an amount to the purchase of its shares at any particular time if such would reduce its surplus below 6 per cent of its assets or as approved by the Minister.

3. The amounts paid for the shares in excess of the value at which they stand in the balance sheet of the company must be written down to that value in not less than five years, with a minimum amount to be applied in any one year of one-fifth of the sum to be written off.

4. When the company acquires 90 per cent of its shares the conditions of sale become binding on the remaining shares.

In 1965 further steps were taken through additions to the Canadian and British Insurance Companies Act to counter the danger of transfer to foreign ownership of a federally registered Canadian life insurance company. These additions aimed at restricting the non-resident ownership of shares of Canadian life insurance companies, and in some cases, limiting the voting rights of non-residents. The amendment is applicable only to stock life insurance companies that were not under foreign control at the time the amendment was introduced in Parliament on September 23, 1964; there were thirteen such companies at that time.

Apart from preserving existing rights at the date mentioned the effect of the amendment is to limit to 25 per cent the proportion of shares of any of these companies that may be transferred to non-residents, and to limit to 10 per cent the proportion of shares that may be transferred to any one non-resident together with any other shareholder associated with him.

More recently, by way of the Foreign Investment Review Act of 1973, the federal government has moved in a general way to control foreign ownership by bringing under review acquisition of control of any Canadian business enterprise or the establishment of a new business in Canada. The purpose of the review is to allow for an assessment of the existence of significant benefit to Canada. The newer provisions are additional to but do not supplant the specific life insurance provisions.

DESIRABILITY OF MUTUALIZATION?

In Canada, as outlined above, mutualization was used to avert the control of major life insurance companies by foreign interests. It has been made clear that so far as policyholders are concerned there is little or no advantage whether a company is mutual or stock. In Canada, both mutual and stock companies issue both participating and non-participating policies, although in the U.S.A. mutual companies are confined to the issue of participating policies by the laws of New York and several other states. In a mutual company the profits of non-participating business, where written, accrue to the general profits of the company and thus to the participating policyholders.

It is a matter of opinion whether the existence of a share capital makes for greater efficiency in a life insurance company. Undoubtedly where the directors and management have a substantial interest in the shares of the company there should be that extra keenness and effort which may mean much to any organization. That in the event of trouble the policyholders, through their elected directors, are in a position to exert their authority is important. In the final analysis the real protection for policyholders, whether the company is stock or mutual, rests in the continuing supervision of the Superintendents of Insurance.

The funds of life insurance companies represent in most cases the life savings of policyholders and protection for the aged, the widows, and orphans. Life insurance companies have long been regarded as different from other commercial organizations and, in Canada, the insurance laws have determined that this shall be so. The diminishing role of the capital of a life insurance company as a company becomes established does indicate that mutualization is justifiable, even desirable, and possibly more so in Canada than in other countries.

CHAPTER TEN

Head Office and Sales Organization

THE LIFE INSURANCE COMPANY IN OPERATION

We continue with our description of an actual life insurance company in operation. In its simplest form the life insurance company in Canada sells policies granting benefits based on the contingencies of life and disability. The premiums received after meeting expenses have to be invested to accumulate assets to cover the liabilities being incurred. A technical staff is required to develop the product; a sales staff to distribute it; an administrative staff to handle the details; an accounting staff to record the collections; and an investment staff for the investment of the funds. It follows that in its simplest form a life insurance company in operation consists of four major divisions: actuarial, sales, secretarial (administration), and investment.

SOME STATISTICS

There were at the end of 1974, actively engaged in the life insurance business in Canada, 166 companies: 84 Canadian companies (58 federally registered and 26 provincial companies), 65 American, 9 British and 8 European (all federally registered).

The personnel of these companies in Canada at the end of 1968 comprised 48,300 persons, 29,900 engaged in administration work and 18,400 in sales. Of the administrative employees, 22,300 work in company head offices and 7,600 in branch offices of the companies located throughout the country.[1]

THE COMPANY: INTERNAL ORGANIZATION

In outlining the internal organization of a typical Canadian life insurance company we realize that the companies will differ in detail but the main

[1] *Canadian Life Insurance Facts, 1975.*

functions will follow a common pattern which will be outlined in this chapter.

By law the supreme control of a company is vested in the board of directors. The president is generally the chief executive officer of the company and a full-time official. Except where full-time officers of the company have been promoted and elected to be directors, the directors are generally men engaged in other lines of business and their duties with the company are essentially part-time. The top organization of a life insurance company is usually determined by the particular abilities of its senior officers, not only currently, but also in its history.

A life insurance company is undoubtedly the most complex organization in the business world (we are considering here a company doing one class of business, in this case life insurance with its associated annuity and pension business). A brief summary of its various operations will illustrate this:

1. There is the periodic billing of tens, hundreds of thousands, or even a million or more of policyholders; the recording of the individual payments; the various procedures to be set up if premiums are not paid. There are also the individual records for each policy to be kept up to date.

2. Every new application has to be "selected," i.e., according to medical and other standards, as to whether it is acceptable at standard rates or, if not, the special terms of acceptance and in a small percentage of cases the declination of the risk. In 1974 some 800,000 new policies were effected in the ordinary life business class by the life insurance companies operating in Canada. This indicates the magnitude of this process and also that of issuing the policies.

3. The majority of business in Canada is with participation in profits and there is the work of calculating the dividends to be allotted to each policy and their recording and accounting.

4. A yearly task of some magnitude is the computation of the policy-reserves; each policy has to be accounted for, and the final results have to be available within a few days of the end of the year.

5. Other items involving the actuaries are the computation of premium rates and the preparation of the rate manual; the calculation of cash surrender and loan values, settlement options, and non-forfeiture values.

6. The detailed reports of operations which a life insurance company in Canada has to submit annually (and as regards certain items, more often) to the superintendents of insurance, both provincial and federal (when federally registered) exceed by far those of any other type of business and form a major task.

7. The payment of claims, the recording of changes of beneficiaries, drafting of policy forms and endorsements, taxation and the attention to statutory requirements, all require special knowledge of the taxation and insurance laws.

8. The investment of the funds, representing mainly the policy-reserves, is one of the most important functions of a life insurance company and may well determine the better, or worse than average, performance of a company. Some life insurance companies are holders of substantial amounts of real estate and this requires the service of specialists. Mortgages on real estate in Canada held by the life insurance companies exceed $8,705 millions, including a multitude of relatively small sums on individual dwellings.

9. The head office administration of the agency organization and branch offices is a major sphere of operations in every company.

10. *Electronics*. The enormous detail of life insurance administration which the foregoing illustrates has made the Computer Section a key division of a life company's operations. The importance of mechanical equipment was realized by life insurance companies and they have been leaders in its development and use from the early days of punch-card equipment to the latest most modern electronic computers. These are used not only to replace a multitude of routine clerical tasks but for much specialized calculation.

ORGANIZATION CHART

From the above summary of the operations the pattern of organization of a life insurance company is self-evident. The set-up of the company may be represented by the chart in Figure 13. They may be enumerated by function as: (1) management policy, (2) sales, (3) actuarial, (4) medical, (5) legal, (6) investment, (7) secretarial. The last comprises administration in its widest sense and specialized functions, such as personnel, planning, accounting, and auditing, and such administrative details as may not be covered by other sections. We have avoided allocating specific duties to each division of the chart for they could in some aspects vary with different companies, and further this might tend to minimize the degree of co-operation necessary among the various divisions to ensure an effective, efficient organization.

The official in charge of sales is known as the *agency vice-president*, *agency director*, or a like title. The actuary needs no additional comment here (see Chapter 1). The inclusive duties indicated above by the "secretarial" division is divided between two officials in some companies designated as, say, *secretary* and *comptroller*, respectively.

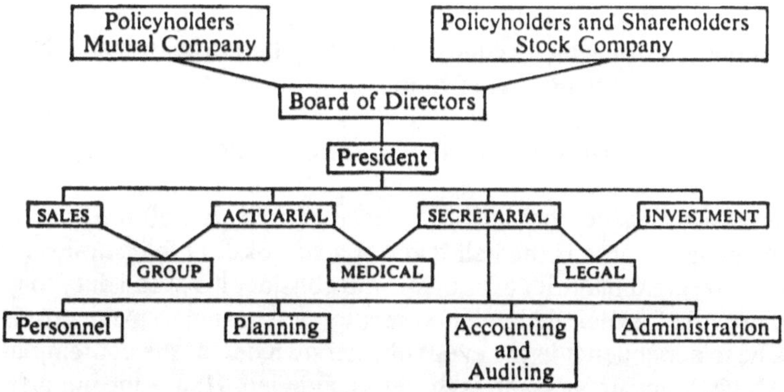

FIGURE 13. Organization Chart, Canadian Life Insurance Company

The officer in charge of investments is designated as *treasurer* or *investment vice-president*, or like title. It is usual for the directors or a committee of them to keep in touch with the company's investment policy and the investment officers, more closely than would be possible or even desirable as regards other divisions of the company's operations.

Group. The great development of group business in the life, pension, and sickness fields by Canadian life insurance companies has meant that the officer now in charge often ranks with the top-level management; in other companies the division may be under the chief actuary. Owing to the specialized knowledge required of agents engaged in the sale of group lines, particularly pensions, it is often found necessary to form a special division of sales and actuarial personnel for this work, hence the link with both "sales" and "actuarial" in the chart.

Medical. In some companies the *medical director* or *chief medical officer* and associated medical officers will act in an advisory capacity only to the *vice-president, underwriting* or *underwriting executive* as the lay head of the division dealing with selection of risks may be named. This is particularly the case where these medical men continue to engage in the practice of their profession outside the company, as is often preferred, and the principle of reducing their administrative duties to a minimum is followed. The department dealing with the selection of risks is called the *underwriting department* or in some companies the *medical department*.

Legal. The position of the *general counsel* or *vice-president, legal* varies with companies. In many smaller companies his services will be as consultant and he may be a partner in a local firm of lawyers; often in this case the preparation of policy forms, etc., is in the hands of one of the actuarial staff subject to his supervision. There are many aspects of investment work which require legal consultation which explains the link with "Investment" in the chart.

SALES ORGANIZATION OF A LIFE INSURANCE COMPANY

The phrase "agency organization" is also used. A well-organized and efficient sales force is the hall-mark of a successful life insurance company. The great majority of people, who consider it a proud duty to work and provide for their dependents, require persuasion to make provision for these dependents in the event of their own death, the contemplation of which, being unpleasant, is therefore avoided. Hence the importance of the salesman in the life insurance industry.

The Agent. In the life insurance industry the salesman is generally referred to as the *agent* or *life underwriter*.

The remuneration paid originally to the agents of the Canada Life when it was organized in 1847 was, on the straight life plan, 5 per cent of the premium in the first year and 2½ per cent on subsequent premiums (renewals). Shortly afterwards these were increased to 7½ per cent first year and 5 per cent on renewal premiums. On these terms selling life insurance could only be a part-time vocation associated with other means of livelihood. As companies became established and better able to meet higher costs the trend, stimulated by competition for business among companies, was to increase first year's commissions, even to excess. It is of interest to note that one of the restrictions imposed by the New York insurance laws following the Armstrong-Hughes Investigation was to limit the commissions and remuneration paid to agents on the straight life plan to a total of 55 per cent of the first year's premium and 5 per cent on each of the following nine renewals. (Note that the total commissions represented one full annual premium spread over ten years.)

Trends in recent years in Canada (and the U.S.) have been to professionalize the business of selling life insurance; to make it a whole-time occupation and a desirable career. This has obliged the companies to choose the men carefully and to spend considerable time, money, and effort in training them. It also obliges the company to remunerate the agent while he is being trained; to encourage him in his studies of the profession leading by examination to qualify for the designation of Chartered Life Underwriter (C.L.U.). The association of agents in Canada is known as the Life Underwriters Association of Canada.

It is maintained by some that the agent is an independent contractor and his results are governed by the time, effort, and judgment he chooses to put into his work, so that payment other than by results must mean needless expenditure of policyholders' funds. To meet this, the importance of which is not denied, the recent trend has been, as with the branch manager, to set certain standards of performance and to remunerate the agent partly by commission and partly by his achievement of these standards. The "quality" of the business, i.e., its persistency after being sold, is stressed above all other considerations. The trend in financing of new agents during the first year or two is for the company to guarantee a minimum scale of remuneration based on personal and family needs with any excess earnings based on performance accruing to the agent. After this initial period, earnings are based entirely on commissions and standards of performance.

The agency system undoubtedly adds to the cost of conducting the life insurance business, but it is a service which is to the benefit of policyholders and must be paid for. The relationship between client and agent is fostered in recent trends; the service which the agent performs after the business is sold and which should continue during the lifetime of the policy and on its maturity is a valuable one and the necessary costs should be faced.

It may be accepted as proven that agents are an essential part of the life insurance industry. There are life insurance companies which operate without agents, such as the Presbyterian Ministers Fund and the Teachers Insurance and Annuity Association of America, but they confine themselves to special classes of the population.

Branch Office Organization. This is the system almost exclusively used in Canada for the sales organization. The person in charge of a branch office, known as the *branch manager*, is usually considered as an employee of the life insurance company remunerated in part by salary. All the expenses of the branch office: rents, staff salaries, equipment, and overhead expenses are paid by the company. Agents are appointed as under contract to the company and before appointment have to be approved by the company; their remuneration is paid by the company. The branch office staff is generally under a *branch secretary* who often reports directly to the head office. The branch secretary and the clerical staff at the branch office all rank as head office personnel for pensions, group life, and sickness benefits. These details are given to indicate the difference between a branch office and a general agency system; the details of the latter will be outlined below.

In the development of the branch office system it has become general to tie the branch manager's remuneration quite closely to his performance so that his fixed salary represents a minor part of his remuneration. Such performance may be determined by the results of his branch as to: (1) volume of new business or what is a better criterion: the premium income of such new business or the commission earnings of the agents from that business; (2) increase in business in force; (3) number of new agents appointed and their performance in the early period of their service; (4) rate of persistency of business; (5) number of agents exceeding production quota; (6) rate of expense of operating the branch office.

General Agent. This type of sales organization is not used in Canada to any extent. Historically the general agent was given a franchise for certain territory; he supplied his own office, clerical staff, and equipment. The agents employed were his appointments and under contract to him and paid by him. The general agent had his term of remuneration settled by a contract with the company but generally was a free agent (subject to the laws of the state) in regard to what he paid his agents. This system played a great part in developing the huge land area of the United States in the pioneer days of life insurance in that country. However, as the business developed, the companies have increasingly assumed responsibility for financing the costs of operation particularly as regards new general agencies. Presumably the companies found that the number of men with sufficient capital to finance a general agency was limited; this may be the result of present-day income tax rates.

It will be noted that under present-day conditions the differences between a branch office and a general agency organization have been considerably reduced.

Professional and Other Associations of the Life Insurance Industry

It would be expected that the many specialists serving the great life insurance industry would organize themselves into bodies dealing with their various specialties to obtain the advantage of the exchange of ideas and the study of trends and developments. There are also associations which may be said to represent the life insurance companies in their corporate capacity.

The geographical situation of Canada with a common frontier, three thousand miles long, with the United States, the contiguity of some important centres of Canadian population to the U.S. centres, the close trading relations between the two countries—all mean that in life insurance, as in other industries, the organizations covering the industry are international covering both Canada and the United States. With a population ten times that of Canada it would be expected that U.S. companies and their officers would tend to dominate these bodies. Yet, the outstanding position of the leading Canadian life insurance companies and the calibre of their senior officials result in Canadians playing a far greater part in these international bodies than the proportion of population would indicate.

Another reason for indicating these various bodies by name and location of head office, is that any readers of this text who wish to pursue their studies of the business further or keep in touch with trends and new developments must necessarily move to the published proceedings of these bodies. This would also apply to specialists in certain fields who would wish to study their specialty at greater depth than is possible in a general text book like the present one. These published proceedings and, in some cases, reports and special studies are an essential part of the literature of life insurance, annuities, and pensions.

The actuarial organizations of Canada, the United States, England, and Scotland have already been dealt with in Chapter 1.

CANADIAN LIFE INSURANCE ASSOCIATION (C.L.I.A.)

The head office is in Toronto and it was founded in 1894, being the oldest life insurance company organization on the continent. It includes in its membership almost every company doing life business in Canada. It is considered as the official body representing the life insurance companies in Canada. The corresponding body representing the life insurance companies in the United States is the *American Council of Life Insurance* (Head Office, Washington).

The C.L.I.A. is in charge of the public relations of the industry and the programme of institutional advertising in newspapers and magazines. It publishes *Canadian Life Insurance Facts* which has been quoted throughout this text. The corresponding organization in the U.S. for this work is the *Institute of Life Insurance* (Head Office, New York), which is a part of A.C.L.I.

Probably the most important function of the C.L.I.A. is to represent the Canadian life insurance industry in its relations with the various government bodies both federal and provincial. Prospective or impending legislation, briefs to Royal Commissions and other investigating bodies, taxation, and every matter concerning life insurance as an industry are the subjects of studies by the staff of the Association and committees of members utilising the specialist staffs of the companies. The provincial uniform life insurance legislation in which Canada was a pioneer was instigated largely by the Association, and the late R. Leighton Foster, Q.C., Managing Director of the Association was a leading figure in this achievement.

LIFE UNDERWRITERS ASSOCIATION OF CANADA (L.U.A.C.)

This is the central organization of the 83 local associations of licensed life insurance agents throughout Canada. L.U.A.C. was founded in 1906 and today represents more than 90 per cent of the active, full-time licensed life insurance agents in Canada. L.U.A.C. has done much to raise the business of selling life insurance to a professional level by maintaining and administering a code of ethics and professional practices. It also acts as a source of information on many subjects of interest to life insurance agents, and presents the views of the members to governments and other interested bodies.

L.U.A.C. also acts as a training and educational body creating and administering courses designed to help life insurance agents to better serve the insurance buying public. Graduates of the program are eligible to receive the title and designation of Chartered Life Underwriter (CLU).

LIFE OFFICE MANAGEMENT ASSOCIATION (L.O.M.A.)

This is a company association founded in 1924 with head office in New York which seeks to improve life insurance company management through the exchange of experience and research by its member companies. One of its main functions is the training and education of head office and branch office employees. There was a corresponding Canadian body named the Insurance Institute of Toronto from 1899 to 1936 and the Life Insurance Institute of Canada from 1936 to 1951 engaged in this work when the examination activities of the Canadian body were merged with those of L.O.M.A.

The L.O.M.A. have a number of standing committees, in areas of Personnel Planning & Control, Personnel Systems & Procedures, etc., whose reports and the discussions thereon at the meetings of the Association play an important part in the development of the business on its administrative side.

LIFE INSURANCE MARKETING AND RESEARCH ASSOCIATION (L.I.M.R.A.)

In 1946, as the result of a merger between the Association of Life Agency Officers (founded in 1916) and the Life Insurance Sales Research Bureau (founded in 1922), this co-operative company organization was established, based in Hartford, Connecticut.

Its purpose is to initiate and conduct research and to generate and disseminate information in order to assist Marketing Officers with all aspects of Agency Management.

Through the use of sound principles and high standards, L.I.M.R.A.'s research work has become well known throughout the business. It has developed an aptitude index to aid in the selection of agents as well as conducting training and educational activities; producing the yearly Buyer Study describing the life and disability income consumer in North America; and providing useful tools in the areas of compensation and financing, to mention only a few.

Among the bodies dealing with more specialized fields of life insurance work are the following.

SELECTION OF RISKS AND MEDICAL ASPECTS OF LIFE INSURANCE

There are the *Institute of Home Office Underwriters* and the *Home Office Life Underwriters Association* of which company executives engaged in the selection of risks are members. There is also the *Association of Life Insurance Medical Directors of America*. These bodies publish their proceedings.

LEGAL AND CLAIMS WORK

There are the *Association of Life Insurance Counsel* and the *International Claim Association*.

There are other associations of those engaged in life insurance work, but we will conclude this chapter by referring to one other only: *Insurance Accounting and Statistical Association* dealing particularly with the application of electronic equipment to life insurance tabulation, accounting, etc.

There are associations of fraternal insurance officials and of government supervisory officials which will be referred to when these subjects are discussed in Chapters 32 and 28 respectively.

CHAPTER ELEVEN

Various Plans and Premium Practices

In this chapter and the next we deal with the wide variety of life insurance plans available to the public and some of the practices associated with life insurance premium payments.

In Chapter 5 we dealt with the three basic life insurance plans: term, straight life, and endowment insurance. It might be said with much justification that there are only three plans in life insurance, namely these three, the rest being variations or combinations of them. It is impossible to refer to every variation and every combination, but the principles underlying them are important. There is also the difficulty of naming them, for a company may adopt a plan which for some years has come to be recognized by a definite title and still use a different name for it. A good rule to follow is never to judge the plan by its name but rather by the provisions of the policy.

In Chapter 3 we dealt with the many situations: personal, family, and business, to illustrate the variety of needs for and the uses of life insurance. Life insurance is based on voluntary purchases by the public and hence sales appeal and amount of premium must always be considered. This explains the variety of plans offered.

PLANS WITH PREMIUMS LIMITED BY NUMBER

Had this text been written fifty or more years ago, pride of place would have been given to the 20 Payment Life Plan under which the sum insured is payable on death but premiums are payable until the death of the life insured but on no account for more than 20 years.

Prior to 1911, when the law was changed, "tontine" dividends were very popular with some companies. The substantial cash value of the 20 payment life policy at the end of twenty years plus the "tontine" dividend (not payable unless the life insured survived to the end of twenty years from entry) appeared attractive to those who were looking solely for a twenty-year insurance policy with an attractive investment feature. For many years, however, the emphasis has been on providing protection for dependents combined in some cases with saving for retirement.

On the participating plan the limited payment life policy, when paid up (that is to say, all premiums have been paid), will continue to receive dividends. Companies as a rule publish the rates for 10 payment life, 15 payment life, and so on; also rates for plans where the premiums cease at the policy anniversary corresponding to the sixtieth or sixty-fifth birthday of the life insured, called Life Paid-Up at 60 or 65 as the case may be. Considering 65 as the present normal retirement age and the need for relief from premium payments under life insurance policies after that age, the Life Paid-Up at 65 deserves more prominence than it now receives in Canada.

Endowment insurances with limited premium payments such as endowments maturing at age 60 or 65 with premiums limited to, say, twenty years have some popularity presumably owing to their substantial cash values in the early years. Such plans are used as an alternative to twenty-year endowment insurances for juveniles.

Companies issuing more than one series of plans which are in effect straight life plans will distinguish between them by using additional names as Life Paid-Up at 85, Endowment at 85, Life Paid-Up at 90 and so on. These plans differ from straight life plans as the policies will become paid-up or mature as endowment insurances at the ages stated but for the usual ages at entry this has quite a minor effect on the rate. In Table 5.1 compare the rates of endowment insurance to age 90 with those of the straight life plan.

SINGLE PREMIUM PLANS

As stated in Chapter 6, when the premium for a life insurance policy is paid in one sum at the commencement of the insurance, on the understanding that no part of the premium paid will be refunded in addition to the sum insured on death, it is described as a single premium plan.

In practice single premium policies are not often sold. For those who wish to prepay a number of annual premiums there has been developed an alternative which is more flexible. Companies will permit the discounting of annual premiums for periods up to twenty years and even longer when investment conditions are favourable. In this way the purchaser is assured of the full competitive advantage of rates, dividends, and cash values on annual premium policies. On death, the discounted value of the premiums not due is refunded in addition to the sum insured. On a participating policy, at the end of the period for which the premiums had been discounted, the accumulated dividends could be used to discount the premiums for another period of years if desired.

PLANS WITH MODIFIED PREMIUMS

The pattern is of the premiums payable under a policy can be modified provided the total present value of the modified premiums at the commencement of the insurance is equal to those before modification. Thus under a straight life policy the premiums in the first five years can be made to be exactly one-half of those payable subsequently provided the equivalence mentioned is borne in mind. The premiums after the first five years must be greater than the level annual premium payable throughout life for the same benefit.

Another type of modified premium plan is where the stepping up of the premium is done by stages, say in two or three stages at intervals of five years. The greater the ultimate premium payable the lower is that payable in the first five years.

The purpose of these modified premium plans is to offer as low an initial premium as possible to a prospect on a permanent life insurance plan. For plans participating in profits it may serve to compete with nonparticipating plans.

PLANS WITH MODIFIED SUMS INSURED

There are a number of plans where the sum insured payable is modified for specific purposes.

Increasing Sums Insured. There are plans where the sum insured may be said to increase with duration. Any plan under which a guaranteed amount is added to the sum insured each year that the policy is in force may be said to belong to this class. It can be a fixed percentage of the sum insured (called *guaranteed bonus policies*), the return of the premiums paid, or the addition of any other guaranteed amount. When these are added to the amount payable on death or maturity we get a guaranteed increase in the sum insured. There is no technical reason why these amounts cannot be added to the sum insured provided they are allowed for in the premium charged.

Decreasing Sums Insured. On the general assumption that a man's life insurance needs will be reduced considerably at age 60, 65, or 70, or at an age representing the end of his expectation of life at entry, policies are issued where the sum insured is reduced by a half at the critical age mentioned. As a rule the premium remains unchanged throughout life. The premium being unchanged means that it is less than for the straight life plan up to the critical age for the initial sum insured, but greater after the critical age for the reduced sum insured. It follows that the cash surrender value at the critical age is substantially less than for a straight life policy for the same initial sum insured. Under some of these plans, the cash surrender values may actually decrease shortly before the critical age. Remember that the cash surrender value is based on the policy-reserve which is the value of the benefits less the value of the future net premiums to be paid. A variation of this plan is when the premium as well as the sum insured is reduced at the critical age.

JUVENILE POLICIES

The attitude of companies towards insurance on the lives of children varies considerably. With some companies a substantial proportion of the business sold is on the lives of children, whereas with other companies such business is discouraged unless the family concerned is in a class where the premiums payable are of little financial significance to them.

Some fifteen years ago amendments to the laws of the provinces of Canada removed the restriction on the total amount of life insurance which may be paid (by all companies) on the death of a child before the fifth birthday. Prior to these amendments the limit was $200 before age one, increasing by equal steps to $1,000 from four to five years of age. Prior to 1931 the limits ranged from $20 to $400 for ages one to ten years and liberalizations were made in 1931 and in 1950. Many companies still continue to restrict the amount of insurance payable on the death of a child under one year of age.

Juvenile life insurance meets the need "to sell the idea of life insurance young" and to encourage thrift represented by the long-term saving on a life insurance policy bought for a child. There is also the short-term endowment to provide a fund for university education etc., in other words a policy to mature at, say, age 21 or age 25. To complete the insurange programme, provision is also made for the waiver of the premiums in the event of the death of the parent paying the premiums. This additional benefit which only covers premiums payable to the child's twenty-first (or twenty-fifth in some cases) birthday, is decreasing term insurance for the discounted values of the premiums. The advantage of this benefit is obvious and its cost is usually small on account of the young age of the parent and the limited period for which it is payable. Corresponding to this "waiver on death of parent" there is a waiver of premiums on total disability of the parent which can also be obtained. This disability benefit follows closely in its conditions the waiver of premiums on total disability which will be discussed later.

Jumping Juvenile Policies. This is an adaptation of a children's plan which has been popular in Britain for many years. In Britain, to avoid the problems of granting insurance on the lives of children, no death benefits, other than the return of premiums with or without interest, were paid before age 21. At age 21 a substantial amount of insurance went into force without any change in premium and without any evidence of insurability at that time. Various options were available at age 21 and the policy could be continued with a choice of various plans. The cash value available at age 21 was quite substantial.

In Canada the modification is that $5,000 insurance goes into effect at age 21 for each $1,000 insurance to age 21, without changing the rate of premium or requiring further evidence of insurability. Companies in Canada vary in their practice as to the plan which goes into effect automatically at age 21. With some it is the straight life participating plan, with others the life to age 65 or endowment insurance at age 65. Options are available at age 21 under which, in lieu of the automatic plan, other plans with a greater investment element and hence with a reduced sum insured can be chosen—all without any increase in the premium payable since entry. The title "jumping juvenile" describes this type of plan although various names are used by different companies.

A point to be noted is that whatever plan is chosen on which to continue the policy beyond age 21, the premium payable is less than if that plan had been entered upon at the outset for the sum insured applicable after age 21. The attraction of setting up a future estate for a child is particularly stressed in this plan; some companies have used the name *estate builder* for it.

INSURANCE PENSION PLAN

It is the practice in Canada for life insurance policies to contain settlement options whereby, on the maturity of an endowment, the sum insured and any accumulated dividends can be exchanged for a life annuity, the rates for which are guaranteed in the tables of settlement options. As was mentioned in discussing the straight life plan, the same is usually permitted with the cash surrender value on life plans so that most insurance plans do provide for insurance and pension benefits.

However, when the desire is to provide for a specific number of units of pension at a specific age, say $100 a month to be guaranteed for life at age 65, the object is to provide a sum at age 65 which is equivalent to the pension desired. Policies providing units of both definite insurance amounts and definite guaranteed pension benefits, e.g., $1,000 with $10 a month, $1,200 with $10 a month, or $1,000 with $5 a month, are called *insurance pension policies* or *income endowments*. It is desirable to retain the word "insurance" as part of the title to distinguish them from annual premium pension plans which contain no insurance benefits other than a return of premium.

An important feature of these plans is that the cost of a pension of $10 a month for life at the usually required pension ages of 60, 65, or 70, exceeds $1,000. Thus with a $10 a month pension, a form of endowment insurance has to be provided which will mature for an amount exceeding the life insurance of $1,000. For a female life at age 60 with a pension guaranteed for ten years, and thereafter for life, the equivalent cash value of $10 a month pension may exceed $2,000 and for a male at 65 it may exceed $1,500. The cash maturity value is sometimes called the *cash option*.

An endowment insurance commencing at $1,000 with a maturity value at age 65 of, say, $1,500 will have policy-reserves increasing to $1,500 at 65 and as cash surrender values are based on the policy-reserves, at some point they will exceed $1,000. Thus the amount payable on death will be $1,000 or the cash surrender value, whichever is the greater. A critic may enquire why, if the cash option is X, we do not sell an endowment insurance providing X on maturity or previous death and save all the bother. These insurance pension plans are quite costly on account of their high endowment values, but for professional men and others, who wish to provide a specific amount of pension to be available at a specific date, the emphasis on the pension benefit relative to the insurance protection is what the applicant desires.

JOINT LIFE POLICIES

When two or more lives are insured under a policy so that the sum insured is payable on the first death it is called a joint life policy. The most obvious combination is that of husband and wife; the next is that of two or more partners. Some companies publish rates on the straight life, 20 payment life, and endowment insurance plans for two lives of equal ages, with a table indicating how two different ages can be reduced to the equivalent equal ages for the purpose of arriving at the amount of the premiums.

The only advantage in a joint policy is that the premium is less than the total for individual policies on each life for the same amount. But the first death leaves the others unprotected, for the policy terminates on the first death.

Drawbacks to *partnership insurances*, apart from the serious disadvantage mentioned, are (1) the lack of adaptibility of one policy covering all the lives; (2) the possible need for different amounts on different lives; (3) the continuous need for revising partnership agreements; (4) the difficulty of adding new lives. All these disadvantages have tended to restrict the use of joint life policies and some companies make no reference to such plans in their published rates.

There have been two interesting developments in recent years concerning insurance on more than one life. (1) Some companies now permit insurance to be continued on the survivor after the first death, without evidence of health, but at the premium applicable to the attained age. The principle may be extended to policies on more than two lives. (2) Introduction of capital gains tax which applies on death but not if property is transferred to the spouse, has led to a demand for insurance payable on the *second* death to occur; such insurance is not *joint-life* insurance as defined; it is more correctly called *last survivor* insurance.

Premium Payment Practices

ANNUAL AND FRACTIONAL PREMIUMS

The demonstration of the calculation of net premiums in Chapter 6 assumed that the premiums were payable annually in advance. For the convenience of policyholders premiums may be paid half-yearly, quarterly, or monthly. The desire of people to budget their expenditures on a monthly basis and the ability of an increasing proportion of the public to buy ordinary life insurance has led to a great development of monthly payments in ordinary life insurance.

Pre-Authorized Cheque Plan. The problem in monthly premium payments in ordinary life insurance is the cost of billing of the amounts, that is, sending out monthly premium notices; this is apart from the collection and accounting of the monthly payments.

In Britain the "banker's order" developed first, i.e., a depositor requested his bank to remit a stated amount each month to the insurance company and debit his account accordingly. The difference in banking systems made this idea unacceptable to the Canadian banks and some companies obtained twelve monthly post-dated cheques signed by the policyholder once a year to cover the following year's premium. However, co-operation between the banks and life insurance companies resulted in the *pre-authorized cheque plan* being developed where one authority signed by the policyholder and filed with the bank suffices and the insurance company bills the bank monthly for the required amount.

Charge for Fractional Premiums. It should be noted that the annual premium is calculated on the assumption that it is payable in one sum and in advance. If it is payable more frequently than annually, it is necessary for three reasons to make an additional charge.

First, there is a loss of interest to the insurance company. It is readily seen that if the premium is payable half-yearly, interest is lost for half of the year on one-half of the premium; a charge equal to one-quarter of the annual interest on a premium is therefore necessary. For monthly premiums the charge required is nearly one-half of such annual interest.

Secondly, the question arises whether on death the balance of the fractional premiums for the policy year of death should be deducted from the sum insured payable. Under a monthly premium policy with the life insured dying in the first month of any policy year, eleven monthly premiums remain unpaid on account of that year's premium.

Thirdly, there is the expense of doing the billing, collecting, and accounting of a premium, say twelve times a year instead of once, and clerical costs are a very substantial item of overhead.

In Canada considerable variation has developed in the charges made for fractional premiums. There used to be some degree of uniformity, and the additional yearly charge for half-yearly payments was 3 per cent of the annual premium, for quarterly payments 5 per cent, and for monthly payments with monthly premium notices 6 per cent. For the pre-authorized cheque plan the 6 per cent was reduced to 4 per cent by one company. The development which disturbed the uniformity is the recognition that the additional cost for fractional premium payments was better expressed as a percentage of the annual premium plus a constant. Thus one company charges an additional $1^1/_2$, 2, and 3 per cent of the annual premium for half-yearly, quarterly, and monthly premiums respectively *plus* fifty cents on each payment; for pre-authorized cheque payments the addition is 3 per cent of the annual premium plus ten cents on each payment.

Balance of Yearly Premium on Death in Fractional Payments. There are various procedures which could be followed with regard to policies on which premiums were payable more frequently than annually, when on the death of the life insured the full premium for the current policy year has not been paid.

1. Deduction of the remainder of the year's premium from the insurance proceeds. This was the general practice some years ago and such premiums are called *instalment premiums.* This practice has practically ceased in Canada.

2. No deduction to be made of the balance of premiums which have not fallen due in the current policy year. Such premiums are called *true premiums.* This practice of true premiums is now almost universal in Canada.

3. A refund of the proportionate premium paid beyond the month of death. Thus in an annual premium there is a possibility of a refund of eleven-twelfths of the annual premium if death takes place in the first month of the policy year. Refunds are also possible in the case of half-yearly and quarterly premiums.

If the extra charge for fractional premium payments is equitable, that is, it takes into account the particular method of the treatment of the balance of the year's premium on death, then there is no objection in theory to the use of either of these plans. This proviso also applies to the extra charge for fractional premium payments to cover the additional cost of billing and accounting where the pre-authorized cheque plan and similar systems are used. The fundamental principle in Canadian life insurance is that: "Equity must always be preserved between policyholders."

RATE OF PREMIUM AND SIZE OF POLICY

Preferred Risk Policies. In 1908 the Metropolitan Life issued in both Canada and the United States a straight life "special" plan in amounts of $5,000 and over. The policy was presumed to be issued to specially selected lives. It was the intention to keep these policyholders in a separate class and to allocate dividends based on their mortality and expenses—almost as a company within a company. This experiment proved so successful that it was in due course widely imitated and special straight life plans with substantial minimum sums insured became the rule in Canada and are still widely used.

In 1908 a $5,000 policy represented a substantial sum and this in itself ensured some selection. Throughout this text we emphasize the remarkable improvement in social conditions and living standards which have taken place, so that the difference in mortality between the "labouring classes" and the "professional, executive, and clerical classes" has been decreasing. Even as recently as 1930 if the mortality of the professional man could be rated as 100 that of the factory worker was found to be 144.[1]

The issue of policies at reduced rates for larger sums insured has taken on a wider significance due to the inflation which began after the Second World War, i.e., after 1945. Inflation has meant a substantial increase in the average size of policies bought. Thus the selective mortality expected from a minimum sum insured of $5,000 ceased to apply. Further, the inflation of costs forced consideration of the equity of charging the same rate per thousand for a $1,000 policy, a $10,000, and a $50,000 policy. The problem of overhead costs has overshadowed that of any possible difference in expected mortality.

A Canadian company (London Life) was the first company to introduce the procedure of a differentiation between the rates charged for policies of different sizes on all plans of life insurance.

Graded Premium Plans. The subject of the overhead costs of the life insurance business will be discussed in a later chapter, but it will suffice here to state that a substantial part of the cost of issuing and maintaining a life insurance policy is independent of the size of the policy. The first year's costs are much greater than in subsequent years but, spreading the first year's costs over the duration of the policy, an average is obtained; an amount of about $15.00 would apply in many companies.[2]

Thus the part of the expenses that can be represented as "Per policy" would be $15 on a $1,000 policy, $3.00 per thousand on a $5,000 policy and so on. Writing these costs down for policies of different amounts we get Table 11.1. If these assumptions were correct they would justify

[1]See "Occupation, Social Class and Mortality," by the author in *Transactions*, Society of Actuaries (Chicago, 1960), vol. 12, Table 5, p. 235.

[2]For the ten largest Canadian companies doing ordinary business only, the average life insurance premium per new policy effected in 1974 was $355 and the corresponding sum insured was $24,707.

TABLE 11.1

Amount of sum insured	Cost per thousand
$ 1,000	$15.00
2,000	7.50
5,000	3.00
10,000	1.50
25,000	.60
50,000	.30
100,000	.15

charging a $2,000 policyholder $7.50 a thousand less than a $1,000 policyholder and similarly a $5,000 policyholder $1.50 a thousand more than a $10,000 policyholder. Note that as the sum insured increases the "step rate" decreases to a trivial amount: a difference of only 15 cents per thousand between a $50,000 and $100,000 policy. In practice one set of rates is published and the policies are graded by size in broad bands and the differences per thousand are given as between one band and another.

Policy Fee Method. An alternative method to the above which is followed by some companies is to quote the premium rates per thousand sum insured for all plans less the "cost per policy" charge and the resulting total premium obtained corresponding to the sum insured required is then increased by the "cost per policy." The "cost per policy" charge is called the "policy fee"; it varies between companies, generally in the range from $9.00 to $15.00; some companies charge as much as $20.00 or $25.00 for term policies because the first-year cost is spread over a shorter than average period.

The full policy fee may not be charged for the smallest policies. Thus one company uses a $9.00 policy fee, but reduces it to $3.00 per thousand for policies under $3,000.

REDUCED RATES FOR FEMALE LIVES

It has been known for many years that the population mortality rates of females has been lower than for males of the same age and in recent years this has become increasingly evident where insured lives are concerned. The lower mortality of females at the older ages was of major importance as regards the cost of annuities and had been taken into account for that type of policy. However, as regards life insurance, policies on female lives were, on the average, much smaller than on males and generally it was considered that there was an offset here between mortality and expenses. Also, on the grounds of simplicity, there was some advantage in using the same rates for males and females, particularly considering the relatively few annuity policies and the multitude of life insurance policies.

When the graded premium plan was adopted, i.e., relating premium to size of policy, there was an obvious inconsistency in charging females increased rates for annuities based on their lower mortality and ignoring the matter for life insurance; this was particularly so when a substantial amount of insurance was involved. Further, succeeding investigations of the mortality of insured lives in recent years indicated that not only was the trend of mortality of female lives downwards but increasingly so when compared with male lives.

It is now the almost universal practice in Canada to charge lower rates for females than for males on straight life and higher premium plans where the insurance benefits are identical. As illustrating current practice, one company reduces the rates on its straight life plans, at age 35 at entry, by $1.72 per thousand sum insured. For the same age at entry the reduction on the endowment insurance maturing at age 65 is 76 cents per thousand and for the 20 year endowment 45 cents per thousand. In some companies the differential is assumed to be three years, i.e., on those life insurance plans where lower rates are granted, a woman of, say, 35 years at entry would be charged the rate for a man of age 32 at entry, but the cash values and dividends (where applicable) would correspond with the true age.

CHAPTER TWELVE

Term Riders and Special Plans

In Chapter 11, reference was made to the basic Life, Endowment, and Term Plans. In addition to these plans insurance companies have offered a wide variety of special policies which they think will meet a particular need or appeal to a certain market. They have also offered *riders*, that is, supplementary benefits which may be added to a regular policy and make it more attractive; often these supplementary benefits may be cancelled without affecting the basic policy.

There has been a wide variety of such special policies and riders; some have proven unattractive and been removed from the market; others have proven popular and continue to be sold in large volume. To illustrate this aspect of life insurance, we shall describe the introduction of the *family income* plan and the subsequent development of a wide variety of *term riders*; the *family plan* and the *guaranteed insurability benefit*. These are to be found in the rate manuals of most companies but may vary in detail.

FAMILY INCOME AND TERM INSURANCE RIDERS

The Family Income Concept. If the proceeds of a straight life policy are left on deposit at interest, or used to buy a life annuity, the resulting income may well be insufficient for the needs of the beneficiary, particularly a widow with young children. The original family income concept was that if death occurred before a fixed date—generally chosen so that children would then be grown up—the proceeds would be left on deposit at interest until that date and in the meantime the interest would be supplemented by an additional monthly income. At the fixed date, the proceeds would still be there undiminished.

Thus if the fixed date were 20 years from issue, and death occurred in the first year, the income would be payable for 19 years plus odd months; if death occurred in the 20th year, the income would be payable for the remaining months only. Because the additional insurance would be greatest when the life insured is young and select, the level premium for the benefit would be relatively small.

A paper by the author traced the history of the Family Income Plan and broke new ground in advocating the extension of the income benefit period to age 65 of the life insured.[1]

For many years the *family income policy* provided a monthly income of $10 for each $1,000 of sum insured, e.g., $100 per month with a $10,000 policy. If the company's guaranteed minimum interest rate is 3 per cent per annum (with excess interest payable as described in Chapter 14: Settlement Options) the guaranteed interest will amount to $2.46 per month per $1,000. (Note that 12 × $2.46 is $29.52, a little less than 3 per cent of $1,000, or $30.00; $2.46 payable each month is equivalent to $30.00 payable at the end of the year.) The balance of the $10.00 monthly payment ($7.54) is provided by the family income benefit; the extra premium is calculated on the cost of insurance of the value of $7.54 per month, not of $10.00 per month.

Development of the Family Income Rider. At first the additional insurance was completely integrated with the straight life protection in a *family income policy*. The extra insurance could not be terminated on request except by rewriting the policy, nor could it be converted to permanent cover. Then came the idea of the *family income rider* which could be added to straight life, limited payment life, endowment, or even term, provided the basic policy had a term not less than the family income period. The rider could be terminated, if desired, without affecting the basic policy; conversion privileges were granted; moreover, a rider could be added to a policy already in force, subject to evidence of insurability.

Once the rider idea was established, it became apparent that there was no reason to limit the total monthly income to $10 per $1,000 sum insured; riders were offered under which it was $15, $20, or more. (Note that a "$20 rider" costs more than twice as much as a "$10 rider" because additional income of $17.54 has to be provided instead of $7.54; the ratio of $17.54 is approximately 7 to 3.)

Another idea which has gained wide acceptance is to pay the sum insured immediately on death but still pay a fixed monthly income until the fixed date. The premium for this must obviously be greater than when payment of the sum insured is deferred.

A further step was an *independent family income policy* with no

[1]*Record*, American Institute of Actuaries (Chicago, 1941), Vol. 30, page 76; see also the discussion of dependency on page 586 of the volume.

underlying level insurance. In this case, the premium has to provide the total income; it also has to be higher than for a rider to take care of expenses which are provided for in the premium for the basic policy, if a rider is added.

Decreasing term. In some cases there might be reasons why the beneficiary would be better served by a cash benefit than by an income followed by payment of the sum insured. This was allowed for by giving the beneficiary the right to *commute* the benefits. At first, commutation was not permitted unless arranged for by the life insured during his lifetime; now it is common practice to make commutation available unless specifically prohibited by the life insured.

The amount payable on *commutation* will evidently depend on the number of years remaining in the family income period. Table 12.1 gives specimen values, calculated by two different methods, which, however, as they must, give identical results.

TABLE 12.1

Commuted Value of a Family Income Benefit. Effective Rate of Interest: 3% per annum

	Method I			Method II	
Remaining Period	Value of $10.00 per month	Value of $1,000 at end of period	Total	Value of $7.54 per month	Add $1,000
35 years	$2,620	$355	2,975	$1,975	$2,975
30 years	2,390	412	2,802	1,802	2,802
25 years	2,123	478	2,601	1,601	2,601
20 years	1,814	554	2,368	1,368	2,368
15 years	1,456	642	2,098	1,098	2,098
10 years	1,040	744	1,784	784	1,784
5 years	558	863	1,421	421	1,421
1 year	118	971	1,089	89	1,089

For Method I, we simply look up in interest tables the values of the income of $10 per month for the remaining period and of the lump sum of $1,000, payable at the end of the period, and add the two together.

Under Method II, we find the value of the *additional income* of $7.54 per month (remembering from above that $2.46 comes from interest on $1,000): e.g., for 35 years .754 × $2,620 is $1,975; adding the $1,000 gives $2,975 as before.

The figures for Method II show that in addition to the basic sum assured we have *additional term insurance* which *decreases*, if the original term is 35 years, from $1,975 to zero, for each $1,000 sum insured; hence the expression *decreasing term insurance*.

From the figures under Method I, we can see that in cases where there is no basic sum insured, an income benefit of, say, $100 per month, is equivalent to decreasing term insurance starting at $26,200, if the original term is 35 years, and running down to zero.

Decreasing term is now available as a rider or as a separate policy. It is frequently used as *mortage insurance*, to pay off the mortgage on the family home in the event of death, because the unpaid balance of a mortgage decreases with time in the same way as the commuted value of an income.

Level term riders. Term insurance policies have been issued for many years and are described as one of the three basic plans in Chapter 5. The idea of adding a *level term rider* to a basic policy, thus saving the additional expense of issuing separate policies, has been widely accepted.

In summary, the introduction of term riders, whether decreasing or level, has been a revolutionary development. Combined with the practice of *programming*, that is, a study by the agent of the total insurance needs of the individual, and a prescribed combination of permanent and term insurance to meet these needs, term riders have brought the prospect of providing adequate insurance protection for dependants within the reach of the majority. The conversion privilege under riders is an important element because it guarantees that temporary life insurance may be extended indefinitely, without further evidence of insurability.

THE FAMILY INSURANCE PLAN

We have dealt with the development of term insurance riders which can be added to a basic plan at a low premium if a large part of the expenses can be borne by the basic plan. The idea of covering a whole family with the basic plan on the husband/father and term insurance on the wife and children would seem to be a logical development. One criticism already made has been the disproportionate amount of life insurance on women and children in some companies in relation to that on the breadwinner. However, the need for some insurance for funeral benefits on each individual of such a family is obvious.

A plan to meet this need was introduced in 1956 by The Prudential Insurance Company of America[2] and given the name "Family Policy." The plan enables companies to serve the public better by providing

[2] Credit should be given to Valentine Howell, executive vice-president of the company. President, Society of Actuaries, 1950–51.

insurance on every member of the family at moderate cost. The plan has been widely adopted in both Canada and the United States.

We outline the main features of one type of "Family Policy" with explanations of the principles involved. Some of these features may be regarded as old-fashioned, or worse, because of the distinction between husband and wife; following the description we mention some of the more modern developments.

1. Each unit provides the following benefits (summarized in brief).

Life insured	Plan	Amount
Husband/Father	Straight Life	$5,000
Wife	Term Insurance expiring when husband is 65	$1,000 if same age as husband (modified if otherwise)
Children entering from 15 days old until 18th birthday	Term Insurance to 21st birthday of child or 65th birthday of father if earlier	$1,000

2. A level premium is payable during the lifetime of the husband/father reducing at age 65 to that comparable to a straight life plan when all benefits on wife and children cease. The premium rate depends only on the husband's age; not on that of the wife, children, or the number of children. The cost of term insurance on children, limited to their 21st birthday, is relatively small if attached to a basic policy. As children yet to be born are covered, the over-all premium for the children's benefit is based on population averages: between two and three children per family in Canada, if childless families are excluded. It follows that there is no change in premium if a child dies or children are added by birth. Children legally adopted are also included.

3. The cost of term insurance on the wife for the period until the husband attains age 65 varies considerably with the age of the wife. To keep the premium constant irrespective of the age of the wife, the amount of the term insurance payable on the wife's death is varied. Thus, if the wife is 17 years younger than the husband, the amount of the term insurance is $3,100 per unit with one company and if 11 years older than the husband it is $460 per unit, this being the range of ages accepted by that company.

4. Waiver of premium in the event of total disability is on the husband's life only.

5. A maximum of five units is permitted by some companies so that the insurance on each child can be as much as $5,000.

6. If the husband/father dies before the policy anniversary nearest his 65th birthday, the insurances on the wife and children continue without further payment of premium until the date when they would have expired had the husband/father lived.

7. If the wife dies before the husband, whatever the amount of her insurance it is replaced by $1,000 of term insurance per unit to age 65 on the life of the husband (with no conversion privileges). The amount of the wife's insurance was equivalent to $1,000 per unit if she was the same age as the husband. This benefit is given so that there is no need to reduce the premium when the wife dies.

8. Conversion privileges. At the policy anniversary nearest the husband's 65th birthday, the wife's term insurance expires and it may then be converted into permanent insurance without evidence of insurability. On the policy anniversary following any child's 21st birthday or nearest father's 65th birthday if earlier, such child's term insurance expires. However, it may then be converted into permanent insurance for an amount up to five times the amount of the term insurance on the child's life.

9. The cash surrender values, etc., guaranteed in the policy are based on the husband's insurance only. The settlement options included in the policy apply only on the husband's death.

10. Family income riders and similar benefits may be added to the husband's insurance.

By covering an indeterminate number of insured lives under one policy at a rate of premium fixed at the outset and other special features, the Family Policy has broken new ground in the development of life insurance. For a man of age 35 who would pay, on the average, $90 a year for a $5,000 straight life policy, the additional life insurance benefits as outlined above for wife and children would cost about $25 a year. As companies differ considerably in the benefits offered under their corresponding plans this premium is illustrative only.

Due to the increasing importance in recent years of wives' incomes in the family budget, some companies now issue additional insurance, by way of riders, on the lives of wives. Also in the market are policies under which the wife is the principal insured and the husband's life is insured for a lesser amount.

Furthermore, for one-parent families, or for cases where one parent is uninsurable, it is possible to buy a "Parent and Children" policy. Another step in the direction of flexibility is the introduction of spouse term riders (level or decreasing) and children's term riders which some prefer to the "package concept" of the original Family Plan.

GUARANTEED INSURABILITY RIDER

The *guaranteed insurability rider* was introduced first in the United States in 1957, and soon afterwards in Canada.

The desirability of introducing young lives to the advantages of insurance combined with long-term savings has been mentioned, but the anticipation of future life insurance needs, many years in advance, introduces a problem. Satisfactory evidence of being a normal life as regards longevity is an essential requisite to obtain life insurance at standard rates. There is always the possibility of an impairment arising which may mean that additional life insurance can only be obtained at special rates and possibly unobtainable at any rate. The G.I.R. has an appeal not only to the very young life but also to the applicant in his twenties and thirties who wishes to ensure that he can obtain additional life insurance, as his needs may dictate, in the future, at standard rates. We outline here, briefly, the plan issued by several companies in Canada with particular reference to one company's plan.

The G.I.R. may be attached to any new policy where the age at issue is 0 to 37 inclusive. It gives the right to purchase, without evidence of insurability, additional insurance on the life insured on certain specific future dates, the limit on each such option date being the face amount of the basic policy with a maximum of, say, $25,000; the maximum varies with companies. The option dates are ages 25, 28, 31, 34, 37, and 40, i.e., six dates for those age 24 or less at entry, five dates for those age 25 to 27 and so on, with one option date for those age 37 at entry, namely age 40.

It should be noted that for an entrant under age 25 effecting a basic sum insured of $5,000 the additional insurance which can be purchased is $30,000; for a basic sum insured of $10,000 it would be $60,000. With this particular company the maximum option allowed to a life insured age 24 or less is $25,000 which would allow total additional insurance of $150,000. The right to effect additional insurance cannot be carried forward; if not effected on any particular option date, that option expires.

The company referred to also allows the policy owner to exercise the right to purchase the additional insurance of the next option date during the 90 day period following the date of marriage of the life insured; birth of a child to the life insured and his wife or the legal adoption of a child. Further, if the life insured dies during the 60 day period preceding an option date or marriage or birth of a child an amount equal to the additional insurance available at that option date will be added to the death benefit payable under the basic policy.

Where the premiums under the basic policy are payable to at least age 40 the additional annual premium for the G.I.R. benefit for a teen-ager is about $1 per thousand basic sum insured; for a man in his twenties it is about $1.50. Although current rates have an actuarial basis, the plan introduces new considerations which future experience alone can determine.

CHAPTER THIRTEEN

Annuities

ANNUITIES AND PENSIONS

We now discuss the other major activity of the life insurance industry in Canada: the sale and servicing of annuities and pensions.

Again we must refer to the lack of precision in terminology. In practice the words annuity and pension have become almost synonymous. Yet, more particularly, the word *pension* should mean an income for life granted for services rendered as by an employer to an employee or by a government to its aged citizens. The word *annuity* should more properly be reserved for the technical processes involved, namely a series of equal payments made at equidistant intervals as will be defined below. Thus a pension is an annuity, but an annuity is not necessarily a pension.

A person could be said to buy an annuity, not a pension, from an insurance company. Yet such annuity policies are often referred to as pension plans particularly in sales material and advertisements. Further, pension contracts effected by employers to cover employees are referred to as group annuities.

In this text we have separated the material dealing with pension plans arranged by employers for their employees or by governments for aged citizens from annuity contracts on individual lives. The first are called *pensions* and the subject is dealt with in chapters 26 and 27. The latter are called *annuities* and are covered in this chapter.

DEFINITIONS

An *annuity* originally meant a series of *annual* payments, but it has come to mean any payments made periodically. It is essential when speaking of annuities to specify clearly the interval between the payments—thus, a *monthly annuity* is an annuity where the payments fall due on the same day of each calendar month, that is, twelve payments each year; a *half-yearly annuity* is an annuity where the payments are made twice a year at six-month intervals, and so on. Unless definitely stated otherwise, it will be assumed throughout this text that the term annuity means a series of equal payments made at equidistant intervals.

If the annuity payments are contingent on the survival of a given life or a combination of lives, the annuity is called a *life annuity*. If the annuity payments are not contingent on the survival of any life or lives, it is called an *annuity certain*.

INCREASING IMPORTANCE OF ANNUITIES IN THE LIFE INSURANCE INDUSTRY

Annuity business has been of rapidly increasing importance to life insurance companies in recent years. This was illustrated by the figures given for premiums for Ordinary Annuities in Chapter 2, viz. $32 millions in 1960, $117 millions in 1970, and $495 millions in 1974. (The annual reports of the Federal Superintendent of Insurance divide annuities into *ordinary* and *group*. Some ordinary annuities are purchased for employees by pension funds established by their employers and are thus *pensions* according to the definition given above; further, some Registered Retirement Savings plans are issued under Group Pension policies, although they are *annuities* by our definition. Thus it is not possible to obtain exact figures for *annuities* as defined, but the ordinary annuity figures reported by the Superintendent are the best guide we have.)

Other figures illustrating the growth of Ordinary Annuities are also available in the Superintendent's Report; these are shown in Table 13.1.

TABLE 13.1

Ordinary Annuities in Canada—Federally Registered Companies

		1960	1970	1974
NEW EFFECTED				
Deferred:	Number	10,106	18,062	85,164
	Annual Payment	$ 6,707,861	$21,903,118	$156,886,865
Vested:	Number	684	3,834	9,361
	Annual Payment	$ 693,196	$ 5,157,399	$ 19,093,716
IN FORCE				
Deferred:	Number	100,876	111,925	305,779
	Annual Payment	$50,499,302	$88,999,663	$428,274,238
Vested:	Number	18,778	41,460	75,627
	Annual Payment	$10,169,051	$35,963,620	$ 95,322,856

Note that at the end of 1974, over 75,000 annuities for over $95 millions per annum were being paid in Canada; at the same time provision was being made for eventual payment of over $400 millions per annum under more than 300,000 contracts.

The main reason for the increase in individual annuity business has been the increasing public interest in Registered Retirement Savings Plans. Another reason has been the introduction of Income Averaging Annuities. Both of these arrangements, which permit substantial deferment or spreading of income tax, are described in more detail in a later chapter.

ANNUITIES IN HISTORY

The history of annuities is a long one and goes back to the earliest records of mankind. The first table of the value of a life annuity of which we have any record, called the Ulpian Table (devised by a great Roman jurist, Ulpianus), arose out of the Falcidian Law. This law, enacted in B.C. 40, prevented a testator leaving more than three-quarters of his property to others than his legal heirs. It therefore became necessary to set a value on any legacies which were in the form of annuities payable for a fixed term or for life.

What rates of mortality prevailed in Roman times we do not know. In Table 13.2 we show specimen values of the Ulpian Table. It is believed that discount factors were ignored, so that the value of an annuity was determined by multiplying the amount of the annual payment by the number of years purchase indicated. We also show in the table the

TABLE 13.2

Comparison of Ulpian Table with Others

Ulpian Table		Expectation of Life*		$\mathring{e}_x$
Age	No. of years purchase	Age	Northampton Table	1937 Standard Annuity Table Males
Birth to 20	30	20	33	51.2
20 to 25	28	30	28	41.9
25 to 30	25	40	23	33.0
30 to 35	22	50	18	24.8
35 to 40	20	60	13	17.6
44 to 45	15	65	11	14.4
49 to 50	10	70	9	11.6
Age 60 and up	5	75	7	9.2

*See Chapter 4 for explanation

expectation of life according to the Northampton Table[1] and the 1937 Standard Annuity Table (referred to later in this chapter). The latter is currently used in Canada for valuing annuities for income tax purposes. However the use of discount factors reduces the values considerably at a young age.[2]

It would be too much to expect that the Romans based their values on an actual actuarial investigation, but it is remarkable that legal and actuarial problems which concern us today had their exact counterpart in Roman days. The Roman achievement is all the more remarkable for throughout more than a thousand years afterwards annuities were sold with little reference to the age of the party on whose life the payments were determined. In 1693 the astronomer Halley published a mortality table and showed how it could be used to calculate the value of an annuity on the life of a person based on his or her age. Governments raised huge loans by offering life annuities in lieu of interest and capital repayment and it was the practice of purchasers to nominate a very young healthy life on whose survival the annuity was to be paid, as the rate of the annuity was the same for young and old.

Annuities grew in importance in mediaeval times due to the prohibition by the Church of lending money at interest. The Bible contains many edicts[3] against "lending upon usury" and in ancient times it was generally associated with "famine and tribute" and the borrower who defaulted was enslaved, or some of his family were sold into slavery to redeem the debt.[4] Only gradually did understanding develop as to the essential differences between usury and interest. The alternative to interest payments which was adopted was annuity payments or in other words instalments including capital repayments and interest. The following which appeared in a book published in 1554 in England, and quoted by Walford in his Insurance Cyclopaedia is worthy of note: "A corporation taketh a £100 of a man to give him 8 in the £100 during his life, without restitution of the principal. It is no usury, for that here is no lending, but a sale for ever of so much rent for so much money."

[1] This was the first mortality table used to any extent for life insurance purposes. It was published in 1783 and was based on the deaths in a parish of the town of Northampton in England. Some of the early rates of the Old Equitable were based on this table.

[2] Under the Income Tax Regulations the present value of an annuity for a male aged 20 is 17.90 times the annual amount; at age 60 the factor is 10.64.

[3] Exodus 22, v. 25. "If thou lend money to any of my people that is poor by thee, thou shalt not be to him as an usurer, neither shalt thou lay upon him usury." Also, Leviticus 25, vv. 35–7; Deuteronomy 24, v. 19.

[4] 2 Kings 4, v. 1. "Thy servant my husband is dead . . . and the creditor is come to take unto him my two sons to be bondmen." (Bondman meant slave.)

IMMEDIATE ANNUITIES

In a life annuity when the equidistant periods of payment date from the commencement of the contract and the first payment falls due at the end of the first period of payment it is called an *immediate life annuity*. The person during whose survival the annuity is payable is called the *annuitant*. If the annuity is payable annually, the first payment of the annuity falls due one year after the date of commencement of the annuity if the annuitant be then living; if it is a monthly annuity, the first payment falls due one calendar month after commencement, and so on. Immediate annuities, by their nature, are single premium contracts.

In Chapter 6 (see Figures 5 and 8) we showed how the value of a series of annual premiums was obtained as a single premium at entry and we referred to the single premium as the present value of an annuity represented by those premiums. Using an appropriate table, the net cost of an annuity is determined in exactly the same way and when the loadings, i.e., additions, for expenses and commissions are added, the cost, i.e., the purchase money, of an immediate annuity is obtained. Note that under the simplest form of immediate annuity which we can call a *straight life annuity*, the annuity payments are made to the survivors only, all payments ceasing on death. In this way the highest return on the purchase money can be obtained; in other words, an annuity for a given amount on the straight life annuity plan costs the least.

To meet the requirements of those who desire that a definite minimum amount be paid out under an immediate life annuity whether the annuitant lives or dies, other plans are available as the following list of various plans indicates.

1. *Straight life annuity*. This was outlined above. Here the annuity payments cease on death.

2. *Minimum guaranteed payments*. Under this type of annuity a minimum number of annuity payments is guaranteed: e.g., for 10 years, 15 years, or 20 years, whether the annuitant lives or dies but continuing during the annuitant's lifetime after the minimum number of guaranteed payments has been made.

3. *Instalment refund annuity*. This is when the minimum guaranteed period is such as to return exactly the amount of the purchase money; the minimum period thus varies for each age.

4. *Cash refund annuity*. Under this modification the balance of the purchase money is returned in one sum on the death of the annuitant.

Comparing (3) and (4), note that for a stated amount of annuity (4) would cost more than (3). This is because the balance of the purchase

TABLE 13.3

Illustrative Immediate Life Annuity Rates (1976). Annual amount, payable in monthly instalments, which $10,000 will purchase

Age at entry	Straight life annuity	Minimum Guaranteed Period			Cash refund annuity
		10 years	15 years	20 years	
		Male lives			
55	$1,071	$1,036	$1,008	$ 981	$1,028
60	1,156	1,095	1,050	1,010	1,090
65	1,268	1,166	1,095	1,035	1,169
70	1,431	1,247	1,135	1,051	1,277
75	1,664	1,327	1,164	1,060	1,418
		Female lives			
55	$1,000	$ 985	$ 971	$ 956	$ 979
60	1,069	1,041	1,016	990	1,036
65	1,166	1,111	1,066	1,022	1,109
70	1,304	1,195	1,114	1,046	1,206
75	1,510	1,287	1,153	1,058	1,338

money under (3) is payable in instalments and hence the value of the benefits under the policy is reduced.

In Table 13.3 specimen illustrative immediate annuity rates are shown as offered by a prominent Canadian life insurance company in Canada in 1976 where the purchase money is $10,000. Note that rates for types 1, 2, and 4 above are given.

Immediate annuity rates are closely related to the current yield on investments for, being single premiums, the company is guided in the rate it offers by the yield it would get on the date of purchase from suitable investments. At the time these specimen rates were quoted, the rate of interest being earned by Canadian life insurance companies on new investments was at a high level; hence the rates might appear unusually favourable if examined at a time when interest earnings by the companies were on a lower level. The rates in Table 13.3 are for an immediate annuity payable in monthly instalments of one-twelfth of the amount shown, the first payment being due one month after payment of the purchase money. The annuity could be made payable quarterly, half-yearly or annually with a slight progressive increase in the amount of the annuity payable each year.

On examining Table 13.3 one may question whether any real purpose is served by the purchase of an immediate annuity with a minimum guaranteed period of as long as 20 years. Taking a practical retirement age, e.g., a male age 65, the return of both principal and interest on such a plan (20 years guaranteed) is 10.35 per cent of the purchase money each year. Under a 10-year guarantee it is 11.66 per cent and under a straight life annuity it is 12.68 per cent. For a male age 75, the three rates of return are even wider apart as one would expect, namely 10.60 per cent, 13.27 per cent and 16.64 per cent. Where a substantial amount of purchase money is involved it is well to compare what is lost in annuity income as against the lengthening of the guaranteed period. It would be to the advantage of an individual without heirs or dependants and not interested in leaving an estate to take the straight life annuity.

We have mentioned how the mortality of female lives is substantially lower than that of males. As a result a smaller annuity is payable for a given amount of purchase money to a woman than to a man of the same age as indicated in Table 13.3. In the widely-used annuitant table, the 1937 Standard Annuity Table, the difference is equivalent to a rating down of the female life by five years. In other words, the vitality of a woman of 70 is taken as equal to that of a man age 65. This uniform rating down is convenient but it will be noted that it has not been used in obtaining the rates given in Table 13.3 which indicate a smaller rating down at the older ages.

Immediate annuities are purchased at the older range of ages, where the variation in mortality and hence the cost of an annuity between one age and the next is considerable. As it is single premium business, such differences may amount to a considerable sum; thus the rates are usually based on the last completed month of age.

JOINT AND LAST SURVIVOR

A form of immediate life annuity which has considerable practical value is an annuity payable to two people during their joint lifetime and the life of the survivor. Husband and wife are the most common combination but it has wider applications than that. The name *joint annuity* means that the benefits cease on the first death. Hence it is important to indicate that the benefit carries on during the lifetime of the survivor and use the name *joint and last survivor annuity*, usually abbreviated to *joint and survivor*. It is possible to calculate the rates for such an annuity to cover more than two lives, the payments continuing until the death of the last survivor. However, such plans are not met with frequently in practice.

Although joint and survivor annuities are available with a minimum guaranteed period, the need for such is far less than with a single life annuity for on the early death of one life the annuity continues to the survivor. Further, the income being smaller for a joint and survivor annuity as the survivorship of two lives is involved, it is, generally, inadvisable to depress the income further by bringing in a minimum guaranteed period.

ANNUITY REDUCING ON FIRST DEATH

It is an interesting exercise to note how, by combining a joint and survivor annuity with annuities on the single lives, various practical combinations can be made to meet particular needs, as the following examples indicate.

1. Consider the combination of the following three immediate annuity benefits:

Husband	\$100 a month
Wife	100 a month
Joint and survivor on them both	100 a month

While they are both alive an annuity of \$300 a month is payable and on the first death the annuity is reduced to \$200 a month, namely two-thirds.

2. To obtain a larger annuity for the husband should the wife die first, note the following combination:

Husband	\$150 a month
Wife	75 a month
Joint and survivor on them both	75 a month

While they are both alive \$300 a month is payable; if the wife dies first the annuity is reduced to \$225 a month payable to the husband, and if the husband dies first the annuity is reduced to \$150 a month. The benefits as outlined above or any other combination can be combined in a single policy.

SPECIAL TERMS FOR IMMEDIATE ANNUITIES

We shall show later in this chapter that mortality rates for those who buy annuities are higher than for the population generally, This is due to *self-selection*; that is, that only people who expect to live a long time will normally buy life annuities.

If, however, the purchase is motivated by some consideration other than simply to obtain an income for life, for example, to reduce the burden of income tax, the effect of *self-selection* is lessened. For this reason, many insurance companies offer somewhat more favourable terms for annuities which are purchased out of funds coming from registered pension plans or registered retirement savings plans; for example, the single premium may be reduced by 1 per cent.

Furthermore, in occasional cases of severe impairments, the insurance company may be prepared to grant special terms by *rating up the age*, that is, charging the premium for an age greater than the true age. This is not done frequently because of the difficulty of assessing impairments at older ages (at which immediate annuities are usually purchased) particularly because exaggeration of such impairments would benefit the prospective annuitant.

DEFERRED ANNUITIES

Definition. Where a life annuity does not commence to be payable until the expiry of a specific number of years it is called a *deferred life annuity* or *deferred annuity*, and it is usual to specify the number of years for which it is deferred. As a rule, deferred annuities are quoted as commencing to be payable on the policy anniversary corresponding to a definite pension age, such as 60 or 65. In their most modern form deferred annuities are arranged so that the annuitant may have the annuity commence at any age from 50 to 71, the amount of the annuity increasing as the date of commencement is deferred. (The reason for using age 71 is that the law covering registered retirement savings plans imposes that maximum.)

Deferred annuities can be purchased either by single premium or by annual premiums; the annual premium can be made payable until the annuity commences or for a shorter period.

History. The deferred annuity policy was originally designed to provide an annuity for pension purposes only. To give the maximum annuity for the premium paid, the factor of survivorship was introduced and if the annuitant died before the annuity commenced, all the premiums paid were forfeited. However, the idea of forfeiting the premiums paid, in the event of death, which might occur a long time in the future when circumstances and obligations may have changed, did not prove practical. The plan was changed to provide, on death before the annuity commenced, for the return of premiums paid, with or without interest, the latter being an attempt to introduce some benefit of survivorship. Although different companies may vary the plan somewhat, the type of deferred annuity currently sold is, in effect, a long-term savings plan with no life insurance benefits other than the return of premiums with or without interest. The policyholder then has the option on the maturity date of taking cash or converting the accumulated amount into an annuity, the amount of which is guaranteed in the policy, per $1,000 of accumulation.

Cash Option. The amount of the cash value available at the time the annuity option can be elected is generally known as the *cash option.* Various forms of annuity are available corresponding to the types of immediate life annuity outlined above and the cash option may be considered as the purchase money. The annuitant can use the cash option to buy an immediate annuity at the time of maturity at the rates then current if thereby a larger benefit can be obtained than is guaranteed in the policy.

The policy-reserve of a deferred annuity will necessarily increase to the amount of the cash option. As the cash surrender value is based on the policy-reserve, at a certain point of time the cash surrender value will exceed the premiums paid. The death benefit on deferred annuity policies should death occur prior to the maturity date is, as a rule, the return of the premiums paid or the cash surrender value if greater.

Types of Deferred Annuity Plans. Under one type of deferred annuity plan, the cash option is determined as the equivalent of a definite amount of annuity of one type becoming payable at a specific pension age. The other types of annuities are then quoted as "options." Premiums are then based on units of the basic type of annuity. Under another type the plan is based on an annual premium, say of $100, and the accumulations at the end of successive years are quoted irrespective of age at entry or sex and a table of options is given indicating the amounts of annuity of various types obtainable for each $1,000 of accumulation at the pension age.

In recent years there has been far more interest in these deferred annuity plans than formerly because of the growing interest in pension plans, particularly in cases where contracts on individuals are required.

SURVIVORSHIP ANNUITY

This is also called a *reversionary annuity.* It is an annuity payable during the lifetime of one party but commencing to be payable after the death of another party. If we consider an annuity payable to a wife for her lifetime and commencing after the death of the husband, we see the value of such a plan. It is, in effect, a slowly decreasing insurance on the life of the husband and the usual rules of insurability, etc., would apply to him. It could be purchased by annual premiums payable until the first death. However, if the wife dies first, the policy terminates without value and thus there are no cash surrender values payable at any time.

Survivorship annuities provided as supplementary benefits to basic plans had some popularity in the past but have disappeared from use largely because of their lack of flexibility. It is interesting to note here the present-day approach as given in Chapter 12.

Annuity Mortality

SELF-SELECTION

In Chapters 5 and 12 we referred to the possibility of selection against the insurance company in the exercise of the conversion privilege under term insurance policies and family income riders. A similar point arises in the purchase of immediate annuities but operates in the reverse direction. People do not readily exchange their capital for a life annuity unless they feel fairly sure of enjoying an average or longer than average span of life. This *anti-selection* by life annuitants—the phrase *self-selection* is a better one—has been very evident in the history of annuities.

We have referred and will refer again to the continuous decrease in mortality in past years and the fact that in recent years it has also been experienced among older lives. Among those who purchase immediate life annuities, the continuous trend to a lower mortality has been obvious for many years, particularly among female lives. Immediate life annuities have been quite popular in Britain for many years and British actuaries have investigated the mortality of their annuitants over a long period of time. With every investigation the death rate among their annuitants has shown a decrease. Among British female annuitants over the long period 1880 to 1945 the decrease in the rate of mortality was about one per cent per year in the important age group 60 to 65. What this has meant is shown by the following figures (based on 3½ per cent interest and being net rates before allowing for expenses or margins for fluctuations).

$1,000 a year annuity payable annually to a female life age 65 cost: in the year 1875, $9,941; in the year 1925, $11,343; in the year 1955, $12,090. If $9,941 is taken as 100, the other figures are 114 and 122 respectively.

MORTALITY PROJECTION

It follows that as the rate of mortality of life annuitants has been decreasing for many years it is likely to continue to do so and in calculating life annuity rates this should be brought into account.

Under life insurance contracts a lower future mortality than may have been allowed for in the calculation of rates will give an additional margin and under participating plans result in increased dividends to policyholders; other factors being the same. In annuities the liabilities involved are very substantial in relation to the number of policies or the number of people involved and a lower mortality than allowed for can result in very heavy losses. This has occurred on many occasions in the past and a historic instance is that of the British government which in 1808 began to sell annuities as a form of raising funds and used the Northampton Table for the calculation of its rates. It had proved most satisfactory for the sale of life insurance, but resulted in very heavy losses when used for annuity rates.

However, the anticipation of a lower mortality in the future than the present is a matter of quite recent date. It was first made use of at the time of the disestablishment of the Anglican Church in Wales in 1912 when the question arose of compensating the retired and older clergy. The British actuary consulted pointed out that in placing a value on the pensions, not only should allowance be made for the fact that clergy were much longer lived than other people but as longevity was improving yearly, allowance should be made for that also.

ANNUITY MORTALITY TABLES

We give below some details of a number of annuity tables which have been and still are in use in Canada for the calculation of policy-reserves and in some cases for the calculation of annuity premiums also. In each case the method of mortality projection is noted.

British Offices Annuity Tables. When an investigation was made into the mortality of annuitants under British life insurance companies' policies covering the years 1900 to 1920, estimates were made of the future mortality and these tables, designated as the *a*(*m*) and *a*(*f*) tables were the first ever published to include an allowance in annuity values based on forecasts of future mortality. British actuaries make a continuous investigation into the mortality under their annuity contracts and periodically tables are published giving the mortality experienced; the *a*(*55*) is such a table.

The 1937 Standard Annuity Table. This table has been used extensively in Canada in recent years for the calculation of premium rates and the setting up of annuity policy-reserves. The 1937 Standard Annuity Table is not a projected table but the basis (from age 65 on) is that of the experience of immediate life annuitants resident in the U.S.A. of twenty American companies up to and including 1917, but rated down two years. This rating allows for the decreases in mortality from that time to 1937. It is under the 1937 Standard Annuity Table that female lives are assumed to have the same mortality as male lives five years younger. For ages under 65 the mortality experience of clerical workers under group life insurance for the years 1932–36 was used indicating the resources actuaries fall back upon when the data available are inadequate or unsatisfactory.

The 1937 Standard Annuity Table has been adopted by many states in the U.S.A. as the minimum standard for setting up policy-reserves for annuities. Allowance is made for the decrease in annuity mortality since the 1937 table was published by rating down the ages. In stating policy-reserve bases the abbreviation 1937 SA (—2) means that policy-reserves for lives two years younger than actual ages are set up. Rating down the lives in this way gives increased values for annuities thus increasing the premiums and the corresponding policy-reserves.

The Annuity Table for 1949. The continuous decrease in annuitant mortality led to a detailed investigation by Messrs. W. A. Jenkins and E. A. Lew. The results were published in the Transactions of the Society of Actuaries in 1949. Based on actual annuity experience as obtained by the Joint Mortality Committee, the basic table known as the "Annuity Table for 1949" is represented by "*a*–1949." Various factors were then obtained to allow for the projection of improvements in mortality beyond 1949 and when factors B are used the table is known as "*a*–1949 (Proj. B)." Messrs Jenkins and Lew applied the projection factors B to calculate tables which might be said to represent annuitant mortality in 1959 and this table is represented as "*a*–1959." Similarly "*a*–1979" denotes annuity values which continue to improve on the same scale to 1979 and then remain unchanged.

In Table 13.4 we show the effect of the mortality projection factors we have discussed above both for the Annuity Table for 1949 and the Standard Annuity Table, when the annuity values are calculated on a 2½ per cent basis. They are the policy-reserve values which would be required for immediate annuities on the mortality assumptions given and 2½ per cent net rate of interest.

Some companies have begun to use projection factors in their annuity values for deferred annuities and settlement options; the longer the deferment the lower the guaranteed rate of annuity. Other companies prefer to quote a safe annuity option value which holds unchanged

TABLE 13.4

Effect of Projected Mortality on Annuity Values
Net Value of Immediate Straight Life Annuity of $1,000 per annum Payable Annually, Male Lives, Rate of Interest 2½ per cent

				1937 Standard Annuity Table		
Age	*a*–1949	*a*–1959	*a*–1979	Actual	(−1)	(−2)
	$	$	$	$	$	$
60	13,676	14,080	14,835	13,016	13,423	13,832
65	11,496	11,841	12,492	11,013	11,408	11,806
70	9,351	9,622	10,140	9,107	9,478	9,855

throughout the duration of the policy. When the policy matures, the current annuity values may be more favourable than the safe values guaranteed and the policyholder or beneficiary will be able to take advantage of this as already explained above. At the time of writing (1976) the current annuity rates are much more favourable than the rates guaranteed in the policies to apply at the maturity dates of the policies.

1971-IAM and IAF Tables. In 1971, the Society of Actuaries published tables of mortality based on experience under individual annuities for males and females, separately, covering a period centred around 1963. The rates of mortality developed from the experience were projected to be representative of mortality expected in 1971, and reduced to provide a margin so that the resulting tables would be suitable for valuation purposes.

At the same time, tables known as GAM and GAF were published based on experience under Group Annuities. The central year was 1968. Extracts from the basic tables given in Table 13.5, illustrate vividly, first, the great difference between mortality of males and of females, and second, the difference in mortality resulting from individual selection.

TABLE 13.5

	Deaths per thousand				
	Age 65	Age 70	Age 75	Age 80	Age 85
Individual experience 1963					
Males	22	33	51	81	122
Females	12	18	32	58	103
Group experience 1968					
Males	24	40	61	96	142
Females	15	23	39	65	108

CANADIAN GOVERNMENT ANNUITIES

In 1908 the government of Canada began to sell annuities with the object of enabling people of small means to provide for their old age. By selling annuities at attractive rates it was thought that the country would stave off the introduction of a government old age pension plan which was then much under discussion. Unfortunately, when the Canadian government introduced its plan in 1908 it used an annuity table which was out of date at that time, and no change was made until 1936, or 28 years later, and then only after a great deal of pressure. With the growth of group annuity business the premium income of the Government Annuities Branch became quite substantial amounting to $68.6 millions in 1955.

Annuity business is one of the most difficult businesses in the world to transact and only time will tell whether it can be transacted at all without heavy loss. With the increasing complexity of the economic life of a country one would have thought that the government had all it could manage to regulate the economic life of Canada and not compete with those aiming to render a service to the public at a fair price. Flexibility in rates and adjustment to changing conditions of which current rates of interest is one, are essential in operating this difficult business.

In its 1962 Report, the Royal Commission on Government Organization[5] recommended that the sale of government annuities in Canada be discontinued and in part stated that the "programme has been very costly to the government" and also: "Apart from a periodic attractiveness when premiums are allowed to get out of line, some inflexible aspects of government annuity contracts make them less popular than competing forms. It is not unfair to suggest that the only circumstances in which they will be sold in volume is when they are priced below the current market; thus the cost of making good future deficiencies will be substantial indeed."

All annuity business in Canada is under the supervision of the Superintendent of Insurance at Ottawa, or the Provincial Superintendents of Insurance except that transacted by the government!

In 1962 the British government discontinued the sale of annuities, the government spokesman stating that there appeared to be no longer any significant public need for the service and the amounts obtained from their sale were no longer of any significance in relation to the National Debt.

[5](Ottawa: Queen's Printer, 1962), vol. 3, pp. 286–8 (the Glassco report).

In 1967, the Canadian government decided to discontinue the active sale of government annuities. One or two regional offices remained open to service existing annuities and write any new contracts which came unsolicited. In 1975 all sales were terminated, and the remaining offices were merged with those of the Unemployment Insurance Commission, which now administers the Annuities Branch.

At March 31, 1975, liabilities in the Annuities Fund were $1,251 millions, receipts were $4.5 millions plus $49 millions in interest from the government. Disbursements were $74 millions, representing vested annuity payments, commuted or death benefits and refunds of premiums.

VARIABLE ANNUITIES

The purchasing power of the payments received under an annuity has received a great deal of attention because of inflation since the 1939–45 war. This resulted in the development of annuities based on units of "value" rather than units of currency, the "value" being determined by the market value of a block of assets invested in common stocks. Such annuities are called *variable annuities* and will be discussed in Chapter 30.

CHAPTER FOURTEEN

Settlement Options

PROVISION OF INCOME

One of the earliest points made in the text was that the major purpose of life insurance was the "protection" of dependants and the idea of "protection" was extended to cover one's declining years; we have emphasized that "protection" means "provision of income."

In the later years of the last century various policies were introduced to guarantee an income to beneficiaries on the death of the insured. In the last chapter we referred to one such plan which incorporated a survivorship annuity benefit and mentioned certain disadvantages of the plan. A later development was to make every life insurance policy providing for a lump sum on death or survival of the life insured into an "income policy" at the option of the insured or beneficiary. These options allowing alternative settlements for the lump sum payable under a life insurance policy are called *settlement options*.

In recent years these settlement options have become most elaborate. In "programming," that is, indicating how an insured's actual needs may be met by his life insurance, an elaborate technique with legal and taxation aspects has been built up. We here confine ourselves to fundamentals and do not touch on the legal aspects.

We referred in a previous chapter to the straight life insurance plan as being in effect a special kind of long-term endowment insurance if we consider the cash surrender value as the endowment. Further we stated that if the cash surrender value was converted into an annuity, we had a "pension with insurance" plan. We have also referred to a deferred annuity policy as in effect an accumulation of premiums (less expenses) with the accumulated amount being converted into an annuity at a pension age.

This "multiple purpose" use of life insurance and annuity plans has been enhanced by the universal adoption of guaranteed settlement options in life insurance company policies. By their use, on the maturity of an endowment policy, or on the attainment of a "maturity age" should the policy be surrendered, various modes of settlement are available in lieu of the payment of the amount due in one sum.

Where settlement options are used on the death of a life insured it is an extension of a life insurance policy beyond the "maturity" of the policy in the form of a trust for the beneficiaries. This is peculiar to the North American continent and in this Canadians have followed the U.S. rather than the British practice. It has its dangers, as we shall indicate, but its value is unquestionable and with proper safeguards is undoubtedly a great advance in the service that life insurance gives to the public. These settlement options are available to the life insured and he can determine how the policy proceeds shall be payable on his death; further, if no election has been made by him, the beneficiary has the right to make an election when the sum insured becomes payable.

INCREASING USE OF SETTLEMENT OPTIONS

In 1925 only 3 per cent of life insurance benefits in Canada were payable in the form of income whereas in 1974 18.7 per cent of life insurance benefits were so used. By the end of that year, the total "amounts on deposit" due to policy proceeds and policy dividends were $1,600 millions. Even so, these amounts are likely to increase considerably in years to come due to the increasing use of settlement options as well as the growth of the business.

The settlement options fall into two main categories: where interest only is involved, and where the survival of one or more lives is involved. Companies vary in the number and detail of the options guaranteed in their policies but the principles involved are similar and will be understood from the outlines given below.

OPTIONS INVOLVING INTEREST ONLY

1. *Deposit Option.* The company here agrees to retain the policy proceeds at interest until the death of the beneficiary or for a specified period, the interest being payable periodically at a rate which may be varied from time to time according to financial conditions but with a minimum rate guaranteed. The beneficiary generally has the right to withdraw the proceeds unless the insured had indicated otherwise. The deposit option is also allowed to the insured on the maturity of an

endowment insurance. The interest paid over and above that guaranteed is referred to as *excess interest.*

The right to withdraw the amount left on deposit without restrictions can involve the insurance company in difficulties. It is in effect a banking privilege and banks arrange their investments so that large sudden demands can be met. This is not the case with life insurance companies, whose investments are generally in long-term bonds and mortgages which may be secure but cannot readily be realized in cash in a time of crisis except at a loss. In the United States the standard policy conditions permit life insurance companies to delay cash withdrawals under settlement options for a period up to six months to cover this possibility and some Canadian policies contain similar restrictions. We mentioned above the figure of "amounts on deposit" which was $1,600 millions and was increasing yearly. The same point arises in connection with cash surrender values which will be referred to later in the text.

Under some older policies in Canada the minimum guaranteed rate is as high as 4 per cent per annum, but during the long period of low interest rates from 1935 to 1955 the tendency was to place these guaranteed minimum interest rates on a $2^1/_2$ per cent or 3 per cent basis. As the beneficiary receives an "experience" rate of interest based on financial conditions, there is no practical advantage in placing the guaranteed minimum rate at a high figure. Also there is no justification for doing so particularly if there are no restrictions on withdrawal. In the calculation of its policy-reserves, a company assumes a certain rate of interest which will be earned over the long term future and the minimum guaranteed rate should not exceed this.

2. *Instalments for a Definite Period.* This is an annuity certain, namely, so many dollars payable for a fixed period of years. The amount and period of the annuity certain are known in advance as they are based on the minimum guaranteed rate of interest. Each year an additional amount may be paid by the company as excess interest. As the discounted value (commuted value) of the annuity certain falls each year, the excess interest payable will decrease year by year if the rate of excess interest remains unchanged.

3. *Instalments for a Definite Amount.* In this case the insured or beneficiary arranges for a specific sum to be paid periodically. The sum insured is thus held at interest and the fixed sum is paid periodically as arranged until the proceeds are exhausted. Note that the higher the guaranteed rate of interest allotted each year the longer is the period of

payment. The minimum guaranteed rate of interest ensures a minimum period of payment. The excess interest paid over and above the guaranteed rate can be paid out yearly as in 2 above or added to the balance remaining on deposit which would thus extend the period of the fixed payment.

LIFE INCOME OPTION

The sum due under the policy may be taken in the form of a life annuity. If the sum due is on the maturity of an endowment or the surrender of a life policy, the annuity could be taken on the life of the life insured or as a joint and survivor annuity on his life and that of his wife. If the sum due was on the death of the life insured then the beneficiary could have the annuity payable on his or her own life.

The life annuity option on a single life is generally available on the straight life basis and also with minimum guaranteed periods of 5, 10, 15, or 20 years or on the instalment refund or cash refund basis. The joint and survivor annuity option is generally without any minimum guaranteed period. The author's comments in the previous chapter on the choice of an immediate life annuity with or without a guaranteed period also apply to the choice of a life annuity under a settlement option. Under life annuity options, different amounts apply to male and female lives.

Projected mortality factors, as noted in Chapter 13 have been introduced by some companies in determining their life annuity settlement options and in such cases the annuity is based not only on the age and sex and type of annuity chosen, but also on the year the option is entered upon.

The settlement option clause usually provides that if the sum due would purchase, using the current annuity rates of the company at the time of settlement less a discount (e.g., 2 per cent), a larger annuity than that guaranteed, the larger amount will be payable.

PRECAUTIONS IN THE USE OF SETTLEMENT OPTIONS

Discretion in Their Use. The great value of settlement options to the public is indisputable, but many desirable things can be made harmful by incorrect use. Small policies should not be tied up under settlement options except, of course, when they are part of a large plan of settlement and thus have been effected for a specific purpose. In most cases the proceeds of life insurance policies will be needed for essentials and lengthy statements directing how the proceeds should be paid involve needless expense to all concerned and are not in the interests of the beneficiary.

No charge is made by the insurance companies for the use of a settlement option. On account of the costs involved in carrying out settlement options the companies require minimum payments to avoid the burden of small payments.

Circumstances change and people do forget what was endorsed upon or attached to the policy, at their request, when it was issued. We referred above to the avoidance of settlement options where small policies were concerned. One may question whether any policy should be tied so rigidly that the beneficiary cannot make changes in accordance with changing circumstances. Cases have arisen, and in recent years, where the beneficiary has found it necessary to appeal to the courts for the removal of such restrictions.

Discretionary Powers. Companies cannot be expected to exercise "discretionary powers" in the execution of trust agreements disposing of the sums due under policies and involving the settlement options. The handling of trusts is a highly complicated and specialized legal business and life companies should not be expected to undertake the cost and risk involved in such matters, as a "free" service. This also applies to accepting trust agreements involving a remarriage clause or similar restriction making it necessary for the company to satisfy itself as to the fulfilment of certain conditions before paying an instalment. When instalment payments have to be made by the ten thousand, a routine procedure is essential, otherwise the cost becomes prohibitive.

Need for Legal Advice. It is poor policy to dispense with proper legal advice or the services of a trust company when such is called for. There is no charge made by the company issuing the policy for filing trust agreements, etc., disposing of the sums insured due under the policy. It would be unfortunate if companies filed dispositions of their policies without the most careful scrutiny. To save future trouble and litigation is also a service to policyholders.

PAYMENT OF SUM INSURED IN INSTALMENTS AND EXCESS INTEREST PAYMENTS

In Chapter 12, we pointed out that when the plan of life insurance provides for the payment of the sum insured in instalments it is a common practice to calculate the instalments on a conservative basis as regards interest—well within the expected rate of interest earnings of the company. The company adjusts matters by allotting excess interest payments representing additional interest earnings on the value of the unpaid instalments remaining in its hands and based on its actual interest earnings.

It will have been noted that this, in principle, is followed in the payment of instalments of a sum insured under a settlement option. In fact the family income rider and similar plans where the sum insured is payable in equal instalments for a definite period following the death of the life insured may be considered as lump sum insurances where a particular settlement option of payment has been chosen at the outset, namely "instalments for a named period." In the family income rider the period of payment of the instalments is reduced each year the life insured survives as is shown in Figure 14 in Chapter 12. The excess interest payable follows the same pattern if the rate of excess interest remains unchanged.

Under family income riders some salesmen stress the advantage of permitting the beneficiary to adjust the amount of the instalment payable in accordance with needs at the time of the death of the life insured. To do this the beneficiary is given the right to commute the instalments due under the policy and by means of the settlement options arrange for a different set of instalment payments.

We have avoided the use of the phrase "interest dividend" when referring to excess interest. The word "dividend" implies a participating policy from the outset whereas excess interest payments only enter into the picture after the sum insured has become payable. All that has been stated above regarding instalment settlements and excess interest payments applies irrespective of whether the policy is with or without participation in profits. This stresses again the indefiniteness of life insurance terminology.

CHAPTER FIFTEEN

Participating Policies

THE ORIGIN OF POLICYHOLDERS' DIVIDENDS

Life insurance deals mainly with long-term contracts. The difficulties of forecasting the long-term future rates of interest, mortality, and expenses on which the premiums are based have meant that the business developed from its early days by charging premiums expected to be more than adequate. As compensation, the policyholders were given a share in the resulting "profit" as it might be called. It might be said that life insurance became established successfully because in its early years the premiums charged proved to be more than adequate.

We outlined in the early chapters of this text the origin and the organization of the Old Equitable which was established in 1762 without any share capital or, as we would now describe it, as a mutual life insurance company. It was the first organization to transact life insurance on permanent plans. When the management of the Old Equitable realized that the premiums which it had been charging were more than adequate it had to decide what reductions should be made in the premiums and further what disposition to make of the surplus which had accumulated. The principle was finally adopted that premiums should remain unchanged from entry but that the surplus in hand, over and beyond the limits which the management and their technical advisers, the actuaries, deemed necessary to meet possible fluctuations in earnings and investment losses, should be returned to the policyholders.

The same principle was followed by "stock" or "proprietary" life insurance companies when these were established. Although the company was owned by the shareholders the policyholders were given the right to participate in the "profits" of the company. This is how participating life insurance developed. It should be noted that on a *participating policy* the benefits are guaranteed but are minimum benefits, and the premiums are guaranteed but are maximum premiums, for, except in the case of insolvency, the benefits cannot be reduced or the premiums increased. When the policyholder has no right to participate in the profits and has a policy with fixed benefits payable by the company and with fixed premiums payable by the policyholder, it is called a *non-participating policy*.

From the above it is evident that in dealing with participating life insurance we are concerned with overpayments and the determination of the amount of these overpayments. Their origin and their distribution have become an important part of actuarial knowledge and practice known as *distribution of surplus*. The refunds to policyholders have become known as *dividends*, and here is another expression used in the life insurance business which can readily be confused with a similar term used in commerce. In a commercial corporation the shareholders share in the profits from trading and each share represents a definite proportion of the ownership of the corporation. A life insurance company is a co-operative business, the policyholders doing business with each other only, so to speak. The overpayments may vary with plan, age at entry, and duration of policy; hence the word *surplus* is far more appropriate than "profits." This also explains why the expression "premium refund" is so often used in place of *dividend* when referring to a participating life insurance policy.

PARTICIPATING VERSUS NON-PARTICIPATING BUSINESS

Of the total of all life insurance owned by Canadians, over 60 per cent is participating. If term insurance and temporary additions to the sum insured are omitted, the ratio is over 80 per cent. Canadian life insurance companies, whether "mutual" or "stock," issue both participating and non-participating plans of insurance; this is also the practice with British companies.

The U.S. companies follow a different practice. The largest U.S. mutual life insurance companies are subject to the laws of the state of New York and other states with similar laws. These mutual companies are required to confine their life insurance operations to participating plans only. The stock companies, on the other hand, confine their business mainly to non-participating business.

Separate Accounting for Par and Non-Par Business. According to Canadian federal insurance law as given in Section 83 of the Canadian and British Insurance Companies Act, "Every company, notwithstanding anything to the contrary in any special Act or elsewhere, shall keep separate and distinct accounts of participating and non-participating business.'' This applies to all Canadian life insurance companies subject to supervision by Ottawa. Each company has to outline the methods it uses in apportioning items of income and expenditure between the various funds of the company and in particular between the participating and non-participating funds. In the periodic inspection of companies by officials of the Department of Insurance at Ottawa these items are checked to ensure that full justice and equity are preserved regarding the interests of participating policyholders. The details are published in the Superintendent's report for each company and the results summarized in Volume I of the reports. Thus the position of the participating and non-participating funds is clearly given so that, except that there is no separation of assets (that is cash, investments and securities) between the two, they might as well be separate companies under the same management. At the end of 1974 the participating fund of Canadian life insurance companies was $12,636 millions and the non-participating fund $5,920 millions.

The rights of participating policyholders are strictly set out in the law and the proportion of divisible surplus of the participating business which can be paid to shareholders is strictly limited as will be noted later in this chapter. However, the distribution of the surplus in the non-participating fund is entirely at the discretion of the directors, subject to the usual restraints of good management. Canada is a keenly competitive field for life insurance and this applies particularly to non-participating business which is often required for business purposes and may involve large sums insured. In a stock company the losses (and profits) of non-participating business accrue to the shareholders. In mutual companies any loss incurred on the non-participating business has to be met by the participating policyholders and any profits accrue for their benefit. The fact of mutual companies doing non-participating business at all might be questioned, but the tradition in Canada has been against restrictions by law of practices which should be left to the judgment of the management.

RIGHTS OF PARTICIPATING POLICYHOLDERS

The rights of participating policyholders of a Canadian life insurance company are set out in Sections 6 and 26 of the federal act already referred to, and some reference to them has already been made in Chapter 9.

The life insurance company has to advise participating policyholders at least once a year of their right to attend and vote in person or by proxy at general meetings of the company. The Act specifies the various ways in which it might be done including a statement on the premium notice, receipt, or dividend notice, and where any such notice is not required to be sent the advice may be sent less frequently but at least once every five years.

LIMITATION OF SHAREHOLDERS' PARTICIPATION IN SURPLUS

In a mutual company the whole of the surplus earnings belongs to the participating policyholders. In a Canadian life insurance company with share capital (a stock or proprietary company) the federal law, Section 84 of the Act referred to above, limits the proportion of distributable surplus arising from participating business which can go to the shareholders. The law states that at least 90 per cent must go to the participating policyholders where the mean participating fund does not exceed $250 millions; at least 92½ per cent where the mean fund is between $250 and $500 millions; at least 95 per cent for between $500 millions and $1,000 millions and at least 97½ per cent where the mean participating fund exceeds $1,000 millions.

Canada is unique in this restriction of shareholders' rights but it is only fair to state that some companies voluntarily had been paying out to participating policyholders a larger proportion of the surplus earned than the law required when in 1951 the legislation indicated was passed.

Distribution of Surplus

How much of a life insurance company's funds may be considered as surplus; in other words, what is surplus? How much of the surplus should be distributed to policyholders? How often should such surplus be distributed? How should the distributable surplus be divided among individual policyholders, considering plan, duration, age at entry and premium paid?

These questions arose in the earliest days of the history of life insurance, some two hundred years ago and are still as much a matter of controversy as ever.[1]

[1]Robert T. Jackson, "Some Observations on Ordinary Dividends," *Transactions*, Society of Actuaries, vol. XI (1959). P. R. Cox and R. H. Storr-Best, *Surplus in British Life Assurance* (London: Cambridge University Press for the Institute of Actuaries, 1962).

In Volume III of the report of the Superintendent of Insurance of Canada, an account is given of the method used by each company to obtain the dividend scale used to distribute surplus to participating policyholders. The descriptions are difficult to follow and illustrate the complexity of the subject. It is not the object of this text to elucidate these actuarial procedures but to illustrate the compromise between theory and practice in this important branch of life insurance administration.

WHAT IS SURPLUS? HOW MUCH SHOULD BE DISTRIBUTED?

A valuation of its liabilities has to be made each year by a Canadian life insurance company at a fixed date, usually December 31, to ascertain the policy-reserves of its business in force. As outlined in Chapter 7 the policy-reserves represent the amount which the company must have in hand to ensure that with future premium payments it can fulfil its contracts as they fall due for payment. At the same date all the securities and other assets of the company are valued; also the accounts are made up indicating all amounts owed to and owed by the company. Thus the company ascertains at that date each year its *liabilities* (i.e., policy-reserves and amounts owing by the company including amounts on deposit by policyholders) and its *assets* (i.e., the value of its securities etc. and amounts owing to it). The deduction of the liabilities from the assets indicates the *surplus* of the company at the date specified.

A company may be accumulating special reserves to strengthen its policy-reserves or have a reason for setting aside special investment and contingency reserves and these special reserves would be added to the total liabilities. Also it is the practice of Canadian life insurance companies, after deciding on the amount of surplus they intend to distribute to policyholders in the forthcoming year as a result of the previous year's operations, to set up this amount as a liability. When the total of these items is taken into account the phrase *free surplus* could be used to describe the balance.

Before the amount of surplus to be distributed is decided upon, a comparison of the free surplus at the end of the previous year and the surplus indicated at the date of the annual statement shows the surplus which has been earned in the year. The decision then has to be made as to the apportionment of this surplus between (1) participating policyholders; (2) shareholders' funds (in a stock company, and this is limited by law as described previously); (3) special reserves; (4) carried forward to increase the existing free surplus. This decision is an important one for the directors to make, advised by the company's management and the technical adviser, namely, the chief actuary of the company. The opening words of R. T. Jackson's paper on dividends referred to in footnote 1 are: "Dividend apportionment may well be the actuary's most important job in a mutual company."

Too generous a distribution of surplus may weaken the company and once money is paid out it cannot be retrieved. Competition forces the management to be as generous as possible, and after all it is the policyholders whose overpayments generally created the surplus available. Here we touch on one of the criticisms of the life insurance business: that huge surpluses are accumulated from one generation to the next without regard to the need for such and life insurance costs more on that account.

The New York law, which determines U.S. practice to a large degree, in 1907 placed a limit on the amount of surplus which a life insurance company could hold—for a company transacting participating business the figure is now 10 per cent of the policy-reserves and liabilities. In the case of Canadian companies, surplus funds and special reserves equalled 8.4 per cent of assets at the end of 1974. The problem of how much surplus a company requires and how much of the surplus earned in any year should be distributed is not answerable by any formula. The intent of the New York law is clear, namely, that current policyholders should participate in the surplus they have made and companies should not accumulate excessive surpluses.

The free surplus of a life insurance company corresponds to the reserves of a commercial business. However, some life insurance companies are prepared to justify every dollar of their free surplus by indicating the various contingencies it is intended to cover and the reasons for the amounts so set aside. It follows that when the outlook is favourable a larger distribution of earned surplus is justified and when the reverse is the case the company will tend to conserve its strength and increase its free surplus and special reserves.

A historical note is of interest. In 1800 the Old Equitable through a by-law obligated its officers not to distribute more than two-thirds of its surplus as indicated by its valuation.

HOW OFTEN SHOULD SURPLUS BE DISTRIBUTED?

Although in Canada some companies still issue policies on the quinquennial dividend plan, i.e., the dividend on an individual policy is allotted at the end of every five years from entry, the tendency is more and more towards distributing the surplus on all business annually. By inference the federal law in Canada requires the distribution of surplus due to participating policies at least once in every five years. If this is not done the policy is called a "deferred dividend policy" and these deferred dividends will be referred to later.

In 1907 the New York law was changed so that all dividends had to be paid annually and this set the pattern for U.S. life insurance companies. In Great Britain the companies have to publish their position at least every five years when the opportunity is taken to distribute the surplus to all policies entitled to participate although several companies now do it every three years and some including some of the largest like the Prudential Assurance do it every year. Where distributions by the British and Canadian companies are made otherwise than annually an interim bonus is allotted to cover death claims and maturity of endowments which arise between distributions.

One advantage of distributing surplus less frequently than annually which explains the historical five-year British system (every ten years was the practice adopted by the Old Equitable in 1800) is that it permits an averaging of surplus earnings over five-year periods. A fluctuating dividend year by year (unless it is always upwards) is most disturbing and hence an annual dividend distribution introduces problems which may be avoided in a five-year distribution. It could be said that an annual distribution requires a greater cushion of free surplus than the five-year distribution so as to be able to draw upon it in adverse years.

In Canada and the U.S. policy dividends are invariably allotted to fall due on policy year anniversaries whereas in Britain the allotments are made for all policies at the valuation date, generally December 31.

DISTRIBUTION OF SURPLUS: THE BRITISH SYSTEM

The underlying ideas of surplus distribution are best illustrated historically; this is the reason for examining the British system first and explaining the departure from it by Canadian and U.S. companies.

The Old Equitable in 1782 adopted the principle that as the purpose of life insurance was to provide insurance, any over-payment of premiums should be allotted in the form of an addition to the sum insured. They are called *bonus additions* or *bonuses* and are paid-up additions to the sum insured. This became and still is the British form of bonus or dividend allotment. When the bonus is allotted as a percentage of the sum insured it is called a *simple bonus*; when it is allotted as a percentage of the sum insured plus bonus additions already attaching to the policy it is called a *compound bonus*. As a rule the same rate of allotment applies to all participating policies, irrespective of age, plan, or duration and hence the phrase *uniform reversionary bonus* system; reversionary means payable on death. On endowment insurances the bonus is payable on the same conditions as the sum insured, namely at the end of the endowment period or on previous death. Bonus additions may be cashed for their surrender value at any time without affecting the sum insured.

The simplicity of the British bonus system is in its favour. A 2 per cent simple bonus allotment for any year means an addition of $20 paid-up insurance to a $1,000 policy. If the same bonus is allotted for five years the total addition is $100; for ten years it would be $200 and so on.

Should conditions change and it is assumed by the company that such changes are likely to continue for some years the company may modify its premium rates for new entrants to correspond with the changed conditions and to preserve equity with existing policyholders. Thus all participating policyholders pay premiums corresponding to the bonus outlook at the time of their entry and then share equally in the fortunes of the company throughout the history of their policy with the company. The companies have adjusted allotments to changing circumstances: a period of low interest earnings justified a lower bonus to endowment insurances than life plans; a period of high appreciation of equity investments by some companies resulted in special additional terminal bonuses payable on death, or on death or maturity of an endowment policy; such adjustments, of course, result in loss of simplicity.

The determination of the cost of a certain rate of bonus is relatively easy under the British system. The sums insured in force under all policies are divided into two groups; life plans and endowment insurances (term plans are not issued with participation in profits). Each group is then subdivided according to age attained for the life plans and for endowment insurances by age attained and period to the end of the endowment period. A single multiplication in each case by factors from a book of tables gives the cost of a simple bonus. For a compound bonus the bonus additions must be similarly grouped with the sums insured. On the CM(5) 3 per cent Table a bonus addition of $10 to a life plan with life insured age 40 attained would cost $4.31 and on an endowment insurance, age attained 40 and 15 years to maturity the cost would be $6.66. The cost of a 1 per cent bonus being determined and the amount of divisible surplus known the rate of bonus to be allotted is a matter of proportion.

DISTRIBUTION OF SURPLUS: THE CONTRIBUTION METHOD—CANADA AND U.S.

The criticism of the British system is that a more exact relationship should hold between the share of surplus allotted to each individual policy and the contribution of that policy to the surplus being distributed. How exact a relationship can in practice be maintained? This is the nub of the matter and explains the continuing controversy referred to earlier in this chapter.

In 1863 two U.S. actuaries, Sheppard Homans and D. P. Fackler, announced and demonstrated the Contribution Method of distributing surplus, the object being to determine the sources of the surplus earned and to return to each policy its contribution to that surplus. The three main factors which determine the surplus earned by a company are the same as those described in Chapter 4 as the three "mysteries" of life insurance, namely: mortality, interest, and expenses. The surplus arising from them is technically known as the mortality profit, interest profit, and loading profit respectively.

It is beyond the scope of this text to develop the actuarial formulas relating to these three main sources of profit or surplus. However, there are a number of facets which illustrate most of the points which a study of these formulas would give.

ASSET-SHARE ACCUMULATION

In Chapter 7 we outlined the method of calculating the policy-reserves under any plan of life insurance. We assumed a number of entrants of the same age effecting the same plan of insurance for the same amount. We accumulated the net premiums paid at the valuation rate of interest and deducted the claims paid assuming mortality on the valuation table of mortality; the resulting accumulation at the end of the year was the policy-reserve for the survivors.

If we repeat the calculations made in the previous paragraph but use the actual gross premiums paid less expenses (which we will call the *deloaded premiums*) and accumulate them at the rate of interest actually earned by the company on its funds, year by year, and deduct the actual claims which arose among those lives year by year, the amount in hand is known as the *asset-share* and will be referred to frequently in this and subsequent chapters (see Chapter 17 and Table 17.5). However, the policy-reserve is the amount which the company must set aside for the survivors each year as a test of its solvency. The total of the asset-shares resulting from a year's operation less the policy-reserves required to be set up should indicate the surplus earned in that policy year. The process would also indicate the surplus earned by each class of policyholder according to plan, age at entry, and duration.

The factors of loading, interest, and mortality used in calculating the asset-shares vary year by year. The asset-shares are usually calculated when the gross premium rates are first adopted and the plan issued; they may be calculated again should a change in the policy-reserve basis be made. Thereafter the actuaries computing the dividend scale are interested in the changes in the individual factors: loading, interest, and mortality, from year to year and how they are affecting the surplus as indicated by the original asset-share calculations. We now consider these factors in the order named.

LOADING PROFIT

The excess of the deloaded premium (i.e., the gross premium charged less expenses) over the net premium used in calculating the policy-reserve determines the *loading profit*. It follows that the higher the rate of gross premium charged for a given plan of insurance and age at entry and the lower the rate of expenses incurred the higher will be the deloaded premium and so the higher the loading profit.

First-year expenses are far heavier than in other years, for not only are the expenses incurred in that year of the issue of the policy and all the processes involved before the policy is issued, but a large part of the commission paid the agent for the sale of the policy is concentrated in the first year. We have throughout Chapters 6 and 7 assumed that all expenses and overhead are spread evenly over the duration of the policy and the level net premium and level net premium policy-reserve have been calculated on this basis.

If the full first-year expenses incurred are deducted, the asset-share at the end of the first year will, in most plans, not cover the first year's policy-reserve and the balance must be drawn from the surplus earned by other policies. However, the principle of charging all first-year expenses to the first policy year can be challenged as contrary to the co-operative nature of the business; if there were no new entrants there would be, in due course, an insufficient number of policyholders to keep the insurance process going. Thus we reach the first difficulty in relating dividends to surplus actually earned: what part of the first year's expenses should be charged to the first year?

First-Year Dividend. What has been stated above in this section has an immediate bearing on the question of whether any dividend can be justified at the end of the first policy year.

The New York law which determines the general U.S. practice is of interest. It states that no dividend shall be apportioned for the first policy year unless it can be shown to have been earned. The point could be made that where a level annual premium is charged the arrangement is implied that all expenses and cost of insurance, however they may vary from year to year, are spread evenly over the duration of the policy. Also, why should the policyholder be concerned with the commission terms that the company uses to pay its agents? In Canada, under annual dividend policies, some companies pay the first dividend at the end of the first year while others, and these include some of the largest companies, pay the first dividend at the end of the second year only.

Trend of Loading Profit with Duration. If we omit consideration of the first year's loading profit or loss, expenses tend to be constant over the duration of a policy so that it could be said that, on the net level premium policy-reserve basis, loading profit tends to be constant with duration.

INTEREST PROFIT

In Table 29.2 we show the average rate of interest earned by Canadian life insurance companies on their funds. The net rate of interest earned (i.e., allowing for investment expenses) in recent years has varied from 4.18 per cent in 1955 to 7.11 per cent in 1974. As interest profit is represented by the excess interest earnings over and above that required to maintain the policy-reserves, if the latter were 3 per cent the interest profit would have varied from 1.18 to 4.11 per cent on the funds of the company. Thus in 1974 the interest profit would be nearly four times what it was in 1955.

Trend of Interest Profit with Duration. On all permanent plans of life insurance the policy-reserves increase with duration. As the policy-reserves increase so will the interest profit earned for policy-reserves form the greater part of the fund on which excess interest is being earned. The interest profit is higher, duration for duration, on endowment insurances than on straight life plans and higher on short-term endowment insurances than on long-term endowment insurances.

We are aware that the lower the rate of interest assumed in calculating the policy-reserves the higher are the policy-reserves (see Table 7.5).

Should a company lower the rate of interest assumed in calculating its policy-reserves (as several companies did in the mid-1940s when interest rates fell continuously), the increase in policy-reserves will reduce the surplus available for distribution in the year the change is made, but the result should be to increase the interest profit each year thereafter above what it would otherwise have been.

An Essential in Dividend Scales. One of the essentials in a dividend scale to policyholders is that the cash dividend allotted or the cash value of the bonus addition should increase with duration, In paid-up insurance the cash surrender value increases with age attained and duration so that the cash value of the same bonus addition allotment does increase with duration. This desirable attribute does illustrate, when dividends are allotted on the Contribution Method, the importance of excess interest earnings for as indicated above excess interest profit on individual policies will increase with duration if the rate of interest earnings remains constant or increases.

MORTALITY PROFIT

We showed in Chapter 7 that the "cost" of insurance in any year is based on the "net amount of risk," i.e., the sum insured less the policy-reserve. The formula for the *cost of insurance* was shown to be:

Rate of Mortality at Attained Age × Net Amount at Risk.

In Chapter 7 we were dealing with the policy-reserve and when the amounts relate to the mortality table on which the policy-reserves are calculated we get the cost of insurance on that basis, i.e., the *expected cost of insurance*. If the actual rate of mortality experienced is inserted in the above formula the *actual cost of insurance* is obtained and the excess of the expected cost over the actual cost determines the *mortality profit*. If the actual cost of insurance exceeds the expected cost then a *mortality loss* is incurred.

Trend of Mortality Profit with Duration. As the duration increases so, on permanent plans of insurance, the policy-reserve increases and so the net amount at risk decreases. With increasing duration the attained age increases and so does the rate of mortality. Thus from the formula for the cost of insurance there appears to be no obvious answer to the trend of the cost of insurance or of the mortality profit, with duration. However, the higher the investment element in a plan, that is, the higher the policy-reserve with duration, the less is the net amount at risk and hence the less the opportunity for mortality profit. There is more opportunity for mortality profit on a straight life plan than on a 20-year endowment insurance, for instance. Under an endowment insurance the mortality profit must decrease to zero as the maturity date of the endowment approaches.

In practice it is generally found that under normal conditions the mortality profit relative to the life insurance business in force is approximately constant.

SOME PRACTICAL POINTS IN SURPLUS DISTRIBUTION

It follows from the previous sections that the analysis of surplus is no simple matter. We have already referred to the problem of allocation of expenses by duration. The policy-reserve is invariably calculated on an ultimate table of mortality and we are aware that the mortality experienced in the first few policy years (select mortality) is definitely less than the ultimate and hence the resulting "mortality profit" when based on such an ultimate mortality table may be questioned. It should be noted how this mortality profit in the select period could be used to offset the high expense rate of the early policy years.

We indicated in an early section of this chapter how the asset-share was calculated indicating the surplus by entry age, plan, and duration. We have also indicated how the individual items of mortality, interest and loading profits are derived. When a company uses all three factors in determining the dividends under a Contribution Method it is called a *three-factor method*. In the previous paragraph we indicated how expense and mortality factors could offset each other in the early policy years and some companies do combine the two and are said to use a *two-factor method*, excess interest earnings being the other factor.

As a rule, on account of the cost, Canadian and U.S. companies will avoid an annual revision of their scale of dividends to policyholders although, as would be expected, the three factors, interest, mortality and loading, will vary from year to year. However, when as in recent years (Table 29.2) interest earnings have moved steadily upwards and mortality has been favourable, frequent revisions have been made; competition between companies is a factor in this.

A question which has been receiving attention is the possibility of introducing the *new money* concept into the determination of the interest element of the dividends. As has been explained, one rate of interest, generally a little lower than the average yield on the fund, is used to determine the interest element. It would be more equitable to use different rates according to the durations of the policies to recognize the fact that premiums received in recent years have been invested at higher interest rates than those received some years ago. To do this is known as the *new money* approach, as opposed to the *average yield* approach. To introduce it for annual premium policies would involve complex calculations because the results of every step in the investment process—viz. purchases, sales, investment of interest income—would have to be allocated to policies of each year of issue. To date it has been considered that the advantage of greater precision would be more than offset by the expense involved in establishing and maintaining a complicated system.

There are other sources of profit or loss besides the three main factors which have been discussed and they will be referred to in connection with the subjects to which they relate—in particular the profit or loss due to lapses and surrenders.

One further point may be mentioned here. The surplus factors outlined above were applied to the policy-reserves. There is the free surplus carried forward from the previous year and the various special reserves which have earned interest which have gone to increase the amount of surplus earned in the year. The allocation of this surplus is another problem in surplus distribution.

EQUITY IN SURPLUS DISTRIBUTION

The principle that surplus should be allotted in proportion to the individual contribution of each policy to that surplus is beyond dispute if equity is to rule in surplus distribution, but the difficulty arises in carrying it out in practice, as will have been realized in the outlines given above of the British system on the one hand and the Contribution Method on the other as practised by Canadian and U.S. companies.

The author is of the opinion that the differences between the two systems are more than actuarial. Where, as in Britain, the investment angle of life insurance is stressed particularly (encouraged by income tax relief on premiums paid), the uniform reversionary bonus system has many advantages. Except in times of sudden change when equity may be of minor importance, it gives as fair and equitable a deal to policyholders as is needed to justify its use. Long-term changes can be adjusted if desired by changing the premium rates for new entrants. The system tends to give relatively high rates of premium particularly for endowment insurances as the investment angle is paramount, namely the amount of the bonuses which will be accrued by the maturity age.

In Canada and the U.S. the protection of life insurance is stressed undoubtedly more than the investment angle. The practice has developed of policyholders taking their dividends in cash to reduce the premiums payable although, as will be noted later, other options are available. The purpose of cash dividends is to enable the policyholder to carry as much life insurance as possible for a given outlay. Further in Canada and the U.S. the straight life plan is preferred to the endowment insurance.

We have already quoted the late Henry H. Jackson at the head of Chapter 8. He was an American actuary who illuminated every subject he touched. Robert T. Jackson quoted earlier in this chapter is his son and it is a unique opportunity to quote both father and son on the same actuarial problem, at periods of thirty-seven years apart. In 1922 the late Henry H. Jackson wrote as follows:[2]

> In the very nature of things—and I do not care what the basis of distribution may be, whether it be the British or whether it be what we are pleased to term the scientific American system—it must of absolute necessity be an extremely approximate affair. . . . It seems to me, then, that any dividend scheme which is soundly conceived, which is properly subjected to changes when conditions change, and which in the broadest possible fashion results in reasonable equity to all concerned is doing everything that can be humanly expected of it.

DIVIDEND ILLUSTRATIONS

The prospective purchaser of a participating policy may be expected to wish to have information concerning the dividends likely to be paid on his policy. He may wish to make a comparison with the premiums and probable dividends of the participating policy of another company or with a non-participating policy.

One method is to look at the past; for example, to ascertain what premium the company charged for the same plan at the same age, say, 10 or 20 years ago, and what dividends it has since paid. As an absolute measure, the net costs (premium less dividends) obtained in this way are unlikely to provide a satisfactory guide to *future net cost* particularly because of the rapid increase in interest rates in recent years. As a relative measure, that is, to compare one company with another, the expectation that the company with the lower net cost in the past will have the lower net cost in the future is not without validity, but is not a certainty.

Figures on past premiums and dividends are given by many companies in commercial publications. The Federal Superintendent also

[2]*Fragments* (Montpelier, Vt.: National Life Insurance Company, 1922), p. 212.

TABLE 15.1

Illustrative Dividends to Policyholders–Straight Life; Age at Entry 35

	Duration–Years in Force				
	3	6	9	12	15
Premium per $1,000	$17.52*	$17.52*	$17.25*	$17.25*	$21.49
Dividend per $1,000	2.02	3.19	4.00	5.45	10.31

*$9 policy factor must be added

publishes figures for each company in his annual report. A sample for one company for 1974 is shown in Table 15.1. The tables gives figures for ages 25, 35, 45, and 55 at entry and for 20-payment life and 20-year endowment as well as straight life.

Another method is to project the current dividend scale, that is, to show the dividends which will be payable if the factors currently used to determine dividends remain unchanged. Until recently it was usual to show the average annual *net cost* over 10 or 20 years, or sometimes to age 65. The average *net cost continued* over, say, 20 years, would be one-twentieth of the excess of twenty yearly premiums over the sum of the dividends projected over the twenty years. In determining the average *net cost surrendered*, the twentieth year cash surrender value would be deducted before making the division; the result would frequently be negative indicating a *net profit*.

The objection was raised that this did not give a true picture because it left out the *time value of money*. To answer this objection, it is now common practice to use instead of the totals of the premiums and the dividends, their accumulation with interest at 5 per cent, which rate is considered to be an approximation to the net rate after tax that an individual might be able to earn on long-term investments.

In presenting illustrations companies are careful to include a *safeguarding clause* to the effect that the dividends are "based on the current year's dividend scale remaining unchanged throughout the period and are in no sense estimates or guarantees; future dividends will depend on the actual earnings of the company."

Much attention has been paid in recent years to the question of the best method of comparing participating policies of different companies. Very sophisticated measures have been proposed. All seem to be beyond the comprehension of the average buyer; all are based on the continuation of the current dividend scale. Since the continuation of the current scale is not guaranteed, one may question the wisdom of basing involved calculations on the assumption that it is.

TERMINATION DIVIDENDS AND EXTRA DIVIDENDS

Some U.S. companies doing business in Canada allow special *termination dividends* when the policy terminates by death, maturity, or surrender after having been in force for a certain minimum period. The theory is that the policyholder has contributed a certain amount to the undistributed or "free" surplus of the company and he should receive this on his withdrawal. Any system which favours the long continuing policyholder is to be commended, particularly if he or his beneficiary has suffered due to the depreciation of the purchasing power of the amount payable on withdrawal.

On the other hand, the permanence of the company requires a continual flow of new entrants. The policyholder on entry enjoys the security and benefit of the "free" surplus; in fact he undoubtedly gets a larger dividend and at an earlier date than if that surplus had not been there, for otherwise the company would have had to accumulate a surplus from his premiums before it could pay any dividends to him. Hence the argument that he should leave the company in as good shape as he found it and not withdraw any part of the "free" surplus. Also the question may be asked: what is the real "free surplus" of a company at any point of time so that a portion can be hived off as somebody's share?

Another case of a special termination dividend is when the guaranteed cash surrender value is less than the policy-reserve which the company holds. The company may have strengthened its policy-reserve basis at some time in the policy's history. The argument here is that the policyholder suffered a decrease in dividends while the company was strengthening its policy-reserve basis and so should get it back on surrender. This argument is particularly forceful if the surrender is at a pension age.

The danger of these termination dividends is that they may be extended to fanciful promises and estimates used for competitive purposes only. Although the use of termination dividends can be justified, they have in them the possibility of abuse and thus require the strictest supervision by the authorities. The resemblance of termination dividends to tontine dividends which are described in the next section is too close for their casual acceptance as a proper development of life insurance.

There have also been special additional dividends added to policies at the end of every five policy years. Of course, if one dollar dividend is withheld from each annual dividend the additional dividend payable at the end of five years is much greater than $5 for there is (1) interest on the accumulation, (2) benefit of survivorship, and (3) the benefit of the dollars from those who have surrendered their policies. The 20-year net cost of such a contract is lower than if regular annual dividends had been paid without the withholding. Such larger dividends at certain intervals are contrary to the accepted notion of dividends that they should increase each year under normal conditions. One can appreciate the value of any system which would encourage the continuing policyholder, but anything which would put the better managed company at a disadvantage should be avoided.

The point to be emphasized is that the regular annual dividend is lower on account of the payment of these special dividends.

TONTINE DIVIDENDS

Lorenzo Tonti was an Italian banker who settled in France about 1650, and proposed a scheme to the French authorities to raise funds for the French government which was a combination of bonds and life annuities. This gave a new word "tontine" to our language. We referred to the 1700's as the "gambling century" and a number of tontines were issued in France, Holland, Germany, England, and Ireland throughout that century. They were quite successful in Ireland, but not in England. Great ingenuity was displayed to make the offer attractive but in essence those who entered and died, or rather whose nominees died, forfeited part or all of their investment, the benefit of which was shared among the survivors.

Tontine Dividends: U.S. The tontine idea has been applied to dividends under life insurance policies where it had the name "deferred dividends," under which the dividends allotted were shared out among those surviving a predetermined period of ten, fifteen, or twenty years. Such policies had quite a vogue in the U.S. from about 1870 to 1907 and were strongly supported by such outstanding actuaries as Sheppard Homans and D.P. Fackler already mentioned in this chapter. However, following the Armstrong-Hughes Investigation, in 1905–6, into abuses in the life insurance business in the U.S. and the revision of state laws, the deferred dividend was banned and as already stated the annual dividend system has been universal throughout the U.S. since 1907 on participating policies.

The abuses to which the plan was subjected were:

1. There was no accounting of the huge sums which accumulated out of the surplus which was being earned each year but not distributed.

2. These sums were treated as "free surplus" and not only led to extravagance but attracted an undesirable type of life insurance official.

3. Extravagant figures were issued by the companies to illustrate the effect of the "tontine" but were not realized in practice.

4. The penalty of forfeiture of all dividends on death or withdrawal caused dissatisfaction.

Life insurance is, in so many cases, the only long-term investment held by the public and full value for every dollar paid should be given in protection and investment. It should not become a lottery.

Deferred Dividends: Canada. In Canada deferred dividend policies continued to be used until the law was changed in 1911. The law now requires a company to allot dividends to a policy at least every five years and to set up the amounts and their accumulation as a liability, that is, as money owing to the policyholders and not as "free surplus." With this enactment deferred dividends under new insurances faded out in Canada although they can still be written, if desired, by Canadian companies. The five-yearly dividends written in Canada are not "tontine" for on death "interim" dividends are paid.

DIVIDEND OPTIONS

In Canadian and U.S. life insurance companies a dividend is declared as a cash allotment and the policyholder has the option of (1) taking it in cash; (2) using it to reduce premiums; (3) converting it into a paid-up addition to the sum insured; or (4) leaving it as a cash deposit to accumulate at interest.

Other options are offered by some companies, such as (i) the use of the cash dividend to purchase one-year term insurance of an amount not exceeding the current cash surrender value of the policy with any balance of dividend being carried forward to offset the increasing cost of term insurance with advancing age. (This has had some vogue under the name of the *fifth dividend option.*) (ii) accumulation of cash dividends in a segregated fund.

"The recent trend among Canadian policyholders is strongly toward using policy dividends to buy more insurance. In 1974, 42 per cent of dividends were left on deposit, 28 per cent were taken in cash, and 30 per cent were used to purchase additional amounts of life insurance. By comparison, in 1960 the respective figures were 46 per cent, 39 per cent and 15 per cent."[3]

[3]*Canadian Life Insurance Facts*, 1975 ed. (Toronto: Canadian Life Insurance Association).

We referred in an earlier chapter to the use of the accumulated dividends to mature a straight life policy as an endowment for its face value, when the cash value of the accumulated dividends plus the cash surrender value equal the face value of the policy. The accumulation may either be as in option (4) above or as the cash value of total paid-up additions. The "endowment option" as it may be called, is an obvious one and companies stress this in selling participating straight life policies.

Another option is to use the accumulated dividends to make the policy paid-up. This could be done by (*a*) commuting future premium payments or (*b*) paying premiums as they fall due from the accumulated dividends, or (*c*) waiting until the reduced paid-up value of the policy plus the total paid-up additions equalled the face amount of the policy. It is important to consider what effect, if any, the method used will have on the future participation of the policy in surplus earnings.

Participating Annuities

IMMEDIATE ANNUITIES

Under this type of annuity the annuity payments commence on receipt of the purchase money by the insurance company. Historically, immediate annuities have been non-participating. The large New York mutual life insurance companies, which issue all their life insurance on participating plans only, nowadays issue their immediate annuities only on the nonparticipating basis.

In theory there is no reason why rates for immediate annuities should not be calculated on definitely conservative lines regarding mortality, loading, and interest, and dividends paid as the surplus emerges. Let us consider these three items in the case of immediate annuities.

1. As we are aware, mortality among annuitants has been decreasing and although decreasing mortality may give "mortality profit" for a life insurance policy, it may result in a loss to the company in the case of an annuity if the mortality experience is lower than that assumed in the rate charged. In fact this has happened and the losses to the companies have been substantial.

2. Loading margins are small; expenses of payment of the annuity are likely to increase with the passage of time leading to reducing dividends or to losses.

3. Each year the immediate annuity continues the annuitant gets older

and the value of the future annuity payments, that is, the policy-reserve must decrease. Excess interest earnings can only arise from the policy-reserve and these perforce diminish each year.

Thus with possible losses on mortality and expenses and decreasing excess interest earnings year by year, the picture of surplus earnings is entirely different from that of a life insurance policy. In effect, under normal conditions, a decreasing surplus must arise each year from an immediate annuity.

Immediate annuities are purchased at the older ages when the future lifetime is necessarily limited and the object of buying the annuity is to obtain the largest possible return on the money spent. The need is for a fixed or if possible an increasing income, certainly not a declining one.

It has been suggested as a means of providing an increasing income, that dividends should be allotted in the form of paid-up additions, that is, each year's dividend would buy a little more annuity; the fear has been, however, that the annual increases in annuity would be so small as to cause dissatisfaction and the result is that immediate annuities are not sold on a participating basis.

RETIREMENT ANNUITIES OR DEFERRED ANNUITIES

By their nature, annual premium retirement annuity policies are savings policies with interest being the dominating factor until the annuity payments commence. Thus the two sources of surplus, namely loading and interest, present no difficulties; the first being generally a constant after the first year and the second, namely surplus interest, increasing generally as the policy-reserve increases.

CHAPTER SIXTEEN

Policy Provisions

Life insurance is property; in fact it forms the major part of most estates. Hence the document which sets out the amount payable, the conditions of its payment, and the party or parties to whom it will be paid is of the greatest importance. This chapter is devoted to the study of the provisions of life insurance policies.

HISTORICAL: THE FIRST CANADIAN LIFE POLICY

As stated in Chapter 2, the first policy issued by a Canadian life insurance company was dated as from November 9, 1847. It was issued by the Canada Life on the life of its president and founder, Hugh C. Baker. This policy consisted of just one sheet. On the face were given the usual details of name, age, amount of premium, how and when payable, and the sum insured. On the other side were given the "Conditions of Assurance." It is stated in the Canada Life records that they adopted the policy form of one of the British companies operating in Canada, so that we may assume that the policy was representative of that in use in Canada at that time.

One is first struck by the brevity of the policy: one sheet compared with at least five of the present-day policy. However, the face of the policy followed the usual verbosity of British legal documents of its day with "Whereas," "And Whereas," "Now this Policy Witnesseth," "Provided Always," and "Provided Also" (twice).

In those days a policy of life insurance was first considered as a legal contract drawn up by lawyers, and for centuries lawyers in English-speaking countries were steeped in the traditions of Roman law and the form and sound of the wording was as important as its meaning. It is only in recent years that we are attempting to get our policy wording in simple "everyday" English, but tradition dies hard. One reason for the much lengthier life insurance policy forms of the present day is the inclusion of tables of guaranteed cash surrender, loan and extended insurance values with very extensive tables of settlement options with the necessary explanations, i.e., present-day policies go beyond the payment of an amount on death.[1]

One is struck in this early policy with the prohibitions on travel. Residence was confined to Europe and Canada and the northern states of the U.S. This early policy did not even cover travel between Europe and North America, although shortly afterwards this prohibition was removed, following the general trend in Canada. The policy became void if the life insured "enter into or engage in any Military or Naval service whatever, or shall engage in navigating the seas, lakes or rivers." In this, this life policy resembled the U.S. life insurance policies of the same date, but in some ways was more liberal. Thus, it had days of grace for paying the premium and provided for reinstatement if it lapsed due to non-payment of a premium. It also provided for a reduced paid-up policy as an alternative to revival with payment of back premiums, in the event of lapse.

The policy also became void if the life insured "shall die by the act of Self-destruction, whether such act be in law felonious or otherwise, and whether such person shall be of unsound mind or otherwise, at the time of committing the same; or shall die by the hands of justice, or in consequence of a duel." However, in such cases the premiums were not forfeited as was the usual case with U.S. policies at that time; instead, the policy provided for the payment of the "amount which would have been paid by the Company for the purchase of the Policy on the day before such decease." This last statement referring to a cash surrender value at this early date in the history of the business is of interest.

One other interesting point in connection with this early policy was that the Board of Directors claimed the right to recall the policy on payment of the "full value thereof" if the life insured "abandoned himself or herself to the use of fermented liquors, to such a degree as shall render him or her an habitual or confirmed drunkard," and in the early days of the Canada Life this was actually done. It is a reflection on the hard drinking habits of those days. However, the policy expressly stated that where it had been assigned for the security of a debt this recall of the policy could not be exercised. The same kind of protection was

[1]Perhaps this paragraph should be modified. In February, 1894, the agency organ of one Canadian life insurance company announced: "A policy in the Manufacturers Life involves one condition only, that of payment of premiums. The contract consists of 232 words framed in language as simple as the Proverbs of Solomon."

given to a *bona fide* creditor where the policy was voided by death due to suicide, duelling, or dying at the hands of justice.

This first *Canada Life* policy issued over 120 years ago deserves the comment that it was in advance of its time and was fair and equitable having in view the development of the life insurance business at the time of its issue. Historically, its importance is that it set a high standard in liberality which other Canadian companies had to meet when they were organized. The early records of Canadian insurance companies refer repeatedly to the removal of restrictions to face the competition of other companies which had removed them.

THE POLICY AS A CONTRACT

A life insurance policy is a legal contract. Such detailed and comprehensive laws dealing with life insurance have been passed that they tend to overshadow the basic fact of it being a legal contract and subject to the general rules of law regarding contracts. These general rules provide that to be binding on the parties entering into the contract:

1. There must be an offer and an acceptance;
2. There must be valuable consideration (e.g., the payment of a premium);
3. The parties must be legally capable of making a contract (children call for special consideration here);
4. The contract must be for a lawful purpose and not contrary to public policy.

Moreover, under an insurance contract there must be "the most perfect good faith" between the parties to the contract.

Throughout this chapter these points will come up for consideration, but it is well to bear these conditions in mind when considering a life insurance policy as a complete document. A contract of life insurance is *not a contract of indemnity* as is the case with most other forms of insurance. Under a contract of indemnity the insured is not entitled to profit by reason of the existence of the insurance; the insurance company's liability is limited to the amount of the loss. A life insurance contract is one where a specific amount of money is payable—the distinction is an important one.

PROVINCIAL UNIFORM LEGISLATION

In Chapter 28 the development of insurance regulation and supervision will be discussed and in particular the dual supervision in Canada by the federal and provincial governments. We there cover the development of the present subdivision of powers whereby it is accepted that the provincial legislation has exclusive jurisdiction regarding the provisions of insurance contracts entered into within the province.

One objection to provincial jurisdiction in insurance is that as there are ten provinces there is the danger of conflicting legal requirements not only troublesome to companies doing business in a number of provinces, but also to policyholders moving from one province to another. The province of Quebec follows its own laws based on the Code Napoleon, while in the other nine provinces the law is based on the common law of England which is also the basis of the laws of the United States. The Quebec Act Respecting Insurance proclaimed in force October 20, 1976 contains provisions similar to those in existence in the common law provinces; nevertheless differences remain. Later in this chapter, some reference will be made to the insurance laws of Quebec.

In tackling this jurisdictional problem Canada has set a pattern for other federated states to follow. The first step towards uniformity was taken in 1914 when the Superintendents of the four western provinces met to consider standardization of their insurance laws. The Association of Provincial Superintendents of Insurance was organized in Winnipeg three years later and jointly with the Canadian Bar Association there was drafted a Uniform Life Insurance Act in 1923 which was subsequently enacted in all nine common law provinces. Revisions to the original Act were made in 1935–36 and in 1948 and further extensive changes were made which came into force simultaneously in all nine provinces on July 1, 1962. The great benefit of this uniformity to the life insurance business in Canada is obvious and the efforts of the Superintendents of Insurance of the nine common law provinces in maintaining it over the past forty years deserves the highest praise.[2]

It is important to note here that the benefits granted by life insurance companies and the removal of restrictions were the result of the development of the business and competition among the companies. They did not arise through legislation, although in some cases the practice of some of the leading companies was made the general practice by being incorporated into the law. We refer here particularly to the existence of privileges and provisions in the modern Canadian life insurance policy such as days of grace for payment of premiums, guaranteed cash surrender, loan and non-forfeiture values and benefits, the incontestable

[2]The late Eugene Lafleur, K.C., a renowned leader of the Quebec bar, as early as 1915 made a plea for such uniformity including Quebec. (See Presidential Address, R. D. Taylor, K.C., Life Insurance Institute of Canada, 1946–7.)

clause, and the wide non-restrictive policy conditions. These will be referred to in some detail in this chapter.

Canadian versus U.S. Practice. There is a difference between Canadian and U.S. practice regarding policy provisions. In the United States each state has detailed regulations regarding policy provisions as to what must or may not be inserted and policy forms have to be approved by the various state insurance commissioners. This approval of policy forms is not the practice in Canada (although there has been a move towards requiring approval in the field of policies providing variable benefits under segregated funds) and the legal requirements as to what must be contained in a life insurance policy are of the most elementary nature as outlined in the next section. Competition has been the determining factor and has been to the advantage of the insuring public.

A movement towards uniformity of policy provisions has been taking place in the U.S. similar to that which has been so successfully accomplished in Canada. When we refer to "U.S. standard" policy provisions, we will be referring to those current in New York state. The insurance laws of New York state have served as a model for other states.

In all our comments in this chapter we are referring only to policies of ordinary life business and annuity business, that is, excluding group, industrial, and fraternal business.

THE UNIFORM LIFE INSURANCE ACT

Although the uniform legislation referred to in the previous section is commonly referred to as "The Uniform Life Insurance Act" or more briefly the "Uniform Act" it is actually a part of a general Insurance Act in all nine provinces except Newfoundland where it is a separate enactment. The Uniform Act is the determining body of legislation regarding policy provisions in Canada and repeated reference will be made to it. For convenience when sections of the Act are referred to the numbers given to them in the Ontario Insurance Act will be used. The actual wording of the Act will be quoted occasionally, and for those who wish to refer to the actual provisions of the Uniform Act the book by E. H. McVitty, Q.C., is recommended.[3]

POLICY PROVISIONS

The Uniform Act, Section 149(2), requires a life insurance company to

[3]*The Life Insurance Laws of Canada* (Life Underwriters Association of Canada, 41 Lesmill Road, Don Mills, Ontario, M3B 2T3).

set out in its policy (ordinary life insurance or annuity) the obvious particulars regarding: the identity of the life insured; the sum insured, its amount, and the conditions under which it becomes payable; the premium, its amount, and how payable. In addition the policy is required to set out: (*a*) whether the policy provides for participation in profits; (*b*) the conditions upon which the policy may be reinstated it if lapses, and (*c*) the options, if any, of surrendering the policy for cash, of obtaining a policy loan, and of obtaining paid-up or extended insurance. Although this section of the Act requires that the period of grace, if any, within which the premium may be paid must be stated in the policy, Section 148(2) prescribes a statutory minimum period of grace of thirty days.

The provisions of a life insurance policy may be said to come under nine distinct headings and will be described in that order: (1) days of grace, (2) statements made are representations, not warranties, (3) incontestability, (4) policy is entire contract, (5) mis-statement of age, (6) dividend clause, (7) cash surrender, loan and non-forfeiture clauses, (8) reinstatement, (9) exclusions: War, Aviation, and Suicide. Not every one of these is covered by the Uniform Act and an effort will be made to indicate specifically the points covered in the Act.

1. DAYS OF GRACE

According to the Uniform Act and as already stated, a minimum period of thirty days must be given for the payment of each premium after the first; the period allowed by most companies is 31 days. As the policy would not go into effect until payment of the first premium the days of grace apply to renewal premiums. Further, during the days of grace the policy must remain in full force and if death occurs during the days of grace the premium due and interest, if any, can be deducted from the insurance money. (Sections 156(2) and 156(3))

2. STATEMENTS MADE ARE REPRESENTATIONS NOT WARRANTIES

Warranty. If a statement is made as part of the completion of an insurance contract and it is stated to be a *warranty*, then its literal truth is vouched for and the contract can be set aside if it is established that it is untrue. There is no question of a warranty being *material to the contract*, that is, that the insurance company would have been influenced by the statement made or concealed in accepting the risk or determining the rate at which it was accepted.

The doctrine of warranty, or the literal truth of statements made in an application for insurance, developed in connection with marine insurance where the property to be insured might be at the other side of the world and at one time it applied to all branches of insurance. The obvious injustices perpetrated under this legal device led the life insurance companies to waive their legal rights to claim that statements made in life insurance applications were warranties. Later this became incorporated into life insurance legislation in Canada and the U.S. There is no law regarding this in Britain, but the principle is universally accepted there. In life insurance the company is in a position to examine the applicant in person, to ask all sorts of questions, and to make various enquiries as to the insurability of the life to be insured, which justifies a different attitude.

The Uniform Act, Section 157(1), requires that the applicant for insurance and the life to be insured, disclose to the insurance company every fact within their knowledge "that is material to the insurance." Apart from the Incontestability Provision which will be referred to in the next section "a failure to disclose, or a misrepresentation of, such a fact renders the contract voidable" by the insurance company. (Section 157(2))

Representation. Where a statement is not given the force of a warranty it is a *representation*. The important point is that for a misrepresentation to affect a contract it has to be *material to the contract*. If any court actions develop as to misrepresentations or concealments in the application, etc., for an insurance policy, the court must decide whether the statements made or concealed influenced the insurer in deciding to accept the risk or the rate at which it was accepted. The "test of materiality" is often a matter of some difficulty for the courts to decide.

Fraud. Fraud in connection with a life insurance policy may arise when a mis-statement is deliberately made or a material fact deliberately withheld with the intention to defraud; an intention to deceive is a necessary element of fraud. It is a fundamental rule of law that fraud renders a contract voidable. We referred in a previous section to a general rule of law regarding insurance contracts; that there must be "the most perfect good faith" between the parties to the contract.

Void and voidable. When a policy is said to be *void* it means that it has no legal force or effect and is incapable of ratification; an illegal contract is void from its inception. When a contract is said to be *voidable* by the insurer it means that the insurance company can withdraw from the contract if it desires, returning the premiums paid.

3. INCONTESTABILITY

The difficulties and legal actions arising from alleged misrepresentations by an applicant or a life insured led to the practice among life insurance companies of waiving their rights to challenge any statements made in connection with an application for a life insurance policy after the policy had been a number of years in force. In April 1880 the directors of a Canadian life insurance company announced that all its policies were to be "incontestable" after having been three years in force. Many years later laws were introduced making this a requisite condition of all life insurance policies in Canada and the United States, the incontestable period having by that time been reduced by competition to two years and in some cases to a shorter period.

Under Section 158(2) of the Uniform Act when a life insurance policy has been two years in force during the lifetime of the life insured any non-disclosure or misrepresentation, in the absence of fraud, does not render the contract voidable. We have emphasized the phrase "in the absence of fraud." Any mis-statement of age or statements made in connection with the disability provision attached to the policy are exempted from the incontestability provision. (Section 158(1))

In the United States, the law, following the practice of the companies, has gone further and even fraud does not vitiate the contract. It means that where the incontestability period is two years, the company has that period to challenge any statements made and to dispute the policy after which the company has no remedy and the claim must be paid. The justification given to override the principle of law that fraud vitiates a contract is that after the death of the life insured, the beneficiary who is generally the widow or an orphan of the deceased may find it difficult to meet the company's accusations possibly many years after the offence. The incontestability provision has one good point both in Canadian and U.S. practice: it cuts down litigation.

4. POLICY IS ENTIRE CONTRACT

As statements made by the insured and the life insured may invalidate a life insurance policy it is most important that copies of any statements made in applying for the policy are available at all times. Hence the practice has arisen of attaching copies of the application and any declarations made regarding health, etc., to the insurance policy. In case this has not been done, an insured or a claimant under the policy has the right to be furnished by the insurance company with a copy of the application. (Section 148(4))

According to Section 148(2) of the Uniform Act, the application, the policy, any documents attached to the policy when issued, and changes to the policy agreed upon in writing after the policy is issued, constitute the entire contract with a life insurance company.

When Policy Goes into Force. It is important to note when a life insurance policy becomes effective. Unless determined by the *interim insurance* stated in the application or in the policy there are three requisites as specified in S. 154 of the Uniform Act: (1) the delivery of the policy; (2) the payment of the first premium; (3) that no change has taken place in the insurability of the life insured between the time of completion of the application and the delivery of the policy. Where a policy is issued as applied for, delivery of the policy to an agent of the company for unconditional delivery to an insured, his assign or agent, or to a beneficiary is tantamount to delivery to the insured.

5. MIS-STATEMENT OF AGE

A mis-statement of age is considered in a different category to other mis-statements in an application for insurance, yet it is important, for age at entry generally determines the premium payable. The Uniform Act provides that where the age of the person whose life is insured is mis-stated to the insurance company, the insurance money provided by the contract shall be increased or decreased to the amount that would have been provided for the same premium at the correct age. (S. 160(2))

6. DIVIDEND CLAUSE

As already stated above, Section 149(2) of the Uniform Act specifies that a policy must state whether it participates in any surplus or profits which may be declared. Note there is no stipulation as to the period of distribution of dividends to policyholders or other details regarding dividends. Under the Canadian federal insurance laws, where dividends are distributed at intervals less frequently than every five years the liability has to be calculated and set aside every five years and the policies are called "deferred dividend policies." This has been discussed in Chapter 15.

The U.S. Standard Provisions require that the insurer shall annually ascertain and apportion any divisible surplus accruing on the policy. Hence all participating policies in the U.S. are on an annual dividend basis. Where premiums are modified for the first three or five years or when dividends are first payable at the end of the second policy year this does not necessarily contravene the law, for a company does not have to apportion surplus to a policy unless the policy has earned it.

The dividend clauses of policies generally cover the details of apportionment and the various options which the policyholder may elect: (1) cash; (2) reduction of premium; (3) paid up addition of the sum insured; (4) cash left on deposit at interest; (5) cash dividend applied to purchase a one year term insurance addition. These have been discussed in Chapter 15.

7. CASH SURRENDER, LOAN, AND NON-FORFEITURE BENEFITS

On account of their special importance the clauses of a policy dealing with cash surrender and loan values and non-forfeiture benefits are dealt with separately in the next chapter.

8. REINSTATEMENT

As mentioned previously, the policies issued in Canada over a century ago were in advance of their time by containing a reinstatement privilege if the policy lapsed, that is, ceased to be in force due to non-payment of a premium. Provincial law requires that every policy may be reinstated within two years from the date of lapse subject to evidence of good health and insurability, unless the policy has been surrendered for cash or the options of reduced paid-up or extended insurance exercised. (Section 163(2)&(3))

The rate of interest permitted to be charged on back premiums and other indebtedness under the policy is restricted to a rate not greater than 6 per cent per annum (S. 156(3) & S. 163(2)). It is also stated that mis-statements, etc., in the application for reinstatement can nullify the policy just as for a new application and the period of incontestability dates from the date of reinstatement and not the date when the original policy went into force (S. 163(4)). The word "insurability" is included in the phrase *good health and insurability* to safeguard the company against the possibility of deterioration of the risk due to bad habits or unsatisfactory financial standing.[4]

Most companies go beyond the two-year period from the date of lapse

[4] In May, 1877 the Canada Life had its first lawsuit, some thirty years after its founding! It had refused to reinstate a lapsed policy as evidence showed intemperance in habits; the company won the case.

during which the policy may be reinstated and with some companies the period stated in the policy is five years. In practice, the genuine desire of the policyholder to reinstate the policy is the determining factor. The evidence of good health and insurability required depends, as a rule, on the amount of insurance and the time elapsed since the policy lapsed. It may vary from simply signing a form that there has been no change in health or insurability since the date of lapse to a non-medical questionnaire or a medical examination.

Redating. When a policy has lapsed for some time (a year or more) reinstatement effected by paying the back premiums and interest does not take into account the fact that the life insured has had no protection for the period the policy was not in force. There is also a further problem when the lapsed policy is burdened with debt due to a policy loan or a loan due to premiums being advanced as a debt against the policy. In such cases, companies will quote for a redating proposition whereby the original date of entry will be advanced. In this way on payment in the future by the insured of the higher premium, due to the assumed higher age at entry, the policyholder avoids payment of arrears of premiums for a period for which no protection was given. These redating propositions require special calculation and quotations by the home office and involve the companies in considerable expense.

9. EXCLUSIONS: WAR, AVIATION, AND SUICIDE

The Uniform Act gives no directions to companies regarding the inclusion or exclusion of the war or aviation hazard in life insurance policies but, as will be indicated below, it does refer to suicide. We are dealing here with the life insurance benefit only, the total disability and double indemnity benefits being dealt with separately in Chapters 19 and 20.

War. As a rule, Canadian life insurance companies, in times of peace, insert no restrictions in their policies regarding war hazards, although where larger amounts of insurance are effected on a member of the armed forces some restriction regarding the war hazard would be prudent.

Aviation. In Canada, policies are issued to civilian lives free from any restriction regarding aviation hazards except where it is known that by occupation or travel the life insured is likely to be exposed to more than the normal aviation hazard which is expected of a business man using air travel freely. As will be indicated in Chapter 22, these normal hazards include all but a few exceptional cases.

Suicide. It was mentioned above that for a contract to be binding it must be for a lawful purpose and not contrary to public policy. In common law it has been held to be contrary to public policy for a life insurance company to pay the insurance money when the life insured commits suicide. Cases will arise where one can comprehend this principle of common law, but it is an awkward problem for life insurance company officials to face in practice. It will be noted that the incontestability provision was introduced to avoid just such problems.

Policies issued by Canadian life insurance companies generally exclude the risk of death from suicide or self-destruction within two years from the date of issue of the policy or from the date of reinstatement following a lapse. The Uniform Act contains the following references to suicide. Section 162(2) specifies that any period of exclusion regarding suicide contained in a policy will also apply from the date of reinstatement if the policy lapses and is subsequently reinstated. Also Section 162(1) clarifies the position implied in Canadian policies that although the policy is voided by the suicide of the life insured within two years from the date of issue the company will pay the claim if suicide occurs after this two-year period. Neither S. 162(1) or S. 162(2) stipulate a two year limitation period; S. 162(2) contains the phrase "within a certain period of time" but as a matter of company policy the usual suicide period is two years.

The common law rule that payment of the sum insured on suicide was contrary to public policy was affirmed in a famous case in England in 1938 (Beresford *v*. Royal) and the above section of the Uniform Act makes it legal for a company to pay the sum insured on suicide if it is stated or implied in the policy that it will do so after two years after entry or date of reinstatement, i.e., as stated in present-day Canadian policies. If the contract lapses and is reinstated subsequently on one or more occasions, the period of time commences to run from the date of the latest reinstatement (S. 162(2)).

The U.S. Standard Provisions do permit the exclusion of the risk of death by suicide, within two years of the date of issue, from policies and although many U.S. companies reduced the period to one year the tendency has been to increase the period to two years being the longest period permitted in view of the incontestability provision.

In the early days of life insurance the business had to be safeguarded against unjust claims and it can be understood that the common law plea of non-payment on death by suicide would be fully supported. Nowadays we are in a position to treat suicide as any other cause of death provided the company is protected against cases where the policy may have been taken out originally with the object of suicide. The possibility of suicide has to be taken into account by the home office in selecting the risk.

Other Life Insurance Policy Provisions

We have dealt with the main provisions of life insurance policies excepting the items of cash, loan and non-forfeiture values and settlement options which are covered in other chapters. We now deal with a number of matters of a more general character in connection with life insurance policies.

INSURABLE INTEREST

In Chapter 1 the importance of the existence of an insurable interest in a life insurance transaction was emphasized; it differentiates life insurance from gambling. The Uniform Act Sections 152(1) and 152(2)(*b*) state that where there is no insurable interest "at the time a contract would otherwise take effect" the contract is void unless the person whose life is to be insured has consented in writing to the insurance being placed on his life. The latter point *re* consent was a change introduced in the 1962 revision. The Act makes it clear that the insurable interest must exist at the time the policy would take effect; any subsequent change in the matter of insurable interest would not affect the validity of the contract.

At common law no person has an insurable interest in the life of another unless he has a pecuniary interest in the duration of the life of that person. We have already noted that where the life insured has given his consent this need not apply. The Uniform Act specifies certain definite cases where insurable interest may be presumed to exist irrespective of pecuniary interest and hence extends the common law. Under Section 153 a person is stated to have an insurable interest in: (1) his own life and in the life of his spouse, child and grandchild; (2) his employee; (3) any person upon whom he is wholly or in part dependent, or from whom he is receiving support or education; and of course, (4) any person in the duration of whose life he has a pecuniary interest.

The question of "pecuniary interest" is very broad and in practice no question is raised if persons insure each other provided the reasons for such insurance appear legitimate and the amount of the insurance corresponds to the interest. As we have noted there are a multitude of commercial transactions which call for life insurance such as to cover debts and for partners to insure each other's lives to buy out the deceased's share on the first death.

Although this matter is so important, it rarely gives trouble in practice for the interests of people in each other's lives, which are the reasons for insurance being taken out, are generally obvious.

RIGHTS OF BENEFICIARIES

The most important change made in the Uniform Act which went into effect on July 1, 1962, was with regard to the rights of beneficiaries under life insurance policies. As the rights of *preferred beneficiaries* in existence on June 30, 1962, are preserved under the new law, it is necessary to consider the position under both the old and the new laws.

The word *beneficiary* is derived from the Latin word meaning "favour" and in law means the person to whom the amount of an insurance policy or annuity is payable.

PREFERRED BENEFICIARIES: POSITION AT JUNE 30, 1962

Under the old Uniform Act if the insured named a beneficiary in the preferred class, a trust was created in favour of the beneficiary and the policy and its proceeds are protected against the claims of any creditor of the insured and does not form part of the estate of the insured. This is a most important modification of the common law and cuts across many laws, including the laws of contract and bankruptcy. It does indicate the special nature of the life insurance policy in the eyes of the law. The laws of Quebec also have a similar protection against the claims of creditors. Under the old Uniform Act the preferred class of beneficiaries was defined as the spouse, child, grandchild, or parent of the life insured.

Further under the old Uniform Act the insured could make changes within the preferred class but could not change to anyone outside that class without the consent of the named preferred beneficiary. Many years' experience indicated that complications arose from this restraint on the insured regarding the policy he took out and various devices were in use to circumvent this. Further, it became apparent that more and more policyholders were declining to name their wives and children as beneficiaries, thus defeating the whole purpose of the legislation in their favour. Hence the change made in the 1962 revision of the Uniform Act.

However, where on June 30, 1962, a preferred beneficiary was named under a life insurance policy the old law continues to apply to it and the rights of preferred beneficiaries are protected as outlined at the beginning of this section. Should the policy monies, at any time, become payable to anyone other than a preferred beneficiary the new law becomes effective.

Policies also generally state that if any beneficiary dies before the insured the interest of such beneficiary reverts to the insured unless expressly stated otherwise.

BENEFICIARIES UNDER UNIFORM ACT, JULY 1, 1962, AND THEREAFTER

We outline below some of the main provisions of the new beneficiary laws as given in the new Uniform Act which went into effect on July 1, 1962.

1. *Designation of beneficiary.* An insured may in a contract or by a declaration designate his estate or a beneficiary to receive the insurance money. The declaration if used must be signed by the insured and must identify the contract. (Sections 164(1) and 145(*f*))

2. *Irrevocable designation of a beneficiary.* The insured may designate a beneficiary irrevocably. Such a designation may be in the contract or by a declaration (but not as part of a will) filed with the insurance company during the lifetime of the life insured. In such a case while the beneficiary is living the insured cannot alter or revoke the designation without the consent of the beneficiary and the insurance money is not subject to the control of the insured or his creditors or forms part of his estate (S. 165(1)). It is not expected that these irrevocable designations will be used frequently but the result of such a designation should be realized.

3. *Insured may alter designation.* An insured may alter or revoke the designation of a beneficiary subject to the exception mentioned in (2) above where an irrevocable designation is made. The declaration must be signed by the insured and must identify the contract. (Sections 164(2), 145(*f*) and 171)

4. *Beneficiaries where policy exempt from seizure.* When a designation is in favour of a spouse, child, grandchild or parent of the life insured "the rights and interests of the insured in the insurance money and in the contract are exempt from execution or seizure" (S. 170(2)). These beneficiaries are identical with those of the "preferred class." In some of the provinces, at this point appears the following definition: "'child' includes an adopted child and 'grandchild' includes the child of an adopted child." In the other provinces (including Ontario) this definition is omitted as it is covered in the general laws of the province.

It should be noted that under the new law except where there is an irrevocable designation the insured has complete freedom to alter or revoke the designation.

5. *Insurance money free from creditors.* Where a beneficiary is designated, apart from (2) and (4) above, the insurance money payable to the beneficiary is free from the claims of creditors of the insured and does not form part of his estate but only from the time the insurance money becomes payable (Section 170(1)). In designations (2) and (4) above the freedom from the insured's creditors applies both before and after the insurance money becomes payable.

It should be noted that "beneficiary" in the Uniform Act does not include the insured or his estate. This is from the definition of "beneficiary" in S. 145(*b*). Thus the meaning of "beneficiary" is made narrower than that usually inferred (see Chapter 1).

6. *Rights to dividends.* During the lifetime of the insured the beneficiaries have no vested rights in the dividends allotted to a policy; also the insurance company may apply any dividends or bonuses allotted to keeping the policy in force. These are, of course, subject to any specific provisions in the policy to the contrary. (Sections 172(1) and (2))

Beneficiaries in the U.S. are designated with or without the right to change them and if the life insured has reserved the right to change the beneficiary then he can exercise all rights, benefits, options, and privileges without the consent of the beneficiary. Thus the changes in the Uniform Act have been along lines which have been in use in the United States for many years.

Life insurance policies are such an every-day concern to millions of people that everything that can be done to simplify the naming and changing of beneficiaries is desirable. Great care should, therefore, be taken to avoid complicated dispositions of policy monies by the beneficiary clauses of a policy for such create difficulties later on if circumstances change.

ASSIGNMENTS

A life insurance policy like any other contract is freely assignable, that is, its ownership can be transferred. The person to whom it is assigned (called the *assignee*) ordinarily secures all the rights (but no better rights) of the *assignor* (the person who assigned the policy). Every life insurance policy includes in its conditions an assignment clause in the nature of a warning that (1) the company assumes no responsibility for the validity or effect of an assignment; and (2) any assignment of the policy, to be binding on the company issuing the policy, must be in writing and be filed with the company. From the earliest days, life insurance policies have been transferred as security to cover a debt, or have been sold for cash.

The Uniform Act, Section 174, actually spells out much of the common law which has grown up regarding assignments and in particular provides that assignees take priority in the order, not of the dates of their assignments, but of the dates of their notice in writing to the insurance companies. It is most important for an assignee to register his assignment with the company, for the company is protected by law if it pays out any amounts due under a life insurance policy to the parties entitled according to its records. An assignee who did not register his claim could sue the party to whom payment was made.

The question of "insurable interest" is not material when the assignee claims under an assignment. We stated previously that the only necessity was for an "unsurable interest" to exist at the time the policy was effected and subsequent changes do not affect the validity of the contract.

MINORS

Changes were made in the 1962 revision of the Uniform Act regarding minors. These are summarized below to give the present position.

1. *No limit on insurance.* There are now no restrictions as to the amount of insurance which a life insurance company may issue or the sums payable on the death of a minor. It is now an underwriting matter for the individual company and is discussed in Chapter 22 on Selection of Risks.

2. *Minor as contractor.* A minor who has attained the age of sixteen has every right to enter into a life insurance contract on his own life or on the life of another. (S. 176)

3. *Minor as beneficiary.* A minor who has attained the age of 18 can, as beneficiary under a life insurance contract, receive the insurance money payable to him and give a valid discharge for it. This provision gives a minor who has attained the age of 18 the capability of a person 19 in those provinces where 19 is the age of majority, i.e., B.C., Newfoundland, New Brunswick and Nova Scotia. In the remaining provinces where the age of majority is 18, the provision is redundant.

POWERS OF AGENTS

Section 197 of the Uniform Act reads as follows: "No officer, agent or employee of an insurer and no person soliciting insurance, whether or not he is an agent of the insurer, shall, to the prejudice of the insured, be deemed to be the agent of the insured in respect of any question arising out of a contract." It is a unique provision in Canadian insurance law and is not applicable to other lines of insurance. It places a great responsibility on life insurance agents and employees of life insurance companies in completing applications and otherwise carrying out the wishes of applicants and policyholders.

Two general rules of agency law are: (1) that the insurance company is bound by the acts of its agents particularly if performed in the course of their regular and expected duties; (2) that the knowledge of the agent is presumed to be the knowledge of the insurance company, so that material facts communicated by an applicant to the agent are presumed to be passed on to the company. However, these statements oversimplify the law and the circumstances of each case and the powers vested in the agent are the determining factors. It is clear from the above quoted section of the Uniform Act that the interests of the insured and his beneficiaries are paramount. The company, of course, can take action against the agent where it has suffered through any wrong-doing by the agent.

Life insurance companies generally warn policyholders in one of the clauses of the policy that only certain officers specified by title have the right to waive or modify any conditions of the policy. This would particularly apply to extending the time for payment of a premium or by binding the company in any way. This not only applies to agents but also to all other unauthorized persons in the service of the company. To be sure that any waiver of the conditions of a policy is effective one should insist on it being in writing and on head office letterhead and over the signature of the authorized officer.

Quebec Insurance Law

As already stated, a policy of life insurance is a contract and only varies in principle from other contracts where special laws have been passed modifying these principles. As the Uniform Act does not apply to the province of Quebec, separate consideration has to be given to the laws of that province regarding life insurance. Historically, it may be said that in Quebec the principles of English law govern in constitutional, criminal, and certain commercial matters, but the old French customs and laws govern in civil matters. In 1866 there came into being "The Civil Code of Lower Canada" which reduced to writing in both English and French the civil law of the province. Parts of the Civil Code deal with certain phases of insurance.

Until 1976 life insurance was also subject to the Insurance Act (quite limited in scope in comparison to the Uniform Act) and to the Husbands and Parents Act which, in effect, designated certain classes of preferred beneficiaries.

In 1974 "An Act respecting Insurance" was adopted which was not proclaimed until October 1976. It repealed the Insurance Act, the Husbands and Parents Act, the Diocesan Montreal Insurance Companies Act, the title of the Civil Code respecting insurance (except the chapter on marine insurance), and finally the Claims Adjusters Act, and in their place incorporated extensive new material concerning life insurance in the Civil Code. The new material is contained in Chapter Second of the Code, Articles 2501 to 2561 inclusive. Chapter Second deals with insurance of persons and covers accident and sickness insurance as well as life insurance.

The requirements of the law concerning such matters as policy contents, insurable interest and so on are much the same as under the Uniform Act. One difference is that there is no provision for a minor to insure his own life; thus, a person may not enter into a contract of life insurance until majority (age 18) is attained.

The effect of the new provisions concerning beneficiaries is also similar to the provisions in the other provinces. An important exception is that the designation of the consort is irrevocable unless otherwise stipulated.

The new law provides as a transitional measure that beneficiaries designated under the Husbands and Parents Act become irrevocably designated except that the policyholder has the right, once only, within twelve months of the coming into force of the new Act, to make a change within the classes named in the former act; the new designation is then irrevocable. If he does not make a change within 12 months, the last beneficiary in standing within the classes named in the former act will be irrevocable as of the effective date of the new law.

It also provides that designations of other beneficiaries made before the coming into force of the new Act are revocable except (*a*) if the policy or document appointing the beneficiary stipulated otherwise; (*b*) if the policyholder had not reserved the right to change the beneficiary, then the beneficiary may within twelve months after the coming into force of the new Act, by giving notice to the insurer, before the nomination is revoked, of his intention to accept the stipulation in his favour.

Variable Contracts

These are policies issued in connection with segregated funds where some or all of the benefits provided are not expressed in constant dollars but depend on the value from time to time of the assets in the segregated fund.

Different forms of variable contracts are issued. Under one form, cash dividends are invested in the segregated fund, all other benefits being fixed in constant dollars. Under another, a part of the premium is used to provide term insurance, either level or decreasing, the rest going into the segregated fund; the death benefit is then the sum of the term insurance and of the current value in the fund; at the end of the term the policy matures as an endowment of the amount of the value in the fund.

Under a somewhat more complicated plan the policy is similar to a normal straight life or other form of policy. However, each year, the increase in the reserve, or of a specified part thereof, determined in advance, such as one-quarter, or one-half, is invested in the segregated fund. The dividends or benefits are then adjusted to reflect the difference in the growth rate of the fund (investment income plus capital gains less capital losses) and normal interest earnings. Thus dividends or benefits will be greater than normal if "growth" exceeds normal interest, but in other circumstances they will be less than normal.

Under another plan both the *premiums* and the *benefits* are expressed in terms of the value of the segregated fund, so that the premiums vary as well as the benefits.

It is apparent that a variable contract must contain certain information not required in policies expressed in constant dollars. For that reason, special regulations concerning them have been issued by provincial governments.

These regulations require that the policy state in bold print that it includes benefits which are not guaranteed. It must describe the benefits and indicate which are guaranteed and which fluctuate with the market value of the fund. It must also indicate the method of determining the benefits related to the market value and, where applicable, state the proportion of the premium to be allocated to provide the benefits related to the market value of the fund.

The policy must also mention the times at which the fund will be valued (which must be at least once monthly) and must describe how the charges against the fund for taxes, management or other expenses are determined.

The insurer is required to provide a prospective purchaser with an information folder concerning the fund and the contract. The insurer must also provide to an insured, at least once a year, a statement showing the amount allocated to the fund under the contract during the year, the value of the benefits related to the market value of the fund, and information concerning the holdings of the fund.

CHAPTER SEVENTEEN

Premiums, Expenses, and Non-Forfeiture Values

GROSS AND NET PREMIUMS

The calculation of a *gross premium*, i.e., that actually charged by the life insurance company involves consideration of the actual mortality, interest, and expenses being experienced or expected to be experienced during the life of the policy. Allowance has to be made for contingencies or as it might be expressed: margins of safety, in each of the following items: (1) to cover the possibility of a higher mortality in the future than in the past or an abnormally high mortality over a short period of time; (2) allowance should be made for investment losses and a downward trend in interest earnings on the insurance funds; (3) allowance should also be made to cover the upward trend in expenses and taxation which has been in evidence for some years. The force of competition acts as a restraint on the margins used in practice.

A net premium is first calculated based on mortality and interest factors on the principles demonstrated in Chapter 6 where we calculated the valuation net premium. This net premium is increased by an amount to cover expenses, taxation, and contingencies which is called the *loading*.

The difficulties in life insurance terminology are again in evidence when we refer to "net premiums." The phrase "net premium" is used in at least three different connections. It is used to denote the *level net premium* to which, if an allowance for expenses and contingencies be added, will give the "gross premium." There is the *valuation net premium* based on the mortality and interest used for calculating the policy-reserves. There is also the net premium which the company has left over after expenses have been deducted and we will call this the *deloaded premium* to distinguish it from the others.

We outline below the analyses which are required to determine the factors used for mortality, interest, and expenses in the calculation of gross premiums. As has been already stressed, in both participating and non-participating plans, once the policy goes into force the premium rate is fixed as is given in the policy.

CALCULATION OF GROSS PREMIUMS: MORTALITY

Our illustrations in Chapter 6 were based on the Canadian Men Ultimate Table CM(5), being the experience of Canadian insured lives over the period 1900 to 1915, more than five years after entry.

Companies determine their death rates, or as we call it their mortality experience, each year, but it is only the largest companies whose experience would be extensive enough to be the basis of a mortality table on which gross premiums could be based. Further, gross premiums for participating policies are based on net premiums which are related to the policy-reserves which, in turn, are based on legislation. There is also the heavy expense of calculating the innumerable tables required in actuarial practice based on the mortality table. This is the background of the co-operation of companies to pool their experience and publish a joint mortality experience.

We have referred to the continuous investigation by the Canadian Institute of Actuaries into current mortality in Canada and the experience of a group of companies combining their figures for the years 1958 to 1964 called the "CA 58–64 Table" which has been published. In Table 8.1 actual specimen rates of mortality are given for ages 20 to 70 at entry, taken from the original table. For convenience the select portion of the table is given for quinquennial ages only, and from age 75 on the ultimate rates of mortality are given for quinquennial ages to age 105, being the end of the table. The CA 58–64 Table gives rates of mortality which are the lowest of any of the mortality rates of insured lives in Canada published to that time.

In the calculation of gross premiums on the participating plan a life insurance company has no need to modify the rates as the mortality improves. Under such participating plans the policyholder receives the benefit of mortality improvement as explained in Chapter 15 on Participating Policies.

Regarding non-participating plans, companies do take into their calculations the latest mortality being experienced. The CA 58–64 Table gives the lowest mortality of any table to the time it was published. In using it actuaries have to make allowance for the possibility of future higher mortality due to war, epidemics, or just fluctuations; mortality rates may go up as well as down. Actuaries have the option of using a mortality table giving somewhat higher mortality rates than those of the latest table or using the latest table and adding a margin for "contingencies." As noted above the joint mortality experience of the companies is examined year by year.

CALCULATION OF GROSS PREMIUMS: INTEREST

In deciding on the rate of interest to be used in calculating the gross premium rates an actuary has to allow for the cyclical fluctuation of interest earnings which will be discussed in Chapter 29 and also the particular earnings of his own company. In 1974 the average net rate of interest earned by Canadian life insurance companies on their insurance funds was 7.11 per cent and the range for individual companies varied from a high of 10.45 per cent to a low of 5.71 per cent. (The high figure is that of a new company which, although registered, had not commenced business; the low is that of one which ceased doing an active business some years ago; the rate earned by 46 out of 56 companies was within a range of one per cent on either side of the average, that is, from 6.11 to 8.11 per cent.) The "net" rate is that obtained after deducting investment expenses from the investment earnings. One cannot consider one year's interest only, for a policy taken out in 1950 may well be in force in the year 2000. The final results of dividends on a participating policy or the profit or loss to the company on a non-participating policy issued in 1950 may depend to a large extent on the interest earnings over the following half century.

Under a participating plan the rate of interest used in computing the premiums will generally be that on which the policy-reserves and the guaranteed cash surrender values are to be based. The lower the rate of interest used in calculating a net premium, the higher will be the premium. It follows that where policy-reserves are based on 2½ per cent interest the premiums, and, as a rule the cash surrender values, will be higher than where the policy-reserves are based on 3 per cent interest. In both sets of premiums the net premiums so calculated will have to be increased to cover expenses and taxation. This explains why, in the same company, there may be a series of high premium policies with high cash values and another series of lower premium policies with lower cash values; different scales of policy-reserves would apply to them.

Under non-participating plans the estimated rate of interest expected to be earned in the years following issue, will determine the rate of interest to be used in their calculation. The actuary has the option of using a rate of interest quite close to what he anticipates will be earned and adding a margin for contingencies, or he can use a lower rate of interest than this, which automatically creates a margin for adverse fluctuations.

CALCULATION OF GROSS PREMIUMS: EXPENSES

Again we note that under a participating plan the actual loading for expenses can be an arbitrary amount but there is some advantage in having it follow the pattern of the actual expenses incurred so that the gross premiums of the numerous plans sold by a company will appear realistic when compared with each other. In determining dividends payable under these various plans, the actual expenses are taken into account. One system of loading for expenses used for many years in Canada for participating plans was 15 per cent of the net premium plus 15 per cent of the corresponding straight life net premium. If the net premium was loaded only with a constant percentage of the net premium, e.g. 20 per cent, it would represent so much more on a short-term endowment than, say, on a straight life that it would be unrealistic, for expenses are not proportionate to the net premiums. By taking part of the loading as a constant percentage and part as an amount which is the same under all plans for the same age at entry, a more realistic loading is obtained.

We show below (Table 17.1) how gross participating premium rates can be obtained from the net level premium if the policy-reserve basis is the CM(5) 3% Table. We take the three main plans for age 35 at entry. The net level annual premiums were given in Table 5.1. The sum insured is $1,000.

TABLE 17.1

	Straight life	20 year endowment ins.	30 year endowment ins.
Net level premium	$17.88	$39.44	$25.08
Add 15%	2.68	5.92	3.76
Add 15% straight life	2.68	2.68	2.68
Gross premium	$23.24	$48.04	$31.52
Average 5 companies	$20.84	$46.87	$30.86

We show in Table 17.1, for comparison purposes, the average participating gross premium rate being charged in 1976 in Canada for a $10,000 policy based on the rates of five of the largest Canadian companies; for a $25,000 policy the gross rates would be lower owing to the grading of premiums by size of sum insured. In Chapter 15 we indicated that the trend of participating premium rates in Canada has been downwards and this is in spite of increased unit expenses to which we have referred. Mortality has declined in recent years, but the companies could have continued to use the same participating rates and relied on the dividends to adjust the cost to the policyholder. The average rates quoted were those where the cash values and hence policy-reserves were on a 3 per cent basis.

For non-participating plans an arbitrary loading is not possible and the actuary has to assess the expense as accurately as he can. He must distinguish between the incidence of the various expenses as to whether they are first-year, second-year, and so on. Also he must decide whether they can most accurately be expressed as a percentage of the premium, a charge per thousand of the sum insured or a cost per policy irrespective of size. What a company spends is only too obvious from its accounts, but the analysis of these expenses into a system for loading its premiums is quite difficult and in spite of its importance, or perhaps because of it, there is no uniform practice among actuaries.

The subdivision into first-year expenses and expenses in other years presents the first difficulty. Should all the expenses of procuring new business be considered a first-year expense and recouped from the new entrants? Or, as new business is essential to the continuity of the company should it be considered as a general charge on the whole business and be paid by all policyholders. Life insurance only became a powerful influence for family protection, retirement pensions, and long-term saving when the companies decided to make its selling a whole-time occupation and commuted a level yearly commission into a higher first year's commission with a much smaller commission payable thereafter for a limited period.

To decide on the expenses for regular ordinary business one has to segregate the expenses due to group insurance and group annuities which are so different to regular business. Of course, if the company does health and accident business on either a group basis or on individual lives these expenses must be separated from the rest. There are also the expenses relating to total disability and double indemnity business.

Some expenses depend on the policy itself and the same cost is incurred whether it is a $1,000, $10,000, or $100,000 policy. Equity between policies of different amounts is maintained by the "graded premium" plan which was discussed in Chapter 11.

ANALYSIS OF EXPENSES

Canadian actuaries have been pioneers in the investigation of life insurance company expenses. The Canadian Institute of Actuaries has a committee on expenses which each year has gathered details of their expenses from a number of Canadian life insurance companies. The figures indicate that unit insurance costs have been increasing almost year by year from 1952 to the latest year for which figures are available. This is in spite of an increase in average policy and premium. In this section some indication of the results of this work is given.[1] Where figures are given it is important to note that they vary considerably between one company and another.

TABLE 17.2

	First year expenses	Expenses after first year
Per policy	$88.00	$7.70
Per $1,000 sum insured	5.60	0.60
Percentage of premium	100%	7½%

A company might, for example, adopt an expense formula such as that given in Table 17.2. These amounts would be intended to include overhead, agents' commissions, overridings, premium taxes, costs involved in claims settlements, servicing of policy loans and surrenders; in fact, every charge and cost of a regular insurance policy in an ordinary insurance company apart from the expenses inherent in investing its funds.

As an example, we apply the expense formula to a $15,000 policy, with an annual premium of $309.00. This gives Table 17.3.

TABLE 17.3

	First year	After first year
Per policy	$ 88.00	$ 7.70
Sum insured	$ 84.00	$ 9.00
Premium	$309.00	$23.17
Total expenses	$481.00	$39.87

It will be noted that the first year cost is about twelve times the renewal cost. A ratio of ten to one has been used as a rough guide for

[1]Details are given in the proceedings of the Canadian Institute of Actuaries. For an account of the work reference may be made to two papers by the author in *Transactions*, Society of Actuaries, vol. IV (1952), and vol. XIII (1961).

many years; although costs have risen sharply in recent years because of inflation, the use of computers has helped control the annual costs of administration. They have had little effect on new business costs; this may explain in part the higher ratio now apparent.

ASSET SHARES

We referred to asset shares in Chapter 15 in connection with the contribution to surplus of individual policies. When we accumulate the gross premium deloaded for actual expenses, year by year, at a rate of interest corresponding to that actually earned and deduct the claims according to the mortality being experienced, the resulting fund per thousand sum insured is called the *asset share*. Many questions such as (*a*) what is the cost of new business; (*b*) what cash surrender value can be paid and when; (*c*) what dividends can be paid under a participating policy and when can they be paid; (*d*) what is the profit or loss on a non-participating policy; and many others can only be decided by working out the asset shares.

ILLUSTRATION OF CALCULATION OF ASSET SHARES

Let us work out the asset shares for the first five years on a straight life policy, age 35 at entry, and to keep the calculations as simple as possible let us ignore the effect of lapses and surrenders. Let us assume:

1. The annual premium is $309 and the sum insured $15,000;
2. The expenses are those indicated in the previous section;
3. Rate of interest is 6 per cent per annum;
4. The mortality being experienced is that of the CA 58–64 Select Table (Table 8.1).

Then (*a*) the gross premium of $309 when deloaded for expenses will give an expenditure of $172.00 above receipts in the first year and a receipt above expenses of $269.13 in all the following years.

(*b*) The number of deaths per 1,000 lives exposed for each of the first five years for age 35 at entry will be:

Year 1	Year 2	Year 3	Year 4	Year 5
.831	.976	1.154	1.358	1.590

Assuming the entry of a unit of 1,000 lives at age 35, the number of deaths in the first year will be .831 so that the survivors entering the second policy year will be 999.169. We could, by taking a larger number of entrants, eliminate the decimals but there is no point in doing so; we are dealing with units only. These 999.169 lives are subject to a mortality of .976 per thousand in the second policy year so that the number of deaths in that year is .975, so that the survivors entering the third policy year number 998.194, and so on. As on each death we have to pay $15,000, the amount of claims paid in the first year is $12,465, in the second year $14,625, and so on. Table 17.4 should present no difficulty with this explanation. Note that the rate of interest is 6 per cent per annum.

TABLE 17.4

Asset Shares
Straight Life Plan, Number of Entrants 1,000
Mortality CA 58–64, Age 35 at Entry
Deloaded Premium: 1st Year $–172.00, Renewals $269.13, Each Policy $15,000

Year	Number living beginning of year	Deloaded premiums received	Fund at beginning of year	One year's interest at 6%	Death claims paid	Fund at end of year
		$	$	$	$	$
1	1,000	–172,000	–172,000	–10,320	–12,465	–194,785
2	999.169	268,906	74,121	4,447	–14,625	63,943
3	998.194	268,644	332,587	19,955	–17,280	335,262
4	997.042	268,334	603,596	36,216	–20,310	619,502
5	995.688	267,970	887,472	53,248	–23,745	916,975
6	994.105					

If we divide the Fund at the end of the year by the number of survivors at that time we get the asset shares corresponding to the $15,000 sum insured and dividing this by 15 the asset shares per $1,000 sum insured. These are given in Table 17.5 with the corresponding CM(5) 3 per cent terminal policy-reserves, specimens of which were given in Table 7.5.

ASSET SHARE VERSUS POLICY-RESERVE

According to Table 17.5 the asset share of the straight life participating plan at the end of the fifth policy year is less than the net level premium policy-reserve. It should be noted that we are taking the extreme case where the whole of the first year's expenditures are charged against the first year's premium. On such a basis there is no contribution to surplus, no profit earned, and hence no dividend could be paid until the policy had been over five years in force.

In fact, companies for which these asset shares might be regarded as typical pay dividends beginning either at the end of the first, or of the

TABLE 17.5

Comparison: Asset Shares with Policy-Reserves, Straight Life Plan, Age 35 at Entry, per $1,000 Sum Insured

End of year	Asset share	Terminal policy-reserves CM(5) 3%	
		Net level premium	Canadian modified
	$	$	$
1	−13.00	14.04	Nil
2	4.27	28.44	14.60
3	22.42	43.19	29.56
4	41.48	58.29	44.88
5	61.49	73.73	60.54

second, policy year. This indicates that, for purposes of determining dividends, they spread part of the first year cost which, as has already been mentioned, is a justifiable procedure, because the foundation of level premium life insurance is the distribution of risk over the duration of the policy (see Chapter 15).

NEW BUSINESS STRAIN

Note that the asset share per $1,000 sum insured at the end of the first year is −$13.00, i.e., the company has spent $13.00 more than it received. Further, as it would have to put up a policy-reserve of $14.04 on the CM(5) 3% net level premium basis if its policy-reserves were on this basis, the *new business strain* at the end of the first year is $27.04 per thousand sum insured. For a company doing $10,000,000 of new business each year on the straight life plan it would represent a strain of $270,400 a year on that business.

LAPSATION: PROFIT OR LOSS?

One occasionally hears the criticism that life insurance companies make large profits on the lapsation of policies, i.e., policies which are forfeited due to non-payment of premiums in the early policy years. Table 17.5 indicates that on the basis noted in calculating the asset shares there is a loss to the company of $13.00 per thousand sum insured on each straight life policy which lapses at the end of the first year. The $13.00 loss is only an example; with some companies the loss is much greater.

If the company calculates its policy-reserves on the CM(5) 3% net level premium basis it would have to set up $14.04 at the end of the year as policy-reserve on this policy which would have to be drawn from the surplus earned on other policies. When the second year's premium remained unpaid and the policy lapsed this $14.04 would be returned to the general surplus from which it was taken; it is a book-keeping entry and not a profit.

Cash Surrender Profits or Losses? The same point arises when the cash value of a policy is paid out on surrender. Competition will tend to make cash values as large as possible and rarely will they be less than the asset share discloses. Companies will, with reason, seek to minimize the losses involved in cash surrenders and keep the surrender values as close to the asset shares as possible. Again, when the policy-reserve exceeds the surrender value it does not necessarily mean that a profit to the company is involved on surrender as the policy-reserve may exceed the asset share which is the amount to be considered.

From Table 17.5 it should be noted that as we are dealing with participating policies and in most cases dividends will have been allotted from the end of the second year onwards and in some cases at the end of the first year, the asset shares there given will be reduced by such dividends as they are paid.

Modified Policy-Reserves

It would be expected that this question of new business strain would receive particular attention in a new life insurance company. Also when a country is expanding rapidly, much new business is written and the new business strain might mean that dividends to policyholders would have to be cut drastically or surplus severely reduced in order to put up the net level premium policy-reserves required.

A partial solution to the problem was found by permitting companies, at their option, to set up policy-reserves on a reduced basis which gives particularly low policy-reserves at the end of the first year, provided this reduction was made up over the life of the policy or over the premium-paying period. We earlier demonstrated (Chapter 7) the following and it follows from first principles:

At any time in the history of a policy,

The Policy-Reserve = Value of the Benefits
− Value of the Future Net Premiums.

If we assume that we will be getting a higher net premium after the first year we increase the value of the deduction in this equation and so reduce the policy-reserve. Such policy-reserves with an increased net premium after the first year are called *modified reserves* or *modified policy-reserves*. The above equation holds whether the policy-reserves are on the net level premium basis or on a modified policy-reserve basis. In the one, the net valuation premium is the same throughout the premium paying period. In the other there are two valuation net premiums, one applying to the first policy year, the other to the remainder of the premium paying period.

The whole point of the use of modified policy-reserves is that the amount of policy-reserves required to be set up by a life insurance company is determined by law. How far should legislation go in reducing the net level premium policy-reserve basis to assist a company in reducing the new business strain due to the payment of a higher commission in the first year and other new business expenses? From one point of view it could be said that the effect could well be to encourage excessive expenditures.

There is a tradition in Canada in favour of net level premium policy-reserves and against the modified policy-reserves. Many companies prefer to set up net level premium policy-reserves at the outset and avoid having to make up the deficiency over the lifetime of the policy. However, a viewpoint may be expressed that it might be advisable in many circumstances to keep the policy-reserves somewhat lower if thereby the free surplus available for contingencies is increased. A reduced new business strain in times of expansion would be beneficial not only to the company but also to the policyholders.

We outline briefly the modified policy-reserve bases in use in Canada and the U.S.A.; it should be noted that at the time of writing (1976) it was expected that some change would be made in the Canadian system within the next year or two.

FULL PRELIMINARY TERM

Consider the straight life plan at age 35 at entry and after the first year assume the net premium to be received will be as for age 36 at entry. At the end of the first policy year, i.e., at age 36 attained, the policy-reserve would be zero for if the life were entering at that age the value of the benefit and the value of the future net premiums would be the same; this is what the valuation net premium means.

The actual figures on the CM(5) 3% basis are as follows: the valuation net premiums would be $17.88 for age 35 and $18.55 for age 36 at entry, so that by assuming a net premium after the first year increased by 67 cents per $1,000 sum insured we obtain a set of policy-reserves for age 35 at entry which require no policy-reserve to be set up at the end of the first year. Thus the company could spend the whole of the first year's premium under the straight life plan, providing only for first-year claims, without incurring any new business strain. In Table 17.5 we show these modified policy-reserves on the straight life plan at age 35 at entry compared with the level net premium policy-reserves.

Where, under any system of modified policy-reserves, it is assumed that the full first year's premium is absorbed by expenses and first year claims, so that the policy-reserve is zero at the end of the first policy year, the basis of policy-reserves is called the *full preliminary term*. The first year is thus treated as if it were a one-year term insurance, the actual plan being entered upon at the end of that year. This explains the name used.

Under a straight life plan where there is a possibility of the policy being in force for 50 years or more, the assumption that initial costs absorb the first year's premium is not unreasonable, but this would hardly be the case, say, with a 10-year endowment insurance or a 10-pay life policy. This explains the limitations indicated by the Canadian and U.S. systems which follow.

MODIFIED POLICY-RESERVES: CANADA

In Canada the full preliminary term plan is permitted by law on the straight life plan, but no greater amount of allowance is permitted for higher premium plans. Thus the deficiency of policy-reserve permitted in the first year is the same for all plans with net premiums equal to or higher than the straight life: note this in Table 17.6. Also note that the $14 per thousand deficiency in policy-reserve has to be made up in the remaining 19 years of premium payments under both the 20-pay life and the 20-year endowment insurance plans.

According to Volume I of the latest reports of the Superintendent of Insurance for Canada, the largest Canadian companies almost without

TABLE 17.6

Policy-Reserves Comparison: Full Net Level Premium (N.L.P.) with Canadian Modified Preliminary Term Basis (Can. Mod.), Age 35 at Entry, $1,000 Sum Insured, CM(5) 3%

End of year	Straight life		20-pay. life		20-yr. end. ins.	
	N.L.P.	Can. Mod.	N.L.P.	Can. Mod.	N.L.P.	Can. Mod.
	$	$	$	$	$	$
1	14	0	22	8	36	22
2	28	15	46	32	74	60
3	43	30	70	57	112	100
4	58	45	94	82	152	140
5	74	61	119	107	193	182
10	156	144	256	247	419	410
15	245	234	412	407	683	679
20	339	330	590	590	1,000	1,000
30	530	523	709	709		

exception, compute their policy-reserves on the net level premium basis and hence make no use of this proviso permitting reduced policy-reserves.

MODIFIED POLICY-RESERVES: U.S.A.

After several years of negotiation the National Association of Insurance Commissioners of the various states in the U.S. were able to agree on the adoption by the various state legislatures of a uniform minimum basis for valuation of policy-reserves which became effective after December 31, 1947. This provided for a modified policy-reserve based on the full preliminary term basis so long as the premium is not greater than the 20-payment life plan; where the premium is greater the allowance is restricted to that which is given under the 20-payment life plan.

As in Canada, the leading and old established companies do not avail themselves of the permitted modified policy-reserve basis, but set up their policy-reserves on the net level premium basis.

Cash Surrender and Non-Forfeiture Values

Originally a life policy was a contract under which the insurance company agreed to pay a certain sum on death if the insured paid a definite premium on a certain date each year. If the policyholder omitted to pay the premium on the due date the policy and all premiums paid under it were forfeited. It has been stated that in the early history of life insurance large profits were made by the companies on these forfeitures. It is to the credit of Canadian life insurance that, from the very first, Canadian life insurance company policies provided for a paid-up policy on the lapsing of a policy due to non-payment of a premium. This provision against forfeiting the value of a policy due to non-payment of a premium is referred to as the *non-forfeiture benefit* and is quite important in the development of life insurance. There are four forms of non-forfeiture benefits:

1. The payment of a *cash surrender value*;
2. The conversion of the policy to a paid-up policy for a reduced amount called *reduced paid-up policy*;
3. *Extended term insurance.* The continuation of the policy as term insurance for a definite period for the face amount of the policy. Should the policy be an endowment insurance the term insurance may extend to the maturity date of the endowment when the balance of value, if any, would be paid in cash.
4. *Automatic premium loan.*

As we indicated in Chapter 16, the Uniform Life Insurance Act of the Canadian provinces (Section 148) provides for a period of grace for payment of premiums and the conditions upon which it may be reinstated, if lapsed (Section 155). It also provides that every policy must give the particulars of any options existing for surrendering the policy for cash, taking a policy loan or reduced paid-up or extended term insurance (Section 141). It is important to note that although there is no requirement of payment of such values or the amounts which should be paid, all companies in Canada do grant such values in their life insurance policies excepting for term insurances, particularly short term insurances, where it would not be practical to do so.

In the development of non-forfeiture benefits certain states in the U.S. have been pioneers. In 1861 the State of Massachusetts passed a non-forfeiture law to the effect that a life insurance company must grant extended term insurance when the premium was not paid and established a basis for the calculation of the benefit. In 1880 the Massachusetts legislature passed a law requiring that cash surrender values be guaranteed by the terms of the policy; a law which through imitation by other states and the force of competition led, by the end of the century, to the inclusion of such clauses in most life insurance policies.

During the quarter century preceding the Armstrong-Hughes Investigation of 1905, non-forfeiture laws became general throughout the U.S. Tables of guaranteed cash surrender values and reduced paid-up and extended insurance values appeared in policies. To this period belongs the development of an automatic non-forfeiture benefit which went into effect immediately the premium remained unpaid beyond the days of grace, if no choice had been made by the policyholder. To this period also belongs the practice of granting the full policy-reserve as a guaranteed cash surrender value after a definite period—generally 20 years. These developments which relate to U.S. life insurance made their impression on Canadian practice.

U.S. STANDARD NON-FORFEITURE LAWS

Following the Armstrong-Hughes Investigation of 1905 these non-forfeiture benefits became written into the law and the efforts of the Insurance Commissioners of the various states toward uniformity led, by 1948, to the almost universal adoption by the states in the U.S. of a series of Standard Non-Forfeiture Laws. There are no such laws in Canada, although as already stated Canadian life insurance companies grant similar privileges to their policyholders. The Standard Non-forfeiture Laws require:

1. That cash surrender and paid-up values and extended term insurance periods be shown in the policy;
2. That the policy include a description of the actuarial basis on which its cash surrender values and non-forfeiture values are calculated;
3. That cash values must not be less than those produced by a certain procedure derived independently of the policy-reserve;
4. That paid-up values and extended term insurance periods be given when a cash value is indicated by the formula.

A *delay clause* is permitted by these laws, enabling a company to defer payments in respect of a cash surrender value or loan value for a period of six months. This does not apply to any death benefits. This clause was introduced in the U.S. in 1934 due to the "bank holiday" which occurred there; the purpose is to prevent demands for cash from life insurance companies which could not possibly be met as a result of a "panic."

Note that items 1 to 4 are minimum requirements; the policies of most companies are more generous in their provisions. This is also the case in Canada. There will be further references to the above items in this chapter.

CASH SURRENDER VALUES: THE PRINCIPLE

The return of a cash amount on the surrender of a life insurance policy, under certain circumstances, was envisaged in the earliest policies issued in Canada and the records of the Canada Life indicate that almost from the very beginning cash surrender values were granted after five years' premiums were paid. The records of 1854 infer the deduction of one-third of the policy-reserve before paying a cash surrender value "to cover the loss through the withdrawal of sound lives." It can be understood that people would not give up their life insurance when they were seriously ill, but it has never been proved that those who surrender their policies have a lower mortality, that is, are sounder lives than those who continue. In fact, as will be mentioned later, there is much support for the view that surrenders are entirely economic in origin and that mortality is not of the best when economic pressures exist. However, in Canada and the U.S. the principle of granting the full policy-reserve after a certain period such as 15 to 20 years has been in existence for many years.

The right of the policyholder to surrender his policy and to request the guaranteed cash surrender value treats the cash surrender value as a bank deposit payable on demand. As stated above under "Delay Clause," U.S. companies are safeguarded against the danger of abnormal demands for cash surrender values in times of crisis. It is most unlikely that this will occur in Canada or in the U.S. with their present banking systems. The enormous expansion of group pension business in recent years, which business would not present the same cash withdrawal hazards as individual policies and representing very large funds, has reduced this danger. However, the fact that the cash surrender value and the loan value based on it represent "cash on demand" should be considered in the increasing liberality in this regard engendered by competition among companies.

There is a further point when cash surrender values, based on the policy-reserves, are guaranteed in policies. It means that on no account can the company change its policy-reserve basis to give lower values for these policies. During a period of gradually increasing interest rates the company faces a depreciation in the value of its bonds which depreciation has to be made up out of existing surplus and current earnings which means reduced dividends to policyholders. As interest earnings reach a definitely higher level the company could assume higher interest earnings in the future, in other words, lower policy-reserves would be justified. However, the company is tied to the policy-reserves on existing business, for it has guaranteed the cash surrender values on these policies, based on those policy-reserves and the former equals the latter very often after 15 to 20 years, as has been stated.

In the United Kingdom most of the life insurance companies decline to guarantee cash surrender values in their policies and where they do guarantee them they are generally on a definitely lower basis than the policy-reserves. The reasons for this are clear. The companies thus have greater flexibility in meeting changing conditions.

In Canada we accept the guaranteed cash surrender values in life insurance policies as fundamental, a benefit only second to that of the sum insured under the policy, and any disadvantages of granting them we consider as a hazard of the business the companies must accept.

CASH SURRENDER VALUES: THE AMOUNT

The amounts of the policy-reserves and free surplus represent the funds in the hands of the company. What relation should hold between these and the guaranteed cash surrender values in the policies? First of all we would exclude the "free surplus" which is required for the effective continuance of the company as a going concern and should not be reduced by payments to a withdrawing policyholder who may possibly weaken the company by his withdrawal due to the essentially co-operative nature of life insurance.

Further, it will be agreed that no policyholder has a greater claim on the company's funds than the amount of his contribution to those funds after allowing for the costs of the services rendered to him. The debatable point as to the allocation of the higher first year costs has been referred to on several occasions. When this has been decided upon the resulting adjusted asset shares indicate the relationship between the actual contribution of the policyholder and the policy-reserve held by the company. Under participating plans the dividends paid year by year have also to be taken into account.

Prior to the introduction of the 1948 Standard Non-Forfeiture Law in the U.S. a common provision required by state laws for minimum guaranteed cash surrender values was that on permanent plans of life insurance a cash value had to be granted at the end of the third policy year and the deductions from the legal policy-reserve held by the company could not exceed $25 per thousand sum insured. Thus the minimum cash surrender values were the policy-reserve per thousand at the end of the third year less $25, the deduction reducing year by year until the full policy-reserve was given at the end of the twentieth policy year. This was similar to the practice adopted by Canadian companies.

The trend both in Canada and the U.S. has been to increasing liberality. Some Canadian companies now grant guaranteed cash surrender values at the end of the first policy year on certain policies and guaranteed values at the end of the second policy year are quite usual. Also the full net level premium policy-reserve is granted by some companies at the end of the fifteenth policy year or at the end of the premium paying period if less than fifteen years.

With non-participating policies some companies may decide to offer a gross premium at the lowest possible figure irrespective of the cash surrender value such a rate would justify. In such a case it would be expected that the asset shares on which cash surrender values would be based would be substantially lower than for the corresponding participating plans in the same company. This is also the reason for companies setting up lower policy-reserves on such plans, but, of course, not less than federal Canadian law will permit. (For the minimum policy-reserve basis see the last section of this chapter.)

Basing the guaranteed cash surrender value on the policy-reserve as was required by law in the U.S. has this disadvantage. When during the 1940's rates of interest declined to a low figure, the companies sought to strengthen their position by increasing their policy-reserves. However, according to the laws then in force in the U.S. an increase in policy-reserve meant an increase in guaranteed cash surrender values and the other non-forfeiture benefits which did not give the flexibility being sought.

The 1948 Standard Non-Forfeiture Law made an effort to separate the minimum legal guaranteed cash surrender basis from that relating to policy-reserves as indicated by the Standard Valuation Law promulgated at the same time. It was done by defining a special type of modified policy-reserve to be used as the basis for surrender values only. Unfortunately U.S. laws require that the basis be set out in the policy with the result that a clause which must be incomprehensible to all but a very few policyholders disfigures the policy.[2] This point is mentioned to justify the Canadian attitude which does not approve such rigidity in life

[2]In the well-known text, Maclean's *Life Insurance* (9th ed., New York 1962) it is stated that the description of the method of calculating cash values "involves the introduction into the policy of technical language which the majority of policyholders will not understand." This is a delightful understatement. It could also be applied to the majority of the head office staffs of the companies issuing the policies! Some states appreciate this by waiving this requirement.

insurance supervisory practices. Canadian life insurance companies doing business in the U.S.A. have to conform to the local laws with regard to their business in that country.

REDUCED PAID-UP POLICY

Where the cash surrender value is applied in exchange for a paid-up policy, payable at the same time and in the same manner as the original policy, the sum insured is of course reduced and the amount of the new benefit is referred to as the *reduced paid-up policy.* As the cash surrender value of any paid-up policy (excepting term insurance) increases with duration, one advantage of this benefit is that the cash value is preserved and increases with time. Where the plan of the original policy contains a high investment element, this non-forfeiture benefit can be of considerable value. In the U.S. and with some companies in Canada these reduced paid-up policies when granted on participating policies still continue to participate in profits.

From the company's point of view the great objection to the reduced paid-up policy as an automatic non-forfeiture benefit, i.e., which goes into operation immediately a premium remains unpaid, is that it would encumber the books of the company with a large number of very small policies. These are burdensome from an expense point of view, particularly with recent inflation of costs; this explains why some companies do not allow dividends on such reduced paid-up policies when arising from participating policies.

With endowment insurances and limited payment life plans the amount of the reduced paid-up policy is roughly proportionate to the number of premiums paid. Thus on a 20-year endowment insurance, after five years the reduced paid-up policy would be roughly one-quarter of the sum insured, i.e., $250 per $1,000 policy.

EXTENDED TERM INSURANCE

When at any point of time the net cash surrender value under a life insurance policy is applied as a net single premium to purchase paid-up term insurance for an amount equal to the sum insured at that time, the resulting insurance is called *extended term insurance.* Note that the resulting protection is that of a paid-up term policy and as such the equivalent policy-reserve decreases with duration until at the moment of expiry it is zero (an exception is that, when applied to an endowment policy, the *extended term* may be long enough to run to the maturity date of the endowment; in that case, the remaining value would be paid on that date).

The extended term insurance is invariably non-participating partly to save costs and partly to make the period of the extended term insurance as long as possible. The extended term insurance benefit has a special significance in the U.S.A., as with most U.S. life insurance companies the extended term insurance goes into effect automatically when a premium has not been paid during the days of grace. In other words, it is the *automatic non-forfeiture benefit* under the policy.

Most Canadian life insurance policies contain guaranteed extended term insurance values available as an option on application by the policyholder, but the option is not often exercised and some companies have withdrawn it from their policies. We give an example of the values granted by one prominent Canadian company: under a straight life plan, participating, age 35 at entry, the period of the extended term insurance is 3 years 360 days at the end of the third policy year; 8 years 31 days at the end of the fifth policy year; 14 years 58 days at the end of the tenth policy year, and so on. Canadian life insurance companies generally use the *automatic premium loan benefit* as the automatic non-forfeiture benefit; this will be referred to later.

Thus the essential difference between the extended term insurance in a U.S. company's life insurance policy and that of a Canadian company is that in the former it is automatic whereas with a Canadian company's policy it has to be specially elected by the policyholder. It is generally acknowledged that the mortality under the extended term insurance benefit with U.S. companies is higher than under continuing policies, thus indicating that policyholders who do not pay their premiums are not as good risks as those who pay them regularly. It would be expected that when a policyholder deliberately chooses to convert his policy into a paid-up term insurance he is selecting against the company and the resulting mortality would be substantially higher than normal.

It is essential to eliminate all indebtedness under a policy when it is converted to extended term insurance, for the policy-reserve of a paid-up term insurance decreases with duration, and it is impracticable to carry a fixed debt against a policy which decreases in value. If the policyholder did not pay his interest there would be an increasing debt with a decreasing policy-reserve. An alternative to the repayment of the indebtedness in cash is to reduce the amount of the term insurance by the amount of indebtedness and to recalculate the period of the term insurance based on the cash value less the indebtedness.

DISADVANTAGES OF EXTENDED TERM INSURANCE

The disadvantages of the extended insurance benefit when used as an automatic non-forfeiture benefit are:

1. The nature of the policy is changed to term insurance from whatever plan it may have been. Hence the policy can only be restored to its original plan with evidence of good health and insurability. If the non-payment of the premium was accidental and the policy has been in force some years this may prove a hardship.
2. All additional benefits such as those of total disability and double indemnity accident are terminated when the policy is continued under the extended insurance benefit. This is necessary as the extended term insurance benefit is determined by the basic policy and no further premium payments can be expected to cover additional benefits.
3. Any additional benefits contained in the policy, such as term riders, family benefits, and guaranteed insurability benefits, must all be terminated.

An interesting development by some U.S. companies seeking to avoid the disadvantages stated in disadvantage (2) should the non-payment of the premium be due to temporary or accidental circumstances is to use an automatic premium loan for the first or the first two unpaid premiums after which any balance of cash value would be applied as an automatic extended term benefit.

AUTOMATIC PREMIUM LOAN

Canadian life insurance companies as a class utilize the automatic premium loan benefit as the automatic non-forfeiture privilege when premiums remain unpaid at the end of the days of grace.[3] The unpaid premium or such part of it as is covered by the cash surrender value of the policy is paid by the company as a loan against the policy and the policy is continued in force until the next premium due date or for whatever period has been covered by the premium loan. Where cash surrender values are payable only after three years' premiums have been paid some companies grant a special value at the end of the second policy year in order to make the privilege effective as early as possible.

An important point is that the policy is continued in force without change or cancellation of any benefits. Further the unpaid premiums or

[3]This procedure originated in Australia and was used by the Sun Life in 1894 but not adopted for its Canadian policies until 1900. It is now the general practice for all Canadian companies.

any part of them may be paid at any time while the policy is continued in force with no need of evidence of good health or other proof of insurability. Further, in the early years of a policy the cash surrender value increases rapidly with the number of premiums paid and the payment of the premium by loan thus enables a higher cash surrender value to be used for the automatic premium loan benefit when the following premium falls due.

Undoubtedly when a premium is not paid, due to accidental circumstances or oversight, the automatic premium loan has considerable advantages over the extended term insurance privilege. However, generally speaking, the period by which the policy can be continued in force is greater under the extended insurance privilege than under the automatic premium loan. This is the justification of extended insurance as an automatic non-forfeiture benefit: as a rule it gives the maximum cover for the longest period possible, provided that, in moving to extended insurance, there is no deletion or termination of term insurance riders or similar benefits.

POLICY LOANS

All ordinary life insurance policies issued in Canada contain a privilege enabling the policyholder to borrow from the life insurance company on the security of the policy an amount within the guaranteed cash surrender value of the policy. For many years the maximum rate of interest charged was 6 per cent per annum and this was stated as a policy provision; for a period of low interest earnings the Canadian companies reduced the rate charged to 5 per cent per annum. However, in the later 1960s the high rates of interest current in Canada led most companies to omit mention of a guaranteed maximum rate of interest to apply on policy loans which enables them to follow market trends in interest charges if they wish to do so. This, of course, would not affect older policies containing a maximum guaranteed rate provision. It is the practice to specify a maximum rate in the loan agreement form, prepared at the time loan is made, if no maximum is stated in the policy. The rate actually charged is generally less than the maximum; in 1976, rates of 8 to 9 per cent were commonly charged, while maximum rates were sometimes 10 per cent or higher.

Most states in the U.S. have laws specifically limiting the rate of interest to be charged on policy loans. The U.S. Standard Non-Forfeiture Law (1948) referred to previously, obliges life insurance companies operating in the U.S. to place a *delay clause* in their policies regarding policy loans similar to that mentioned above in connection with cash surrender values. It has never been invoked since its introduction in 1948 and it is extremely unlikely it ever will be. There are no such laws or regulations in Canada as have been referred to in this paragraph.

The advantages to a policyholder of borrowing from the life insurance company issuing the policy are the privacy and lack of formality. The production of the policy and the signing of a form are all that is necessary. It is doubtful if any security exists on which a loan can be obtained with less formality than on a life insurance policy. In fact, it is this very simplicity which can be a source of danger for a policy loan is often the first step to the termination of the policy. This explains why, although even in times when interest rates are low and policy loans represent a remunerative investment, the life insurance companies discourage policy loans. Life insurance represents the only long-term savings of the great majority of people. Thus a policy loan, so easy to obtain, indicates the economic pressure which generally results in the termination of the policy. All companies will accept repayment of a policy loan in small monthly instalments and they give every facility for doing so in spite of the expense involved.

Banks and Policy Loans. The banks compete with the life insurance companies in granting loans on the security of life insurance policies and the quotation of cash values to the banks, even when such are given in the policies, involves the life insurance companies in considerable expense. U.S. life insurance companies may charge a lower interest rate on policy loans than Canadian companies, but interest rates have always been lower in the U.S. than in Canada. Canadian companies doing business in the U.S. follow local conditions in this regard, as would be expected.

As the granting of policy loans on life insurance policies is a benefit guaranteed in the policies and a company has no right to refuse a policy loan however small the amount may be, the average policy loan is quite small. Thus the cost of handling such loans is disproportionately heavy considering the computation of the amount of loan available, its recording, the mailing of interest notices, and the acceptance of any amount at any time in repayment, and the accounting of these amounts. Actual figures of the extent of the policy loans with Canadian life insurance companies will be given in Chapter 29.

A Criticism and a Fallacy. The question is sometimes asked, "Why should I pay interest on a policy loan on my own policy? Is it not borrowing my own money?"

As was shown in Chapter 7 the life insurance company must earn a certain rate of interest at which to accumulate the level net premium and the policy-reserve, otherwise it would not be able to meet the claims as they fall due. Also in the calculation of the premium it is assumed that a definite rate of interest will be earned. Thus a policy loan must be treated as any other investment and produce interest earnings. Also to preserve equity between policyholders who take policy loans and those who do not, the company should charge as much interest on policy loans as it can obtain on other investments, subject, of course, to any maximum rate stated in the policy and allowing for the different rates of expense associated with different types of investment.

MINIMUM GOVERNMENT POLICY-RESERVE REQUIREMENTS

This is a suitable point at which to indicate the minimum standards of policy-reserves required by law in Canada and the United States to be set up by life insurance companies. We deal here with Ordinary business only; Industrial business is covered in Chapter 31. There were, at the time of writing, no minimum standards imposed by law in Britain, but steps were being taken to establish a minimum reserve requirement.

Canadian Policy-Reserve Standards. We here refer to federally registered companies only, as they stand in mid-1976; as mentioned earlier, changes are expected. The requirements are set out in the Third Schedule of the Canadian and British Insurance Companies Act. A net premium valuation is required as has been demonstrated in Chapter 7. For life insurance plans the net rate of interest used may not exceed $3^1/_2$ per cent per annum. Eight tables of mortality of insured lives are named as the mortality basis, but any other table approved by the Superintendent is acceptable. Those tables named are those on which extensive tables of premiums and values have been published. We have already outlined in this chapter the modification of the net level premium policy-reserve which is permitted. In volumes I and III of the Superintendent's Reports, details are given of the bases used by the companies; the volume of business and policy-reserve are shown for each basis.

For life annuities, individual or deferred, or those arising out of settlement options, four annuity tables are named but others may be used subject to the Superintendent's approval. The rate of interest used in computing the annuity policy-reserves may not exceed 4 per cent per annum.

In March 1965 a change was made in the Canadian federal insurance laws regarding the maximum rates of interest which may be used in the valuation of policies as stated above: life insurance $3^1/_2$ per cent, life annuities 4 per cent. The Superintendent of Insurance is authorized to permit such higher rate of interest for a particular class of policies issued by any company on receipt of evidence satisfactory to him that the higher rate is appropriate. Such authority is generally sought for single premium annuities. Rates as high as 8 per cent are in use, but it is the practice of the Superintendent to require that such rates be assumed to continue only for, say, 15 years, after which more normal rates apply. The Superintendent may at any time withdraw such authorization.

U.S. Policy-Reserve Standards. We referred earlier in the chapter to the action of the Insurance Commissioners of the various states in the U.S. in deciding on a uniform minimum policy-reserve basis and the modification of the net level premium policy-reserve adopted. The maximum rate of interest allowed for the calculation was $3^1/_2$ per cent, but 4 per cent is now permitted in several states as a temporary measure applicable to policies issued up to 1986. The mortality basis adopted was the C.S.O. 1941 Table, replaced later by the C.S.O. 1958 Table, both of which are referred to in Chapter 21. For life annuities, the 1937 Standard Annuity Table was adopted as the minimum standard as referred to in Chapter 13. The a-1949 Table and the 1971 (IAM and IAF) tables have also been approved. Interest rates up to 6 per cent may be used for single premium annuities but only with the 1971 tables of mortality. When changes are made in policy-reserve bases they are usually confined to new policies issued after the adoption of the new basis for reasons given in Chapter 8.

CHAPTER EIGHTEEN

Taxation

The demand for increased taxes from every level of government appears insatiable in this modern age. The subject of taxation is therefore one of much importance.

One of the main causes of the considerable and increasing burden of taxation is the increasing responsibilities assumed by governments to meet demands for the support of the aged and widows and orphans. It would thus appear to be in the national interest to encourage in every way possible the voluntary action of people to provide for their dependants in the event of their death or their own old age. In the past this principle has been accepted by the Canadian federal government.

Apart from the provincial taxes on life insurance premiums, details of which follow, Canada, in the past, maintained a beneficent attitude to life insurance and annuities in taxation matters which set an example to other countries. We have repeatedly throughout this text stressed the important part the life insurance industry in Canada has played in fostering savings and the great social value their investments have been in the past and are in the present in developing the resources and industries of Canada. However, the demands of the tax gatherer changed the situation in 1969.

Carter Report and 1968 Budget. In 1962 the Royal Commission on Taxation was set up and, after four and a half years of labour and employing a staff of up to 150 researchers, it published early in 1967 six volumes of 2,600 pages with hundreds of detailed recommendations. Unfortunately a knowledge of life insurance theory and practice was not one of their strong points and the Commission's proposals relating to mortality gains, policy dividends, and allocation through to policyholders were unsound, unworkable, or both. The spirit and philosophy of the Commission (referred to as the *Carter Report*) are expressed in the following statement taken from the Report:

> If a man obtains increased command of goods and services for his personal satisfaction, we do not believe it matters from the point of view of taxation whether he earned it through working, gained it through operating a business, received it because he held property, made it by selling property, or was given it by a relative. . . . By adopting a base that measures in power, whether exercised or not, to consume goods and services, we obtain certainty, consistency, and equity.

This reads like the taxation plan of a crushing despotism or a back-room theorist, hardly appropriate to a people still largely in a pioneering stage of social and industrial development. However, in his October 22, 1968 Budget, the Minister of Finance announced a new tax system for life insurance as the first step in an overall reform of the tax system of Canada. The objective, he stated, was to remove "a considerable inequity in the treatment of insurance companies compared to other companies and in the treatment of the returns from investment in insurance policies as compared with other forms of savings." A Bill to enact the Budget proposals became law in June 1969.

Undoubtedly the United States *Life Insurance Company Income Tax Act* of 1959 had a major influence on the Carter Report and those responsible for the 1969 amendments to the Income Tax Act of Canada. One of the objectives in the U.S. act was stated to be to devise a formula reasonably acceptable to the life insurance industry in that country which would produce approximately $500 millions of revenue in 1958. In Canada the amount of additional revenue expected to be produced in 1969 from this new additional taxation and which was part of the Budget calculations was $95 millions. "Recognition of the social desirability of life insurance through preferential tax treatment . . . has accordingly been abandoned in Canada."[1]

In Britain companies are taxed on their investment earnings less expenses of operation. However, life insurance premiums, within certain limits, are deductible from income in the calculation of personal income tax. It was officially estimated in Britain that the cost of this tax relief exceeded the taxes paid by the companies so that the net result was a subsidy of the life insurance business by the government.[2]

Before dealing with the 1969 amendments we will outline the taxes levied on insurance companies by provincial authorities and certain federal taxes.

[1]Raymond L. Whalley, F.S.A., *The Taxation of Insurance in Canada, Transactions*, Society of Actuaries, 1970. Also: Discussion, *Transactions*, Society of Actuaries, Vol. 21, D263 April 1969; *Reports*, Canadian Institute of Actuaries, Nov. 1968.

[2]Submission to Royal Commission on Taxation, C.L.I.A., 1964.

Premium Taxes. Each province in Canada imposes on life insurance companies a premium tax payable on the life insurance premiums paid in the province less the dividends to policyholders. The tax was 2 per cent in all provinces, but in 1976 Ontario introduced an additional tax of 1 per cent applicable only to the *protection portion* of premiums on policies issued after April 1976. (As will be explained later under Registered Retirement Savings plans, premiums other than for term insurance may be divided into *protection* and *tax-deferred* portions.) In 1975 the revenue to the provinces was $26 millions. Only a trivial part of this is used to cover the cost of the supervision of the life insurance business by the provinces and in the provinces of Quebec and New Brunswick the cost of supervision is charged to the companies in addition to the premium tax.

It should be noted that in Canada annuity premiums are excluded from this premium taxation. This recognizes the very special nature of annuity premiums paid to life insurance companies as provision for old age or akin to deposits in a savings account. Further, by the deduction of dividends before the tax rate is applied to life insurance premiums, it is recognized that dividends are "refunds of over-payment of premiums" and not "profits."

A plea could be made that there is no more justification for taxing life insurance premiums than in placing a "sales tax" on bank deposits. However, this tax has been in existence for many years and the need by the provinces for sources of taxation is so urgent that there is little likelihood of its removal.

Apart from premium taxes the life insurance companies pay to the provinces licence fees for doing business in the province, fees for filing statements, and agents' licence fees. There are also corporation capital taxes in British Columbia and Manitoba.

Federal Taxes on Dividends to Shareholders. Until the 1969 amendments, the only federal corporation income tax levied on life insurance companies was that levied on stock companies and the taxable amount was the "profits" for the year which was assumed to be the amount transferred to the shareholders' account; this is the account from which shareholders' dividends are paid.

Expenses of Federal Government Supervision. The federally registered life insurance companies pay the cost of their supervision by the federal Department of Insurance at Ottawa.

1969 AMENDMENTS TO INCOME TAX ACT

The 1969 amendments to the Income Tax Act resulted in three major additional taxes:

1. *Tax on Excess of Proceeds over Cost.* This tax is paid by the individual policyholder as part of his personal income tax and is based on the gain, if any, realized on an individual policy or group certificate when it matures or is surrendered or terminated (but not on death). The amount to be included in taxable income is the excess, if any, of the amount due less the premiums paid since entry; dividends allotted are deducted from the premiums paid (unless applied to purchase additional insurance). The point here is that this amount is considered to represent the interest included in the amount withdrawn and all interest is considered taxable. To avoid making taxes retroactive, if the policy was in force on the budget date then any excess of value over premiums paid as of the policy anniversary between 23 October 1969 and 22 October 1970 is deductible.
2. *Tax on Investment Income of Company.* This tax is levied at the rate of 15 per cent on the taxable life investment income applicable to Canadian business. This taxable income is found by deducting from the gross Canadian life investment income certain amounts among which are: (i) investment expenses; (ii) interest paid such as on dividends and policy proceeds on deposit; (iii) investment income attributable to non-participating policies in force on 22 October, 1968. (For participating policies, it was considered that the company could recoup the tax by reducing dividends.); (iv) investment income attributable to policies under tax-sheltered arrangements, such as registered retirement savings plans and registered pension plans; (v) the company's corporate profit for the year; (vi) amounts paid to policyholders and taxable in their hands as described in section 1. It should be noted that the idea behind this tax is that, since the nature of the insurance business is such that it would be impossible to attribute investment income to individual policyholders and to tax them on it each year, the company pays tax on their behalf. Thus, when they pay direct, as on interest allotted or on profit on disposition of a policy, the income is not taxed in the hands of the company.

From the 15 per cent of taxable investment income there may be deducted (i) one-half of provincial premium tax paid (subject to an upper limit of 1 per cent of premiums); and (ii) a portion of the dividend income from shares to compensate for the dividend tax credit policyholders would pay if taxed directly.

3. *Tax on Company Operations.* Corporation tax (average, including provincial tax, approximately 52 per cent) is to be paid on the net "profit" or "surplus" from operations or whatever term one would apply to the income less outgo of the operations of a life insurance company as would be charged to any other corporation. The increase in policy-reserves and numerous other items are allowed as deductions to indicate the special nature of life insurance operations. However, only the "company share" of dividends received from taxable Canadian corporations can be deducted.

The above tax system applies only to the Canadian operations of the life insurance companies. The three taxes outlined are inter-related. Thus the final tax on investment income (item 2) is a deductible expense for the business income calculation (item 3); the business "profit" in item 3 is a deduction under item 2. Thus if the taxable gain or "profit" from operations before interaction is less than 15 per cent of the taxable investment income, item 3 cancels out and the total tax is 15 per cent of the taxable investment income. If the taxable "profit" from operations is greater than the taxable investment income before interaction, item 2 cancels out and the total tax is the corporate tax of, say, 52 per cent on the "profit" from operations. Working the process algebraically it can be shown that in the intermediate position where both 2 and 3 above are operative the total tax is approximately 44 per cent of "profit" from operations plus 8 per cent of taxable investment income.

TAXATION OF POLICY PROCEEDS

(*a*) In item 1 of the previous section we dealt with the amounts received by a policyholder when a policy is surrendered or matures (but not by death) and where the policy proceeds exceed the premiums paid.

(*b*) Amounts received or premiums waived under a disability income benefit are not taxable as income. (There is a provision in the Act for taxation of payments under a disability insurance plan to which an employer contributes but this does not apply to the normal ordinary or group *life* policy.)

(*c*) Under a settlement option of a life insurance policy where the sum insured or cash surrender value is left with the company at interest this interest when received by the policyholder or beneficiary is considered as income to them for income tax purposes.

(*d*) A double indemnity accident benefit would be treated as part of the sum insured for taxation purposes.

TAXATION OF ANNUITIES

We first illustrate the principle involved with an *annuity certain*, that is, where the annuity payments are to be made for a fixed period and are not dependent on the survival of any life or lives.

Annuity Certain and Income Tax. Each payment under an annuity certain consists partly of interest and partly of a return of capital. The principle behind the treatment for income tax is that the interest portion alone should be treated as taxable income.

Let us assume that under a settlement option of a life insurance policy the beneficiary, instead of $1,000 cash, elects to take an annuity certain of $218.36 a year for five years with the first instalment due one year hence. If we assume 3 per cent per annum interest, the interest earned on the $1,000 which paid for the annuity certain is $30.00 so that of the $218.36 received, the balance $188.36 must be the return of capital. Starting the second year with $811.64 we could go through the same process analysing the instalment into interest and the return of capital and so on.

For income tax purposes, such an analysis year by year would be impracticable. The rule used in practice is to average the interest and capital returned over the period of the annuity payments. In the above example, $1,000 is the cost of the annuity certain of $218.36 payable yearly for five years. The total of the instalments payable is $1,091.80 (five times $218.36) so that the total amount of interest payable is assumed to be $91.80 or $18.36 a year. Thus for income tax purposes each instalment of $218.36 is assumed to be made up of $18.36 interest and hence taxable and $200.00 repayment of capital which is not taxable. Excess interest (see Chapter 14: Settlement Options) would be taxable as paid.

The above is given as an illustration of principles only; it is advisable to follow the current regulations of Revenue Canada in any particular instance. This also applies to other illustrations in this chapter.

Life Annuity and Income Tax. The same principle that only the interest element of an annuity payment is treated as taxable income applies to life annuities where the payments are dependent on the survival of a life or lives. (Employee pension fund annuity payments and those under Registered Retirement Savings Plans are exceptions and will be dealt with later on in this chapter.)

The practical method adopted in Canada should be credited to two Canadian actuaries, C. C. Ferguson and A. D. Watson; the procedure has been followed by other countries. It is assumed that for taxation purposes the annuity is payable for a fixed term of years equal to the complete expectation of life at the time the annuity began to be payable. The purchase money for the annuity is divided by this term of years and the answer gives the capital repayment each year; the balance of the annuity payment received each year is treated as interest received and therefore as taxable income.

The annuity table approved by Ottawa is the *Standard Annuity Table 1937* described in Chapter 13, the complete expectations of life for which are given in Table 13.1. Since 1972, to allow for improved mortality, it has been required that the age be reduced by two years before entering the table for the annuity value.

As an illustration assume a male life age 65 bought a straight life annuity, paying $10,000 for it. Assuming the rate in Table 13.3, he would receive $1,268 each year. The complete expectation of life at age 63 being 15.62 years, dividing this into $10,000 we get $640 as the capital repayment each year; the balance of $628 is the interest element which has to be considered as income for taxation purposes. Each year and however long the annuity may be paid the same figure of $628 applies as the amount subject to taxation.

For types of annuities other than straight life, the complete expectation of life has to be calculated by an actuary, but the arithmetic is similar to the above once the modified expectation of life is obtained. The subdivision into interest and return of capital, once having been determined, applies unchanged throughout the duration of the policy. When the policy is taken out or when the annuity first becomes payable, the insurance company from whom it is purchased is required to advise the annuitant how the annuity payment is to be "split."

The capital versus interest principle outlined above applies to any form of annuity paid: immediate, deferred, or annuity option of a life insurance policy. However, the 1969 amendments provide that, when a policyholder elects for the proceeds of a policy to be paid as an annuity, the capital portion of the annuity shall be deemed to be the net cost (premiums less dividends) and not the proceeds due at that time, the effect being to tax the interest element during the accumulation period over the period of payment.

Segregated Funds. It has been mentioned that tax is levied on the investment income of the company because it would be an impossible task to tax policyholders directly. In the case of segregated funds, where the number of units in the name of each policyholder at any time is known, it is possible to apportion the income to each one and tax directly. Thus, the company is required to report to each policyholder each year his share of the interest and dividend income of the fund as well as his share of net realized capital gains which amounts must be included in the policyholder's income tax return.

Of course, much of the money accumulated in segregated funds is under registered pension plans or registered retirement savings plans; in that case the company is not obliged to report, nor the policyholder to include, investment income (or gains) on a yearly base; tax is payable on amounts paid out of the fund as explained under registered plans.

REGISTERED PENSION PLANS

We refer here to a plan covering a number of employees of the same firm or associated firms where specific rules are set out and apply to all persons covered under the plan as to the amount of pension, pension age, amount of contribution, return on death prior to retirement, etc. They are variously described as "pension plans," "superannuation plans," or "employee pension plans." As special taxation regulations apply to the contributions put into such plans by both employees and employers and the payments made out of the funds, it is most important to distinguish them from annuities on individual lives, which we have so far dealt with in this chapter.

When the income tax was first introduced into Canada in 1917 (during the First World War; it was presented as a temporary measure), employees contributing to a pension fund had the privilege of deducting their contributions to such pension funds from their earnings before computing their liability for income tax. In many cases membership in these pension funds was compulsory and the contributions were deducted from salary or wages and in one sense could be said not to form part of the earnings of the employee. There was a maximum limit of $300 for permissible income deductions for income tax for the years 1936 to 1946, it was then raised to $900, later to $1,500 in 1954, to $2,500 in 1972, and to $3,500 in 1976. Contributions for past service are allowed in addition.

For these taxation concessions to apply the plan has to be registered with Revenue Canada at Ottawa and hence the term "registered" is applied to them. Care must be taken to avoid confusing them with registered retirement savings plans described in the next section.

Contributions made by an employer to such an employee pension fund are, subject to certain rules, chargeable as a legitimate expense of operation by the employer just as if they were an addition to the payroll.

All payments received from such an employee pension fund are subject to taxation, in particular on retirement the pension received is fully taxable as income; the separation between interest and capital repayment does not apply in such cases. The principle here followed is that where contributions to a pension fund are exempt from taxation as they are paid, the entire pension benefits when received are taxable as income. Any lump sum paid on withdrawal from an employee pension fund or on the death of the employee before retirement is subject to income tax; the burden of tax on the lump sum may be spread by the general averaging provisions of the Income Tax Act or by the purchase of an Income Averaging Annuity.

REGISTERED RETIREMENT SAVINGS PLANS

Here we are dealing with individual policies covering individual lives and generally referred to as registered retirement savings plans.

The privilege of deducting from income premiums paid for pension purposes, within certain limits, before earnings are assessed for income tax was extended in 1957, in Canada, to all citizens. The particular purpose was to enable professional men and women and other self-employed people to provide for their retirement. The law also enabled a member of a registered employee pension fund to add to his pension within limitations.

The maximum contribution in any one year is 20 per cent of earned income subject to a maximum of $3,500 for employees enrolled in registered pension plans and of $5,500 for others. Amounts received under other registered plans or income from Old Age Security or the Canada or the Quebec Pension Plan may be contributed without regard to the limit. This is called "rolling over."

Whether registration is advisable in any particular case is a matter for careful consideration. The main advantage is the deferment of taxation which for those in a high income tax bracket who will be in a much lower one on retirement can be of considerable advantage. However, the benefits in the registered policy are locked in and cash and loan values are eliminated.

We summarize the main points bearing on *registered retirement savings plans*:

1. The corporations authorized to issue these plans are (i) a life

insurance company, (ii) a Government Annuities Office (the federal government and Alberta have these; the federal Annuities Branch no longer writes new contracts; annuities are issued by the Alberta government, but the volume is very small), (iii) a trust company, and (iv) a company licensed to issue investment contracts. In the case of (iii) and (iv), the accumulated funds under the contract must be used at the pension date to purchase an annuity for life from a body licensed to sell annuities as (i) and (ii). The Income Tax authorities are advised by these organizations of the contracts they have issued which qualify for exemption and the amount of the exemption.

2. In addition to deferred annuity policies, all life insurance policies which include an element which will provide an annuity are eligible for registration but only the portion of the premium required to produce the annuity will qualify for tax exemption. This will be discussed later in this chapter.

3. To be eligible for registration:

(*a*) The contract must provide for an income for the taxpayer or for his spouse for life commencing not later than age 71 or, in 1 (iii) and (iv) above, it must provide for the purchase of such an income. The right to receive a lump sum settlement at retirement must be eliminated.

(*b*) The contract must not contain any cash surrender or loan privileges. In the event of default in the payment of premiums the policy must provide for automatic conversion to a reduced paid-up policy.

(*c*) The contract must contain a provision that it cannot be assigned.

Income Tax on Retirement Income. Under a registered retirement savings plan the annuity payments as received must be considered as taxable income; there is no splitting up of the annuity as between interest and capital repayment. The treatment is thus similar to annuities or pensions payable under employee pension funds.

Death before Retirement. On death before retirement of the annuitant, that part of the payment made (accumulated premiums or deposits) which is considered to represent the tax-deferred portion accumulated up to the date of death, is taxable income of the recipient. Rules define what the tax-deferred element is in such a case.

"De-registration." The holder of the contract may apply to the company to have the special provisions cancelled, i.e., "de-registered." This would apply if the contract were surrendered. In such a case the individual concerned has to include the payment in his taxable income for the year.

Separation of Insurance and Savings. We stated above that all life insurance policies which include an element which will provide an annuity are eligible for registration but only the portion of the premium required to provide the annuity will qualify for tax exemption.

The division of the premium into its component parts is beyond the scope of this text, but the principle involved can be appreciated by those who have read Chapter 7 on the calculation of policy-reserves.

In the chart of the endowment insurance at 65 in Figure 12 (Chapter 7), the shaded part represents the amount at risk or the insurance part of the policy. If this were term insurance, i.e. payable on death only, and were paid for by a level annual premium duly loaded for expenses, it would represent, in a practical way, for the purpose in view, the insurance part of the premium paid and, if it were deducted from the gross premium actually paid, the balance would represent the part required to provide the annuity, or that portion of the premium which may be tax-deferred.

TABLE 18.1

A. Endowment insurance at age 65 participating	Gross annual premium	$30.09
	Protection portion	5.39
	Tax-deferred portion	24.70
B. Life paid-up at 65 participating	Gross annual premium	$24.74
	Protection portion	6.84
	Tax-deferred portion	17.90
C. Straight life participating	Gross annual premium	$21.22
	Protection portion	7.65
	Tax-deferred portion	13.57

Table 18.1 shows, for illustration only, the split as applied to the premiums of one particular company, per $1,000 sum insured, age at entry 35. It will be noted that the plans with the highest policy-reserves give the lowest "protection portion" cost where the number of premiums payable is the same.

It is essential to realize that the division of the premium into the two portions described above is an artificial one adopted only for purposes of income tax. The life or endowment policy premium is, in fact, one and indivisible.

Deferred Profit Sharing Plans. Another way in which life insurance policies and annuities may be used in deferring income tax is to use them for investment of funds of Deferred Profit Sharing Plans. A discussion of these plans is outside the scope of this text. However, the Life Underwriters Association of Canada publishes a text which details this plan.[3]

[3]*Taxation – a handbook for insurance and estate planners*, 1st ed., 1976 (Life Underwriters Association of Canada, 41 Lesmill Road, Don Mills, Ontario M3B 2T3).

Income Averaging Annuity. The law provides that certain lump sums, which would otherwise be considered as income in the year received, may be used to purchase an income averaging annuity contract. The lump sum is then excluded from income, but the annuity payments, as received, are included as income in full (i.e., not the interest element only). In this way the taxpayer may avoid paying a high rate of tax on an unusually large income. This privilege is available in respect of (i) income from literary, dramatic, musical, or artistic works; (ii) income of an athlete, musician, or entertainer; (iii) capital gains; (iv) various lump sums out of pension plans or paid on termination of employment; and (v) certain other payments. The annuity must start within ten months and may be either a life annuity with or without a guaranteed period or an annuity certain; the guaranteed period or the term of an annuity certain may not exceed 15 years nor may it extend beyond age 85.

Interest and Dividend Deduction. Every taxpayer may, in determining taxable income, deduct the first $1,000 of income from interest and dividends. Interest for this purpose includes the profit on disposition of an insurance policy, as well as interest on proceeds or dividends left on deposit, and the interest element of annuity payments. It does not apply to amounts received under registered plans or income averaging annuities.

Pension income deduction. Similarly, there is a deduction of the first $1,000 of pension income. Up to age 65, the deduction applies only to income from an employer pension plan or to income arising on the death of a spouse. After age 65, it is extended to include income under a registered retirement savings plan, or a deferred profit sharing plan, or the capital element of an annuity. It does not include income under an income averaging annuity, or from Old Age Security, or from the Canada or Quebec Pension Plans.

CHAPTER NINETEEN

Total Disability Benefits

In May 1857, an eminent British actuary, John H. Higham, wrote to the *Journal of the Institute of Actuaries*: "The man who has insured his life, or contracted for an endowment or an annuity yet deferred, and who is disqualified by sickness from continuing his premiums and even from maintaining himself, is in sad case, and to this case we can at present apply no remedy."

This close relationship between life insurance and long term disability was thus recognized over a century ago but it took some fifty years before there was a general attempt by life insurance companies to meet the need. The difficulties of transacting income disability insurance are illustrated in its history as outlined below and the withdrawal of the great majority of companies from the field in 1932. Several Canadian companies continued to issue the benefit and since then, those Canadian companies which withdrew, have returned to the field.

Although this text is primarily confined to life insurance benefits, total disability and double indemnity accident benefits have become an integral part of the life insurance business in Canada and have been made so by federal insurance laws; this chapter and the next will be devoted to them.

HISTORY OF DISABILITY BENEFITS

The voluntary banding together of workers to provide sickness benefits on a co-operative basis has a history much older than life insurance and many British friendly societies existed before 1800 with this as one of their main objects. "Disability" is not identical with "sickness" for it implies illness of a serious or even permanent nature. It is as well to use the term *total disability* in referring to the benefit attached to life policies in Canada, to stress the fact that serious illness or accident, which has a disabling character preventing the sufferer from earning a livelihood, is meant. However, friendly societies and fraternal orders have played an important part in the development of disability insurance, for it was from their published experience that the early sickness and disability rates were obtained. In this connection one would refer to the Manchester Unity of Oddfellows, a British order whose published sickness experience for the years 1893–97 is still one of the landmarks of the business.

In the history of total disability benefits attached to life insurance policies the different forms of the benefit should be noted.

FIRST PHASE: EARLY HISTORY: WAIVER OF PREMIUM AND PAYMENT OF SUM INSURED

The first disability benefit issued in Canada in connection with life insurance benefits was in 1881 by a Canadian fraternal order, the Independent Order of Foresters. Upon proof of total and permanent disability commencing before age 70, 50 per cent of the life insurance certificate was paid in cash and the remainder was kept in force without further payment of premiums. The experience under this benefit was published by the I.O.F. actuary, Sidney H. Pipe, and formed part of the first official table regarding total and permanent disability benefits adopted in Canada and the U.S.A.

In 1896 the Fidelity Mutual Life of Philadelphia was the first life insurance company on the North American continent to issue a disability benefit as part of a life insurance policy. The benefit was payable on proof that the life insured had become "totally and permanently incapacitated" and consisted of the option of either taking a fully paid up policy or taking an annuity on the surrender of the policy.

From 1906 on, various U.S. life insurance companies began to issue a waiver of premium benefit on proof of total and permanent disability. In 1910 the Canadian federal insurance laws were changed to permit life insurance companies to issue a disability benefit as part of their life insurance business. Under this benefit, in the event of total and permanent disability, the premium was waived and the sum insured became payable in instalments at the rate of 10 per cent a year, reducing the amount of the sum insured. By 1913 the benefit had been generally adopted in Canada.

SECOND PHASE: MONTHLY INCOME DISABILITY

The second main step followed a change in the Canadian federal insurance laws in 1917, permitting, besides the waiver of premiums, the payment of a disability benefit without reducing the sum insured. The benefit issued by the companies paid 1 per cent of the sum insured ($10 a month per thousand sum insured), the monthly income commencing to be payable on proof of total and permanent disability of the life insured.

THIRD PHASE: THE THREE-MONTHS CLAUSE

In practice the interpretation of "total and permanent disability" caused considerable difficulty. This led to the third main development in 1921 when the practice was adopted by certain companies of paying the monthly income under the disability benefit after total disability had continued for a certain period although the permanence of the total disability could not then be determined. This provision was made a part of the policy. The lead set by one company of making this qualifying period or *waiting period* three months rapidly became the general practice.

The above brief summary should not disguise the continuous series of changes from 1906 to 1921, each with the object of extending the benefit and this became a subject of competition among the companies. Note that in 1921 the benefit which had started out as "total and permanent disability" became a "non-cancellable sickness benefit" with a maximum waiting period of three months. Under regular sickness policies the company has the right on any renewal date to cancel the policy. Life insurance companies, had they referred to the literature on the subject, might have been warned of the dangers to them inherent in the benefit; they might also have learnt that the rates being charged for this "non-cancellable sickness benefit" were totally inadequate.

The significance of the three-months clause is better realized if it is stated that when the experience of this clause was examined under the auspices of the Society of Actuaries (1952 *Report*) it revealed that the chance of a person suffering total disability of three months or longer is much greater than the chance of death occurring during his working lifetime. At age 40 the hazard of such disability is 2.3 times as great as the risk of dying (see also Chapter 3). Thus what was presumed to be an addition to a life insurance policy became the major benefit.

The above developments, although referring mainly to U.S. companies, may be said to apply to Canada also, allowing for some time-lag between the general adoption or any practice in the U.S. and its acceptance in Canada. The importance of the disability benefit among the U.S. life insurance companies in the 1920s may be grasped when it is stated that in some companies over 75 per cent of the life insurance policies issued carried some form of disability benefit.

In the years prior to the stock market crash of 1929 certain casual underwriting practices developed among U.S. life insurance companies. The same applied to disability benefits except that retribution was earlier and if anything the losses proportionately heavier. Even before the stock market crash the disability benefit began to involve the U.S. companies in heavy losses and troublesome litigation and drastic changes in policy conditions were made with premiums substantially increased. When the business depression began (the most severe in modern history) it became obvious that the life insurance companies were faced with many serious problems in the conduct of their regular life insurance business. It is difficult nowadays to recapture the "new era" psychology of the years immediately preceding 1929 when elementary precautions were thrown to the wind. Even had the disability benefit been written cautiously and with adequate premiums the recession would have meant heavy claims and losses.

FOURTH PHASE (1): WITHDRAWAL OF THE INCOME BENEFIT

The fourth phase of the development of the total disability benefit was reached in 1932 when one prominent U.S. company decided to restrict the disability benefit offered to its life policyholders to the waiver of premium benefit only, thus eliminating the "monthly income" from all new issues. This action was followed by most U.S. and Canadian companies.

It must be emphasized that the withdrawal of many Canadian companies from the "income disability" field in 1932 was not so much due to heavy losses, for the Canadian companies had been rather more conservative in their business methods and the recession was relatively milder in Canada. Their action was due more to a desire to concentrate on the many current problems and to avoid adding to them by continuing to write a benefit which seemed to bring only dissatisfaction, worry, and criticism.

FOURTH PHASE (2): SOME CANADIAN COMPANIES CONTINUE INCOME BENEFIT

However several Canadian companies decided to continue the income benefit but with a restricted form of benefit.[1] The waiting period before

[1] "Additional Benefits in Life Policies in Canada," James A. Campbell, XVIth International Congress of Actuaries, Brussels, 1960. See also a paper by the author: "Disability Benefits in Connection with Life Insurance," Tenth International Congress of Actuaries, Rome, 1934.

total disability was presumed to be permanent was made six months and the limiting age before which total disability had to occur before any income became payable was reduced to 55. The income payments were $10 a month per thousand sum insured for fifty months only, after which they were reduced to $5 a month for the next one hundred months. At the end of the 150 months if the life insured was still disabled the full amount of the sum insured would be paid and the policy ceased to be in force.

The continuation of the disability income benefit by several Canadian life insurance companies in 1932 is thus described by the late V. R. Smith,[2] one of the leaders in the movement.

> In 1932 a small group of Canadian actuaries placed their professional lives at stake in recommending and obtaining the approval of their boards of directors to the continuance, by their respective companies, of a monthly income disability benefit as part of a life insurance policy. . . . The six months waiting period eliminated certain types of malingering which occur particularly in seasonal occupations where disability appears to be more prevalent and recoveries more numerous at certain seasons of the year. . . . (*Record*, American Institute of Actuaries, vol. 24 (1935).)

FIFTH PHASE: TO THE PRESENT TIME

The continuation of the income disability benefit by certain Canadian companies turned out to be a successful decision. By 1936 the continuing companies had changed the income from 150 months to the period to age 65 and maintained the income at $10 a month per thousand throughout the period of its payment. The adoption of the six-month waiting period was the important factor as well as maturing the policy if disability continued to an age which could be considered as a pensionable age.

Canadian companies as a class have gradually returned to issuing the income benefit, and some have liberalized their benefits in recent years as mentioned below. The latest development is that a few companies have withdrawn the income benefit as an addition to a life insurance policy, but continue to offer disability income under separate policies through their personal sickness and accident branches.

TOTAL DISABILITY BENEFITS: CURRENT LEGISLATION

We have already referred to the changes in the Canadian federal insurance laws permitting life insurance companies to include disability

[2] V. R. Smith (1883–1947), a Canadian actuary, who made a definite contribution to the development of life insurance. He filled in succession the posts of actuary, general manager and finally president of the Confederation Life. He was president of the American Institute of Actuaries in 1937.

benefits in their life insurance contracts and treat them as part of their life business. Currently (1976), the law permits the following disability benefits to be included:

1. Waiver of premiums during "disability caused by accident or sickness."
2. A "disability indemnity" during the continuance of such disability payable for a period not exceeding 100 weeks at a weekly rate not exceeding $^1/_2$ of 1 per cent of the sum insured and thereafter not exceeding one half of that rate. It will be noted that these limits are fractionally more than \$20 and \$10 per month per thousand respectively; thus a company subject to federal legislation may not pay a \$20 monthly benefit for more than 100 weeks.
3. A lump sum disability indemnity in respect of total and permanent disability which together with any other disability indemnity shall not exceed the sum insured.
4. In a deferred annuity contract a disability indemnity not exceeding the rate of annuity provided by the contract.

WAIVER OF PREMIUMS BENEFIT

So long as the benefit is confined to the waiver of premiums benefit only, many problems of disability insurance are avoided. Excepting in extreme cases as where a large annual premium in relation to the sum insured is involved (as a short-term endowment), there is no incentive to select against the company in seeking the waiver benefit. The benefit is desirable, costs very little, and in underwriting presents no special problems other than those presented by the basic life insurance benefit.

Proof has to be submitted that the life insured has been totally disabled for a certain period, usually six months, and that the disability commenced before the limiting age, which is generally 60. On such proof future premium payments are waived during the continuance of the total disability. It is common practice, but not universal, to make the benefit retroactive to cover any premiums which fell due during the waiting period if the claim is admitted.

Some companies, under their waiver of premiums benefit, mature the policy and pay the full sum insured or declare it fully paid up if total disability continues to a specified age, generally 65. This obviates the necessity for obtaining proof of the continuance of total disability after that age; such proof is generally of doubtful value owing to the difficulty of distinguishing between total disability and old age.

DISABILITY INCOME BENEFIT

There is considerable variety in the benefits issued by Canadian companies but the most common provides, in addition to waiver of premium, a monthly income of $10 per thousand sum insured on proof of disability occurring before age 55 and continuing for a waiting period of six months. The first payment is made at the end of the waiting period and the income continues during disability until age 65 or to death or maturity if earlier. At age 65, if the insured is still disabled, the income ceases and the sum insured is payable in settlement of the policy.

Variations on the above include:

(*a*) cover to age 60 instead of 55;

(*b*) waiting period of three or four months;

(*c*) income of $20 per month per thousand; a federally registered company which has this provision reduces the income to $10 after 24 months;

(*d*) policy made paid-up, rather than matured, at 65;

(*e*) income continuing after 65 but reduced to $5 per thousand, the policy remaining in force.

CURRENT STATISTICS

At the end of 1974, according to the report of the federal Superintendent, one ordinary life insurance policy in every two in force in Canada included a disability benefit ($4.8 millions out of $9.6 millions); by sum insured the ratio was 47 per cent. The ratios of Canadian and other companies are of interest:

	By number	By sum insured
Canadian companies	44%	47%
British and foreign companies	61%	47%
All companies	50%	47%

The high ratio by number for non-Canadian companies reflects the fact that the two largest companies include a waiver of premium benefit automatically in the great majority of their policies.

The 50 per cent by number is made up of 42 per cent with waiver of premium only, 6 per cent with waiver of premium and payment of the sum insured in instalments, and only 2 per cent with an income benefit.

The premium income for disability benefits during 1974 was $23 millions, approximately 1.8 per cent of the total premium income for ordinary insurance.

DEFINITION OF TOTAL DISABILITY

In life insurance, there is no need to define "life" and "death"; with the exceptions of a period of a few minutes at the end of life, and of occasional cases of disappearance, there is no question whether a person is alive or dead. Unfortunately, it is not equally clear whether or not a person is totally disabled, so that it becomes necessary to define the condition.

It must be remembered that whether or not a person is totally disabled is to some extent within his own control. One person may be strongly motivated to struggle to resume activity; another will accept his condition. An income payable during disability, particularly of a large amount, may lessen the motivation to struggle; waiver of premium is unlikely to be of sufficient importance to do so.

Consider these cases, all of which have come within the author's experience: a surgeon with a muscular impairment of his hand who could not operate but could make a good living as a physician; a farmer able to direct the operations of a large and profitable farm from his bed; an insurance broker doing business by telephone from his home; the owner of a small hotel, who had had a heart attack and sat all day in the bar keeping an eye on business. Are they totally disabled or not?

Because a contract drawn up by one party is usually construed by a court in favour of the other, if there is a lack of clarity, and because courts, particularly juries, tend to give the benefit of doubt to individuals as against corporations, companies have found it necessary to define total disability rather strictly, although they are usually more liberal in their actual interpretation, if there is a claim.

A typical clause defines total disability as inability due to sickness or bodily injury to perform any work for compensation or profit or to follow any gainful occupation. This is known as an "any occupation" clause.

There is a tendency to adopt what is known as an "own occupation" clause; this defines disability as the insured's inability to follow his regular occupation. An intermediate definition is the inability to follow any occupation for which the insured is fitted by education, training, or experience. Frequently, a liberal definition applies at the commencement of disability but a more strict one applies after, say, 24 months. In practice, there may be much less difference in treatment of claims than the wording would indicate.

Sometimes the definition states that total blindness or double amputation is considered as causing total disability regardless of whether or not the insured could work.

Generally, under an "own occupation" clause, even if the insured would be totally disabled as defined, the benefit does not apply if he is, in fact, gainfully employed.

EXCLUSIONS

Companies vary in their exclusions and a stricter attitude may be taken regarding a disability clause with an income benefit than with a waiver of premium benefit only. Usual exclusions are disabilities resulting from (i) self-inflicted injuries (ii) riot, insurrection, or war or hostilities of any kind, and (iii) service in the armed forces of any country in a state of war.

With a benefit of such an uncertain nature as the "total disability" benefit any possible additional hazards either known or which may develop in the future must be eliminated if possible.

WOMEN

Women are better life insurance risks than men, but definitely worse where sickness and disability are concerned. Hence many companies do not allow the "disability income" benefit to any women either single or married but do grant the waiver of premiums benefit only, to self-supporting single women at the same or $1^1/_2$ times the rate for males.

Where women are granted total disability benefits the limiting age prior to which disability must commence is generally five years less than men. Some companies terminate the total disability benefits granted to single women on their marriage.

So long as women remained in their traditional role of housekeeper, dependent on the incomes of their husbands, it is apparent that disability income presented a risk virtually impossible to underwrite. Single self-supporting women were in a different position, but their situation would change on marriage. The insurance companies have therefore been very conservative in their acceptance of women for disability income.

Under present conditions, problems may well arise in the two-income family, as regards both men and women; either partner may be motivated to enjoy a disability income supplemented by the earnings of the other. It is probable that the trend will be towards issuing the same benefits to women as to men, but differences in premium may remain.

"Human rights" legislation, under consideration at the time of writing, may prescribe such action.

PREMIUMS FOR WAIVER OF PREMIUMS AND MONTHLY INCOME BENEFITS

In Table 19.1 premiums are shown illustrating the current premiums used in Canada for waiver of premiums and monthly income total disability benefits. As premiums for life insurance vary among companies, it would be expected that the waiver of premium rates would also vary. Further, companies differ considerably in their attitude to the disability income benefit and this may be shown by the competitive aspect of the rates they charge.

TABLE 19.1

Illustrative Annual Premiums per $1,000 Sum Insured for Total Disability Benefits, Males, Age 35 at Entry

	Straight life		20-pay life	Life to 65	End. at 65	End. 20
	Par	Non-par	Par	Par	Par	Par
Waiver of premiums only	$0.58	$0.44	$0.68	$0.53	$0.41	$0.48
W.P. and $10 M.I. with maturity at age 65	$2.97	$2.81	$2.73	$2.93	$2.34	$2.04

In the rates illustrated, the waiting period in every case is six months and the limiting age before which disability must occur is 60 for the waiver benefit, 55 for the income benefit. For the waiver of premium benefit the premiums would be waived during total disability to the death of the life insured or the maturity of an endowment policy.

The disability income benefit is $10 a month per thousand sum insured with the sum insured payable at age 65 if total disability still exists at that age. The additional premiums are payable to age 60 or 55, respectively, or until the end of the premium-paying period if earlier.

LIMITS

For reasons outlined in this chapter an upper limit is most important, for the amount of disability income may well prove the determining factor in whether a claim is made. Companies generally have two limits: one which they will accept on their own policies which may be, for example, $1,000 a month and this is subject to an over-all limit in all companies of perhaps $2,000 a month, not exceeding 50 or 60 per cent of earned income. Companies may exceed their published limits in special cases. In writing the benefit much attention is paid to existing "disability income" benefits separating the accident policies from the sickness policies and in particular separating incomes payable for a temporary period of some weeks from "disability income" payable for life or for a term of years. There are, practically speaking, no limits for the waiver of premiums benefit only.

Pro-Rata Benefits. In the literature on the subject, one will read of the need to "prorate" benefits to income. This means that on a claim arising the insurance company will only pay its proportion of the total "disability income" on the basis that it will not exceed a certain percentage of the insured's proven income at the time of the claim. Although theoretically an excellent way to eliminate the dangers of over-insurance, prorating is not generally used in practice because it leads to dissatisfaction among policyholders; their attitude is that if they pay a premium based on a certain amount of income, they should receive that amount, if they are disabled, and not something less. In considering this matter the point should be noted that "disability income" is not taxable, so that in these days of high income tax a disability income of even half a man's current earnings may represent a very high proportion of his net income after tax.

In mentioning income in relation to "disability income" we mean earned income. The investment or other income which will be received irrespective of the health of the insured should be excluded in determining the insurable limits. In fact a substantial investment income reduces the need for disability income and indicates a possible anti-selection hazard.

Over-insurance. In middle age, many a man is ready to take advantage of a minor impairment to give up work entirely in exchange for a small income from a life insurance company. Disability increases with age. A man's income is subject to wide fluctuations, particularly as between boom times and depressions.

The issue by the insurance company of a disability income benefit which is more than say, one half, of a man's current earnings may be said of itself to increase the hazard. When the "income benefit" is added to a permanent plan of life insurance and the disability income is fixed by the amount of the life insurance purchased, the cost of the policy may serve as some restriction on over-insurance. This is why some companies do not permit the disability income benefit to be added to term insurance.

SOME FEATURES OF DISABILITY INSURANCE

Increased Premiums May Mean Increased Claims. One important factor of "income disability" insurance is that it follows other classes of non-life insurance in that, as premium rates are increased, the claim rate tends to increase also. Thus, when the claims experience is unsatisfactory, the solution is not a simple one of increasing rates. As the premium rate increases, so some of the better classes of risks decide not to take the benefit on account of the cost, thus increasing the proportion of the less desirable risks.

Life Insurance Trends Conflict with Disability Trends. The whole trend of life insurance has been towards broadening the basis on which life insurance can be granted and simplifying the procedure. The increasing limits for non-medical insurance is one instance. The interests of the life insured and the insurance company are similar in life insurance, that is, life is desirable to the insured and he will normally do all he can to prolong it. In sickness and disability the reverse is too often the case. The desire to work is not an inherent characteristic in man—the insured may even seek to protract an illness to enable him to draw a substantial income from an insurance company. In the case of nervous or mental disease the very fear of the conflicts of economic life may have brought on the disease.

SELECTION OF RISKS

Almost everything we have written above has some bearing on the home office selection of risks and it must be obvious that disability benefits present problems differing from those of life insurance benefits.

There is much opportunity for selecting against the company in disability insurance. The restrictive attitude of many companies towards the "income disability" benefit has been mentioned. At least one company takes the attitude that the answer to anti-selection is aggressive selling. To this one comment might be added that selectivity in selling is more essential for disability insurance than for life insurance.

Unacceptable Classes. It follows from what has been said that where there is no occupation or it is a part-time or casual occupation that "disability income" cannot be granted. Such classes are students, unskilled workers and labourers, professional athletes, and seasonal workers such as lumbermen and fishermen. Persons with "home occupations'' are also questionable. Cases have arisen which indicate particular difficulties with farmers and farmers' sons, poultry and dairy farmers, cattle breeders, etc.

Medical versus *Non-Medical.* As part of the stricter underwriting of ''income disability'' benefits some companies will not write the benefit except with a medical examination. When non-medical applications for life insurance are accepted, the limits, if the application includes the ''disability income'' benefits, are quite low compared with non-medical applications for life insurance only.

Special Aspects in Underwriting. The following special points in medical underwriting arise in considering disability benefits. They particularly concern the ''income disability'' benefit.

1. Where the occupational hazard requires an extra premium the risk requires special consideration particularly if it is due to the danger of illnesses involving long disability that the extra is required for life insurance. So far as the waiver of premiums benefit only applies many such cases can be accepted at two or three times the standard rate as indicated in the company's Occupational Ratings Manual.
2. Any nervous illness or family history of such (or insanity) will disqualify. Long periods of absence from work may indicate this background.
3. Deformities which in themselves will not disqualify for life insurance will do so for ''disability insurance'': for example, the loss of sight in one eye or the loss of any limbs. A further accident may readily place the insured in the total and permanently disabled class.
4. Alcoholism, even in a modified form, with or without any unsatisfactory business or moral hazard, will generally disqualify for the income disability benefit.

ACCIDENT AND SICKNESS BRANCHES

It has been mentioned that some companies have established separate branches for the transaction of accident and sickness business; this is permitted by federal legislation. A few words about this may be of interest.

The direct premiums written by accident and sickness branches of life insurance companies amounted to $610 millions in 1974. (This is about 20 per cent of the premium income for life and insurance and annuities which total nearly $3 billions.) Almost 90 per cent of the accident and 20 per cent of the premium income for life insurance and annuities which total $3 billions.) Almost 90 per cent of the accident and sickness premiums are for group insurance, covering mainly employees but also creditors.

Individual premiums totalled $76 millions; of this it is estimated that about $65 millions were for income replacement, both short and long term, the balance being for accidental death and dismemberment risks and for insurance of medical, hospital, and dental costs. Comparing $65 millions with the total of $23 millions for all disability benefits in ordinary life policies, it is obvious that most individual income replacement insurance issued by life insurance companies is done through accident and sickness branches. Over half of the business is written by a few U.S. companies which specialize in the line and write relatively little life insurance.

CHAPTER TWENTY

Double Indemnity Accident Benefit

INTRODUCTION

In this chapter we deal mainly with the benefit which, in Canada, may be included in a life insurance policy whereby, in the event of the death of the life insured by accident, the sum insured payable on death from any cause is doubled. The name originally given to the benefit was *double indemnity accident benefit*, represented by the symbol "D.I." which has become accepted in life insurance terminology. It is incorrectly called an "indemnity" for the amount payable is fixed and not limited by the amount of the loss suffered as the word "indemnity" implies. The 1962 revision of the Uniform Life Insurance Act changed the definition from "double indemnity insurance" to "accidental death insurance."

At the end of 1974 there were $19,308 millions of double indemnity accident death benefits, i.e., D.I., in force in Canada with federally registered companies as against $80,515 millions of ordinary life insurance in force. Thus 24 per cent of the business in force has the D.I. benefit attached. In the large U.S. companies operating in Canada as much as 50 per cent of the ordinary business sold has the D.I. benefit attached.

There are some who are critical of the D.I. benefit as being just a frill added to a life insurance benefit, with little economic justification and adding a possible source of litigation to a business singularly free from it. However, we cannot ignore its popularity, which is probably far greater in the U.S. than in Canada, and it has been a popular benefit with both the sales and administrative departments of the companies as indicated by (i) repeated reductions in the rates charged, (ii) extensions of the limiting age to which the benefit applies, and (iii) liberalization of the policy conditions. Considering the extent of the business, litigation in Canada has been trivial but appears to be increasing.

Unlike the total disability benefit, the D.I. benefit makes a strong appeal to the man in the best of health; he thinks death by disease rather remote, but is aware every day of death by accident, to which much publicity is given. By combining the D.I. benefit with life insurance the benefit can be obtained at a very low rate. The suddenness with which accidental death strikes, with the insured's dependants totally unprepared, is justification for it on economic grounds.

The sales appeal of the benefit is important. That for the addition of a dollar or so a thousand to the premium, double the sum insured is payable on accidental death has a major sales appeal particularly as so many people realize they are underinsured. On the other hand the critics of the benefit maintain that it is wrong to concentrate on death from any particular cause. Further they maintain that every dollar available should be devoted to increasing the sum insured payable on death, whatever the cause, and that this can be achieved with little extra cost, for the premiums for term riders at the younger adult ages are quite low.

HISTORY OF THE D.I. BENEFIT

The first life insurance policy containing a double indemnity accident benefit was issued by the Fidelity Mutual Life (of Philadelphia) in 1904. The same company was the first to issue a total and permanent disability benefit. The D.I. benefit did not become popular in the U.S. until about 1917–20. In 1922 when the federal insurance law in Canada was changed permitting Canadian life insurance companies to transact D.I. insurance as part of their life business the benefit took hold in Canada, practically every company issuing the benefit.

The 1922 federal legislation permitted a life insurance company to issue what was in effect accident insurance without the necessity of making it a separate class of business with its own funds, investments, and accounts. In some cases this might have meant a change in the company's charter. By the 1922 change a company could issue the D.I. benefit as part of its life policies without any of these restrictions. In 1961 a further amendment of the federal insurance law extended this right to a triple indemnity benefit, i.e., the payment on accidental death of three times the amount payable on death from any cause. Further, it permitted the addition of dismemberment and loss of sight benefits; all part of a life insurance policy without the need for setting up separate funds, etc. These additional benefits will be discussed separately later, and we confine our present discussion to the D.I. benefit only.

THE RATE OF ACCIDENTAL DEATH

We have referred previously to the inter-company joint investigations of the Society of Actuaries. In Figure 14 we show the rate of accidental death according to age attained for the D.I. benefit attached to life

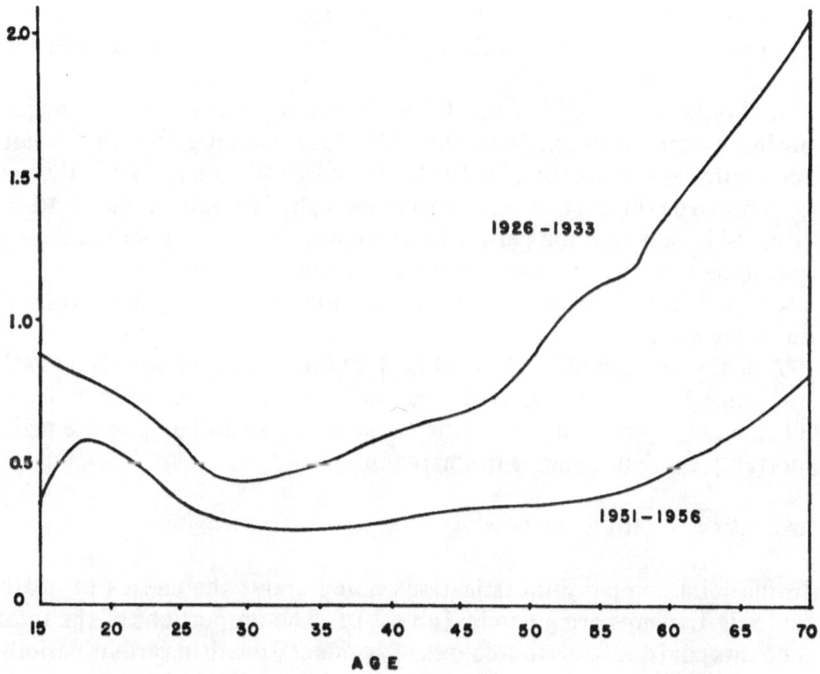

FIGURE 14. Double Indemnity Accident Benefit, Claim Rate per 1000

policies of a number of companies obtained from such investigations covering two periods 1926 to 1933 and 1951 to 1956. The business relates to the U.S. and Canadian business of the companies and is of course mainly that of U.S. policies.[1] Investigation has shown that for *males* in Canada the D.I. rate would be slightly lower at the younger and older ages and slightly higher at the middle ages; in other words a slight flattening of the curves as shown in Figure 14; the latter are based on the sums insured. The D.I. claim rate for women is definitely less than for men.

[1]"Reports of Mortality and Morbidity Experience," *Transactions*, Society of Actuaries, 1958.

Figure 14 shows a definite decrease in the D.I. claim rate in the intervening 25-year period at all ages. We are aware of the fall in the death rate from all causes over this period. However, whereas the fall for all causes of death has been mainly at the younger ages with only a slight decrease at the older ages, for the D.I. benefit the reverse has been the case: a major fall at the older ages and a slight fall at the younger ages.

Another point to note in Figure 14 is the decrease in the D.I. claim rate from ages 19 to 30 in both periods with a definite hump in the 1951–56 period from age 15 to age 30.

It should be noted that the 1926–33 period covers part of a major business depression following the 1929 stock market crash. In a major economic depression suicides and accidental death rates (it is not always possible to distinguish between them) are high. The point intended to be stressed here is that the period 1951–56 may have been unduly favourable to be taken as a measure of the D.I. claim rate over a long period of years and hence unsuitable for the calculation of D.I. rates without adequate margins.

A final point regarding Figure 14 is that the high accidental death rate under age 30 in the 1951–56 curve has affected the rate of mortality from all causes at those ages and is the cause of the slight hump in the male mortality curve in Figure 3 in Chapter 4.

CAUSES OF ACCIDENTAL DEATH

In the joint company investigations noted above the causes of death under D.I. claims are given in Table 20.1. The proportions of the total amounts paid due to certain causes of accidental death in various periods are of interest.

TABLE 20.1

	Years 1951–56	Years 1929–33
Motor Vehicle Accidents	55.2%	40.3%
Accidental Falls	8.8	8.5
Aircraft Accidents	4.7	not available
Suicide (reported as)	0.5	1.1

The substantial increase in claims due to motor vehicle accidents is very striking. The fall in claims due to suicide indicates the abnormality of the 1929–33 period. Suicide is, as a rule, expressly excluded as a cause of accidental death in the D.I. policy conditions but in some states in the U.S. the exclusion is not permitted under certain conditions. Further, in some cases, suicide cannot be established although reported as the cause of death.

LIMITING AGE

The accidental death rate increases with age (after age 35 or so) and the D.I. benefit is generally terminated at age 70. One U.S. company has no limiting age, i.e., the benefit is paid on accidental death whenever it occurs. There are objections to carrying the benefit beyond age 70. Beyond that age, heart attacks and cerebral haemorrhages are common and when falls occur associated with death from these cardio-vascular diseases there is considerable difficulty in establishing the true cause of death. It was never intended that the D.I. benefit should pay double the sum insured if death occurred due to a heart attack and if it were done a substantially larger premium would have to be paid. With every extension of the limiting age the possibility of litigation is increased which companies are most anxious to avoid.

D.I. PREMIUM RATES

On the assumption that the D.I. claim rate increases with age, if we loaded the rate for expenses and allowed for the fact that the average policy increases in size with age a larger loading would be required at the younger ages. This would tend to level out the premium rates at those ages. Based on this conception, with benefit ceasing at 60 or 65, for many years a flat premium of $1.25 per $1,000 sum insured was charged in Canada up to age 45 at entry, after which the rate increased with the age at entry to $1.75 at age 55 which was the maximum age at which the D.I. benefit was issued.

Owing to the favourable experience under this benefit, reductions of rates were made, first of all from the $1.25 to $1.00 and then below the dollar mark. Premiums are now based on the actual D.I. experience curve as shown in Figure 14 as a result of which the premiums are lowest (on the straight life plan) for ages 24 to 34 at entry, being higher below age 24 and increasing year by year above age 34 at entry.

In examining the D.I. rates quoted by companies it should be noted that where the limiting age for a claim is 65 say, the additional D.I. premiums cease to be payable at that age so that the D.I. premiums for an endowment insurance at 65 or a life paid-up at 65 are the same as for the straight life plan. Male and female rates are the same for the Double Indemnity Accident benefit.

D.I. LIMITS

There is some evidence that higher amounts of D.I. tend to give a higher claim ratio. Undoubtedly some speculative element enters when D.I. is granted for large amounts. There is little justification for very large amounts of D.I. benefit. Companies will usually participate in cover up to a total of $250,000 or more on one life. The amount a company retains at its own risk varies with its size, the balance being reinsured with other companies.

The total amount of D.I. held in all companies and the amount of accident insurance held under auspices other than life insurance are factors in deciding the amount of D.I. a company will accept and retain in a particular case. Companies have found it difficult to ascertain the total amount of accident insurance held by an individual and in any case it is subject to wide fluctuations. Hence the tendency has been to concern themselves with the total insurance carried in their own company and its relation to the needs of the applicant rather than how much is life and how much is accident insurance.

Life insurance companies are well aware of the unfavourable publicity attendant on large accidental death claims and the speculative element introduced by granting such insurances. This explains the relatively small amounts granted on the D.I. benefit compared to these companies' limits on regular life insurance.

SELECTION OF D.I. RISKS

The accident hazard in any particular case may present an entirely different picture from that of the general death risk, yet the two are related, as the general death risk includes death from accidental causes. In fact, the pattern of the rate of accidental death as seen in Figure 14 and in both the experiences shown, which decreases from age 19 to age 30, is due to the high accidental death rate among teenagers and those in their early twenties. In considering the D.I. benefit on any risk we must ask (1) whether there is any abnormal hazard of sustaining injury; (2) whether there is the possibility that such injury may prove fatal; (3) whether such death is likely to be confused with death from any existing disease.

Medical Impairments. We have already mentioned that heart disease and cerebral haemorrhage are likely to cause sudden death in circumstances in which a claim for the double accident benefit would be made and yet death was due to disease, not accident. Or, these diseases may lead to a seizure where what would otherwise be a minor accident becomes a fatal one. There are also impairments, such as deafness and badly impaired eyesight, which may make the applicant much more liable to accidents than a normal person. Whenever a case is rated or considered as borderline because of medical history or a physical impairment, a separate estimate of the accidental death hazard has to be made and the risk assessed accordingly.

Habits and Moral Hazards. Any past records of over-indulgence in alcohol, even if it be decided to grant standard life insurance, requires special consideration and the possible rejection of the D.I. benefit. This would also apply to any record or report of reckless automobile driving or involvement in auto accidents.

Occupations. Some occupations involve a health hazard but no abnormal accident hazard. For example, there is the hazard of possible lead poisoning in the manufacture of storage batteries and the hazard of dust due to grinders in the metal trades. Although life insurance may be rated, the D.I. benefit may be granted at standard rates. However, more generally, where there is an occupational hazard, both the life insurance and the D.I. benefit will be rated or the D.I. benefit possible declined, as in the case of mining and underground workers, structural iron workers, and power linesmen.

In some occupations the accident hazard is above normal yet within limits that will permit life insurance to be issued standard. This is the case with some grades of electrical and construction workers and truck drivers. The desire to include as many occupations as possible within the standard class of life insurance and the favourable experience with the D.I. benefit has meant that most classes of occupations taken as standard for life insurance are also taken as standard for D.I.

THE MEANING OF ACCIDENTAL DEATH

In Chapter 19 on Total Disability, it was mentioned that there is no need to define "life" and "death"; with rare exceptions, it is obvious whether a person is alive or dead. Whether or not a death is an "accidental death" is by no means so clear; in some cases it may be difficult to know whether a death was due to accident or to disease; in others to know whether it was due to accident or suicide.

Consider a case of a man, known to have a heart condition, and to have serious personal or business problems; his car collides at high speed with the abutment of a bridge and he is found dead. Did he simply lose control of his car; did he die from a heart attack while at the wheel; or did he deliberately cause the collision? It will never be known.

An insurance company is particularly anxious to avoid having to pay for an accidental death when in fact suicide was involved. There is often a strong suspicion of suicide when death is due to inhalation of carbon monoxide from a car, in a garage with the doors closed, or due to the discharge of a firearm in the hands of the deceased.

One company states: " 'accidental death' means death which (1) results, directly and independently of all other causes, either from bodily injury sustained solely by external, violent and accidental means or from accidental drowning and (2) is not a risk excluded from cover as provided below."

Although the clause refers to accidental means which may be distinguished in law from an accidental result, there is, in practice, little distinction.

The clause states further that for a benefit to be paid death must occur "within ninety days after the date of the accident"; this is intended to eliminate death from disease which may have no connection with the accident but which a claimant may seek to associate with it.

EXCLUSIONS

The clause quoted above excludes various risks as follows:

1. *Suicide, whether sane or insane.* The purpose of insurance is to cover losses from unforeseen contingencies; a deliberate act of the insured to make happen the event on which the insurance is payable is contrary to the principles on which insurance is based.

2. *Inhaling gas, or taking poison, drugs or medicines, voluntarily or otherwise.* Suicide by one of these means is so common and so difficult to prove as being self-sought, that in self-defence the companies exclude death due to one of these causes and try to avoid the question whether it was suicide or not. An exception to the exclusion is if the death is due to an occupational accident incident to the occupation of the life insured; in such a case, the possibility of suicide is virtually eliminated.

3. *Physical or mental infirmity, medical or surgical treatment, illness or disease of any kind.* It is accidental death which is being covered and not death from any other cause.

4. *Committing or attempting to commit a criminal offence.* No one (nor their heirs) should profit from wrongdoing.

5. *Insurrection, civil commotion, war.* Companies must protect

themselves against mass claims and special hazards, of which war is one, the cost of which cannot be computed.

6. *Aviation.* The hazards due to aviation as an occupation or hobby are obviously such as cannot be covered under regular premium rates. Formerly all deaths due to engaging in aviation were excluded, but currently all passenger flights are generally included without extra charge.

TRIPLE INDEMNITY AND DISMEMBERMENT BENEFITS

We have already referred to the amendments to the Canadian federal insurance laws permitting a federally registered life insurance company to issue certain accident benefits as part of its life insurance policies without the necessity of treating such accident benefits as a separate class of business. The law as it now stands permits the following benefits to be so written:

1. Insurance payable on accidental death not exceeding twice the amount of insurance payable on death from any cause (the latter may be described as the face amount of the life insurance policy).
2. Insurance payable on "accidental dismemberment or accidental loss of sight in one eye or in both eyes" provided it does not exceed the face amount of the life insurance policy.

Triple Indemnity. It will be noted that under (1), three times the face amount of the policy could be paid on accidental death. This is an extension of the double indemnity accident benefit which has been discussed in this chapter and which has been a feature of Canadian life insurance since 1922.

Not all Canadian life insurance companies have availed themselves of this extension. A variation of this which comes within the 1961 change of law is offered by some U.S. companies. It is to pay triple the face amount of the policy if accidental death occurs while a passenger in an aircraft or other public conveyance operating commercially to transport passengers for hire.

Dismemberment Benefit. It has been quite common for casualty insurance companies and those life insurance companies doing accident business as a separate branch of their operations to offer benefits payable on the loss of an eye or both eyes and of one or more limbs. Following the 1961 changes in law such benefits can now be attached to a life insurance policy and treated as part of the life insurance business.

One Canadian company has through its accident insurance branch been offering for some years an Accidental Death and Dismemberment Benefit to be attached to its life insurance policies. In addition to the face amount being payable as an additional accidental death benefit: the face amount would be paid on (i) loss of both hands, both feet or sight of both eyes or (ii) one hand and one foot or (iii) one hand or one foot and loss of sight of one eye; half the face amount would be paid on (iv) loss of one hand or one foot or sight of one eye; a quarter of the face amount would be paid on (v) loss of thumb and any finger of one hand.

All these indemnities are doubled if the accident occurs while the insured is a fare-paying passenger in a public conveyance: bus, taxi, train, ship, or commercial aircraft. It should be noted that the triple face amount payment on accidental death is within the 1961 federal life insurance legislative changes, but not the double face-amount payments on dismemberment.

One criticism of this form of benefit added to a life insurance policy is that it is likely to increase considerably the difficulty of settling claims. Thus: what constitutes loss of sight? Another criticism might be that the various dismemberment benefits bear no economic relationship to each other. In casualty insurance this point is rarely questioned but it is traditional in life insurance to do so. This Canadian company has a larger volume of this accidental death and dismemberment benefit in force than of the regular D.I. benefit.

CHAPTER TWENTY-ONE

Mortality Trends and Tables

"The days of our age are three-score years and ten; and though men be so strong that they come to fourscore years: yet is their strength then but labour and sorrow; so soon passeth it away, and we are gone." (Psalm 90, v. 10)[1]

The thousands of years that have elapsed since the above statement was made appear to have made little difference to man's longevity. Yet in the past century major changes have occurred in death rates with a corresponding influence on man's social life and activities.

TRENDS IN POPULATION MORTALITY

In analysing mortality trends we require a broader base than the lives selected by life insurance companies under their policies. Once the selection has been made by the company, the life insured is subject to the environment in which he or she lives, including occupational and recreational hazards. Thus there is a close connection between population and life insurance mortality, particularly in a country like Canada where life insurance covers such a large proportion of the population.

The earliest official population mortality tables for the whole of Canada were based on the census of 1931. In the United States, vital statistics for the whole country are available from 1933 only. Hence we can appreciate the importance of the British tables covering England and

[1] The version is from the Anglican Book of Common Prayer. Gerhard von Rad in *Genesis* (London, 1961) notes in reference to the great ages given to the Patriarchs in the Old Testament (Adam 930, Methuselah 969) that with increasing distance from the Creation the average life span diminished in stages to that noted by the Psalmist.

Wales which date back to 1838. There has always been a similarity in their way of life among English-speaking peoples which is reflected in their rates of death and survival. Further, these English life tables have been an important factor in the sanitary and industrial reforms which have spread throughout the world.

The Dark Ages. We read of sanitary regulations in the Old Testament and the care the Romans took to bring pure drinking water from long distances to their cities; this emphasis on sanitation seems to have been forgotten in the many centuries which followed. Throughout the Middle Ages, and the Tudor and later periods, living conditions of the utmost filth and squalor were accepted as the normal state of living; little care was taken to dispose of human excrement and the contamination of food and water was universal. The infectious diseases took a terrible toll, particularly of the young. Gibbon, the great historian, writing in 1763 quoted vital statistics that more than one-half of the children born in his day died before their ninth birthday! The latest Canadian Life Table covering the years 1970–1972 shows that if present rates of mortality continue one-half of the boys born today will live to age 73 and one-half of the girls to age 80!

The Industrial Revolution. It was due to the alarm caused by the ravages of cholera in England in 1831–33 that the first thought was given by parliament to sanitary reform and it was realized that accurate statistics were necessary. Hence began the annual series of reports on vital statistics and public health measures in which the British were the pioneers.

The growth of cities, particularly the slum areas, during the so-called Industrial Revolution; the terrible working conditions in factories; the unduly long hours of labour; the contamination and adulteration of food; the ignorance of the causes of death: all explain the lack of general improvement in the death rate until comparatively recent times. To give an example on this continent: the death rate in New York City rose almost continuously from 1810 to 1854.

The Modern Era. It may not be realized that the medical discoveries which have had such an influence on our lives are of quite recent development. It was only in the latter half of the nineteenth century (from 1850 on) that Pasteur's researches demonstrated the existence of parasitic organisms, visible under the microscope, which were the basis of infectious diseases. This and his work on the sterilization of food products places the world forever in his debt. To the same period belongs the discovery of anaesthetics by Morton of Massachusetts and the introduction of antiseptic methods in surgery by Lister of Edinburgh. X-rays were discovered by Roentgen in 1895. Just consider what surgery was like before anaesthetics and X-ray and with standards of cleanliness in the operating theatre that indicated complete ignorance of the causes of infection!

During the present century the development of immunization following Pasteur's discoveries has made enormous strides. The attack on tuberculosis, formerly called the "white plague," has been remarkably successful and each year shows an improvement. It is difficult to believe that in 1900 tuberculosis was the leading cause of death. The study of nutritional deficiencies, the discovery of vitamins and their function, has meant that scurvy and rickets have almost disappeared as is evidenced by the straight-limbed youngsters of today.

The discovery of insulin by Sir Frederick Banting in Toronto made 1920 a red letter year in medical history. The enormous development in the past twenty years of chemo-therapy (the administration of a chemical preparation as distinguished from a biological serum) and antibiotics has given man powerful weapons in his fight with disease. Thus since 1900 a new era has dawned for the human race, not only regarding advances in medicine but in the general improvement in standards of living and the elimination of poverty. Reviewing the past half-century, man in the western world has much cause for satisfaction in his fight with disease and death.

Table 21.1 shows the trend of mortality in the past hundred years in the general population. It covers male lives, from 1838 to 1931, according to the life tables of England and Wales and then from 1931 to 1971, according to the Canadian life tables. Both the rate of mortality and the expectation of life are shown for specific ages. As explained earlier, the "expectation of life" being the "average after lifetime" is not too specific as a measure of mortality at any particular age.

At all ages the reduction in mortality has been remarkable over the period covered. Even over the past forty years there have been marked reductions except around age 60 where the rate has remained almost constant: there is also some evidence that further reduction at younger adult ages is unlikely.

Proportion of Older People Increasing. A result of the decrease in mortality, particularly at the younger ages, has been a striking increase

TABLE 21.1

Trend of Population Mortality 1838 to 1971
Male Lives

Period	Rate of mortality $1000\,q_x$				
		Ages			
	At birth	20	40	60	80
England & Wales					
1838–54	163.6	8.3	13.0	32.5	141.8
1881–90	161.0	4.8	12.6	35.9	153.0
1901–10	144.3	3.8	9.3	32.6	141.6
1921	90.0	3.5	6.9	25.6	140.0
1931	71.9	3.2	5.6	24.2	145.0
Canada					
1931	87.0	3.1	4.9	19.4	115.3
1941	62.5	2.4	4.3	20.3	117.4
1951	43.2	1.7	3.3	20.7	108.5
1961	30.6	1.5	2.8	20.0	100.9
1971	20.0	0.8	2.9	19.2	97.0

Period	Expectation of life $\mathring{e}_x$				
		Ages			
	At birth	20	40	60	80
England & Wales					
1838–54	39.9	39.5	26.1	13.5	4.9
1881–90	43.7	40.3	25.4	12.9	4.5
1901–10	48.5	43.0	27.0	13.5	4.9
1921	55.6	45.8	29.2	14.4	4.9
1931	58.7	46.8	29.6	14.4	4.7
Canada					
1931	60.0	49.0	32.0	16.3	5.6
1941	63.0	49.6	31.9	16.1	5.5
1951	66.3	50.8	32.4	16.5	5.8
1961	68.3	51.5	33.0	16.7	6.1
1971	69.3	51.7	33.2	16.9	6.4

TABLE 21.2

Population of Canada
Percentage by Age Groups

Mid-year	Age Group					
	0–9	10–19	20–39	40–59	60–69	70 and over
1971	18.8	20.5	28.1	20.9	6.5	5.2
1931	21.3	20.4	29.8	20.0	5.0	3.4

in the proportion of older people. This is evident even in a relatively young country like Canada in spite of immigration. From 1931 to 1971 the population increased from approximately 10 million to 21½ million and the number of people age 70 and over from 345,000 to 1,124,000 or as shown in Table 21.2 from 3.4 per cent to 5.2 per cent.

FEMALE MORTALITY

The trend of female mortality has not only been downwards but in recent years has far outpaced the downward trend of male mortality. Even at the critical age 60 where the downward trend for male lives was questionable, for female lives the mortality rate per thousand in Canada fell from 17.1 in 1931 to 10.6 in 1961, a fall of 38 per cent. In 1971 the ratios of female to male mortality in the population of Canada at representative ages were:

Age 20	Age 40	Age 60	Age 80
32.1%	59.6%	48.6%	67.2%

A similar trend has been apparent in most advanced countries as in the United States (for both white and non-white lives), Great Britain, Australia, Europe, and Japan.[2] The change must be ascribed to the lower frequency of child-bearing and the reduction in maternal mortality, but this distinct biological difference between men and women is one of the enigmas of vital statistics.

A similar difference between male and female mortality has become evident in recent years in the mortality of insured lives and has resulted in a reduction of rates of premium for life insurance on female lives as has been referred to in Chapter 11.

CAUSES OF DEATH

Statistics Canada publishes very detailed information concerning causes of death. For 1970 this was given under 17 main headings. The deaths in that year numbered 155,961. The five most important causes of death accounted for nearly 90 per cent of the total as follows:

Circulatory diseases (heart, etc.)	77,379	49.6%
Neoplasms (cancer)	30,762	19.7
Accidents and violence	14,443	9.3
Respiratory diseases	10,698	6.9
Diseases of digestive system	5,354	3.4
Total	138,636	88.9%

[2]R. H. Daw, F.I.A., "The Comparison of Male and Female Mortality Rates," *Journal*, Royal Statistical Society, vol. 124 (1961).

The item showing the smallest number of deaths was complications of pregnancy and childbirth; the number of deaths was only 75. It is a measure of the remarkable progress made in medicine that only 75 women died of these causes out of 4,000,000 of child-bearing age; the number of births in 1970 was 371,988.

In the 1960 report it was stated that if the 1921 rates of mortality had applied to the 1960 population the number of deaths would have been 206,000; actually there was only 139,693. Particular reference is made to striking reductions even in the period from 1941 to 1960; comparing death rates per 100,000 of population in the year 1960 with those in the period 1941–45 showed a reduction from 50.0 to 4.6 for tuberculosis, from 8.7 to 1 for the principal communicable diseases (diphtheria, whooping cough, measles, and scarlet fever) and from 69.0 to 40.5 for influenza, bronchitis, and pneumonia.

In different age groups, causes of death are of differing important. From age 45 on, circulatory diseases and neoplasms rank first and second; in the age group 40 to 45, accidents have second place. From age one to 40, accidents are the greatest killer with neoplasms second from age 3 to 40; at age 2 respiratory diseases are second; at age one, congenital abnormalities. In the first year of life the leading cause is perinatal (after birth) diseases, and congenital abnormalities are second.

The principal difference by sex is that females are much less prone to accidents than males, 6.5 per cent of deaths as opposed to 11.2 per cent. The difference begins to be noticeable by age 5, reaches a peak in the age group 20 to 24, and gradually declines until, by age 70, the proportions are approximately equal; but even if accidents are eliminated, death rates at all ages are still considerably lower for females than for males.

A Fallacy. One must avoid the fallacy that a reduction in mortality at the younger ages necessarily means an increase in the rates of mortality at the older ages. The same conditions which tend to reduce mortality at the younger ages as: improved social conditions and all that is implied by a higher standard of living and improvements in medical and surgical techniques and knowledge, also operate at the middle and older ages. More survivors to the older ages may mean more deaths by number at those ages but that does not necessarily mean that the ratio of the number of deaths to the number of survivors must increase.[3]

[3] "The Survival of the Unfit and Its Influence on Mortality," by the author, *Proceedings*, Centenary of the Institute of Actuaries, 1948.

MORTALITY OF INSURED LIVES

When dealing with the mortality of insured lives there are special factors which might influence the trend, some of which are outlined here:

1. Standards of selection of risk may vary at different times. Undoubtedly in recent years a much broader view has been taken as regards the type of risk which would be accepted at standard rates.

2. Economic conditions may influence the mortality in some period, e.g., following the stock market crash of 1929, when suicides and accidents of a suspicious nature increased the claims ratio of larger policies.

3. Social classes included may change. The improvement in wage and living standards has brought large numbers of industrial workers into Ordinary insurance whereas formerly they were almost all in the Industrial class of life insurance business.

4. Different classes of selected lives may be introduced into the experience. For example all the CA Tables include both standard medically examined lives and those taken at standard rates without medical examination, but based on an extensive questionnaire completed by the applicant.

5. The proportion of female lives included may vary between experiences. As already stated the mortality of female lives is substantially below that of male lives of the same age.

In Figures 15 and 16 we show the ultimate rates of mortality, i.e., after the select period, of a number of tables covering insured lives over the past hundred years or so. They relate to Canadian lives or are tables originating in Britain which have been used as standards in Canada for the calculation of premium rates and policy-reserves. It will be observed that there has been a progressive decrease in mortality at every age under 60 when the tables are taken in chronological order. Further, the table relating to Canadian insured lives, the CA 52–56 (as does also the latest Canadian table the CA 58–64) indicates definitely lower mortality at all the ages shown.

Some Well-Known Mortality Tables

An outline is given below of the background of several well-known mortality tables dealing (with one exception) with the mortality of in-

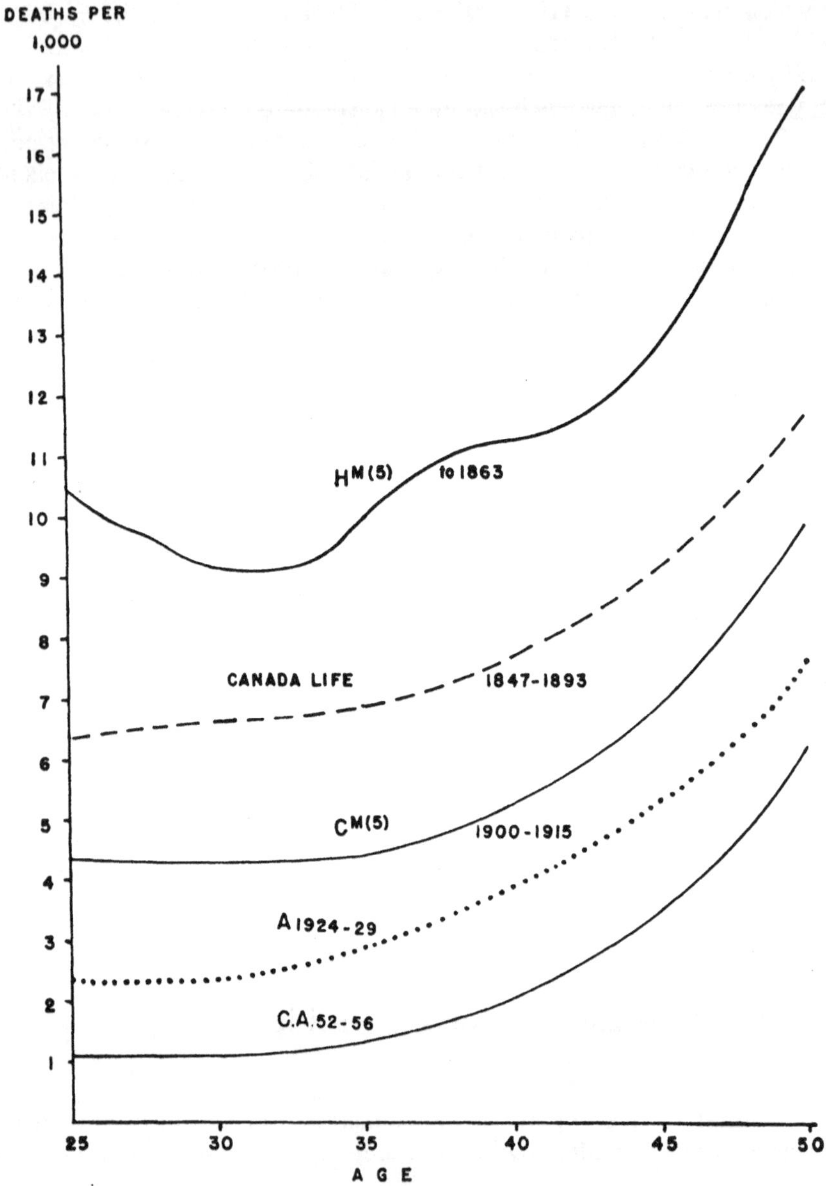

FIGURE 15. Ultimate Rates of Mortality, Insured Lives Ages 25–50, $1000q_x$

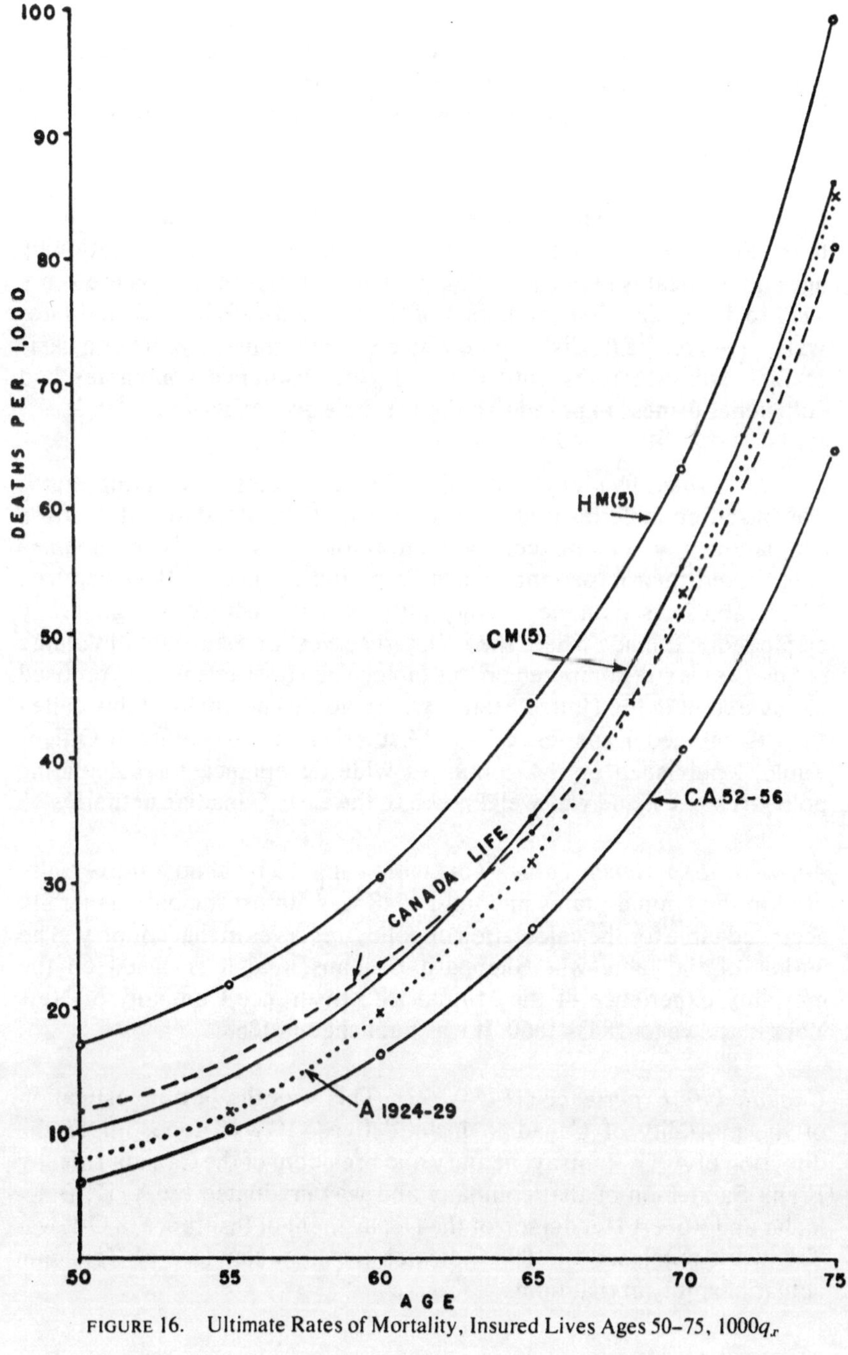

FIGURE 16. Ultimate Rates of Mortality, Insured Lives Ages 50–75, $1000q_x$

sured lives. These have played a part in the development of life insurance in Canada. In most cases extensive tables have been published giving the net premiums at various rates of interest for various life insurance plans and the corresponding policy-reserves at various durations.

The Carlisle Table. This was published in 1815 by Joshua Milne, actuary to the Sun Life (of London) and was based on a census enumeration by age and the deaths in two parishes in Carlisle, England, during the years 1779 to 1787. The first premiums of the Canada Life in 1847 and later were based on the Carlisle Table which served for many years as a basis of life insurance rates until the early life insurance companies had sufficient business exposed to compute their own experience.

The Hm Table. The letters signify "Healthy Males" indicating that it was based on male insured lives accepted at the standard rates of the companies. It was a joint company effort and twenty British companies contributed their experience during a period ending on 31 December, 1863. Tables based on the Hm mortality experience were very generally employed in Canada where the policy-reserves for a substantial volume of business is still computed on this table. The Hm Table was never used to any extent in the United States, where an earlier English table called the "Combined Experience" or "Actuaries" or "Seventeen Offices Table," published in 1843 obtained wide acceptance for calculating policy-reserves, and was well known to the early Canadian actuaries.

American Experience Table. This table came to be almost universally used in the United States and until 1948 was almost the only generally accepted table for the calculation of policy-reserves in that country. The author of the table was Sheppard Homans, and it is based on the mortality experience of the Mutual Life Insurance Company of New York in the years 1843–1860. It was published in 1868.

Canada Life Experience (1847–1893). This was the first investigation of the mortality of Canadian insured lives. It was done, under the direction of A. G. Ramsay, actuary and president of the Canada Life, by Frank Sanderson of that company and was graduated by A. K. Blackadar and Robert Henderson of the Department of Insurance at Ottawa. The work published in 1895 indicates the high standard of Canadian actuarial ability at that time.

British Offices "O" Tables. These tables were based on the joint experience of British life insurance companies over the period 1863 to 1893. This investigation was the most detailed and comprehensive ever made into life insurance company mortality to that date, some sixty British companies giving their experience. These tables are generally represented by the symbol "O," as O(m) the select experience, Om the aggregate experience, Om(5) the ultimate experience which excludes the experience of the first five years following entry, and so on. An investigation into the mortality of the lives covered under their annuity policies was made at the same time by the British Offices.

The Om(5) was extensively used in Canada for the calculation of policy-reserves and is still used in Canada for that purpose. Two Canadian actuaries, Messrs. Thomas Bradshaw and Cecil Moore, published in 1905 a volume containing extensive tables of net premiums and policy-reserves based on this mortality experience.

American Men and Canadian Men Tables. The Canadian Men Table has already been described (Tables 4.4 and 4.5) and has been used extensively in this text. It was the result of an investigation, conducted along identical lines, into the mortality of both U.S. and Canadian insured lives. Fifty-nine companies contributed their experience for the period 1900 to 1915. The tables were published in both select and ultimate forms, the select period being five years. These were the first tables based on amounts of life insurance and not on the numbers of policies or lives thus giving the financial effect of the mortality. A point worth mentioning is that the Canadian Men Table showed, for practically all ages of life, a lower mortality than the American Men Table. The ultimate tables are expressed by the symbols AM(5) and CM(5). The AM(5) table was never widely used in the United States.

The A1924–29 Table. The actuarial organizations of Great Britain, the United States, and Canada have been engaged for some years in compiling and publishing the results of a continuous investigation into the mortality of insured lives in each of their countries. From the results, periodically, a new table is prepared. That of the British actuaries covering the years 1924 to 1929 and the tables of that experience, called the A1924–29 Table, have gained wide acceptance in Great Britain and also in Canada. In this table the select period is three years only. A later report with monetary tables covering the years 1949 to 1952 has been issued.

The CA Tables. The organization of Canadian actuaries now known as the Canadian Institute of Actuaries published in 1953 the results of its first joint continuous investigation of mortality under ordinary life business in Canada covering the years 1949 to 1952. This is known as the CAA 1949–52 Table. A second published table covered the joint experience of a number of companies for the years 1952 to 1956 and is designated as the CA 52–56 Table. These tables are based on the combined data for male and female lives and medical and non-medical business and were published in select and ultimate form. For the latest table 25 companies contributed data representing by volume 84 per cent of the life insurance industry in Canada and again medical and non-medical business were combined, but the data for male and female lives were examined separately. This latest table records the mortality of male and female lives separately and the tables are known as CA 58–64 (Males) and CA 58–64 (Females). The mortality rates of the male table are given as Table 8.1 in this text.

Commissioners Standard Ordinary Mortality Tables. The almost universal adoption by the various states in the U.S. of a series of standard laws governing minimum policy-reserves and the cash surrender values, etc., based on them, gives particular importance to the mortality table on which such policy-reserves are based. The replacement of the American Experience Table in 1948 resulted from the deliberations of a Committee appointed by the National Association of Insurance Commissioners and hence the name given to the table accepted: Commissioners 1941 Standard Ordinary Mortality Table, or 1941 CSO Table. This table was derived from the joint experience of a number of U.S. companies in the years 1930 to 1940 under Ordinary insurance on lives accepted at standard rates. This table is being replaced by one relating to a more recent experience covering the period between 1950 and 1954 policy anniversaries; it is known as the 1958 CSO Table.

Both CSO tables give the ultimate mortality excluding the first five years from entry. Both tables include margins of safety as would be expected if one table is to be used by life insurance companies serving all social classes and covering all areas of the United States. These tables are of importance to Canadian life insurance companies due to the extensive business done by Canadian companies in the U.S. and the simplicity of using one table for both Canadian and U.S. business.

RECENT CANADIAN, U.S., AND BRITISH MORTALITY ON INSURED LIVES

How does the mortality of insured lives under the latest tables published compare with each other? There is the Canadian CA 52–56, the U.S.

1958 CSO covering the years 1950–54, and the British A1949–52. We use the *ultimate* mortality ratios in this comparison, i.e., after the period of selection is presumed to have expired, as otherwise a sudden influx of new business or the reverse, by changing the proportion of those still in the "select period," would affect the mortality experienced quite apart from chronological changes. If we take in order the mortality per 1,000 exposed for the four tables: (i) CA 52–56, (ii) the basic table (without margins) used for the 1958 CSO Table, (iii) the British A1949–52 and (iv) the latest Canadian table, the CA 58–64 (Males), the figures for representative ages are:

Age 20:	1.07	0.84	1.11	1.10
Age 35:	1.35	1.41	1.32	1.23
Age 50:	6.24	6.71	5.99	5.90
Age 65:	26.56	27.61	28.10	26.81
Age 80:	101.62	95.64	113.69	94.12

The Canadian and U.S. rates of mortality are quite close together so that the same tables could be used for premiums and policy-reserves, at least for permanent plans of insurance. The same could be said for the British table except for ages over 65 where British mortality is substantially higher than the others. The mortality rates of U.S. insured lives indicate the following characteristics: they are relatively low at both extremes of the age range—under 30 and over 70—but higher in between.

In this chapter we have referred only to mortality tables used for the calculation of premiums and policy-reserves for standard ordinary insurance. Other tables which deal with industrial, group, and fraternal insurance as well as those dealing with annuities are referred to as these types of business are discussed.

CHAPTER TWENTY-TWO

Selection of Risks: Objectives and Functions

The principle of life insurance operations, as already stated, is that the life insurance company will, on acceptance of the application of the insured and on the payment of specified premiums, obligate itself to pay a certain sum or sums on the death of a specified life insured. Where the premium is payable annually and the life insured is young the sum insured payable may be fifty, one hundred, or even many more times greater than the annual premium. The premium rates charged assume a specific rate of mortality which has been determined from an investigation of the death rates among a definite class of lives who have met certain standards of health and personal history, etc. It is the function of the underwriting or medical department to examine the applications for life insurance and to determine whether the applicants to be insured meet these standards or if not, to decide under what terms they can be accepted, if they can be accepted at all.

One prominent Canadian life insurance company on its Canadian business accepted over a recent period at its normal or standard rates 94 per cent of the applications received for life insurance; 4 per cent of the applications were accepted subject to an extra premium and only 2 per cent of the applications were declined. Figures for other companies in Canada are similar.

Life insurance meets a fundamental public need and it is the duty of the industry to offer life insurance to as large a proportion of those who apply as possible. The figures given indicate that this duty is being fulfilled. In this chapter and the two next following the procedures of the selection of risks will be outlined. It will be noted how closely trends in mortality are followed and as these have been mainly downwards it has resulted in an expansion of the class accepted at normal or standard rates, the lowering of the extra premiums charged to others, and the reduction of the uninsurable class. Further, through the study of the mortality of those accepted the industry has contributed to the advance of medicine and industrial hygiene. U.S. life insurance companies have been pioneers in this, but Canadian companies have made worth-while contributions to the combined statistics and their analysis.

THE STANDARD AND SUBSTANDARD RISK

Those lives insured accepted by a life insurance company at its normal or standard rates and conditions are called *standard risks*. Those lives insured who for any reasons, including those of health, personal, family or medical history, or occupation, are accepted on special terms are called *substandard risks*.

Every company's underwriting department is torn between two desires. On the one hand it wishes to accept as large a proportion as possible of the risks submitted to it at standard rates. On the other hand it wishes to preserve equity by seeing that those whose expected mortality is outside the acceptable normal range should pay a rate of premium corresponding to the estimated extra mortality to be expected from them in the future. At the extreme is the class who may not be acceptable on any terms and who may be called "uninsurable." The word "may" is emphasized, for one company will accept a risk considered "uninsurable" by another. The acceptance of risks subject to extra premiums for every variety of medical, occupational, aviation and other impairments, affects less than 5 per cent of individual life insurance policies issued. The handling of these substandard risks is based on statistical data supported by medical and inter-company mortality research. Many, previously considered uninsurable, can now purchase insurance at reasonable premium rates.

The success or otherwise of a life insurance company in selecting its risks is a major factor in its operations. Careless acceptance of risks may result in heavy losses due to unfavourable mortality and "mortality" is one of the three fundamental factors determining the successful operation of a life insurance company. The whole picture of the competitive position relative to other companies can be affected by a wise and well-operated system of selection of risks. On the other hand an unduly restrictive policy by a company in its selection of risks can antagonize its agency force and prejudice its relations with clients, and this may offset to a large extent the advantage to be gained by a more favourable mortality experience.

ANTI-SELECTION OR SELF-SELECTION

The life insurance company may set its rules and offer its ratings, but it is the applicant who has the final choice whether he will accept the offer or not. In the type of plan he chooses, the applicant often shows a preference which influences the mortality experienced. An applicant who has reason to believe that his longevity is impaired, who is or has been under some special strain, or who expects to be exposed to some extra hazard, may seek an abnormal amount of life insurance. As cost is always a criterion, he may choose a low-premium-rate type of life insurance which for the same outlay will give a much larger amount of insurance. It would be expected that in the aggregate such risks would result in a higher eventual mortality than, say, those who are more concerned with the long-term savings aspect of life insurance rather than immediate protection and choose a plan accordingly.

This *self-selection* is also called *anti-selection* because in practice it may tend to offset the selective practices of the life insurance company.

It might be expected that under policies for large sums insured the factor of anti-selection would become more obvious. The first studies made by the Society of Actuaries of the collective experience of a number of companies confirmed this showing mortality of 96 per cent of normal for permanent plans and 106 per cent for term plans; however, more recent studies of large policies have shown mortality for term plans as favourable as that for permanent plans.

The self-selection exercised by an applicant to whom a policy with a rating is offered is indicated by the proportion of such offers which are not taken up. Investigation has shown that the higher the rating, the higher is the proportion of "not taken." The figures of a joint investigation by a number of Canadian companies reported to the Canadian Life Insurance Association illustrated this. The proportion of policies which were accepted standard and which were not-taken was 3 per cent; when rated substandard the not-taken ratio was 16 per cent. Quite often when a case is known to be substandard, particularly a heavily rated case, it is submitted to more than one company so that the ratio of 16 per cent exaggerates the true position.

Often in practice financial considerations are the deciding factor whether an offer is accepted or otherwise. Here the agent plays an important part. In many cases the agent is discouraged by the offer of a rated policy, yet it follows that a substandard risk requires the insurance more, if possible, than the standard risk.

FACTORS IN THE SELECTION OF RISKS

We list below the factors which are considered, in any particular case, to determine the mortality to be expected and hence which indicate the details required from an applicant. It is after the consideration of these particulars that the underwriter would determine the class of risk in which the application would be placed, namely: (i) standard; (ii) sub-standard and the degree of such; (iii) uninsurable.

1. Age, sex and amount of insurance;
2. Occupation and social environment;
3. Residence and travel;
4. Habits – use of alcohol, drugs and tobacco;
5. Aviation; hazardous sports;
6. Family history;
7. Medical history of personal illness or operation;
8. Height and weight (build);

9 to 13. Results of medical examination or the details of the Non-Medical Declaration made in lieu thereof (outlined in Chapter 23).

THE TOOLS OF SELECTION

In the earliest days of life insurance in Britain an applicant for life insurance had not only to be recommended by an existing policyholder of the company, who was personally acquainted with him, but the applicant had to appear in person before the Board of Directors. This was to decide, in the days when medicine was still in a primitive state, whether or not the applicant was a suitable risk. Note that non-medical insurance is older than insurance by medical examination.

The information on which the final decision is made and which is covered under factors (1) to (5) in the previous section are given in the *application for life insurance*. Where the application indicates that the proposed life to be insured has or intends to fly other than as a passenger on a scheduled commercial airline an *aviation questionnaire* giving details is usually requested. The information given in the Application is often supplemented by an *inspection report*.

The items (7) to (13) in the previous section are covered by the *medical examiner's report* or in lieu thereof, in non-medical cases, the *non-medical declaration*. Consideration of items (6) to (13) will be deferred to the next chapter. There are various supplementary questionnaires used by companies and requested in special cases to give additional information which will be referred to. The above represent the tools used by the underwriter in the selection of risks.

The Inspection Report. To get an independent opinion of the applicant's background, his occupation, his social environment, and his home life and habits, it is the practice of life insurance companies in Canada and the United States to use the services of an inspection company. The applicant is notified that such a practice is part of the routine underwriting process. At one time it was the practice to get an applicant to give the names and addresses of two friends to whom the company wrote to get information, but this practice is now extinct. Neighbours, business associates, and employers are the source of information on which inspection reports are based.

The Medical Information Bureau. The M.I.B. was organized in 1902 as a non-profit association to make possible an exchange of information among life insurance companies. It permits them to detect misrepresentations of fact and thus to guard the interests of existing policyholders. The exchange of information chiefly concerns medical facts. The confidentiality of information exchanged is assured by the Medical Director in each member-company.

Provincial laws in Canada require that an applicant be notified of the Medical Information Bureau and inspection reporting practices. In certain provinces, notably British Columbia, Manitoba, Ontario, Nova Scotia and Prince Edward Island, the applicant must be notified of the cause of adverse action taken on his application.

We now deal in turn with the items (1) to (5): the factors in the selection of risks.

1. AGE, SEX AND AMOUNT OF INSURANCE

Age. Life insurance is granted on lives from birth to, usually age 70. It may be granted at higher ages, on request, if the need is shown and underwriting standards are met.

The amount of insurance which could be written on the life of a child was formerly strictly limited by provincial laws. Such restrictions have now been removed but insurance companies guard against over-insurance by limiting the amount in accordance with the income of the family and the amount of insurance carried by the parents.

Sex. References have been made repeatedly to the lower mortality among females relative to males of the same age and this also applies to the mortality among insured lives according to investigations in recent years. On this account companies grant reduced rates to female lives. This is a remarkable change from the early days of life insurance in Canada when an extra premium was required on female lives and some companies declined them altogether.

Amount of Insurance: Overinsurance. In Chapter 24 we outline the facility of reinsuring any excess above the amount a company desires to retain at its own risk on a certain life. This enables a company to offer life insurance practically without limit should circumstances justify it.

We have stressed to such an extent the inadequate amounts of life insurance owned that the question of overinsurance may be considered to be academic, but it does come up in practice. In selection of risks the amount of insurance applied for is considered in relation to the following: (1) the purpose of the insurance and the party to whom it is payable, (2) the life insurance needs of the applicant, (3) the ability of the applicant to pay for the insurance. In Chapter 1 we referred to the question of the legality of one person insuring another and under provincial laws the scope of insurable interest and the rights of parties to effect insurance on other lives is set out (see Chapter 16). The underwriter must be satisfied that the amount of life insurance applied for and the total life insurance carried bears some relation to the loss of income the man's dependents would suffer in the event of his death.

Regarding personal insurance, one rule used by some underwriters is that the total expenditure on life insurance premiums should not exceed 20 per cent of a man's gross income. One should remember that in the higher income brackets taxation is high, and this 20 per cent applying to the gross income may represent a far larger proportion of his net income after taxation. A rigid rule is difficult to apply for circumstances vary considerably.

Some underwriters assume that the 20 per cent gross income should be considered as if it were used to purchase straight life insurance at the applicant's age and take this amount of insurance as the upper limit irrespective of the plan on which insurance is being sought. A man aged 35 earning $20,000 a year would on this basis have a limit of approximately $200,000 insurance.

When it is a question of a firm insuring a "key man," an amount in excess of five times the man's remuneration from the firm is likely to be questioned, for the firm should be able to replace an executive within five years of his death; this places a measure on the insurable value of his services.

2. OCCUPATION AND SOCIAL ENVIRONMENT

Occupation is a fundamental factor in his probable future expectation of life. It is not only the possible accidental hazards or unfavourable health reactions of certain occupations. Rather it is that the type of occupation determines his earnings and usually his entire social environment. Where, as in England and the U.S.A., investigations have been made into mortality relative to socio-economic class, it has been shown that the professional class has the lowest rate of mortality whereas unskilled workers have the highest rates. This would be expected for all that is conducive to health and longevity and appreciation of such exists in far greater measure in one case than the other![1]

In the last thirty-five years there have been remarkable changes in industrial medicine and engineering. A substantial part of the improvement in mortality in recent years has been due to higher standards of living and improved working conditions. This has been recognized in the life insurance industry in recent years by a considerable reduction in the number of occupations for which an extra premium is required; further, the extras have been reduced in many case. The life insurance companies have investigated their experience according to the occupation of the life insured, in some cases pooling their experiences to do so. The latest published experience is that by the Society of Actuaries, "1967 Occupational Study."[2] Special underwriting considerations apply to the disability benefits and additional accidental death benefit attached to life insurance policies as were considered in the chapters devoted to them (Chapters 19 and 20).

From the underwriting point of view occupations may be divided into two classes: those where there is a definite accident hazard and those where the occupational hazard is other than accident.

Occupational Hazard: Accident. These are self-explanatory:

(*a*) Workers with or near machinery;
(*b*) Building and construction workers, particularly those on high buildings;
(*c*) Underground miners;
(*d*) Power line workers;
(*e*) Lumbermen;
(*f*) Explosives handling and manufacture.

Occupational Hazard: Other than Accident. We note briefly why certain occupations are generally considered to be "rated" occupations and the health hazards associated with them.

[1]"Occupation, Social Class and Mortality," by the author, *Transactions*, Society of Actuaries, vol. 12 (1960) and Addendum to paper by the author in vol. 15, pp. 99–100.

[2]See outline by Sibigtroth and Woodman: *Proceedings*, Home Office Life Underwriters Association, vol. 49 (1968).

(i) *Dust.* Workers in anthracite coal and in metal mines and workers in the stone and abrasive industries are exposed to diseases of the lungs (silicosis, etc.). In the past these have been very serious. One must watch for the case of the man affected by such diseases who has changed to another occupation. There is some evidence that the latest pneumatic drills introduce a greater hazard; they may be effective in reducing labour costs, but are dangerous to health on account of the extra concentration of fine, penetrating dust.

(ii) *Poisons*, as in acid manufacture, smelters, oil refineries, paint and varnish manufacture.

(iii) *Abnormalities of temperature and air pressure.* Divers, tunnel workers, caisson workers; workers in the smelting and glass-making industries and in potteries.

(iv) *Radiant energy.* Exposure to radiant energy may become a major occupational hazard in view of the projects involving the use of atomic energy in industry. However, the dangers are so well known, and the built-in safeguards established almost irrespective of cost, that it is to be hoped the additional hazards may be negligible. The danger to the workers and the general public of accidental leakages of radiation is something realized but as yet unmeasurable.

(v) *Liquor industry.* The problem here is the ready access to alcohol. Undoubtedly the mortality of those engaged in the retail end is substantially higher than average, such as the proprietor of the small hotel where liquor is served, waiters, bartenders, porters, and others. It is a very ancient problem and is further discussed under "habits." The underwriter will pay more than usual attention to the habits of salesmen and others connected with the liquor industry.

(vi) *Amusement industry.* Here the very nature of the occupation calls for late hours, abnormal strains, and long periods of inactivity. Criticisms of habits and morals arise more frequently in this group than others. Individual selection to distinguish between the "insurable" and "uninsurable" is more the criterion here than the assessment of a rating.

When dealing with the extra mortality to be expected under the life insurance benefit due to occupational hazards, Canadian companies assume for practical purposes that the extra hazard can be represented as so many extra deaths per annum per thousand lives insured and that this is the same irrespective of age. Thus a flat premium of so many dollars per thousand dollars sum insured is charged and added to the annual premium payable. As illustrated in Figure 12, Chapter 7, the *amount at risk* (sum insured less policy-reserve) reduces rapidly under endowment insurances particularly where the period of the endowment is short. Allowance is made for this by reducing the period during which the extra premium is payable under endowment insurances or alternatively charging a reduced extra premium for the whole period of the endowment insurance.

Consistent with the desire to extend the range of standard risks as much as possible, most companies will ignore the occupational extra where it represents an extra premium of less than $3.00 per thousand sum insured. The proportion of the population who are subject to occupational hazards has fallen considerably in recent years due to social and industrial changes (the reduction in coal mining is one). It follows from this and what has been stated above that the factor of occupation has decreased in importance in underwriting in recent years.

Armed Forces. In Canada the armed forces are employed full-time and the term "professional" can be applied to them. Canadian life insurance companies differ so much in their attitude to business on the lives of members of the armed forces that only a brief reference will be made here to their insurability.

Apart from the accident hazard connected with modern equipment, men attracted to the armed forces have a higher accident death rate than normally would be anticipated. Further, in the first year or more there is a weeding-out process among the young enlisted men, some of whom would not qualify for standard ordinary insurance on the basis of their civilian occupations. Thus, restrictions are generally placed on the amount granted to those recently enlisted. For those established in the armed forces, receiving "trade pay" due to technical skills acquired, and those of higher grades with family responsibilities, increasing amounts of life insurance are granted and at standard rates provided the equivalent civilian occupation would also be accepted at standard rates. Commissioned officers are accepted at standard rates unless in submarine service, aviation, or paratroops, where all ranks are accepted subject to an extra premium.

It has been the practice, other than in time of war, to issue policies to those in the armed forces giving the same full protection as to all other policyholders, i.e., they are fully covered in the event of war. On this account when there is serious danger of war, restrictions may be applied by the companies on the issue of term plans or plans with a large element of term insurance.

3. RESIDENCE AND TRAVEL

The world may, broadly speaking, be divided into three areas from a life insurance point of view, i.e., with regard to the mortality to be expected in various countries. The lowest mortality is to be expected in the temperate zones, like Canada, U.S.A., British Isles, Europe, South Africa, Australia, and New Zealand. There are variations among these countries and even between different parts of each country as among the different areas in Canada; but the variations are well within what is considered normal. The other two areas may be generally described as semi-tropical and tropical, but from a life insurance point of view the geographic definitions do not hold. It is not only distance from the equator but other factors which count. Thus, besides latitude, the whole picture of public health, sanitation, and racial characteristics determine the mortality of the inhabitants of countries.

A problem arises when a Canadian goes to take up an appointment or makes an extended visit to a country outside the temperate regions named, and wishes to effect life insurance before leaving Canada or during a return visit to Canada. A Canadian may live in such countries under the best conditions of health and medical care. However, heat, humidity, altitude, social life, political background, and the general hazard of contact with a native population living under conditions which result in a high rate of mortality have their effect and may necessitate a rating.

All policies issued in Canada are free from restrictions as to residence and travel provided they are taken out when there is no indication or likelihood of residence in or travel to areas requiring an extra premium. Such policies would remain in full force in event of such residence or travel subject, of course, to the payment of the regular premium.

The possibility of selection against the insurance company arises when life insurance is purchased in contemplation of residence in, or travel to, countries necessitating extra premiums. It is thus obvious that restrictions should be anticipated regarding term plans or additional benefits with a large element of term insurance or additional disability or accidental death benefits.

There are also cases of citizens of foreign countries temporarily resident in, or on a visit to, Canada who wish to effect life insurance in Canada with a Canadian company. Apart from the difficulties of checking on background, medical history and habits, many foreign countries have strict laws against their nationals effecting life insurance abroad as a form of illegal export of capital. Another case which may arise is a Canadian citizen residing in a foreign country wishing to effect life insurance in Canada while resident abroad. Again, apart from the difficulties of arranging for satisfactory medical examinations abroad, this might be considered by that foreign country as transacting life insurance in that country without being licensed to do business there, although the transaction was carried out by mail.

As already stated several leading Canadian life insurance companies do business in many parts of the world and there should be no difficulty in obtaining information as to rates, etc., on a Canadian moving to other parts of the world for business purposes.

Foreign Immigrants. With foreign immigrants there may be a question whether the applicant understands the nature of the contract and the questions submitted to him on the application forms. Further, even where there is no language difficulty, readjustment to life in a new, strange country is hard and may result in emotional strains and may exaggerate any tendencies to disease which otherwise may have remained latent for many years. Companies vary in their attitude to such business but one can appreciate the reasons for their (*a*) insistence on medical examination, (*b*) restrictions on amounts, (*c*) refusal to grant term insurance or special plans containing a large element of term insurance, (*d*) refusing disability and double indemnity benefits. Some companies may even insist on a minimum period of residence in Canada before any insurance is granted.

4. HABITS – USE OF ALCOHOL, DRUGS AND TOBACCO

A life insurance company has no desire to sit in moral judgment on applicants for its policies. It has been established that persons who deviate substantially from the normal in their code of habits, morals, and business ethics have a substantially higher than average rate of mortality. To assess the excess mortality, if any, is the job of the head office. The abuse of alcohol is by far the most frequent cause of rating in this category. It is a most difficult aspect of underwriting for specific information is difficult to obtain.

Statistics indicate a serious toll of accidental deaths and undoubtedly alcohol plays a major part in this. An analysis by the Canadian Institute of Actuaries of the death claims paid by life insurance companies in Canada in the five years from 1969 to 1974 showed that over one-third of the total claims paid within five years of the policy being issued were due to accidents.

One prominent U.S. life insurance company investigated its experience between 1931 and 1948 on lives accepted both at standard and as rated cases where there was a history of alcoholic excess. *Those accepted at standard rates showed a mortality of 225 per cent of the normal.* Other results were as follows, the percentages indicating the mortality experienced as a percentage of normal:

1.	Steady free user, never intoxicated	183%
2.	Intoxicated six times a year for a day or evening only	227%
3.	Intoxicated once a month for a day or evening only	287%
4.	Intoxicated once a week for a day or evening only	328%
5.	Intoxicated not oftener than three times a year but lasting two or three days	332%
6.	Has received treatment or cure for alcoholic habits	293%

The death claims showed a much higher claims ratio than average from (*a*) cirrhosis of the liver, (*b*) automobile accidents at the younger ages, and (*c*) suicide. More recent figures would probably be equally serious.

It must be agreed that excessive use of alcohol is a serious matter in selection for life insurance and with more automobiles with greater engine power its importance is not likely to decrease. The amused toleration of the public is a handicap which has to be overcome. Unfortunately on the highways, it is the innocent traveller who so often pays the penalty.

The background of the applicant who is reported as an excessive user is important; associated with marital troubles, business reverses, or a job just too big for him, it is a warning which should not be ignored.

Alcoholics Anonymous. This organization has done wonderful work. As a general rule a person who required a cure or treatment or moral support to reform was probably a heavy drinker and any relapse is likely to be of a serious nature. Likelihood of the permanence of reform must be tested by the lapse of time and a period of five years' clear record, at least, would generally be required.

Drugs. The non-medical use of drugs has increased drastically over the past ten years. The assessment of the health and mortality hazards of drug users presents the underwriter with a difficult problem. Rules cannot be set as underwriting data are incomplete and statistics unavailable. The applicant, physically dependent on "hard" drugs, is uninsurable. The infrequent marijuana user with an otherwise normal lifestyle is generally considered a normal risk. The concern is the increased use and progression to more potent drugs. What is the personality make-up of such a person? Other drug users fall between these extremes and are considered as individual underwriting problems.

Smoking. One cannot ignore the statistical evidence from various sources which indicates that excessive smoking is detrimental to health. There is, however, a limit to the detail which can be included in the application forms without lowering the value of the overall information requested. Undoubtedly where there is a suggestion of chest pains, signs of bronchial or heart trouble, the degree of indulgence in smoking is a factor in underwriting.

5(*a*). AVIATION

The tremendous development, in recent years, of aviation as a means of travel and the rapid technological changes in aviation mean that any figures will rapidly become dated. The Society of Actuaries has had for many years an active committee gathering and publishing statistics on aviation experience, both of the companies and of governments, so that the industry has been able continuously to compare it practices with current experience. The increasing size of jet aircraft introduces uncertainties in future fatality rates.

Fare-Paying Passengers. As a rule there is no extra premium charged to fare-paying passengers irrespective of the amount of flying done. The Society of Actuaries' statistics indicate that a rate of 10 cents per $1,000 of insurance per 100 hours flown will cover the risk of flying on scheduled airlines anywhere in the world: even less will suffice in Canada and the U.S.A. Considering the average flying time per annum of the fare-paying public it is apparent why no extra premium is charged.

The experience of fare-paying passengers on non-scheduled flights has shown a distinct improvement in recent years and as would be expected is higher than for scheduled flights. It would follow that company-owned planes used to transport their own personnel would, on the average, be more hazardous, partly due to less rigorous inspection and partly due to the same pilot flying many different routes. Taxi-flying as a passenger would call for a higher rating still.

Companies generally have a schedule indicating the risk anticipated through passenger flights and the corresponding extra is based on the amount and type of flying. Any annual extra premium of less than $2.50 per thousand sum insured is generally ignored so that a considerable amount of flying as a passenger, irrespective of type, is generally covered without payment of any extra premium.

Civilian Pilots. There is a wide range in the duties of civilian pilots as from those engaged with a major Canadian or U.S. national air line to those who fly their own planes as a hobby and again to those who make experimental flights as an occupation.

Pilots and crew in the service of major North American air lines operating passenger planes from a North-American terminal are generally taken at standard rates, that is, no extra premium is charged for their flying activities. Others are accepted subject to an extra premium the amount increasing according to the anticipated extra hazard. Companies vary considerably in their practice.

As an indication of the factors considered we quote one Canadian company's practice on private licensed pilots flying their own planes but not as an occupation. No extra premium is charged subject to the following provisos: (1) over age 26 at entry; (2) a minimum of over 100 hours solo flying experience; (3) not flying more than 150 hours a year; (4) satisfactory record of responsible flying; (5) financial ability to maintain aircraft; (6) no history of alcohol abuse; (7) otherwise satisfactory.

Student pilots are graded by age and amount of flying done, a higher extra being charged as a rule at the youngest ages. Helicopter flying is graded with the comparable class of airplane flying.

Aviation Exclusion Clause. Where the aviation risk is uncertain or unusual or the insured prefers this course no extra premium is charged but an aviation exclusion clause is inserted in the policy. This restricts the amount payable in the event of death due to engaging in aviation to the policy-reserve or the amount of the premiums paid. This would apply, of course, to aviation as an occupation or hobby.

Aviation and the Armed Forces. Members of the Armed Forces and others where there is a definite aviation hazard are accepted subject to the payment of an extra premium, and companies generally restrict the sum insured in such cases. Here, too, the extra premiums are graded according to age at entry, the youngest applicants paying the higher extra premiums. The alternative to paying an extra premium would be to have attached to the policy an Aviation Exclusion Clause.

The rapid development and changes in types of aircraft would make any figures on mortality and the accident hazard of temporary value only. Whereas in commercial airlines safety overrides all other factors, in the development of fighting aircraft it stands to reason that performance comes first. Also the development of new types of aircraft with possibly increasing accident hazard explains the companies' restrictions.

5(*b*). HAZARDOUS SPORTS

If we examine the male mortality curve in Figure 3 (Chapter 4), and in particular Figure 15 (Chapter 20) showing the Double Indemnity Accident Benefit claim rate, we note the "hump" in the death rate in the 15 to 24 age group. It is in this age group that we would expect to find those seeking their "kicks" and thrills through some active and possibly hazardous sport. This trend has increased in recent years. This increases further the accidental death rate and mortality rate which we should expect at the younger ages when taking chances is greater than at older ages of discretion.

It is estimated there are some 45,000 sky divers today in Canada and the U.S. and this sport results in an annual death rate of 2.0 per thousand of those engaging in it, which is a considerable extra mortality at the younger ages; the extra risk cannot be ignored. Other forms of hazardous sport requiring the attention of underwriters are skin or scuba diving; automobile, motorcycle and speedboat racing; mountain climbing. Details of these activities are required and the rating determined. When these sports are engaged in professionally, a far more serious situation has to be assessed.

CHAPTER TWENTY-THREE

Selection of Risks: The Medical Side

It is not the intention to make this text an encyclopaedia of impairments or to quote actual ratings for such. The medical aspects of life insurance, particularly its treatment of substandard risks, are of considerable public interest. The principles of underwriting and the medical aspects of a risk do illustrate the combination of statistical evidence, medical opinion, and over-all judgment which are combined to serve the life insurance needs of the public. Where actual ratings, either credits or debits, are quoted they are given for illustrative purposes only. Medical and surgical treatment and techniques have been making giant strides and are reflected in the attitude of the underwriters in the assessment of risks submitted to them. Another purpose of this chapter is to note the terminology used in the medical examiner's Report and give such explanations as may signify their meaning and importance in underwriting.

When an applicant for life insurance states he is suffering from or has suffered from a certain illness or undergone surgery, the assessment of the risk requires a knowledge of medicine and hence the function of the medical director or chief medical officer of the life insurance company. The knowledge of the effect of these illnesses on longevity is derived from the experience of the medical director and the usual text books and published material. The point should be recognized that the results in private practice may differ definitely from what would be expected in life insurance where self-selection is an important factor.

Until some seventy years ago the assessment of risks from the medical point of view was at best an approximate affair based mainly on the personal judgment of the medical director, for statistics, where they existed, were unreliable. Just as life insurance took a major step forward when a set of reliable mortality rates based on insured lives was published (as the Seventeen Offices Table and the Hm) so a great advance in the selection of risks occurred when records of the mortality of those accepted for life insurance with definite impairments were kept and the results published.

For this we are indebted to Arthur Hunter and Dr. Oscar Rogers, the actuary and medical officer respectively, of the New York Life Insurance Company. Over seventy years ago they began to encourage the acceptance of substandard lives at additional ratings. They also began a series of investigations to determine the mortality of the substandard lives accepted according to the impairments known at the time of issue of the policy. This laid the foundations of the science of acceptance of substandard risks. For a number of years these investigations have been inter-company affairs and the published results have not only been of the greatest value to the life insurance industry but have made significant contributions to medical statistics. The latest inter-company investigations are the 1951 Impairment Study[1] and the Build and Blood Pressure Study 1959.[2]

NUMERICAL RATING SYSTEM

The procedure by which the results of these investigations were transformed into ratings was called by Hunter and Rogers the *numerical rating system*.

In essence, the Numerical Rating System assumes that the average risk accepted by a company at standard rates has a value of 100 per cent and each material factor which affects the mortality of the risk is expressed numerically in terms of its variation from 100 per cent. By the summation of these factors subject to certain modifications the risk is evaluated.

Favourable features are expressed as credits, such as an exceptionally favourable family history. This may give as many as 15 points credit, i.e., a group of lives with a similar favourable family history, all other factors being average, would be expected to have a mortality of 85 per cent of that of a group of lives accepted at standard rates.

Unfavourable features are expressed as debits: thus a man age 35 of height 5′ 10″ and weighing 238 lbs. (i.e. 68 lbs. overweight) would receive a debit of 50 points. That is, other factors being average, the mortality expected from a group of lives age 35 each of whom was 68 lbs. overweight would be 150 per cent of that expected from a group of lives age 35 accepted at standard rates.

[1]For an outline of this by Mr. E. A. Lew see *Proceedings*, Home Office Life Underwriters Association, vol. 35 (1954).

[2]Also outlined by Mr. Lew in the same *Proceedings*, vol. 41 (1960).

The Numerical Rating System has been criticized as being mechanical, but when, as in several large companies, thousands of applications may have to be evaluated daily, some simple procedures have to be followed to separate the three-quarters or so of them which are obviously standard, from the others. A company would have certain rules under which the larger cases and questionable cases would be weeded out, to be dealt with by more experienced staff. This ensures uniform treatment in simple impairments and avoids the accusation of decisions being arbitrary. It is also of great assistance in difficult cases which require expert consideration and judgment, ensuring that the statistical evidence is studied and special features of the risk evaluated before a decision is made. The rating for a combination of impairments is not necessarily the sum of the ratings for the individual impairments as will be indicated later.

Among Canadian life insurance companies the Numerical Rating System is not applied to every case, particularly not to those which are obviously standard risks. In practice a great deal of time is given to border line risks to determine whether they should be rated or not and the system is most helpful in such cases. In at least one Canadian company every case before being rated as substandard must be passed upon by the medical director or his associates. This is certainly the rule in all companies before a risk is declined on medical grounds. The Numerical Rating System would generally be applied in rated cases but the final decision would not necessarily be determined by it, as final judgment plays a part.

The Limit for Standard Risks. Companies vary in their assessment of standard risks when evaluated by the Numerical Rating System. Traditionally, a risk indicating a total rating exceeding +25 (i.e. a presumed expected mortality exceeding 125 per cent of standard) was considered as substandard and a rating was imposed. However, there has been a liberalization of this practice in recent years and the figure of +35 (135 per cent standard mortality) would be more representative at the present time, with a lower limit for ages over 40 at entry.

Some companies treat cases where overweight is the only impairment more leniently still, particularly if the life is under age 40. Further, some companies treat as standard any case where the equivalent extra premium to be charged does not exceed $2.50 per thousand sum insured.

There are limitations under the Numerical Rating System to the extent to which credits are permitted to reduce the rating for certain impairments or combinations of them. It will be apparent that a considerable amount of detail can be introduced by a company in the daily working of the system.

OTHER FACTORS IN THE SELECTION OF RISKS

In the previous chapter we dealt with the factors which arise in considering the *application for life insurance* under six main headings. We now deal with those which arise in considering the *medical examiner's report* or the *non-medical declaration* completed in non-medical cases in lieu thereof.

The medical examiner's report consists of two parts. The first part covers a number of questions to be put by the medical examiner to the life to be insured; his answers are recorded on the form and when completed the record is signed by both of them. The questions cover the family history of the life to be insured; his personal history and details of illnesses, operations, etc.; his height, weight and changes in weight; his habits *re* drugs and consumption of alcohol. The second part gives the record of the medical examiner's physical examination of the life including a urinalysis. The object of the two sets of questions is to obtain the fullest information possible to enable the head office medical and lay underwriters to assess the risk. These items will be discussed in this chapter and are summarized under the headings (6) to (13) given below, apart from that of habits which have already been dealt with in the previous chapter as item (4).

Under non-medical applications only the first part of the information given in the medical examiner's report is obtained. The answers are recorded by the agent and signed by the agent and the life to be insured. This is the non-medical declaration which we have referred to previously.

The list of factors (6) to (13) are as follows:

6. Family history;
7. Medical history of personal illnesses, operations, etc.;
8. Height and weight (build);
9. Heart, circulatory system and kidneys (cardiovascular-renal system);
10. Respiratory system;
11. Digestive system;
12. Urinalysis;
13. Other impairments.

6. FAMILY HISTORY

The details requested regarding family history are of the parents, brothers and sisters, and spouse of the life to be insured. If living, their ages and state of health are required; if dead, the ages at and causes of death.

Undoubtedly there are family traits which are hereditary and which influence longevity, but statistics on which to base any practical considerations are lacking. People frequently exaggerate the ages at death of their parents and relatives, and actual causes of death are even more problematical. As already stated, an exceptionally good family history may receive credits of 15 points, that is −15. On the contrary, where there are two or more deaths below age 60 other than from accidents, a debit of 15 points, that is +15, may be expected, and should they both be from heart diseases, cerebral haemorrhage, or kidney disease, a substantially higher debit may be imposed. The 1951 Impairment Study showed that, of those taken at standard rates and where two or more deaths under age 60 from these diseases were indicated in the family history, the actual mortality was 141 per cent of the standard.

It is debatable whether tuberculosis, cancer, diabetes, or insanity are hereditary. Tuberculosis was the leading cause of death at the beginning of this century, but it is relatively insignificant in Canada at the present time. A normal X-ray of the lungs will generally set at rest any question of tuberculosis in the family history; a recent exposure to tuberculosis would be considered of significance. The appearance of any of these diseases in the family history will receive special attention in their bearing on the personal history of the life to be insured.

7. MEDICAL HISTORY OF PERSONAL ILLNESSES, OPERATIONS, ETC.

The statements made by the life to be insured to the medical examiner or, under a non-medical application, to the agent cover this information. Recent illnesses are of particular importance; the length of time disabled is a criterion of the importance of an illness of which an applicant may have only a hazy recollection, particularly its medical significance. The company may wish to write to the doctor, surgeon or hospital regarding any material illnesses and hence the names and addresses of these are requested.

8. HEIGHT AND WEIGHT (BUILD)

Excessive weight has always been associated with higher than normal mortality. The latest of a series of studies on the relation between weight and mortality is the Build and Blood Pressure Study, 1959, already referred to. As regards build it was based on the records of nearly five million policies. A summary of the more important findings have a bearing on the present subject.

1. Substantially the same relative mortality among overweights as in previous studies was disclosed. As there have been substantial reductions in over-all mortality generally in recent years, it indicates that overweights have benefited from the general downward trend in mortality to the same degree as persons of average weight.

2. The excess mortality among overweights was shown to be predominantly due to high death rates from diseases of the heart and circulatory system.

3. The optimum weight, i.e., that with the lowest relative mortality, is from 10 to 20 pounds below the average weight. Some small degree of overweight may be an advantage in the teens.

4. A rule-of-thumb summary of the relation between overweight and excessive mortality according to the latest investigation is as follows:

20 lbs. over average weight	5 to 20% above average mortality
40 lbs. over average weight	20 to 35% above average mortality
90 lbs. over average weight	60 to 90% above average mortality

Average Height and Weight. Table 23.1 gives the average weight by age and height in the 1959 Study. The statistics covered both Americans and Canadians but were predominantly from the U.S.A. Statistics indicate no marked difference in weight between Canadians and Americans although they are both definitely heavier than Englishmen. The figures show that the present generation of men are heavier than their fathers, but women have become lighter which may be due at least in part to lighter clothing, for the weight was recorded as with indoor clothing and wearing shoes.

Build and Underwriting. In the 1959 Study when men were graded according to build, the presence of a minor impairment increased the mortality by about 25 percentage points and when the minor impairment was a slightly elevated blood pressure, the average increase in mortality ratios was 60 percentage points. It also confirmed the finding of the 1951 Study of the relatively high mortality when two or more early deaths

TABLE 23.1

Average Weight in Pounds
Build and Blood Pressure Study, 1959
(in indoor clothing with shoes)

Height	Ages 20–24	Ages 25–29	Ages 30–39	Ages 40–49	Ages 50–59	Ages 60–69
			Males			
5′ 0″	122	128	131	134	136	133
5′ 2″	128	134	137	140	142	139
5′ 4″	136	141	145	148	149	146
5′ 6″	142	148	153	156	157	154
5′ 8″	149	155	161	165	166	163
5′ 10″	157	163	170	174	175	173
6′ 0″	166	172	179	183	185	183
6′ 2″	174	182	188	192	194	193
6′ 4″	181	190	199	203	205	204
			Females			
4′ 10″	102	107	115	122	125	127
5′ 0″	108	113	120	127	130	131
5′ 2″	115	119	126	133	136	137
5′ 4″	121	125	132	140	144	145
5′ 6″	129	133	139	147	152	153
5′ 8″	136	140	146	155	160	161
5′ 10″	144	148	154	164	169	—
6′ 0″	154	158	164	174	180	—

from heart diseases, cerebral haemorrhage, or kidney disease are shown in the family history of an overweight life. Hence when these impairments appear in combination with overweight the sum of the ratings of the individual impairments must be increased further to represent the expected mortality.

In assessing overweights, credits would be given where the occupation presented favourable features of physical activity and outdoor work. Although the 1959 Study indicated that underweight was no handicap, one should discriminate between a man, more than 50 lbs. below average weight, which is an abnormality, and a spare build which has always been conducive to good health.

9. HEART, CIRCULATORY SYSTEM, KIDNEYS (CARDIOVASCULAR-RENAL SYSTEM)

We have already referred to this group of diseases, called c.v.r. for short, and Figure 16, Chapter 21 indicated that it represents the most frequent cause of death. In common terms it consists of heart diseases, cerebral haemorrhage, and kidney disease. They often exist in combination and appear to affect the leaders, the brain-workers, and top executives far more than manual workers.[3] In the Canadian Institute of Actuaries' analysis of death claims for the years 1969 to 1974, deaths from these causes represented about 20 per cent of the total claims paid within five years from the issue of the policy; for policies more than five years from entry this group of diseases represented about 45 per cent of the total death claims paid. Deaths from heart attacks continued to rise until 1967, then between 1968 and 1972 dropped over 8 per cent. Credit for this downward trend in mortality has been ascribed to changes in life-style, less cigarette smoking, and to improvements in medical care of patients with coronary disease.

The Heart. The heart is a muscular bulb, about the size of the fist, lying obliquely in the chest like an inverted cone, in such a way that the broad end (*base*) is uppermost. In front the lungs overlap the heart but there is a notch in the margin of the left lung which allows the *apex* of the heart to come forward to the front chest wall. It follows that one can hear the heart beat most clearly at the apex. The difficulty of determining whether the heart is functioning properly is that we can only do so by listening to and recording its beat, and determining the size of the heart. In spite of this we are still often in the position of only knowing that something has been wrong with the engine because it has stopped! Figure 17 gives a simplified diagram of the flow of blood through the heart; as stated the lungs overlap the heart. The developments in heart surgery require some modification of what has been stated. The living heart can now be seen, studied, and operated upon successfully. Undoubtedly major advances in our knowledge of the heart and diseases which affect it may be expected.

The heart consists of four cavities: right and left auricle (RA and LA) and right and left ventricle (RV and LV). There is no direct communication between the right and left sides of the heart. It has four valves: mitral (4), aortic (5), pulmonic (3) and tricuspid (2), indicated by the figures shown as we move across Figure 17. The arteries are elastic, strong-walled tubes which carry the blood from the heart to the tissues; the veins, which carry the blood back to the heart, are generally of larger calibre than the corresponding arteries and more easily distended as their walls are not so thick.

The Circulation of the Blood. The circulation of the blood through the heart and as shown in Figure 17 is as follows: The blood enters the right

[3]"The Mortality of the Medical and other Professions with special reference to Heart Disease," by the author, *Transactions*, Society of Actuaries, vol. 15 (1963).

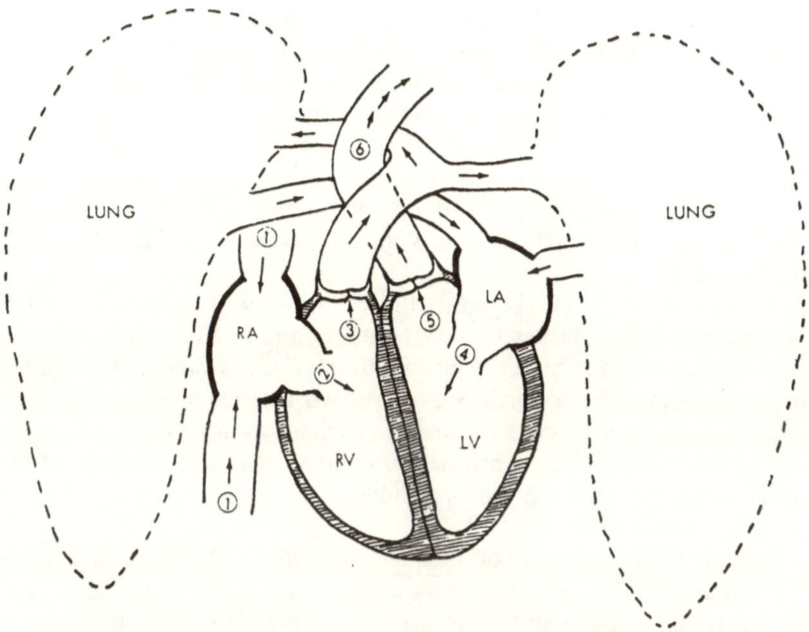

FIGURE 17. Circulation of Blood through the Heart

RA Right auricle
LA Left auricle
RV Right ventricle
LV Left ventricle

THE FOUR VALVES

2. Tricuspid
3. Pulmonic
4 Mitral
5. Aortic
1. Veins carrying blood to heart
6. Aortic artery conveying blood to brain, intestines, kidneys, and extremities

auricle, brought by two very large veins (1) which drain the blood from the body. When the right auricle is filled, it contracts and forces the blood into the right ventricle past the open tricuspid valve (2). The right ventricle then contracts and the pressure closing the tricuspid valve, the blood passes through the other opening in the ventricle, the pulmonic valve (3), into the lungs. The lungs purify and oxygenate the blood. After passing through the lungs the blood returns to the left auricle which on contraction forces the blood past the mitral valve (4) into the left ventricle which on contraction closes the mitral valve, and the blood is forced past the aortic valve (5) into the aortic artery (6) which conveys it by various branches throughout the body, the main areas of which are the brain, intestines, kidneys, and extremities. The blood is then returned by the veins to the right auricle and so the circulation continues.

The action of the valves may be understood by considering the opening from the auricle to the ventricle, which is guarded by flaps of tissue. They do not obstruct the flow of blood from the auricle to the ventricle, but when the ventricle fills, the pressure forces the flaps upwards and together and they normally prevent any flow of blood backwards from the ventricle to the auricle. Both auricles contract together, followed immediately by the contraction of both ventricles, a wave of contraction passing from the auricles to the ventricles—the heart is, in effect, a double pump.

The aorta is the largest arterial trunk of the body. It arises from the left ventricle and first passes upwards then bends to form an arch, continuing downward behind the heart into the body. Coming off from the aorta just beyond the aortic valve are two arteries which divide and subdivide on the surface of the heart in such a way as to supply the heart muscle with blood. These arteries run part way around the base of the heart forming a crown or corona, hence their name *coronary arteries* (not shown in Figure 17).

Disease of the right side of the heart is seldom met with during active life and hence in life insurance we are only concerned with the left side of the heart and its two valves, the *mitral* and *aortic*, (4) and (5).

Heart Murmurs. The rhythmic contraction phase of the heart is called the *systole*; the dilation or relaxation phase is called the *diastole*. The heart beat is characterized by two sounds: the mitral and tricuspid valves snapping closed when the ventricles contract and that when the aortic and pulmonic valves close when the ventricle relaxes. Normally the two sounds, imitated by "lup-dup," are clear but if the blood stream is interfered with as by narrowing or leakage of the valves other sounds or *murmurs* are heard. Disease, such as rheumatic fever or other infection, may cause damage to the lining of the heart and delicate edges of the valves, resulting ultimately in either a narrowing of the opening where the valve is situated (*stenosis* or obstruction) or inability of the valve to close accurately with subsequent leakage (*regurgitation* or insufficiency) or both.

When the murmur is heard during the systole it is called a *systolic murmur*; if heard during the diastole it is called a *diastolic murmur*.

Functional and Organic Murmurs. Functional murmurs are those not associated with any defect of the valves and may be due to many causes, as for instance the heart rubbing against the lung tissue. They may vary with various phases of breathing and different postures of the body, and may be heard only at the apex, that is, they are not heard at the left side or back. Generally such murmurs are ignored in selection at entry ages under 40, but their distinction from *organic murmurs*, that is, those indicating a definite heart impairment is not obvious, and there is sometimes a difference of medical opinion on the matter.

Enlargement of the Heart or Hypertrophy. The normal position of the apex of the heart is in the fifth interspace (between the fifth and sixth ribs) and $3^1/_2$ inches from the centre of the chest (midsternal line). If the heart is enlarged the apex moves to the left and downwards. The amount of enlargement can be determined fairly accurately by noting the point of maximum intensity of the heart beat, but is readily resolved by X-rays. Marked hypertrophy is generally a sign that something is wrong with the heart, for the heart tries to adjust itself to compensate for internal damage which may not be evident otherwise.

Underwriting Heart Murmurs and Hypertrophy. The relation of the various types of heart murmur and of hypertrophy of the heart to their probable causes and their treatment in underwriting is beyond the scope of this work. The 1951 Impairment Study indicated that certain types of systolic murmur had little effect on the mortality particularly if the life at issue of the policy was under age 40. However, other types of murmur indicating valvular damage gave a mortality double the normal and where the murmur indicated obstruction (stenosis) the mortality was five times the normal. Where the heart murmur was associated with a history of rheumatic fever or similar infection the resulting mortality was much higher than when the history was absent. A high rate of mortality was also shown when hypertrophy was associated with a heart murmur, the greater the degree of hypertrophy the higher the mortality shown.

Electrocardiogram. All muscle tissue produces electrical energy when it contracts in response to a stimulus. A galvanometer is an apparatus used to measure electrical energy. These two facts have been used in electrocardiography to study the action of the heart muscle by means of graphic records (electrocardiograms) of the electric current emanating from the heart. A normal electrocardiogram may be obtained even when the valves of the heart are defective or after a heart attack. An abnormal electrocardiogram is however an indication of damage to the heart muscle and serves as an aid to the heart specialist to interpret his findings.

Coronary Disease. The coronary arteries were described above; they supply the blood to the heart muscle. They are liable to the same changes as other arteries and *sclerosis* (hardening) of the coronary arteries may become evident as in other arteries by the formation of a *thrombosis* or clot. If the main coronary arteries or a large branch becomes jammed with a clot then death is instantaneous; if the clot is in a small branch, then recovery may occur as the other branches take on the work of the one which has become clogged. The first warning of coronary artery disease may arise with an attack of *angina pectoris* (pain in the chest). A problem arises when there is doubt if the pains are neuralgic or due to a thrombosis.

Much has been written about the relation of a fatty diet to coronary atherosclerosis (deposits on the walls of the coronary arteries—atheroma being Greek for porridge) and a source of the clots causing coronary thrombosis. Much of this has been disputed. However, the relation between overweight and disease is beyond dispute.

Pulse. The pulse rate is the rate of the heart beat and can be felt at the wrist and other places where an artery is near the surface. The normal beat is from 60 to 80 per minute and when persistently over 90 may call for a rating. An irregular pulse occurs frequently, and will show on an electrocardiogram taken when it is present. It is indicated by the term "intermittent pulse" or *extra systoles*. They vary considerably in importance and may be due to nervous tension.

HIGH BLOOD PRESSURE (HYPERTENSION)

When we speak of blood pressure we ordinarily refer to the pressure within the arteries carrying blood from the left ventricle under sufficient pressure to overcome the resistance of the blood vessels and to continue into the veins to return to the right auricle. The arteries, through wear and tear, become twisty and brittle (sclerosis), losing their elastic qualities whereby they normally expand and store up energy and so help equalize circulation. In such cases there is increased resistance to be overcome by the heart and the pressure has to increase to maintain circulation. If the blood pressure increases for any reason, the work of the heart is increased and the arteries are subjected to increased wear and tear, and danger of rupture (in the brain it causes apoplexy or cerebral haemorrhage).

Without going into the matter as to which is the primary cause it is a fact that much sclerosis of the arteries, most cerebral vascular disease, a

TABLE 23.2

Age	Systolic	Diastolic
20–24	119	73
30–34	122	76
40–44	124	78
50–54	128	79
55–59	130	79
60–64	132	80

TABLE 23.3

Systolic/diastolic	Ages 15–39	Ages 40–69
132/85	125%	115%
132/90	150%	130%
142/90	185%	165%
142/100	275%	215%

greater part of chronic heart disease, and a large portion of kidney disease are associated with persistent high blood pressure.

The blood pressure is highest when the left ventricle contracts and forces blood through the aortic valve into the system. It is called the *systolic pressure* and at age 20 would average 118 mm. that is, would balance a column of 118 mm. of mercury. The pressure is lowest after the ventricles relax: this is the *diastolic pressure*. The diastolic pressure is the constant pressure in the body; the resistance which the heart has to overcome before it can drive the blood forward or even open the aortic valve. The average blood pressures increase slowly with age, and the 1959 Study gives the averages (shown in Table 23.2) according to age, showing little change from those recorded in the 1930's. Low blood pressures are generally ignored where the life is otherwise in good health.

Table 23.3 shows the mortality experienced as a percentage of standard mortality indicated by the 1959 Study for those with slight or moderate elevation in blood pressure and these ratios were higher than shown by earlier studies. However, by the time the study was published the treatment by medication of elevated blood pressure was showing, and continues to show, excellent results so that where, apart from blood pressure, the underwriting picture is favourable, lower ratings than those shown in the table are being used by the companies.

The 1959 Study also indicated that when higher blood pressure was combined with overweight, hypertrophy of the heart, albuminuria, or adverse family history (two or more deaths under age 60 from c.v.r. disease) the resulting mortality was definitely greater than the sum of the individual impairments if expressed by the Numerical Rating System. It would follow that this would be taken into account in assessing the risk for underwriting purposes.

KIDNEY DISEASE

There is a close relationship between the kidneys and the heart and circulatory system and hence the term cardio-vascular-renal disease already referred to (renal means "of the kidney"). There are two kidneys and their main function is to purify the blood and pass the waste products into the urinary bladder. Albumin is destroyed tissue and its presence indicates some breakdown in organic tissue. The presence of albumin in the urine (shown by the urinalysis) may indicate inflammation of the kidneys (Bright's disease, nephritis) and combined with overweight or high blood pressure is considered a serious matter for an applicant for life insurance, as already mentioned when dealing with overweight and high blood pressure.

The deposit of crystals from the urine in the kidney may form one or more stones (renal calculus). Kidney stones may be passed spontaneously or removed by a cystoscope. Cutting into the kidney generally to remove stones is called *nephrotomy*. Surgery involving the entire removal of the kidney is called *nephrectomy*. On removal of one kidney the other could carry on the function of both if it is in a healthy condition; without kidneys, death follows. In most cases of kidney impairments, insurance is obtainable at an extra rating.

EXPERIMENTAL HEART CASES

Some life insurance companies offer policies to properly selected risks covering all the major forms of heart disease including coronary heart disease, hypertension, rheumatic and congenital heart impairments, and irregularity of the heart rhythm. The granting of insurance in these cases may be said to be experimental; the ratings are necessarily substantial. Such offerings not only perform a public service, but also the analysis of the mortality experienced is a contribution to medical knowledge.

10. RESPIRATORY SYSTEM

The lungs are situated in the thorax within the framework formed by the ribs. Two smooth membranes cover the lungs and line the thoracic cavity, called the pleura.

Where there is a personal history of tuberculosis of the lungs and complete recovery has taken place, insurance can generally be obtained, the rating decreasing with the length of time since recovery. X-ray photographs will generally be required and the severity of the previous attack will be a factor in determining the rating or acceptance. We referred previously, under Family History to the phenomenal improvement in the death rate from tuberculosis in recent years.

Chronic asthma not clearly associated with some allergy may be considered as an impairment, as well as chronic bronchitis—both placing a severe strain on the heart; the strain increases with age.

Pleurisy is inflammation of the pleura. Unless associated with an attack of pneumonia when it can be generally ignored, the chances are strong that it is tubercular in origin. X-ray findings are of importance on this account.

11. DIGESTIVE SYSTEM

For life insurance purposes we can consider the digestive system as the stomach, the duodenum, which is the first part of the small intestine (some twenty feet long), and the large intestine or colon (some five feet long). Subsidiary organs besides the kidneys, already mentioned, are the appendix, liver, gall bladder, and pancreas.

The appendix frequently becomes inflamed and may be removed; it is of virtually no importance in underwriting. Other parts of the digestive system may be removed, such as the gall bladder, parts of the stomach and intestines and the patient be little worse off. However, in underwriting such a case considerable attention would be paid to the cause of removal.

Indigestion may or may not indicate some serious impairment, hence it should be referred to as a symptom, not a disease. Ulcers may be the cause, as in the stomach (*gastric ulcer*) or the duodenum (*duodenal ulcer*), the latter being by far the more common complaint. The term *peptic ulcer* is generally applied to ulcers of the stomach and intestines. Applicants with a history of ulcers are insurable, the rating applying in some cases for a limited period since the attack. Surgery in various forms has been applied to the removal of ulcers and the surgeon's report and time elapsed since operation and condition since then are the factors determining the classification of the risk.

The gall bladder is the source of much trouble due to infection or stones (deposits). On recovery after an operation for the removal of the gall bladder, all being well, the case may be considered as standard;

removal of the stones only still leaves the possibility of future trouble. Trouble with the liver or pancreas is a much more serious matter.

12. URINALYSIS

The urine consists 95 per cent of water and various salts in solution and some solid matter, depending to some extent on the time of the year and general habits of the applicant. The examining doctor generally makes a urine test for the presence of albumin and sugar. For larger amounts of insurance and in the case of older lives or where abnormalities are found in the test or there is a history of a kidney disorder, a specimen is required for microscopical analysis at the Head Office. By the microscopical analysis the sediment of the urine is examined for the presence of blood cells, pus cells and casts which may indicate the presence of disease.

Albuminuria. At one time the presence of albumin in the urine was considered as most serious for life insurance purposes, as it was the cardinal symptom of Bright's disease (nephritis, i.e., inflammation of the kidney). It is now recognized that it may occur as a transient phenomenon in adolescents and others and be of no medical significance. However, investigations have indicated that the constant presence of albumin in the urine indicates that an increasing mortality is to be anticipated as the amount of albumin increases. This was confirmed by the 1951 Impairment Study. That study also confirmed that where the presence of albumin is associated with higher than normal blood pressure or other cardiovascular impairment or overweight the combination gave an increased rate of mortality, greater than if the impairments were considered separately.

Sugar and Diabetes. Glycosuria, meaning sugar in the urine, is a symptom of diabetes, a very complex disease. It is a wasting disease and is due to a deficiency of insulin normally produced by the pancreas. The discovery of insulin in Canada by Banting in 1921 marked one of the great epochs in medical science. Normally the glucose in the blood is absorbed by the kidneys and does not pass into the urine. In the *sugar tolerance test* a measured quantity of glucose is given periodically to the applicant and specimens of blood and urine are taken and examined to determine the level of sugar in the blood and the urine.

Again we face the problem that glycosuria does not always indicate true diabetes, i.e., suffering from a deficiency of insulin. When sugar is found in the urine and there are no other signs or symptoms of diabetes and the sugar tolerance test is normal, it may indicate *renal glycosuria* which, if established, is considered of minor importance in underwriting.

If discovered early enough, diabetes can be controlled by a combination of insulin injections and diet. The long-term outlook is, however, clouded by cardiovascular complications. Many diabetics can now obtain life insurance subject to a rating. Occupation, habits, and environment, indicating a high level of intelligence and self-control, with effective medical supervision are favourable features, and the reverse most unfavourable.

13. OTHER IMPAIRMENTS

Some other impairments of general interest are:

Deafness. Impaired hearing alone is not usually rated. Infections of the middle ear indicated by discharges were formerly rated, but now with modern drugs they should lend themselves readily to treatment and the former dangers of bone and brain involvement are much reduced.

Venereal disease. Applicants may hesitate to disclose this impairment but it is as well to know that the advent of modern germ-killing drugs has made cures so effective and permanent that standard life insurance can be obtained in most cases on evidence of thorough treatment and cure.

Pregnancy. The 1951 Impairment Study of pregnancy indicated that the hazards to the mother in childbirth have been reduced greatly in recent years. The hazard is somewhat greater with the first child and increases with age of the mother. Where there is no history of previous complications the practice of one company is illustrative. Within the first seven months of pregnancy if the life is age 40 or over a single extra premium of $5.00 per thousand is charged; if in eighth or ninth month of pregnancy, all ages, the application is postponed. Otherwise, the case is considered as standard.

Arthritis, rheumatism. Arthritis means inflammation of a joint; rheumatism is a far wider term applied generally to all types of arthritis as well as to conditions with little or no relation to the joints. From the underwriting point of view it is important to differentiate between a relatively harmless touch of neuralgia on the one hand to rheumatic fever which invariably leaves a damaged heart. The frequency of attacks, their severity, the time spent in bed, are all features in the assessment of the risk.

Nervous system. A record of an illness vaguely referred to as a "nervous breakdown" or "neurosis" introduces the need to obtain sufficient details to classify the illness for underwriting purposes. Can the illness be associated with a definite cause as business troubles or marital difficulties, now definitely passed? The time elapsed since recovery, the severity and time incapacitated from normal activities and work, the family history, are all factors in the assessment of the risk.

OPTIMISTIC OUTLOOK

A difficulty arises in practice when an applicant is rated on account of an impairment which his personal physician has minimized and advised him to ignore as being of little consequence. It might be said to be the duty of the personal physician to give such advice in many cases and there is not necessarily any conflict between such advice and the action of the life insurance company. Life insurance is based on the law of averages and when statistics indicate that a certain illness or surgery does definitely reduce longevity the company is bound to act on the knowledge.

We have indicated how all trends in the past fifty years have been towards a lower mortality, not only at the younger ages but also to some extent at the older ages. It has also been indicated that some of this improvement has carried over to substandard lives as well. An optimistic outlook is therefore justified. It should be some satisfaction to the rated applicant that the rating can never be increased and there is always the possibility that it may be reduced or removed in the future.

CHAPTER TWENTY-FOUR

Selection of Risks: Other Aspects

THEORY AND PRACTICE

In the previous chapter we discussed the more frequently occurring types of impairments. The next step is to translate the decisions regarding the extra mortality anticipated into the additional premiums to be charged so that equity is preserved between the substandard and the standard lives and also between the various classes of substandard lives.

The difficulties of combining theoretical exactitude with practical necessity are particularly evident in the treatment of lives who may differ materially from what are obviously standard lives. The resentment of the applicant who is offered a rated policy far exceeds any objection to the monetary additional amount he is required to pay and exists however trivial that additional amount may be. It is a factor in the public relations of the company. This, combined with keen competition among companies for business, explains the desire of companies to make the standard class as wide as possible and to ignore small extra premiums which, in strict equity, should be charged.

We have already referred to the practice of companies in ignoring ratings which would represent an annual extra premium of less than $2.50 or $3.00 per thousand sum insured. Some companies use a minimum for temporary extras which are referred to below, and will ignore such temporary extras if the total possible extra premium payable is less than $15.00 per thousand sum insured, i.e., $10.00 per thousand payable for one year would be ignored as would $3.00 per thousand payable for four years. The equity of this practice may be challenged, but the reasons for it have been given above.

THE INCIDENCE OF SUBSTANDARD MORTALITY

In computing the extra premium required for a specified expected extra mortality we require to know how the extra mortality is distributed; that is, whether it varies between younger and older ages at the time when the rating is assessed and whether it is distributed over the whole duration of a policy or concentrated in the earlier or later years of the history of a policy.

In the previous two chapters we referred to the additional mortality of substandard risks as a percentage of the standard mortality and the Numerical Rating System was based on this assumption. As the rate of mortality increases with age (see Figure 3, Chapter 4), the assumption of a constant percentage of extra mortality ordinarily means a trivial addition to the rate of mortality at the younger ages, i.e., in the number of extra deaths expected and a correspondingly large increase at the older ages. This is also seen in the many figures and tables in this text as well as from Table 24.1, Columns 10, 12, 14 and 16, in this chapter.

What is the incidence of substandard mortality as indicated in the various studies? It is as well to point out that statistical evidence is not always precise and in some instances may even be contradictory. However, a pattern does emerge from these studies on which our statements as outlined below are based. Another question is: with advancing medical knowledge and discoveries, and in particular the drastic reductions in over-all mortality at the younger ages and improvements even at the older ages, what weight can be attached to trends of substandard risks over a long period in the future if we did know their trend in the past? It follows that practical considerations should determine the procedure with the over-all results in mind and the service rendered to the public as the criterion.

The different patterns of substandard mortality, with examples of impairments the mortality for which has been noted to follow the particular pattern, are outlined below.

a. A high initial percentage extra mortality, rapidly diminishing so that normal mortality is attained after a very few years. This pattern appears to be followed by a recent personal history of peptic ulcer with or without operation and with full recovery.

b. A percentage extra mortality which appears to decrease more slowly with increasing duration of the policy and gradually approaches normal mortality. Most occupational additional mortality seems to be of this type.

c. The percentage extra mortality appears to remain constant for a number of years. This describes the incidence of the majority of impairments and in particular certain types of heart impairments, a moderate degree of overweight, and a moderate elevation of blood pressure. Some companies have found on investigating their own experiences that for the longer durations and in particular the older ages attained there is a tendency for the percentage extra mortality to decrease although not disappearing entirely. This will be referred to later.

d. The percentage extra mortality increases slowly with duration. This pattern appears to be followed by marked overweights; also those with marked high blood pressure, glycosuria, and diabetes.

Systems of Extra Premiums to Cover Extra Mortality

Several different systems of extra premiums are in use to cover the patterns of extra mortality indicated above. They are (1) temporary flat extras, (2) flat extras, (3) constant extras, (4) multiple table classes, (5) rate-up in age, (6) liens. These are now described.

1. TEMPORARY FLAT EXTRA PREMIUMS

The expression "flat extra" means that the extra is the same irrespective of the age of the life insured at the time of the issue of the policy. Under this classification the extra premium is payable for a limited number of years only. This system is used for an extra mortality incidence of the type (*a*) above, namely, rapidly diminishing to zero. It is generally applied to cases of peptic ulcer and gall bladder disease, after full recovery, the extra being charged to cover a period of five or six years since the last attack or date of the operation.

2. FLAT EXTRA PREMIUMS

This corresponds to type (*b*) above, namely, a slowly decreasing percentage extra mortality and which might be represented by a constant additional number of expected deaths year by year. This is the system universally used by Canadian life insurance companies for occupational extra premiums. It is also used for aviation extras. We have already referred to these extra premiums under occupation and aviation in Chapter 22. The constant extra premium is payable in addition to and in the same manner as the basic premium of the policy. We have also referred to the reduction of the extra premium payable either by amount or by number of premiums payable for endowment insurances in the case of occupational extra premiums. The reason for this is obvious where a decreasing extra percentage mortality is applied to a decreasing "net amount at risk" due to a rapidly increasing policy-reserve.

3. CONSTANT EXTRA PREMIUMS

This is the method used by the majority of companies in Canada for risks other than those already described as covered by temporary extras and occupational extra premiums. It covers type (*c*), namely, a constant percentage extra mortality. The risks are evaluated according to the Numerical Rating System and graded into classes representing on the average +50, +75 and so on, namely 150, 175 per cent and so on, of standard mortality. In one Canadian company additional classes of 137½ and 167½ per cent are used in the lower ranges where the majority of substandard cases arise and beyond 175 per cent there are the additional classes: 200, 225, 250, 300, 400, and 500 per cent standard mortality. The 200 per cent class would represent cases rated as +88 to +112, i.e., from 118 to 212 per cent standard mortality and correspondingly for other classes.

Having decided on the number of substandard classes, percentage extra mortality tables are then computed corresponding to the average of each substandard class and for each of these the net annual premium by age and plan is calculated and loaded for expenses, etc. These extra premiums are payable at the same time and in the same manner as the basic premiums to which they are to be attached. It will be noted they are constant in amount for each age and plan and degree of substandard mortality. As previously mentioned, some companies assume that the percentage extra mortality decreases at the older ages attained. This is put into effect in calculating the extra premiums thus: from age 65, say, the percentage extra mortality is decreased so as to merge into the standard mortality at age 85, or so. This reduces the extra premium charged.

Illustrating the magnitude of the constant extra premium thus obtained: for 200 per cent standard mortality it would represent an extra annual premium on the straight life plan, age 35 at issue, of approximately $5.50 per thousand and for a 20-year endowment of approximately $1.50 per thousand. If the company had a minimum extra premium for rated lives of $2.50 or $3.00 a thousand then this case would be rated on the straight life plan but accepted as standard on the 20-year endowment insurance plan. On a limited payment life plan the annual extra would exceed the $5.50 for the straight life plan as the extra mortality expected would have to be paid for in a shorter time.

An important point to mention here is that in the above three types of extra premiums no changes are made in the guaranteed cash surrender and other values of the basic plan or the policy-reserves, and the regular dividends (on participating plans), as for the corresponding standard policy, apply. It is a general rule that extended insurance values are not granted where the degree of substandard mortality is above a certain level.

4. MULTIPLE TABLE CLASSES

This is the system used to some extent in the U.S.A. corresponding to the constant extra premium method outlined in the preceding section. Rather wider classes representing percentages of standard mortality are used and the total premium is calculated varying by age at entry and plan and based on the percentage of standard mortality.

In some of the largest U.S. companies the substandard classes are grouped and the cash surrender and other guaranteed values in the policy are all calculated on the mortality table representing a broad average of the substandard classes in the group as are also the policy-reserves. As this means in effect the issue of a rate manual for each group of substandard classes it will be understood why this procedure is followed by the very largest companies only. These companies also allot dividends to these policies based on the actual mortality experienced. As a rule occupationally rated cases are excluded and the flat extra premium method applied to them.

5. RATE-UP IN AGE

Historically this is the oldest method and possibly the most obvious method to the layman. It states, in effect, that a certain individual has impairments which should curtail his longevity, on the average, as if he were 3, 5, or 7 years older; in other words a "rating-up" of *n* years places an applicant in the category of one of average health and longevity *n* years older than the applicant is in fact.

In this method the life is treated on every account as at the rated-up age with the increased cash surrender values and dividends applicable to the rated-up age, so that on early surrender the company has received very little for the increased risk run. The company also bases its policy-reserves on the rated-up age.

One of the largest Canadian companies has always used the rated-up age method for its substandard business. It is simple to understand and explain; the higher cash values appear to give something for the higher premiums paid and on participating policies higher dividends further satisfy the policyholder as the policy continues in force.

Table 24.1 shows what a 5-year rating-up in age means in additional mortality to lives ages 30 and 40 respectively at entry, according to the Canadian Institute of Actuaries 1958–1964 Ultimate Table (the latest

TABLE 24.1

Rating Up in Age and Percentage Extra Mortality, C.A. 58–64 Ultimate Table

	True age at issue 30			True age at issue 40		
	Death Rate per 1,000		Extra deaths per 1,000 provided	Death Rate per 1,000		Extra deaths per 1,000 provided
Years in force (1)	True age (2)	Rated up 5 years (3)	(4)	True age (5)	Rated up 5 years (6)	(7)
1	0.92	1.34	0.42	2.12	3.83	1.71
5	1.23	1.91	0.68	3.39	5.90	2.51
10	1.91	3.39	1.48	5.90	9.35	3.45
20	5.90	9.35	3.45	15.88	26.81	10.93
30	15.88	26.81	10.93	41.54	62.37	20.83

	150% Mortality		200% Mortality		150% Mortality		200% Mortality	
Years in force (8)	Death rate per 1,000 (9)	Extra deaths provided (10)	Death rate per 1,000 (11)	Extra deaths provided (12)	Death rate per 1,000 (13)	Extra deaths provided (14)	Death rate per 1,000 (15)	Extra deaths provided (16)
1	1.38	0.46	1.84	0.92	3.18	1.06	4.24	2.12
5	1.84	0.61	2.46	1.23	5.08	1.69	6.78	3.39
10	2.86	0.95	3.82	1.91	8.85	2.95	11.80	5.90
20	8.85	2.95	11.80	5.90	23.82	7.94	31.76	15.88
30	23.82	7.94	31.76	15.88	62.31	20.77	83.08	41.54

published experience of Canadian insured lives which is given in Table 8.1). This is compared with ratings of +50 per cent, +100 per cent, of standard mortality, i.e., 150 and 200 per cent of standard mortality respectively. Note how a rating-up in age gives an almost negligible additional mortality in the first few years at a young age at entry. This can be appreciated for we are aware of the flatness of the curve of mortality up to age 35.

A rating-up in age of 5 years may be taken roughly as the equivalent over the life of a policy of +50, i.e., 150 per cent standard mortality. Thus in Table 24.1, Columns 3, 4, 9, and 10 should be compared for age 30 at entry and Columns 6, 7, 13, and 14 for age 40 at entry. The low rate of mortality at young ages at entry both for standard and substandard lives in the early policy years should be noted.

6. THE LIEN

This is, from the Canadian point of view, the least important system in use. It provides for a deduction from the sum insured in the event of death, the regular premium being payable. The liens generally decrease by a constant amount each year so as to be eliminated over a period of years or they may be constant for, say, five years and then decrease. Under an endowment insurance the sum insured is payable in full at the maturity date and in short-term endowments where the death benefit is the least important factor, a lien to cover additional mortality may be of use. Liens are sometimes offered to cover a temporary additional mortality, as for peptic ulcer, in lieu of a temporary extra premium. It is widely used in Great Britain where short-term endowments are popular for tax-savings purposes.

The objection to the general use of liens in Canada is that they reduce the amount of insurance in the early policy years when it may be most needed. When liens are used, the cash surrender values, dividends, and other features are all as for a standard policy of the same plan and same age at entry and the company sets up the normal policy-reserves for the full sum insured, ignoring the lien. It is usual, when death is due to accidental causes and a lien is attached to the policy, for the full sum insured to be paid on death.

MAXIMUM RATINGS

We mentioned above the various classes of substandard mortality varying from 130 per cent standard mortality to 500 per cent standard mortality. As a rule companies do not accept cases which indicate an expected mortality of more than 500 per cent, i.e., five times the standard mortality for the age of the life in question. However, in the previous chapter we referred to experiemental cases as those recovered from a coronary attack and pointed out the advantage to both the public and to medicine if selected cases could be offered insurance and the selection exercised tested by experience. At least one Canadian life insurance company has been a pioneer in this field. The extra premiums charged are necessarily considerable and in some cases represent an expected mortality of ten times the standard mortality for that age.

REMOVAL OF EXTRA PREMIUMS

A company cannot, once a policy is issued and continues in force, impose a rating or increase an existing rating if it becomes aware that the policyholder's health has deteriorated. For this reason, if the reverse takes place, a life insured who has been accepted as a substandard risk and improves his condition should not in theory, anyway, be rerated and the extra premium reduced or removed.

However, such cases generally arise through an insured being re-examined by the same or another life insurance company and offered better terms so that the refusal to reconsider the case may result in the surrender or termination of the policy and the creation of ill will.

We have already referred to the resentment of applicants on being rated and in practice there is continuous pressure in such cases for the reconsideration or removal of the rating. Further, the removal of an extra premium involves an expense usually out of proportion to the amount of extra premium in question. In an attempt to reduce such pressure one company, on offering a rated policy (if the type of impairment is such that an improvement is to be expected), will specify the actual period after which the rating will be reconsidered.

Another company has been extending the use of temporary extras far beyond the impairments represented by type (*a*) extra mortality outlined above. In particular it has been extended to impairments representing a history of some operation or illness in which an extra mortality can be expected for a number of years following the illness or operation. Thus, if $5.00 per thousand extra premium for 10 years can be assumed as the equivalent of the extra mortality expected from a certain illness or operation, and at the time of the application for insurance four years have elapsed since the illness or operation, then $5.00 per thousand is charged for six years. This has the effect of reducing or possibly eliminating the pressure for reconsideration of the extra. Another thought which may influence this company's practice is that $5.00 a thousand, say, for four or five years is better justified than an equivalent extra of $1.50 per thousand assumed to be payable for throughout a straight life policy and waived as being too small to charge. We may appear to have laboured this matter unnecessarily, but it is important as indicating the conflict between theory and practice.

Non-Medical Insurance

HISTORY AND DEVELOPMENT

The mortality curve in Figure 3, Chapter 4, shows the rate of mortality up to age 35 in the general male population to be under 2 per thousand

and Table 8.1 shows the mortality of insured lives according to the latest table to be not much greater than 1 per thousand in the same age range. It would thus appear that where small sums insured are at risk and for the younger ages, and if some evidence of insurability were obtained in order to eliminate those obviously not standard lives, then one could dispense with the medical examination.

During the 1914–18 War there was considerable difficulty in obtaining the services of doctors for medical examinations for life insurance particularly in sparsely populated rural areas where mortality is known to be very light. After the war the fees for medical services increased and the possibility of dispensing with medical examinations for the smaller policies was forced on companies. The system was first introduced into Canada in 1921 where policies up to $1,000 were issued for applicants aged 20 to 45 without medical examination and it proved so convenient and successful that by 1928 the maximum amount accepted had increased to $5,000. Non-medical insurance has become general not only throughout Canada but also throughout the United States and further extensions in limits have been made.

In recent years the increasing cost of a medical examination, the increasing pressure on medical services, the continued difficulties of obtaining medical examinations in sparsely populated rural areas, and the great practical convenience of the non-medical system have all contributed to its expansion. Added to this, the continued increase in the size of the average policy due to inflation and the popularity of the inclusion of term benefits with the basic sum insured in the same policy and the guaranteed insurability benefit have resulted in pressure for increased limits.

Reference has been made to the earliest days of life insurance when applicants had to appear before the board of directors as a condition of the issue of a policy. This might be considered as non-medical insurance, but in those days a medical examination would have meant little. In Britain a form of non-medical insurance had been in operation for many years prior to 1921, but in essence the company obtained a confidential statement from the applicant's medical attendant in lieu of medical examination. In such circumstances it would be expected that the amounts granted and the age range were far wider than the practice on this continent.

NON-MEDICAL DECLARATION

We have already given the details of the non-medical declaration: the questionnaire which is completed regarding the family history and medical history of the life to be insured. The answers are recorded by the agent and the statements are signed by them both.

Under present-day Canadian practice of handling non-medical insurance the applicant's medical attendant is only referred to if the classification would depend on details of some medical impairment referred to in the papers, or for more specific information regarding illnesses, medical check-ups, electrocardiograms, etc. referred to in the non-medical declaration. The company reserves the right to make inquiries from any source from which details of an applicant's medical history can be obtained and also reserves the right to ask for a medical examination.

MEDICAL VERSUS NON-MEDICAL MORTALITY

The answers recorded by a medical examiner as to the medical history of a life to be insured should be of greater value than those recorded by the agent so far as classifying the risk is concerned. Further, there may be impairments of which the life may have no knowledge which would ordinarily be revealed in a medical examination. These are, for example, heart murmurs, elevated blood pressure, albumin or sugar in the urine as revealed by the urinalysis. An interesting sidelight is that in the early days of non-medical insurance in Canada some companies required a specimen of urine to be sent to the head office in all non-medical cases.

It is possible for the non-medical policies in a particular company to indicate a lower mortality than those of its medically examined lives. As already stated anti-selection may play a prominent part in life insurance and where this was effective in the larger policies, i.e., those medically examined, it would be possible for the medically examined lives to exhibit the higher mortality. However, the results of numerous investigations indicate that generally non-medical mortality is higher than medical mortality for the same ages and durations.

The Canadian Institute of Actuaries has published the results of an investigation into the combined experience in Canada of a number of life insurance companies as to the relative mortality of their non-medical and medically examined policies. For the period 1969 to 1974 the combined results based on amounts of insurance and covering the first ten policy years only, were as follows in Table 24.2, 100 per cent representing the mortality by the CA58-64 Table.

This investigation indicates that the excess mortality at ages 0 to 5 for medically examined over non-medical business would appear to be a statistical fluctuation. Non-medical mortality at ages above 5 was from

TABLE 24.2

Age at Issue	Medical	Non-Medical
0–5	112%	80%
6–30	93%	104%
31–45	85%	97%

12 to 14 per cent higher than that of medically examined lives. Such an excess mortality when expressed in dollars and cents is quite small at a young age at entry but increases rapidly with age. We may note here the traditional acceptance of 25 points excess mortality under the Numerical Rating System for standard lives.

NON-MEDICAL LIMITS

All companies do not have the same limits for non-medical insurance. Table 24.3 is illustrative and gives the limits of one Canadian company. It indicates the reductions which apply as entry age increases above 30. Generally, all lives have to be medically examined above age 45 at entry. Some companies go above the $30,000 limit shown, but many have lower limits. Some companies reduce their limits for term insurances and in some cases restrictive limits apply on very young children.

The limits indicated would apply to the total sum at risk at the time the policy was applied for including any family income, term insurance rider, guaranteed insurability, or similar benefits attached to the policy. Companies have rules regarding the assessment of these benefits to determine the amount at risk. The limits would also include the sum at risk on policies on the same life issued on the non-medical plan by the same company within a specified period or since the last medical examination.

TABLE 24.3

Age of Issue	Amount at Risk
to age 30	$50,000
31–35	25,000
36–40	10,000
41–45	7,500

PARA-MEDICAL EXAMINATION

We referred above to the increasing pressure on medical men which appears to be becoming more onerous to those seeking their services.

We have also noted the increasing amounts at risk on new applications which make for increased responsibilities to underwriters. The para-medical examination is a fairly new type of service which meets this problem. It was first introduced in the United States in 1969 and has been widely accepted in Canada. The applicant appears before a technician who obtains a full medical history, height, weight, blood pressure, electrocardiogram, and a sample of urine. Such a report is of great value to the underwriter and companies will accept application for insurance for far larger amounts than their regular non-medical limits when such a para-medical report is available.

Where applicant is at a young age, say under 40 or 45, a para-medical report could be said to be of more value to an underwriter than the usual medical examination. The additional information obtained may offset the lack of information on possible chest and heart impairments which would be obtained from a medical examination report on a life of that age.

LANGUAGE AND RESIDENCE

We have referred to these factors in discussing classification of risks and it is obvious from the comments there made why in certain circumstances companies would require medical examination as an additional precaution. The accuracy of the replies made to a long questionnaire in either English or French by a person who spoke neither would be suspect. Companies might also require medical examination in the case of individuals who had resided in Canada or the United States for a matter of months only, when the usual inspection report would be of little value.

OCCUPATION

Where an applicant would be rated for occupation on account of exposure to extremes of dust, heat, or cold, a medical examination might be requested to ensure that such exposure had not already left its mark.

Limits and Reinsurance

LIMITS OF ACCEPTANCE

How much life insurance should a company carry at its own risk? A theoretical answer can be obtained based on the business in force, the distribution of the business by size of policy, the amount of surplus, and the mortality it is expected to experience. Other considerations would be the relation of the income to outgo so that the payment of claims should not involve a disturbance of its investments. However, it may be stated that companies do not, as a rule, go to the theoretical limit. In theory a number of substantial claims falling due in any year and within the theoretical limit and involving a marked inroad into surplus would be rectified in the course of time as the law of averages demonstrated itself. However, in practice, in such an event, the explanations to be made, the disturbance of public confidence, and the doubts aroused as to the ability of the company's underwriters and management and the reaction on them would be a serious matter. The result is that limits are much lower than theoretical considerations would justify.

In a new company the amount accepted at the company's own risk might be as low as $10,000 and possibly lower. In a company with billions of assets and a proportionate surplus it could be said there was no limit as regards an individual life and the company could retain several millions of dollars at its own risk. However, apart from the financial considerations already mentioned, there is the quasi-public standing of life insurance institutions and the essentially co-operative nature of the business. Policies should not be considered as individual risks but units of a class, and cases of one million and over in any one company may not be numerous enough to form a class. Further, the unfavourable publicity which an early claim on a very large policy might arouse is a factor to be considered.

The largest amount held at its own risk by a Canadian life insurance company is two million dollars. The largest U.S. life insurance companies, some of which do business in Canada, will carry up to several million dollars at their own risk. The variation in size among these companies in relation to their maximum retention indicates that theoretical considerations are not the determining factor. A company would retain more on a life under several policies taken out over a period of years.

No attempt will be made to indicate limits beyond what has been stated as every company is a law to itself in this regard. Further, by sharing with other companies any risk in excess of their own retentions (called reinsurance), companies can handle almost any amount offered to them.

In determining limits another set of factors have to be considered. We stated above that each policy has to be considered as a unit of its class. The smaller the class, the less homogeneous it is. Further, the higher the expected mortality of such a class the sharper and more sudden will be the fluctuations in the mortality of that class. It is just such sharp and sudden fluctuation which it should be the desire of the management to avoid. Hence the variation of the limits as outlined below.

VARIATION BY AGE AT ENTRY

As the rate of mortality increases so do the claims to be expected. From the curve of mortality we know that the rate of mortality begins to climb rapidly after age 50, so some reduction in the amount accepted from new entrants should be made after age 50 or 55. At older ages at entry, say over 60 or 65, degenerative diseases normally develop very rapidly and the usual life insurance medical examination and other selective tests decrease in effectiveness. Therefore one would expect the maximum amounts accepted on new insurance and held at its own risk to decrease at the older ages at entry.

On the other hand there are the younger ages at entry. Large amounts of life insurance under age 25 at entry introduce a speculative element as the habits of life are not yet fixed. Thus reduced limits generally apply below age 25 at entry.

VARIATION BY PLAN

The loss to a company on the death of a life insured is the net amount at risk, that is the sum insured less policy-reserve. With term insurance the policy-reserve does not increase consistently throughout the term of the policy and under a short-term insurance the net amount at risk is practically the sum insured as at issue. Prudence would thus indicate a lower limit, age for age, for term insurance than, say, straight life.

VARIATION: STANDARD VERSUS SUBSTANDARD

With substandard risks, the anticipated mortality is expected to be greater than with standard lives and as the degree of rating increases so the limit of retention should decrease. From what has been discussed, it will be appreciated that in rating substandard risks, as the rating increases so does the uncertainty and the degree of anti-selection. Another reason for reducing limits considerably is such a case as when members of the armed forces are insured without any war restriction. The uncertainty of the hazard is the reason here.

Some new company might decide to reinsure the whole of its substandard business on the ground that it may not have the experienced underwriting staff to handle it and with its low normal retention on standard business the corresponding limit on substandard business would be trivial.

OTHER VARIATIONS

A company may outline its practice regarding limits and denote specific limits in a schedule for various classes of standard and substandard risks and yet retain a lesser amount than the schedule calls for in a specific case. This may arise when the head office feels that all the facts of a case have not been disclosed or possibly are not obtainable, and being obliged to give a decision, the head office acts prudently by reducing the amount it holds at its own risk.

Another important fact which determines acceptance limits and hence reinsurance is that in Canada separate funds have to be kept for participating and non-participating insurance policies. Where the amount of non-participating insurance written is relatively small compared to the participating insurance, and hence the fund out of which non-participating claims are paid is small, it follows that the amount at risk which a company can accept at its own risk on a non-participating policy will be much less than on a participating policy.

THE NEED FOR REINSURANCE

Life reinsurance is a device for smoothing fluctuations in the claim experience of a life insurance company. The company ceding part or the whole of its risk is called the *principal company* and that accepting the reinsurance is called the *reinsuring company*.

Reinsurance is vital to a new or small company. Such a company would rarely have the necessary surplus to meet an abnormal demand for claims in any one year and sharp variations from the expected average do occur. As already explained above such a company restricts severely the amount it will retain at its own risk. Further, it could hardly expect its agents to restrict their sales to what the company, for financial reasons, decides to retain at its own risk.

However, with the general writing of substandard business by almost every company and the desire to offer insurance wherever possible, even on cases where only a nominal amount would be carried at its own risk by the principal company, the business of reinsurance has become a most important one. Companies exchange reinsurances freely among themselves, that is, of amounts in excess of what they decide to hold at their own risk.

Several companies, writing business themselves with the public (direct-writing companies) have developed departments catering specially to accepting reinsurances from other companies. There are also companies which do reinsurance business only and hence do not deal with the public at all. A substantial part of reinsurance business must necessarily deal with border-line and highly substandard business, where the normal acceptances are cut substantially.

The extent to which reinsurance is used may be measured from the fact that out of approximately $80 billions of ordinary insurance in force in federally registered companies at the end of 1974, some $4 billions of reinsurance have been exchanged between companies.

MODES OF REINSURANCE

Reinsurance may be either *automatic* or *facultative*. Under an automatic agreement the reinsuring company can be placed automatically on the risk for a definite proportion of the principal company's retention and thus accepts the principal company's underwriting rules and selection standards.

Under the *facultative method* copies of all the material papers are sent to the reinsuring company with a statement of the amount the principal company intends to retain at its own risk and the amount of reinsurance required. The statement also notes any amounts the principal company holds under other policies on the life in question. The reinsuring company, with the facts before it, decides whether it will accept the offer. Under the facultative method each case is a separate offer and a separate acceptance. Companies specializing in reinsurance service are specialists in substandard risks and often cases are submitted for their opinion, the principal company deciding its own action after an offer has been made by the reinsuring company.

COINSURANCE AND Y.R.T.

There are two main plans in operation in Canada for handling the payment of premiums for business reinsured. They are *coinsurance* and Yearly Renewable Term Insurance of Net Amount at Risk known as *Y.R.T.*

Coinsurance. Under this plan the reinsuring company in effect reinsures part of the policy issued by the principal company; it guarantees a part of the sum insured and the same proportion of the cash surrender values and options in the principal policy and receives that proportion of the premium paid to the principal company. If the policy is participating it guarantees the same proportionate part of the principal company's dividends. The principal company is also reimbursed by the reinsuring company for its proportion of the commissions and premium taxes, etc., and receives some allowance for its expenses on the principal policy.

Co-insurance involves the transfer of substantial amounts of money to the reinsuring company, thus slowing down the growth of the assets of the principal company. For that reason most reinsurance is now arranged by the Y.R.T. system.

Co-insurance is used largely by smaller companies to assist them in carrying the financial burden of new business. It has been explained that the costs of issuing new policies and the commission payable in the first year generally make it necessary for a company to draw on surplus to finance its new business; if a small company writes more than it can comfortably finance, it may co-insure a proportion of its new business in bulk, thus sharing the financial burden with the reinsurance company.

Yearly Renewable Term Insurance of Net Amount at Risk (Y.R.T.). Here the principal company determines each year the net amount at risk, i.e., sum insured less policy-reserve, of the part of the policy reinsured and pays the one-year term cost of reinsuring this amount. On permanent plans of insurance the policy-reserve increases each year and hence the net amount at risk will decrease each year, thus offsetting the increase in the one-year term insurance premium with age, particularly in the later years of life. It is helpful here to examine Figure 10, Chapter 6, to note how the net one-year term premium increases with age when based on a constant sum insured, and Figure 12, Chapter 7, to note the net amount at risk under various plans. There is usually an arrangement between the companies that when the net amount at risk on any reinsurance falls below a certain figure the principal company has the right to terminate the reinsurance thus avoiding dealing with trivial amounts of sum insured or premium payments.

Reinsurance on any basis costs money and in recent years as policies have increased in size the companies have repeatedly increased their net retentions to keep down the amounts reinsured. It should be noted that under the Y.R.T. plan the policy-reserves and their investment remain in the hands of the principal company. It should also be noted that whatever the method of reinsurance used or however it is paid for, it is an arrangement between companies and there is no relationship either in fact or in law between a reinsuring company and the policyholder under a policy which is reinsured by the principal company.

We have above indicated how the procedures of life reinsurance have changed with changing conditions. Undoubtedly other changes will be made. The adaptation of life insurance procedures to changing conditions and the adoption of simplified procedures are some of the fascinations of the business.

CHAPTER TWENTY-FIVE

Group Life Insurance

GROWTH

Group life insurance may be described simply as insurance covering the lives of a number of persons, such as employees of one employer, by a single contract. It has been developed to cover a wider field as will be described in this chapter. The growth of life insurance in Canada has been outstanding in recent years, but the growth of group life insurance has been spectacular as the figures in Table 25.1 indicate for business in force in Canada of federally registered companies.

TABLE 25.1

Year	Ordinary and Industrial	Group
1939	$ 6,089 millions	$ 687 millions
1944	8,085 millions	1,055 millions
1949	12,259 millions	2,150 millions
1954	17,795 millions	5,339 millions
1959	28,284 millions	12,590 millions
1964	39,012 millions	23,660 millions
1969	54,612 millions	48,173 millions
1974	80,965 millions	96,155 millions

At the beginning of the Second World War, the amount of group insurance in force was only one-tenth of the amount of individual (ordinary and industrial) insurance; by the end of 1972 the amount of group *exceeded* that of individual business.

ORIGIN AND DEVELOPMENT

An examination of Table 21.1 shows the rate of mortality for the years 1901 to 1910 among the general population to have been 3.8 per 1000 at age 20 and 9.3 at age 40. From this it would appear that an employer at a cost of about 50¢ a month per person could provide $500 on the death of his employees where the average age did not exceed 35, say. It would be necessary, of course, to eliminate the costs of individual solicitation, individual collection of the small premiums, and other individual services. Undoubtedly, odd cases existed where this was done, but the move which started group life insurance on its way with considerable publicity was in 1910 when three nephews of Montgomery Ward, who controlled that company, invited quotations from life insurance companies to cover the employees of that company.

The Equitable Life Assurance Society of the United States wrote the policy covering 2,912 employees for approximately one year's salary with a limit of $3,000 per person, under a blanket policy amounting to $5,946,564. Every employee received the cover irrespective of age or physical condition; there was no medical examination of any individual and the employer paid the whole premium. The policy became effective on July 1, 1912.[1] In 1912 just two companies wrote group life insurance in the U.S. and the amount in force at the end of that year was $13 millions. By 1918 sixteen companies were in the field in the U.S. and the amount in force was $632 millions.

In the U.S. there was bitter opposition to the plan in its early years particularly from the smaller companies and the fraternal associations. It was referred to as "imprudent," "unsafe," "fraught with possibility of a most disastrous nature to companies allowed to launch therein" and "a discrimination against regularly examined policyholders." It is well to note these comments made by responsible authorities in the U.S. in 1913 for there *are* such dangers present in group business if it is not properly administered.

DEVELOPMENT IN CANADA

This development in the U.S. raised much interest in Canada, but it was thought at first that group life insurance would not be legal in view of the federal Insurance Act then in force, which did not permit discrimination between persons having the same expectation of life. It was assumed that acceptance of a risk without medical examination would constitute

[1]The Equitable of the U.S. had been developing the idea since 1908 based on a railway employees plan current in England. It had obtained approval for such a policy from the New York State Insurance Department in February 1911. Undoubtedly the magnitude of the Montgomery Ward plan and the attendant publicity was a major factor in establishing the new form of insurance.

such discrimination. During the war of 1914–18, group life insurance continued to expand in the U.S. doubling and redoubling each year from 1916 to 1918. In Canada the federal Department of Insurance changed its views on the matter of discrimination and in 1919 the Sun Life of Canada was the first Canadian company to write a group life insurance policy in Canada. In the same year several U.S. life insurance companies wrote group business on Canadian lives. The amount of group life insurance in force in Canada was $11 1/2 millions at the end of 1919 and $77 millions at the end of 1920. One important development in the 1920s was the payment by the employees of part of the cost, changing the pattern from the example of Montgomery Ward where the employer paid the whole cost.

Group life insurance business in Canada weathered the depression of the 1930s remarkably well, business in force dropping from $498 millions at the end of 1931 to $461 millions at the end of 1933. During the Second World War, owing to restrictions in wage increases and the heavy taxation of profits, many industrial firms found it desirable to grant generous "fringe benefits" which included group life insurance. As a result, as shown in Table 25.1, there was a 50 per cent increase in group insurance in force in the five years from 1939 to 1944; since then the amount has doubled every five years.

While exact figures are not available, it is estimated that over two-thirds of the business is arranged under employer/employee groups; the balance is divided more or less equally between (1) insurance on members of trade unions and other associations, and (2) creditor group life insurance covering borrowers from banks, credit companies, and merchants under instalment purchase plans.

GROUP LIFE INSURANCE AND THE UNIFORM ACT

As many of the conditions required to be included in individual insurance policies would be inappropriate for group insurance, the Uniform Life Insurance Act and the Quebec Insurance Act define group life insurance and establish appropriate conditions for it. The Uniform Life Insurance Act gives the following definition: "'group insurance' means insurance, other than creditor's group insurance and family insurance, whereby the lives of a number of persons are insured severally under a single contract between an insurer and an employer or other person."

The single contract is called the *master policy*. The Uniform Act deals in detail with policy conditions applicable to insurance policies on individual lives, many of which would be inapplicable to group policies.

This necessitates a distinction between group and other forms of life insurance.

Creditor's group insurance has its own particular features which make it necessary to set forth special conditions applicable to it. Family insurance (see Chapter 12), although insuring a *group* of persons, is more closely allied to individual than to group insurance and so is not brought within the definition of group insurance.

Group Life Certificate. The Uniform Act stipulates that every group life insured, i.e., the employee or other primary life insured under a group insurance contract, must have delivered to him a certificate or other document setting forth the following particulars:

1. Identifying the master policy and the name of the insurance company.
2. Specifying the amount (or the method of determining the amount) of the insurance on the life and on any dependents or relations if covered under the contract.
3. Stating the circumstances in which the insurance terminates and the conversion privileges of those insured on such termination. These conversion privileges are quite important and will be discussed later in the chapter.

A MODEL GROUP PLAN

We summarize below the principles which should be followed in establishing a group life insurance plan. These were, in the main, those followed in the Montgomery Ward plan in 1912. Since 1912, in almost every instance, these principles have been modified and in some cases features have been introduced which may be considered as undesirable or which require special vigilance on the part of the insurance company to prevent them becoming so. Following the summary we proceed to discuss these developments in turn. The principles of a model plan are:

1. An employer-employee relationship should exist between the party contracting for the insurance and the lives insured.
2. Every life entering the group should be covered without medical examination or other proof of insurability except that of being at work, i.e., no selection by the insurance company.
3. All employees should be covered and the amount of insurance on any employee should be determined by a fixed formula, i.e., no selection by the lives insured.
4. No individual soliciting, no individual billing for premium, no indi-

vidual collection, no individual servicing, should be required. As much as possible should be done by the employer, thus reducing the overhead on the part of the life insurance company to an absolute minimum.

5. The insurance should be on the one-year term basis and the individual should be covered during working life only.

6. The employer should pay the whole or the major part of the premium. Where the employees contribute, the cost to them should not increase with age and should be definitely less than what similar insurance would cost them as individuals.

7. There should be recognition that the plan is supplementary to and is no substitute for regular life insurance purchased by the employees as individuals.

EMPLOYER-EMPLOYEE GROUPS

We deal first with employer-employee groups where the premium is based on the one-year term basis with a periodical adjustment of the rate charged in the light of experience. It is immaterial to the employer or employees whether this readjustment of rate is a dividend on a participating policy or a readjusted rate on a non-participating policy.

Number and Eligibility. As already stated it is essential under group life insurance, where all lives are to be accepted without any qualifying tests as regards health or insurability, to eliminate any voluntary act by the life insured which might disturb the "average" mortality to be expected of the group. Without some standard of expected average mortality no premiums could be quoted. In the early days the minimum number of employees for a plan to be accepted without medical examination or evidence of insurability was 100. This was progressively reduced as experience accumulated. It became successively 50, 25, and is now 10, which may include executive officers, partners, or proprietors.

The earliest experience under group insurance was in the nature of a surprise—the companies experienced a much lower claims rate than was anticipated. By covering only those actively at work, there was an effective element of selection. Therefore a much lower rate of mortality than for the general population could be expected as the general population would include many sick and incapacitated people. We are assuming here an average type of employment involving no special occupational hazard.

All full-time employers, including executive officers, partners, or proprietors, are eligible. If not actually at work on the effective date they would be covered when they return. All employees hired after the effective date are eligible after a "waiting period," usually three months; the purpose of which is to eliminate temporary and transient help, particularly sick people who might seek temporary employment just to obtain the insurance cover. Note the phrase "full-time employees." Part-time directors or retired employees are not, as a rule, eligible. The selectivity of "full-time work" does not apply to these and the heavy cost of insurance at an advanced age is a reason for eliminating a retired employee. This will be referred to later.

As a rule, it is optional whether employees enter the plan if they are to contribute part of the cost. No evidence of health or other method of selection is exercised by the insurance company if employees enter at the time the plan goes into effect. This also applies to newly hired employees. However, if an employee voluntarily defers entering the plan and later wishes to join, the insurance company has the right to require evidence of good health before admitting him or her. This is to ensure that no deliberate selection against the group is being exercised.

Required Participation. If the employer pays the whole premium (*non-contributory*), 100 per cent of the eligible employees must be included in the group. If the employees pay part of the cost (*contributory*) and the number of eligible employees is 50 or more, one company insists that at least 75 per cent of the eligible employees come into the plan and that that proportion remain in it. With smaller groups this company requires a higher minimum percentage participation, rising to 100 per cent participation for the smallest groups.

Unless a high percentage of those eligible accept the insurance the purpose of the plan will fail and experience shows that indifference spreads and the plan will probably terminate with dissatisfaction to all concerned. The insurance company has to be protected against anti-selection by under-average lives. The 75 per cent minimum participation is on the low side, for a properly constituted group plan is so definitely to the advantage of the employees that every eligible employee should be covered.

Limitation of Cost to Employees. Where employees contribute to the plan, it is desirable that no employee should be required to pay more than it would cost him to take out individual term insurance; otherwise he will be reluctant to join the group, at least for the time being.

For many years, the contribution of employees was limited to a maximum of 60c per month per thousand of sum insured; at the time term insurance at the youngest adult ages cost about that amount.

The cost of individual term insurance has been greatly reduced since the Second World War and is now about 20c per month per $1,000 of sum insured at young adult ages, employee contributions at about that level are now common; however, no figure has received the same universal recognition which was accorded to the 60c limit some years ago.

A step-rate system has been used in some cases, e.g. 20c up to age 35, 40c from ages 35 to 50, and 60c above age 50; however, human rights legislation in some provinces now requires a level rate of contribution from age 18 to 65, except for additional amounts of insurance obtainable voluntarily by the employee or in cases where the employees pay the total cost under an association plan.

Schedule of Amounts of Insurance. The amount for which each employee is covered must be determined by a fixed rule and no arbitrary choice allowed to the individual. Those who know they are uninsurable as individuals or that they would be subject to a substantial rating would be expected to apply for the largest amounts of insurance obtainable, particularly under a plan where the cost to the employee is deliberately kept to a low figure. No plan of life insurance can function where there is any opportunity for discrimination in favour of impaired lives.

In developing schedules of amounts of insurance factors such as salary, status in the firm, length of service, may be introduced. Formerly, it was customary to distinguish between male and female employees, and, sometimes, between married and single males. Again, however, human rights legislation now prevents such distinctions.

An example, based on earnings, might be:

Employees earnings weekly	*Amount of Insurance*
under $100.00	$10,000
$100.00 to $110.00	11,000
$110.00 to $120.00	12,000
$120.00 to $130.00	13,000

and so on, to the maximum stipulated in the plan.

Another example, based on status, might be:

Executives	$40,000
Departmental managers	25,000
Other employees	10,000

Maximum Cover. In some cases the self-interest of a proprietor or an executive results in a demand by that person for an amount which is difficult to justify. This often becomes a factor in competition between companies quoting on the case. This can be a source of abuse of the principles of group life insurance when the proprietor or executive is aware that he is a substandard risk or possibly uninsurable. It must be remembered that we are dealing here with limits of insurance on individuals where no test of insurability is applied.

Different life insurance companies have different formulas for ascertaining the maximum amounts acceptable in any case and they vary as a rule with the size of the case—the larger the case the greater the maximum amount acceptable on any one life. The larger the case the less likelihood there is of any one claim disturbing the over-all experience and hence the company can accept larger amounts on any individual.

For many years the limit on any one life was held at $20,000, and then at $40,000, following laws in force in a number of states in the U.S.A. There has never been any limit imposed by law in Canada and in recent years amounts as large as $100,000 or more are now accepted, with no evidence of insurability, in very large groups.

Certain *underwriting rules* are adopted by companies to reduce the effects of anti-selection. For example, the maximum amount on any one life may be limited to $2^1/_2$ times the average amount per life in the group, excluding the top class. Further, amounts of insurance expressed as a proportion of salary must not be higher for the upper income classes than for others.

Survivor Income. In addition to a cash sum, an annuity is sometimes payable following the death of an employee. For example, a group plan might provide for a lump sum equal to one year's salary, followed by a life annuity to a surviving spouse, equal to 25 per cent of annual salary. In addition, 5 per cent of salary might be paid as an annuity for each surviving child until the age of 21. In these cases the commuted value of the annuity payable on death would be treated as the sum insured to calculate the premium. Under this type of benefit, the acutal value of the insurance may be quite large, particularly for young employees. Thus, the benefit formula mentioned as an example would provide insurance with a value equal to between three and four times the annual salary.

Group life insurance has come a long way from its original purpose of providing a small sum for wage earners who did not or were unable to make some reasonable provision for their dependents in the event of early death. Many persons now depend for a large part of their insurance protection on their employers' group insurance plan. While this provides them with cover at low cost, the situation is not without its dangers and disadvantages. Cover will cease on termination of employment by changing jobs, or by retirement, either at normal age or earlier, and it may be impossible to pay the high rate of premiums required to convert the insurance to a permanent plan at an older age. Moreover, no cash and loan values are built up as they would be under individual permanent insurance.

RETIRED LIVES

An examination of any of the tables of mortality given in this text indicate the enormous increase in the rate of mortality year by year, as the normal period of retirement, say age 65, is approached and attained. Thus in Table 8.1, indicating the mortality of Canadian assured lives on individual policies, the death rate at age 65 is 26 times that at age 25 and at age 70 it is 41 times as great; in the Canadian Population Table 4.2 for males, the corresponding figures are 17 and 25. It follows that on a one-year term basis the cost of the same amount of insurance to a retired individual compared to that for a young employee would be altogether out of proportion to any objective which could be served by including retired people in the group.

Although the additional cost of carrying the death benefit for pensioners would be borne by the employers it would act as a deterrent to an increase in benefits to the active employees. An alternative to termination of all group insurance at pension age is to reduce the amount of insurance in one or more steps over a period so that it finally becomes no more than a last illness and burial fund.

PROVISIONS OF THE GROUP MASTER POLICY

Conversion Privilege. To meet the contingency which arises when an employee leaves his employment and his group insurance terminates, a conversion privilege is inserted in group policies. This enables the employee to obtain, without medical examination or evidence of insurability, an individual policy on any regular life or endowment plan, issued by the insurance company: if the individual prefers, conversion may be made to a one-year term policy and, at the end of the year, to a permanent plan. The permanent policy (or the one-year term policy) would be issued at the premium rates applicable at the age attained at their commencement.

In the early days of group life insurance little attention was paid to this privilege, but as the business has developed it is used in increasing measure by those whose impaired health is the reason for the termination of their employment. The higher mortality experienced on these conversions from group plans has been shown to have a value of $60 or more per thousand of insurance converted.

Group life policies generally provide that the death benefit will be paid if the employee dies within 31 days after he terminates his employment at which time his insurance under the plan would cease. This keeps him covered while he is arranging to convert or obtain group insurance with a new employer.

Many group policies give the life insured the same conversion privilege on the termination of the master policy provided the life insured has been continuously insured under the policy for at least five years but with restrictions on the amount of insurance to which the conversion privilege applies.

Beneficiaries. As with regular life insurance policies, group life insurance policies allow the employee to choose his beneficiaries, subject to the beneficiary provisions of the law of the province of his residence at the time he became insured. There are obvious objections to the employer being named as the beneficiary.

Payment in Instalments. Group life insurance policies do not as a rule contain guaranteed settlement options whereby the sum insured can be taken in various forms or remain on deposit at interest. These guarantees involve additional costs. However, the payment of the sum insured in the form of instalments is generally permitted and some group life insurance policies are drawn up from the outset as a "salary continuation plan" namely, to continue to pay the life insured's wages or salary, for a specified period, to the beneficiary after the death of the life insured.

TOTAL DISABILITY BENEFITS

The history and experience of disability benefits under group plans follows that of similar benefits under individual policies and varies with economic cycles. Up to the early 1930's most group policies providing total and permanent disability benefits before age 60, paid out the sum insured either in one sum or more generally in instalments on proof of such total and permanent disability. The balance outstanding was paid if the life insured died before all the instalments were paid. During the 1930s the experience of the companies on total disability was so unsatisfactory that they ceased to include this benefit in new policies and replaced it by an Extended Death Benefit which provided for payment of the death benefit if the employee died within one year from the date of termination of his employment and was totally disabled continuously from the date of termination to the date of death prior to age 65.

In 1938 companies began to include in group life contracts a *waiver of premium benefit* upon total disability if it occurred before age 60. If as a result of the disability the employment of the life insured terminated, then so long as he remained totally disabled his life insurance continued and no premium was charged. Evidence of the continuance of total disability was generally required once a year. The termination of the master policy would not affect the continuance of the waiver of premium benefit on the disabled life. This benefit was included automatically in the standard group life rates.

The original "pre-1930 depression" disability benefit has been reintroduced by some companies. Under this benefit called *income total disability*, when the employee becomes totally and permanently disabled before age 65 the amount of the insurance is converted into and payable in monthly instalments for a specified number of years in lieu of the death benefit. On death the remaining monthly instalments (if any) are commuted and paid to the beneficiary of the life insured. The charge made by one Canadian company for this benefit is an additional annual premium to the group life rate of 60 cents per $1,000 sum insured.

Long-Term Group Disability Benefit. Most of the Canadian life insurance companies who do a substantial group life business also transact group sickness and accident insurance through a separate branch of the company, the separation of the business being required by law. Among other benefits this group sickness and accident insurance provides for weekly indemnities for a temporary period during total incapacity for work, the benefits being payable for a total period of 13, 26 or 52 weeks according to the plan chosen.

A recent development in group insurance is to cover *long-term total disability* as a separate benefit from life insurance cover. It has grown rapidly and is being offered widely and liberally by many life insurance companies both in Canada and the United States. It seeks to protect and bridge the gap between the expiration of the weekly indemnity payable under the regular group sickness and accident plan and retirement at age 65 in the event of long continuing total disability. Plans are also available where benefits are payable for two or five years only (but not beyond age 65). Thus life insurance companies are venturing again on a major scale into the total and permanent disability income field, the history of which as outlined in Chapter 19 indicates the difficulties and dangers of that class of business.

Although both the above benefits are considered as outside the scope of this text, they are mentioned here as indicating the efforts of life insurance companies in Canada to round out their group insurance services to employers and their employees.

PREMIUM RATES

The initial rate for a one-year term group plan is obtained by dividing the employees according to age and ascertaining the total insurance at each age. These are multiplied by the rate per thousand insurance (either annually or monthly) and the total premium obtained. No short cut as by taking an average age and working on the rate for the average age is feasible. This is because of the sharp increase in mortality with increasing age above 35 so that a rate based on an average age is always too low.

We specifically referred to the "initial rate" because the renewal rate (at the end of the first year) may be modified in accordance with the experience of the group.

The original Equitable of U.S. group rates of 1912 were based on the American Experience Table and proved much too high. We have already mentioned that the earliest experience on group insurance indicated a much lower mortality than anticipated as it had not been realized that "active at work" was an effective method of selection. When this was realized and rate cutting among companies threatened to harm the development of the business the State of New York in 1926 fixed minimum group rates which became the standard group life rates throughout the U.S. and Canada for many years and are referred to as the "T Rates." These T Rates were based on the AM(5) Table of Mortality. Adjustments of the T Rates were made in 1950 (called U Rates) and again in 1958. In 1961 two committees representing the life insurance industry and the Insurance Commissioners of the United States recommended new minimum rates based on actual group life mortality experience; further revisions were made in 1974.

Since the move away from the T Rates the effect on the Canadian market of premiums used in the U.S.A. has become virtually nil.

The premium rates used in Canada depend not only on age but on the total sum insured under the group and on the average size of certificate. Table 25.2 gives a comparison of current rates of one Canadian company with the T Rates.

Note that while the T Rates applied to both males and females and to

TABLE 25.2

Group Life Rates per $1000 Sum Insured. Monthly Premiums

Age 15	25	35	45	55	65	75
T RATES						
$0.46	$0.54	$0.58	$0.86	$1.71	$3.76	$8.31
CURRENT RATES						
Small Policy–Male						
$0.24	$0.21	$0.22	$0.42	$1.07	$2.17	$5.33
Small Policy–Female						
$0.15	$0.16	$0.18	$0.30	$0.62	$1.29	$3.73
Large Policy–Male						
$0.14	$0.11	$0.12	$0.32	$0.97	$2.07	$5.23
Large Policy–Female						
$0.05	$0.06	$0.08	$0.20	$0.52	$1.19	$3.63

all sizes of groups, it is now usual to charge less for female lives, and to reduce premiums considerably for high volume to reflect the savings in administrative expenses. Premiums are shown on a monthly basis, which is by far the most common mode of payment.

OTHER FEATURES OF EMPLOYER-EMPLOYEE ONE-YEAR TERM GROUPS

Hazardous Occupations. Where it is known that certain occupations produce higher mortality than normal it is essential to include the additional charge in the "initial rate." Such occupations are mining and smelting, occupations where there are excessive hazards of dust and heat, and occupations where there is an excessive accident hazard such as police departments, fire departments, explosive manufacture, and the personnel of aviation companies. Employees in breweries are also rated. The matter of occupational hazards has been dealt with in Chapter 22. In group life insurance the extra for such personnel in the group whose occupation calls for a rating is ascertained and is then spread over the whole group. Thus the same extra is paid by everyone in the group, although the life insurance company receives the same amount as if only those who were rated paid their appropriate rating. This is to simplify the computation of rates.

Experience Rating. The amount of the premium adjustment or dividend will depend on: (*a*) the claims experience; (*b*) the size of the policy; (*c*) the time the policy has been in force.

Although the "initial rate" is not the criterion in the ultimate cost of the group insurance over any period of years it does play quite a part in competition. There is a temptation for a life insurance company to quote a cut rate for the initial premium to get the business and trust to actual experience to determine what the correct charge should be with the hope that the cut rate will be justified. Employers resent increases in rates even when they are justified and the practice referred to increases the number of cases where an increase in rates is necessary and this tends to react to the detriment of group insurance and the life insurance industry.

Retention Basis. In larger group life insurance plans some life insurance companies have been willing to indicate in advance what the cost to the employer will be so that the only unknown factor would be the claims for the year. Suppose the gross annual premium for the year is $100,000 and the retention figure quoted is 12 per cent. Assuming the claims for any year amount to $65,000 and the company retains 12 per cent or $12,000 for all its overhead costs, taxation, transfer to reserve for contingencies, etc., the refund to the employer will be $23,000, being the balance of the gross premium after deducting claims and retention costs.

The objection to this basis is that most of the responsibilities of the insurer for the business are surrendered to the employer. There is also the real danger that competition may force retentions below what is actually spent and, although they are not guaranteed, the company may have pressure brought to bear to adhere to its original quotation. In such a case the losses will have to be borne by other group policyholders. If transfers to reserve as margins to cover contingencies are not borne by this "retention basis" business, it means that other groups of policyholders or other classes of the life business transacted have to bear more than their share. The emphasis on cost in dollars and cents at one point of time, to the exclusion of every other factor, is not in the interests of policyholders generally, for life insurance is essentially a business operated for policyholders who share each others' risks.

"Excess" Voluntary Group Insurance. Should any individuals in a group desire larger amounts of insurance in the group than the formula provides, one is faced with the difficulty of costs, the necessity for individual underwriting as to insurability, special accounting and servicing, and the fact that group rates are not loaded for such costs. In the case where a whole class of managers or executives wish to be covered by a formula of, say, double the annual salary and the size of the group policy precludes amounts in excess of, say, $50,000 on any one life, some Canadian and U.S. companies will meet the problem. Taking the

case outlined: the excess amounts over $50,000 are written on the one-year term group rates provided the whole class applies for the excess amounts on the same formula and the usual rules as to insurability, etc., apply to the applicants as individuals. With some companies substandard lives are accepted with an appropriate increase in the rates. The fact that these excess amounts are individually substantial is an important factor in meeting the cost problem.

An important point is that the rating or declination of a particular life for this *excess* insurance on the one-year term basis does not affect the membership of that individual in the basic group or the amount of insurance he is entitled to thereunder.

For obvious reasons the companies issuing such excess amounts insist on the termination of the excess cover at age 65 or the termination of employment whichever occurs first.

The problem that such excess amounts might disturb the experience of the basic group and thus affect the cost of the group life insurance to the detriment of the rank and file is met as follows. These excess amounts and the corresponding premiums and expenses relating to them are *pooled with the excess amounts of other groups* and the over-all experience of the pool affects the premiums charged for these excess amounts and does not affect the premiums for the basic group plans.

DEPENDANTS' GROUP LIFE INSURANCE

Under this plan the group insurance idea is extended to cover the spouse and children of the employee. The purpose is to provide a sum to defray the costs of the last illness and funeral expenses of such dependants. So long as the amount of insurance is consistent with the purpose stated and does not exceed, say, $5,000 for spouse and $1,000 for each child under age 21, its interference with regular life insurance is kept to the minimum. The limitations of group life insurance should be noted here and the fact that it is no substitute for regular life insurance. On death, retirement, disability, or termination of employment of the life insured the dependants' insurance ceases. The wife may convert her insurance in such an event but there is no conversion privilege for the children.

ASSOCIATION GROUPS

These account for about one-sixth per cent of the group life insurance in force in Canada. The extension of the one-year term premium basis to a group in which there is no employer-employee relationship introduces complications. If the association is of such a nature that its membership exists apart from the insurance plan then group life insurance may be satisfactory. Such a group would be an association of school teachers or civil servants where there is no authority for the employers to pay part of the premium and yet most other features of a true group exist. Premiums are deducted from salaries by the employers and remitted in one sum on behalf of the association to the insurance company.

However, the question of the rate increasing as the average age increases is insurmountable although in favourable circumstances many years may pass before this becomes a problem. As soon as the rate increases for the younger entrants beyond the point where it ceases to be a "bargain" and they stay out in increasing numbers thus forcing an even higher rate on the rest, the situation rapidly deteriorates. With the two classes we mentioned where a definite pension age exists and the insurance is terminated at the pension age, there is a possibility of the plan succeeding.

A variation of the employer-employee plan which is based on equal contributions per thousand by all participants is to grade the premiums so that as the lives insured get older they pay more for their cover. Each participant pays the premium according to his age bracket, there being a step-up in rate every ten years or so. This does not eliminate the possibility of a general rate increase in addition but does reduce the cost to the younger members which is so essential for their continuation in the group.

It is well to review the reasons for the success of the employer-employee one-year term group which have been repeatedly stressed. Where these factors do not apply it is doubtful if group life insurance can be applied with any degree of success. The whole theory of group life insurance is the elimination of the individual except when the claim arises. If this is not possible, group insurance cannot be carried on with success. As soon as individual solicitation or billing or collection of the premium enters into the picture it begins to trespass on the field of individual insurance for which group life insurance is no substitute. The costs of individual life insurance are necessarily high and no plan can be devised which can give the same service as individual life insurance and avoid this cost.

Labour Unions. There are strong labour unions with substantial funds and management personnel. If such unions receive contributions of which the insurance premium is not a major part they may be able to operate an "association" group life insurance plan with some degree of success. There is one advantage which labour unions have: their members are in a narrow wage band and hence a uniform amount of insurance is feasible.

Associations of Professional People. There is a difficulty here which is shared with associations of teachers and civil servants. These are people with widely different earnings and a uniform amount of insurance may mean that on the one hand it may be too much and on the other too little; both may result in members staying out of the group for exactly contrary reasons. It has been questioned by some with experience of the difficulties encountered, whether any association group will ever prove completely satisfactory.

It must be acknowledged that a number of "association" groups covering professional people are apparently operating successfully. A benefit of the "family income" type by reducing the insurance at risk with increasing age does tend to offset one difficulty. However, the difficulties stressed should serve some purpose as a warning against undue complacency in these cases.

Associations of Employers. Associations of employers may wish to cover the employees of their members. If it is a well-established association existing for purposes of which the insurance is a minor item and the association has substantial funds and a well-organized staff, the costs of collection and servicing its members may present little difficulty and does not concern the life insurance company. The maximum amount of insurance should be kept quite low in relation to the average in order to reduce selection against the group which would increase the cost. As such an association would contain some large firms who could obtain group life insurance outside the association and possibly on better terms the difficulties are apparent. It has been found in practice that such associations require vigorous and continuous promotion, the cost of which must be allowed for.

TAX POSITION

As at the time of writing (1976) the tax position regarding group life insurance is as follows:

Employer. The employer's contribution is treated as any other operating expense of his business.

Employee. 1. Where the plan is a contributory one the employee is not allowed to deduct the premiums paid by him from his income for income tax purposes although such premiums are, as a rule, deducted from his salary or wages.

2. The employer's contribution towards the employee's group term insurance is not classed as income to the employee *except* where the group term life insurance exceeds $25,000 when the cost to the employer of the excess over $25,000 must be treated by the employee as income to him for income tax purposes.

3. None of the receipts of group insurance benefits are considered as income to the employee and so are not subject to income tax. However, the amount payable on death forms part of the employee's estate for succession duties.

It may be added that the exception noted in (2) above is a very minor restraint on the granting of amounts of group term life insurance in excess of $25,000.

CREDITOR'S GROUP LIFE INSURANCE

In its early development this type of group insurance was used to cover (*a*) unsecured personal loans made by banks, thus saving the banks the expense, delay, and ill will of proceeding against the estate of a deceased debtor. Other fields developed in recent years have been (*b*) auto finance loans; (*c*) finance company loans on furniture and appliances; (*d*) merchants selling heavy goods and appliances on the instalment plan.

At the end of 1966 this form of group insurance represented an in-force in Canada of abut $7 billion or 22 per cent of the total group life insurance in force. Ten years earlier it was about $830 millions or 11 per cent indicating a tremendous growth. Although the rate of growth has declined, the volume has increased steadily and has been estimated as between $15 and $20 billions at the end of 1974.

Definition. According to the Uniform Life Insurance Act: " 'creditor's group insurance' means insurance effected by a creditor in respect of the lives of his debtors whereby the lives of the debtors are insured severally under a single contract."

Note the creditor is both policyholder and beneficiary. The amount of insurance is limited to the outstanding indebtedness and so there is at all times a proper insurable interest. The creditor will generally charge the entire cost of the insurance to the borrower and the factors of cost sharing which apply to other types of group insurance do not apply here. As it is impracticable to obtain details of ages from borrowers a flat annual rate based on the amount of loans outstanding is used.

Practice and Cost. The practice of one Canadian life insurance company is given here, but it is typical of the general practice. The business is limited to loans with a maximum period of repayment of three years. The maximum amount on any one life is determined by the total volume of outstanding loans of the creditor effecting the policy. It varies from a maximum of $1,500 where the total is less than $150,000 to a maximum of $5,000 where the total is $800,000 or more. The insurance company requires 100 per cent participation of all eligible debtors. The premium to cover the insurance risk varies from 50 cents to 70 cents a month per $1,000 of outstanding debt according to the size of the plan and for the largest cases with millions of debt outstanding the rate is reduced to 45 cents a month.

Government regulations are in effect which ensure that excessive costs are not passed on to the creditors and that they receive the benfit of favourable mortality experience.

On selected groups this company will add a total disability benefit covering the balance of the instalments payable on the loan in the event of the total disability of the borrower. The premium rates for this benefit vary according to the duration of the loans outstanding and a composite rate is calculated. The benefit is limited to borrowers who will be under 65 at the maturity date of the loan.

GROUP ORDINARY LIFE INSURANCE

The very success of one-year term group life insurance would encourage attempts to use the mass merchandizing techniques of group insurance for permanent plans of insurance. The increasing standards of living among many classes of working men has made them prospects for ordinary insurance and as a group of employees they can be canvassed readily by agents of all life insurance companies. Further, there is the contribution by the employer for group one-year term insurance which can be applied towards the premium for the permanent insurance plan. It is a way of building up a cash value which is lacking in group term insurance.

There are various modes of operation. One such is outlined here and another in the next section. It is illustrated here for an applicant age 35 who is a member of a group life term plan for whom the employer is contributing $3.74 a year per thousand sum insured (see Table 25.2), which premium rate increases each year and ten years later, when the employee is age 45, would be $8.08 a thousand and so on. These rates would be adjusted according to the size of the group and so on, and the *experience rating factor* credits could reduce the employer's contribution.

Should the employee, age 35, decide to convert all or part of his group term cover to permanent insurance, there is a choice of plans; but here we will give the figures for the *straight life* plan, the annual premium for which (non-par) is, say $17.13 a thousand sum insured. Applying the $3.74 a thousand employer's contribution the payment charged to the employee is $13.39 a thousand for the insurance converted. Each year as the group term premium increases, the charge to the employee reduces; at the end of ten years to $9.05 a thousand ($17.13 less $8.08). At age 53 when the straight life plan has been 18 years in force and the employer's contribution is $16.34 a thousand, the payment is 79 cents a thousand; in the years following, when the group term premium would exceed the $17.13 a thousand, the employer's contribution remains at $17.13 a thousand and the employee has no further payments charged to him. Such a straight life plan, age 35 at entry, at the rate of premium charged, would have a cash value at age 65 of, say, $481 per thousand sum insured.

Should the employer expect his employees to contribute towards the cost of the group term plan such contributions would reduce the cost to the employer as given above. The conversion is purely voluntary on the part of the employee and, should circumstances arise, the employee can remove his policy from the plan and have it transferred back to the group one-year term plan without loss of the group term benefits.

This group ordinary life insurance has the tax advantage of group term life insurance in that the employer's contribution can be charged as a business expense.

GROUP PAID-UP INSURANCE

A plan to provide some measure of group insurance after retirement without burdening the plan for active employees has been developed. Under the plan a definite amount of paid-up life insurance is purchased annually in respect of each employee covered. The difference, between the amount of insurance such employee should get according to the group insurance schedule and the amount of paid-up life insurance, is purchased on the one-year term basis as under the usual group plan. Note that year by year the amount required to be purchased on the one-year term plan diminishes. Such a plan, although more costly, does tend to stabilize costs. When the employee leaves his employer by withdrawal or retirement he becomes entitled to the amount of paid-up life insurance purchased on his behalf and may convert the balance. Or, he may surrender the paid-up policy for cash.

There are a number of combinations which could be used. One might be that the employer pays the whole of the one-year term premium and the whole of the employee's contribution would be used to purchase a paid-up policy by single premium; the amount being small but accumulating year by year. Of course, the employees near to retirement would accumulate relatively negligible amounts of paid-up life insurance, but this could be rectified if the employer was willing to pay the cost.

Under such a group paid-up plan a larger contribution could be expected from the employee; the figure of $1.30 a month per thousand sum insured should be the maximum.

As illustrating the amount of paid-up life insurance obtainable on the plan let us assume that for each $1,000 initial group insurance $1 a month of the premium payable is applied to purchase paid-up insurance. Then in each year, according to the age of the life insured at the beginning of the year, the following amounts of paid-up insurance would be obtained and added to those obtained in previous years.

Age	15	25	35	45	55	65
Amount	$58	$45	$34	$27	$21	$18

CHAPTER TWENTY-SIX

Pension Funds

In Chapter 13 we dealt with individual annuity policies on individual lives and individual point and survivor annuity policies on two lives. In this chapter and the next we deal with *pension funds* or plans, where an employer enters into an arrangement to provide pensions for his employees on retirement. These arrangements are also known by the self-evident names of *employee pension plans* or *superannuation plans*.

The growth of pension funds to their present importance is of comparatively recent origin. Formerly only governments, banks, and railways had formal pension funds for their employees. There used to be a stigma attached to the terms "pension" and "pensioner" which is no longer the case.[1] Strictly speaking the word *pension* should be reserved for periodical payments to a man or a woman or their dependents by an employer and in consideration of past services. Thus a pension is an annuity, but an annuity is not necessarily a pension. However, we do refer to old age pensions, but the implication is clear for it employee pensions were universal and adequate there would be no need for government old age pensions.

Every responsible employer is now expected to provide for the superannuation of his employees, and is encouraged to do so through tax exemptions on money set aside for that purpose. Moreover, employers are required, as are employees and the self-employed, to contribute to the Canada Pension Plan or the Quebec Plan, both of which have benefits and contributions tied to earnings.

In 1973, some $2,991 millions were paid into private pension plans and some $1,305 millions into the Canada and Quebec Pension plans.[2]

[1]Before employee pensions were developed the word pension meant a subvention to retain goodwill or a regular payment to a royal favourite or to a man of learning. It often inferred a dubious relationship. Employee pensions are considered as a form of deferred pay and in the great majority of cases the employee makes substantial contributions to the pension funds from which they are paid.

[2]*Pension Plans in Canada, 1974.* Statistics Canada, Ottawa.

Growth of Insured Pension Plans. Table 26.1 gives statistics for *group annuities* taken from the reports of the Federal Superintendent of Insurance. It does not tell the complete story of the involvement of the life insurance industry in pension funding because it leaves out (i) small pension plans funded under *pension trusts*, (ii) pensions being arranged under *segregated funds*, and (iii) as regards the 1974 figures, pensions being arranged through *deposit administration.*

TABLE 26.1

Group Annuities in Force in Canada in Federally Registered Companies

	Deferred			Vested	
At end of year	No. of Contracts	No. of Lives (000)	Annual Pension ($000)	No. of Lives (000)	Annual Pension ($000)
1939	311	38	22,173	1	307
1944	425	57	37,040	2	727
1949	1,299	136	126,620	5	2,395
1954	2,596	246	272,940	13	6,464
1959	5,850	423	582,117	25	15,846
1964	10,048	571	852,686	46	33,642
1969	13,209	616	937,022	75	61,291
1974 (*a*)	13,518	432	724,319	119	115,175

(*a*) See text.

The last two are of increasing importance and cover many large groups of employees; they are described in Chapter 27.

The figures up to 1969 include the numbers of contracts, and of lives, as well as estimated annual pensions under *deposit administration* plans. The 1974 figures do not include them. Their removal in 1971 accounted for a reduction of about 2,000 contracts covering about 200,000 lives and $300,000,000 of deferred annual pension.

It will be noted that the reduction in the number of contracts was made up by growth between 1969 and 1974, but obviously the new plans cover smaller groups as the figures for numbers of lives and deferred annual pension show. *Vested* annuities (that is, those being paid) were little affected by the change in reporting and the figures indicate the accelerating growth.

Statistics Canada Study. The study referred to in footnote 2 is a most valuable source of information concerning the broader pension field in the recent past. Tables 26.2 and 26.3 are taken from it and the following commentary is quoted at length from it.

"The sharply increasing growth rate that characterized occupational pension plans in the 1950s and early 1960s reached its peak by the

TABLE 26.2

Pension Plans and Members by size of Group

Size of Group	1960 Plans	1960 Membership	1965 Plans	1965 Membership	1970 Plans	1970 Membership	1974 Plans	1974 Membership
0– 4	5,037	24,000	5,032	11,303	6,604	14,429	5,127	11,208
5– 14			3,659	30,843	4,008	33,739	4,232	36,210
15– 99	2,613	101,000	3,351	130,058	3,674	142,892	4,322	163,813
100– 499	892	193,000	1,127	244,577	1,266	273,521	1,504	329,326
500–1,999	249	249,000	345	345,483	406	404,638	451	444,543
2,000– up	129	1,248,000	146	1,583,384	179	1,953,117	217	2,439,145
Total	8,920	1,815,000	13,660	2,345,648	16,137	2,822,336	15,853	3,424,245

mid-1960s and then in the early 1970s leveled off or fell back somewhat. The dampened growth rate, particularly over the last half of the 1960's was attributable to some degree at least, to the introduction of the Canada/Quebec Pension Plan (C/QPP). Since occupational pension plans were a well established institution in Canada by 1966, when the C/QPP was introduced, the new public programme had wide-ranging effects on existing occupational schemes. Some plans were cancelled outright, though these were limited to relatively small plans with comparatively low benefits, while in others some participants cancelled membership, withdrew their accumulated contributions and chose to rely entirely on the C/QPP for retirement benefits.

"Thus pension plans which had grown to 8,920 in number by 1960 increased over 50% by 1965 to 13,660 plans; by 1970 growth dropped sharply to 18% so that pension plans numbered 16,137 and then ceased entirely with plans dropping to 15,853 representing a decline of slightly under 2% in 1974. Over these same periods the growth rate of the plan membership had levelled off at around 20% although in real terms participation continued to rise sharply. Membership in occupational

TABLE 26.3

Pension Plans and Membership by Funding Agency

	1970 Plans	1970 Employees	1974 Plans	1974 Employees
Insurance company contracts	11,067	398,761	11,242	462,073
Trusteed	4,384	1,703,358	4,167	2,170,866
Canadian government annuities	270	2,657	154	1,176
Combinations	367	87,772	250	117,912
Government consolidated revenue funds	19	607,885	21	666,078
Other	30	21,903	19	6,140
Total	16,137	2,822,336	15,853	3,424,245

plans which reached a total of 1.8 million workers in 1960 increased to 2.3 million by 1965, 2.8 million by 1970 and to a record level of 3.4 million by 1974.

"Notwithstanding the modest decline in plans, emerging trends for both plans and membership appeared to point to continued growth but at a much slower rate than in the past. The current reversal in plan growth was largely attributable to an administrative review of pension plan registrations by Income Tax officials. Limitations placed on "significant shareholder" plans (i.e., plans designed primarily for major shareholders and therefore generally limited to one or two persons) resulted in the termination of a number of small plans, which in many cases were converted into either deferred profit sharing or registered retirement savings plans. This review, which took place over a period stretching from the late 1960s to early 1970s resulted in a sharp decline of small plans with less than five members each. This is confirmed in Table [26.2] which shows a sharp decline between 1970 and 1974 in plans with less than five members; and indeed it was the decline in this size group that accounted for the overall drop in plans.

"Notwithstanding this net decline in total, there were changes in the whole range of larger plans. The sharpest increase was recorded in plans with 2,000 or more members which rose 21% over the 1970 level. Since these plans had the greatest weight in terms of membership the loss of the smaller plans had virtually no impact on the total which recorded a continued upswing to reach the record level of 3.4 million persons by the beginning of 1974.

"A key decision in formulating the funding policy of a pension plan is the choice of funding agency. This choice determines the organization or group of individuals who will provide facilities for the accumulation of assets for the ultimate payment of benefits under a pension plan. Funding agencies include insurance companies, Canadian Government annuities,[3] trust companies, and individuals acting as trustees. In this study, pension plans using the facilities of insurance companies or government annuities were called "insured plans"; where the funding agency was a trust company or individuals acting as trustees the plan was classified as a "trusteed plan"; and if both agencies were used the plan was classified as a "combination". Finally the category identified as the "government consolidated revenue funds" consisted of plans for public service employees wherein all contributions were paid into the

[3]Although a widely used funding agency in the 1940s and 1950s, over the past two decades very few plans used this facility because of its limitations so that it currently plays a very insignificant role as a funding agency for pensions plans.

federal or provincial consolidated revenue funds, and used for general government purposes.

"The general pattern of funding arrangements showed relatively little overall change since 1970. As in the past, insurance companies were the most widely used media for funding in terms of plans, but plans using this funding agency tended to be the smaller ones, so that the number of persons covered was comparatively small. Of the 15,850 plans in operation at the beginning of 1974, a total of 11,242 plans were funded with insurance companies but these covered only 13.5% of the members—462,000 out of a total of 3.4 million members. One third of these plans had less than five members each and another third had 5–14 members. The largest plan that used an insurance company as funding agency had fewer than 12,000 members.

"Insurance companies provided a choice of funding arrangements consisting of individual, group, deposit administration and segregated fund contracts as well as combinations of these. The most widely used arrangement was the group contract. Of the 11,242 plans using an insurance company as funding agency, 6,948 were group contracts and had a membership of 171,600. There was a sharp cutback in the use of individual contracts which dropped from 2,300 plans with 10,260 members in 1970 down to 1,756 plans covering 6,500 members in 1974.

"Contrasting with this decline, was the growth in deposit administration and segregated funds as funding arrangements. Deposit administration contracts increased by 48% from 635 in 1970 to 932 plans in 1974, with a corresponding increase in membership from 87,000 to 115, 592, a rise of nearly 33%. The initial modest growth in segregated fund arrangements that occurred over the first few years after they were introduced in 1961, started to accelerate in the late 1960s and by the early 1970s the trend was sharply upward. This growth pattern reflected an increasing interest in this type of funding arrangement by pension managers with a number moving from other funding agencies to segregated funds of insurance companies. In addition, a significant number of larger pension plans split their funds, directing part of their holdings together with a continuing fixed proportion of current cash flows into segregated funds. The net result has been an increase of more than threefold in the number of plans using this type of arrangement, from some 281 plans with 42,000 members in 1970 to 993 plans with 97,000 members in 1974.

"Whereas most small plans tended to use insurance companies as the funding agency, most large plans used trust arrangements. The 4,167 plans that were trusteed in 1974 accounted for only about one quarter of all occupational plans, little changed from the ratio in 1970, but these relatively few plans covered nearly two thirds of all participants, 2.17 million out of a total of 3.42 million persons who participated in pension plans in 1974.

"Three out of four of these plans used a trust company as the funding agency while most of the balance were managed by individual trustees. With this concentration of coverage, trusteed pension funds represented the most significant group of funds both in terms of annual cash flow and accumulated assets. These assets have been growing at the rate of 13% per year and in 1973 reached a record level of over $16 billion at book value with annual contributions of $1.6 billion, nearly 60% of the total contributions paid into all pension plans operating in 1974.

"The smallest category in terms of plans–only 21 in all–was the group classified as government consolidated revenue funds which included some of the largest plans in the country, such as the federal superannuation plan, the Armed Forces, the RCMP and provincial superannuation plans of the provinces. Together they accounted for 666,000 participants some 19% of all members in Canada at the beginning of 1974, down somewhat from 22% of the total in 1970. As the name implies all contributions were paid into the consolidated revenues of the applicable governments and the funds were used for general government purposes. Characteristically, these plans had no invested assets so none of the funds were chanelled into the financial markets."

GOVERNMENT ENCOURAGEMENT OF PENSION FUNDS

One cannot stress sufficiently that pensions cost large sums of money which is one reason for the slow development of pension arrangements until quite recently. A $100-a-month pension to a man age 65 is worth over $10,000.

We have referred in previous chapters both to the increasing longevity of people and the increasing proportion of elderly people in Canada. This means that the accrued liability for pensions will increase both in regard to the increasing numbers of the "retired" population and the increasing cost per unit of pension.

High taxation has become a permanent feature of the Canadian economy since the Second World War, increasing the difficulty of people in making voluntary savings for their old age. As stated above, the government has encouraged pension plans by exempting from income tax the amounts paid into them within certain limits. This has undoubtedly been a major factor in the recent rapid development of pension business.

In Chapter 18 we outlined the taxation incentives to employers to establish pension funds and to employees to contribute towards them and also dealt with the general taxation aspects of payments received from a pension fund.

GOVERNMENT PENSION PLANS AND SUPERVISION

Pension plans in Canada are under provincial jurisdiction, but in 1951 the British North America Act was amended to enable the federal government to enact the Old Age Security Act (OAS). In 1966 the federal Canada Pension Plan (CPP) became effective; Quebec elected to operate its own plan, but the Quebec Pension Plan (QPP) closely follows the federal plan.

The OAS provides pensions to virtually all Canadians over 65 escalated for increases in the Consumer Price Index; by the end of 1976, it paid $139.39 per month. It may be noted that in 1952, the amount was $40.00 monthly, payable from age 70. It was formerly financed by special taxes, but is now paid directly out of the Consolidated Revenue Fund.

The CPP and QPP are related to earnings, the retirement pension being 25 per cent of average pensionable earnings subject to a ceiling, originally $5,000 a year; all amounts are subject to escalation and by 1976 the ceiling was $8,300. Normal pension age is 65. There is a disability pension and survivors' and orphans' benefits. OAS and CPP/QPP are supplementary. Assuming average pensionable earnings of $7,500 a year, a man and wife would have a combined pension at age 65 of $5,219 a year ($1,672 plus $1,672 plus $1,875), which is over two-thirds of average pensionable earnings.

When the OAS was the sole benefit, it was ignored in most private plans and still is; the CPP and QPP are, however, now taken into account in most plans.

The present universal pensions may well be entirely adequate for lower paid employees. In making this statement we assume, of course, that current inflation will be brought under control and some degree of stability in cost-of-living prices attained.

The rate of contribution by the employee under CPP/QPP is 1.8 per cent of earnings between the escalating basic exemption and ceiling; the employer pays an equal amount. Self-employed persons pay 3.6 per cent of earnings on the same basis. Since CPP/QPP became effective, almost every pension plan in Canada has been reviewed by employers and employees. The introduction of disability, survivors' and orphans' benefits in the government plan has given increased interest to such benefits in private plans.

Under the Pension Benefits Act which became operative in Ontario on 1 January 1965 and under similar legislation in Quebec, Alberta, Saskatchewan, and Manitoba, rules have been made by the provincial governments regarding vesting, investments, funding, valuation, and the meeting of any deficits shown.

Furthermore, human rights legislation, now in effect in several provinces, has affected the operations of pension plans by requiring the elimination of certain differences in coverage or conditions based on sex, age or marital status.

Basic Features of a Pension Fund or Plan

We outline below the basic features which should receive attention in the setting up of a pension fund. In discussing these we shall again make reference to the study mentioned in footnote 2, which we shall refer to as the *Stat. Can. Study*.

CONTRIBUTORY OR NON-CONTRIBUTORY

Where the employees contribute to the cost of their pensions the fund is called *contributory*. The points in favour of contributory plans are:
(i) Pensions cost money–a great deal of money. A definite contribution by the employee reduces the total cost to the employer.
(ii) A plan to which employee and employer both contribute serves to stress the joint partnership on which all industry depends.
(iii) The contributions by the employees should enable a more generous plan to be adopted. Pressures for unjustifiable increases in pensions may be restrained if it is understood that additional contributions by both employer and employees will have to be made.
(iv) If the plan is started as a non-contributory one, (i.e., where the employer pays the whole cost), it may be difficult to change to a contributory one at a later date.
(v) The feeling that the pension is "given free" and the employee has no right to question any feature of the pension plan reverts to the old stigma of "pensioner."

(vi) The income tax allowances for contributions by employees is a clear indication that public policy favours contributory plans.

The points in favour of *non-contributory plans* (i.e., where the employer pays the whole cost), are:

(i) The employer retains complete control over the plan and hence it is simpler to introduce and to change. Administration costs are much less as records of payroll deductions and their accumulations for individual employees are unnecessary.

(ii) There are no withdrawal benefits, which reduces considerably the total cost of the plan.

(iii) "Take home pay" may be what counts and the employer can be faced with paying higher wages or salaries where a contributory plan is adopted.

(iv) There is no problem in getting 100 per cent participation. Every employee is covered automatically.

The *Stat. Can. Study* showed that in the public sector (civil servants, etc.) less than 2 per cent of plans were non-contributory. In the private sector, 23.6 per cent of plans covering 43.3 per cent of employees were non-contributory. Many non-contributory plans were of the "top-hat" variety covering small numbers of executives; on the other hand union-negotiated plans covering large numbers of workers are also nearly always non-contributory.

Eligibility

Who should be covered under the pension plan? To eliminate temporary employees, entry of new employees into the plan may be deferred until they have given a minimum period of service or have reached a certain age. Under a contributory plan the question of suddenly having to make contributions from which the employee has been free since entering service may introduce difficulties. There is much to be said for making membership in the pension plan a condition of employment when it is on a contributory basis so that employee contributions start from entry into service.

According to the *Stat. Can. Study* the majority of plans do have restrictions, but the greater part of them permits an employee to join after completing one year or less of service; in some, the period is two or three years or more. There is often a minimum age for eligibility which is generally 21 or 25.

INTEGRATION WITH CANADA AND QUEBEC PENSION PLANS

In 1966 when these plans were introduced, employers and employees already contributing to pension plans had to consider whether they could afford to continue to contribute at the same rate and at the same time pay the required contributions to the government plans. Further, particularly in plans with generous benefits, it became a question whether it was necessary or desirable to continue to provide these benefits in addition to the benefits under the government plans.

As a result many plans were *integrated* by reducing rates of contribution and of benefits in respect of earnings up to Yearly Maximum Pensionable Earnings or YMPE (the "ceiling" referred to earlier in this chapter)—*formula intergration*—or by directly reducing benefits and contributions by the amounts applicable under the government plans—*direct offset*.

Most public sector plans and most in the private sector with comparable benefits are integrated with CPP/QPP. However, many plans in the private sector do not provide such generous benefits and many of them are not integrated.

NORMAL RETIREMENT BENEFITS

At normal retirement age a pension becomes payable for life, usually with a guaranteed period (see *Death Benefits* (below)). The amount of such pension will depend on the terms of the plan which may be classified as follows:

1. *Money Purchase Plans*. Here the contribution defines the benefit. For example, each employee may contribute 5 per cent of pay, or, perhaps 3 per cent up to YMPE and 5 per cent on the excess; the employer usually contributes an equal amount. These contributions are accumulated for the employee and provide his pension at normal retirement age; the amount of his pension depends on the amount accumulated.

This plan is simple and has the advantage, to the employer, that costs are known in advance as a percentage of payroll. The main disadvantage is that while the plan may provide adequate benefits for younger employees, it will usually not provide enough for older members.

2. *Flat Benefit Plans*. The benefit does not depend on earnings and

generally provides a fixed benefit, say $10.00 monthly for each year of service; thus an employee retiring with 20 years service would receive $200 a month. Alternatively, the pension may be the same for everyone after a certain period of service.

3. *Unit Benefit Plans*. The benefit is expressed as a percentage of salary for each year of service. For example if the percentage is $1^1/_2$ per cent, 35 years of service would provide a pension of $52^1/_2$ per cent of salary. If the plan is to be integrated, the percentage might be $^3/_4$ per cent up to YMPE and $1^1/_2$ per cent on the excess; then the pension for 35 years of service would be $26^1/_4$ per cent on salary up to YMPE and $52^1/_2$ per cent on the excess.

These percentages may be applied to the average earnings during participation in the plan (*career average*); to *final earnings*; to the average earnings in the last few years (*final average*); or to the average earnings in the years when earnings were highest (*best average*).

Pensions must be related to minimum needs, and a career average earnings plan can produce quite inadequate pensions if the pension is entered upon at the end of a period of sharp inflation when final earnings have been adjusted to the cost of living, but the pension is based on average earnings over a lifetime. The same applies when a pensioner has entered as a junior at a very low salary and becomes one of the senior officers in the last few years prior to retirement.

However, a pension based on final earnings can cause serious embarrassment to an employer because of the enormous increase in the cost of the plan when any inflationary trend causes substantial increases in the salary scale. Recent experience indicates how, due to inflation, many salaries can be doubled in the ten years prior to retirement. Every increase in salary scale means not only an increase in all pensions for future service but the assumption of an immediate and generally very substantial liability regarding accrued pensions for past service, towards which no contribution by the employees can be expected.

Sometimes, as a compromise, benefits under a *career average* plan are increased by using the salary in a given year instead of the actual salaries in previous years for purposes of computing the average; obviously if this were done every year the result would be a pension based on *final earnings*.

A possible disadvantage of this method is the repeated adjustment of the pension plan. On the other hand this may tend to bring home to employees an appreciation of the realities of pension planning and the efforts made by management to meet them. This is preferable to a smug acceptance of a formula which will "look after everything" and which it is doubtful can ever be achieved.

PAST SERVICE BENEFITS

When a plan is first adopted, the question arises as to what credit should be allowed for past service. As a rule employees cannot be expected to pay towards the cost of past service benefits although such payments would rank within certain limits for deduction from gross income to determine taxable income. The cost of past service pensions thus falls on the employer and he is permitted to charge this as an operating expense of his business which he can spread over a period of years if he so wishes.

This matter of the liability due to past service is one of the great deterrents to the inauguration of a pension plan, in spite of the encouragement of the Department of National Revenue by income tax allowances. If the firm has a number of older employees and has been in business for a number of years, the statement of the amount of the liability on account of accrued pensions to existing employees might well end any desire to proceed with the establishment of a pension plan. However, delay does not improve the situation, for liability due to past service increases the longer it is deferred. The liability due to past service benefits if spread over the longest period possible and expressed as an annual addition to current pension costs is less likely to be disturbing to the employer contemplating the inauguration of a pension fund.

To reduce the liability due to past service pensions, it is quite usual to limit the number of years of past service which qualify on the introduction of the plan. As an illustration, consider a formula of, say, 2 per cent of salary for future service multiplied by the number of years of future service; the past service ranking for and being limited to a maximum of ten years at $1\frac{1}{2}$ per cent of salary as at the time of inauguration of the pension plan. Thus an employee aged 40 who is to be credited with ten years past service and whose salary at the time of inauguration of the pension plan was $1,000 a month would get a pension at age 65 of: for future service ($20 × 25) $500 a month; for past service ($15 × 10) $150 a month. This gives a total pension of $650 a month if salary remained unchanged throughout future service.

EMPLOYEE CONTRIBUTION RATES

Before the introduction of the Canada Pension Plan and Quebec Pension

Plan the most common contribution was 5 per cent of earnings. The *Stat. Can. Study* confirms that 5 per cent is still the most common rate on income above YMPE.

In the private sector 82.0 per cent of plans in force in 1974, covering 55.2 per cent of members, were in plans with a contribution rate of 5 per cent.

RETIREMENT AGE

A pension plan should specify a normal retirement age when the employee will retire with the full pension as provided for under the plan. Until very recently retirement ages were generally 65 for males and 60 for females. It is a curious contradiction that women, who on the average have a greater vitality than men, should be retired at a younger age. As their salaries are generally at a lower level than men, their pensions cost much less. However, the trend now is to make their retiring ages the same, and in provinces where human rights legislation has been enacted the normal retirement age must not be discriminatory on the basis of sex.

Also since the introduction of the Canada Pension Plan and the changes in the Old Age Security Act where 65 is stated to be the common pension age (as against 70), it has tended to become the universally accepted pension age. In the *Stat. Can. Study*, age 65 was shown to be the almost universal normal retirement age for males; for females 77 per cent of the plans had age 65, and 20 per cent had age 60 as the normal retirement age. The tendency to reduce retirement ages is contrary to the fact of increased vitality at the older ages which has been stressed throughout this text. It should be considered a recognition of improved standards of living in the "affluent society".

The acceptance of a normal retirement age still permits retirements at a younger age at a reduced pension should health or other circumstances make this advisable. One reason for not choosing too early a retirement age is the matter of cost.

To provide a given amount of pension at age 60 rather than at 65 requires the accumulation of a larger amount of money in a shorter time so that the cost expressed as a percentage of payroll might be increased by about 50 per cent, or, for the same rate of contribution pensions would have to be reduced by almost one third.

EARLY RETIREMENT

This is generally permitted within ten years of the normal retirement age if the employer approves. Just as deferment would increase the "actuarially equivalent'' pension so the reverse is true for earlier retirement. The pensions to a male at retirement ages 70, 65, and 60 are roughly in the ratios of 9 to 6 to 4.

In many cases an earlier retirement is in the interests of the employer. It is not economic to retain, at full salary, an employee who has outrun his usefulness. Thus, to make it acceptable and to avoid deferring an advisable early retirement, it may be desirable to grant a larger pension on early retirement than the actuarial equivalent. When a long period of service has been given or when retirement is due to total and permanent disability, one way would be to give the accrued pension based on years of service, etc., without deduction on account of earlier commencement.

Most plans permit early retirement within ten years of normal retirement age, but some allow it only within 5 years of normal retirement age. Many plans allow it with a combination of age and years of service: for example, at age 55 provided a minimum of ten years of service has been given.

According to the *Stat. Can. Study*, only 10 per cent of the plans permit early retirement without the employer's consent.

POSTPONED RETIREMENT

In view of what was said about a normal retirement age of 65, postponement above that age might be expected to become more common, and it may do so as the proportion of older people increases.

The question arises as to the amount of the postponed pension. It is simplest to permit the continuation of the employee's contributions. The amount of pension increases the longer it is postponed. The cessation of the employer's contributions could be justified during such deferred period. This may not only serve to offset any additional cost due to earlier retirements but it is undesirable to make the pension advantages of later retirement too attractive. With a trend to greater vitality, there should be a restraint on increases above what is considered as an acceptable pension whatever be the retirement age, on the grounds of cost alone.

VESTING ON TERMINATION OF EMPLOYMENT

Vesting refers to the right of an employee, on the termination of his employment and withdrawal from the pension plan, to the whole or part of the pension accrued on his behalf or the value of that pension; in particular, the part which represents the employer's contribution.

This question of vesting has acquired considerable importance. It has been stated that older workers are discriminated against in seeking employment due to the restrictive maximum ages for entry into the pension plan. It is maintained that if on leaving one employer the employee could carry with him an acquired pension, i.e., a portable pension, relating to his previous service that re-employment would be facilitated and this would aid the mobility of labour.

It was the federal government which first attempted to regulate pension plans through the Department of National Revenue's "approval" of such plans for income tax purposes; it insisted that the benefits provided by the employer's contributions must vest in the employee within a determinable period, and according to its 1950 edition of Principles and Rules vesting had to be absolute on employee attaining age 50 subject to a minimum period of service or participation not exceeding 20 years. The Pension Benefits Act of the provinces (which became effective in 1965 and later) now carry out that task and their current rule on vesting is "at least 10 years service with the employer and having attained age 45." In Manitoba vesting is mandatory after 10 years of service.

Many plans permit vesting to a greater degree than required by law. For example, a contributory plan often provides that on termination an employee may have either: (i) the return of his own contributions with interest, or (ii) a paid-up deferred pension (starting at normal retirement age) of the amount purchased by his own contributions plus a percentage of that purchased by the employer's contributions. The percentage usually increases with service, say, 10 per cent after 11 years, 20 per cent after 12 years, up to 100 per cent after 20 years.

Overruling this would be the provision that after age 45 and 10 years service the employee would be *locked in* with full deferred pension, that is, based on his own and 100 per cent of the employer's contributions; *locked in* means that he may not take cash; the law does, however, allow an exception to the extent of 25 per cent of the value of the pension.

DEATH BENEFITS

Before Retirement. The *Stats. Can. Study* states: "Most plans provide for the payment of some form of death benefit in the event of the member's death before retirement. In contributory plans, at least the employee contributions are refundable in a lump sum. Some plans pay the beneficiary all, or part, of the employer contributions in a lump sum, in addition to the employee contributions, if any. The amount of the employer contributions payable depends upon the vesting conditions applicable on death. A number of plans provide death benefits in the form of a pension payable to the widow instead of a lump sum settlement. A typical widow's benefit provides the widow with a life pension equal to one half of the participant's pension accrued up to date of death."

Because of human rights legislation, if a widow's pension is provided, then a similar pension must be provided for widowers of female employees. Small pensions for dependent children, usually terminating at 21 (or 25, if education continues) are sometimes added.

In the public sector 13.8 per cent of plans with 82.9 per cent of members provided a widow's pension; in the private sector the figures were only 38 and 22.6 per cent.

After Retirement. Most plans provide that if death occurs within 5 years after retirement, pension will continue for the balance of that term. Sometimes the period is 10 years. Another practice is to refund any excess of employee contributions with interest up to retirement, over the total of the pension payments made.

Plans which provide a widow's or widower's pension before retirement usually have a similar provision after, the pension continuing at 50 per cent of the full rate to the widow(er).

Plans generally provide for options; for example, if the basic plan is with 5 years guaranteed, the employee may have a reduced pension with 10 or 15 years guaranteed, or with continuation to a surviving spouse.

PENSION ESCALATION

Again, to quote from the *Stats. Can. Study*: "One of the most pressing problems facing pensioners is the devastating impact of inflation on the purchasing power of their retirement income. At a time when most industrial countries are victims of double-digit inflation the impact on fixed incomes can be catastrophic. Rampant inflation has directed increased attention on "inflation-proofing" of pension plans. A number of employers adjust pensions-in-pay on an ad hoc basis. They regularly review their pension programmes and make adjustments to benefits being paid in the light of current economic conditions and the general financial health of their pension fund. Relatively few plans provide for automatic indexing of benefits based on some objective measurement such as the Consumer Price Index."

The study shows that the number of employees covered under indexed plans increased from 191,700 in 1970 to 607,894 in 1974. "This increase . . . was mainly attributable to the introduction of an indexing formula in some public sector plans, the largest of which was the federal superannuation plan which was amended in 1971 to include this adjustment. Most plans with an escalator clause adjust benefits on the basis of the Consumer Price Index, usually limited to a maximum increase of 2%, or less, per year although some plans provided for a ceiling of 3%. A significant variation to this pattern was introduced in ten plans with a total membership of 502,500, which linked the automatic escalation of pensions in pay directly to the Consumer Price Index, increasing benefits by the full amount of the Consumer Price Index. Included in this group were the plans for the Armed Forces, RCMP and federal public servants."

The study concludes: "The extent to which post-retirement adjustment will become automatic in pension plans is difficult to predict. Although there is considerable concern about the erosion of benefits because of inflation, the cure can be very costly. It is this cost that undoubtedly will deter the growth of automatic indexing."

Because private employers cannot write a blank cheque, as the government has done, there has been considerable public criticism of the indexing of government pensions, particularly those of larger amount.

CHAPTER TWENTY-SEVEN

Funding Methods of Pension Funds

We continue with the subject of pension funds, or employee pension plans or superannuation plans as they are called.

The most important part of any pension fund arrangement is that relating to the means taken to accumulate the funds required to ensure the payment of the benefits; this is called the *funding method*. The subject is a technical one and unfortunately expressions are used which have not been strictly defined as the subject is still in a state of development. It is well not to be guided by terminology alone. In the following two methods, *pay-as-you-go* and *terminal funding*, it could well be said that as no funds are accumulated the expression *funding* should not be used.

PAY-AS-YOU-GO

This was the earliest method used. As pensions become payable they are met out of current income as part of the payroll. No liability is set up for the pensions being paid out or for the undoubted increase in pension payments which fall due with the passage of time. Such plans are non-contributory and often no acknowledgement of any liability to aging employees is made. This is not a satisfactory mode of operation.

A number of plans covering public service employees are on this basis but as they have the taxing power of the province or municipality behind them they are in a special category. The plans of the federal government employees, Armed Forces and RCMP which have been referred to, are not on a "pay-as-you-go" basis. Their liabilities are required to be calculated periodically and Parliament is required to provide for the increased liability through the budget. The total liability is set up in the government accounts as a definite liability of the Canadian government. The total liability under these three plans as at 31 March, 1975, was over

$12.5 billions, having increased by seven billion dollars in the seven years since 1968.

TERMINAL FUNDING

Under this method annuities are purchased for pensioners as and when they attain the date of retirement but no other financial arrangements are made. Thus existing pensioners are fully secured but no others.

This funding arrangement has arisen in connection with pension plans negotiated with trade unions. Over the period of the agreement, which may be from one to five years, the employer agrees to purchase certain annuities for such employees as may qualify for pensions, according to certain specified conditions. Whatever subsequently happens to the arrangement, the employee who retired while the agreement was in effect is fully provided for. It may be assumed that future agreements will ensure continuation of the agreement but the employer has entered into an obligation for a limited period only during which time the cost is treated as part of his payroll. It is a special form of funding devised to meet special circumstances.

FUNDED PLANS AND ACTUARIAL SOUNDNESS

It is socially desirable to promote the establishment of pension funds for employees and hence we should deprecate anything tending to hinder such development. We referred in the previous chapter to this in connection with the cost of past service benefits. It could be said that until the entire liability due to past service benefits is met the pension fund is not *fully funded*. However, one would not criticize such a plan if contributions were made by the employer so that this liability diminished year by year.

The statement that a pension fund is *actuarially sound* may have different meanings to different people. One statement by an authority runs as follows:[1]

> "...An actuarially sound plan is one where the employer is well informed as to the future cost potential and arranges for meeting those costs through a trust or insured fund on a scientific, orderly program of funding under which, should the plan terminate at any time, the then pensioners would be secure in their pensions and the then active employees would find an equity in the fund assets reasonably commensurate with their accrued pensions for service from the plan's inception

[1]Dorrance C. Bronson, F.S.A., *Concepts of Actuarial Soundness in Pension Plans* (Homewood, Ill., 1957).

up to the date of termination of plan. Note that this definition admits of a long time before all the original past service credits reach a funded condition...."

Advance funding implies that sums intended for payment of benefits under pension plans are set aside, under proper legal safeguards, in advance of the actual date of retirement. The phrase *orthodox funding* means that assets have been specially set aside and earmarked to serve the needs of the pension plan which, together with a normal and uniform rate of contribution by the employer and agreed contributions (if any) by the employees, will meet all pension, death, and withdrawal benefits as they arise in the future. We have already used the phrase "fully funded." It goes a step beyond that given above for actuarial soundness. It would require that the entire liability due to past service at the time of the plan's inception had been met and covered by assets in the fund.

It will be appreciated from the above that in any rules which may be adopted by governments regarding the satisfactory funding of pension plans, allowance should be made for the judgment of the supervising officials which should be based on regular periodic reports by qualified actuaries; a rigid set of principles may hinder the growth of pension funds.

INSURANCE AND TRUST COMPANY DEVELOPMENTS

In recent years, life insurance companies, trust companies, insurance brokerage houses, and investment firms have moved actively into the field of employee pensions. There is also the federal Government Annuities Branch. The competition is keen and has resulted in various innovations which have made the plans more attractive to the buyers and in the main this competition has been advantageous.

Judged by the number of plans, the life insurance companies do the largest business (insured plans); by volume of assets and number of employees covered the self-administered (trusteed) plans take the lead. As stated the larger employer appears to favour the trusteed plan and the smaller employer, the insured plan. However, trust companies have made efforts to extend the trusteed plan to the smaller employer by the inauguration of *pooled funds*, thus giving greater opportunities for investment diversification in experienced hands.

Trust companies have also emphasized the advantages of investment in common stocks with growth potential. This did place the life insurance companies on the defensive since their policy has been to hold a relatively small proportion of their assets in common stocks and in any event they were restricted to a figure of 15 per cent (now 25 per cent) by federal insurance laws. Since 1956, no restrictions apply to trust companies regarding the proportion of pension fund assets which may be invested in common stocks.

The life insurance companies have moved to meet this competition and changes in legislation have permitted them to do so by establishing *segregated funds* freed from the restrictions which operate on life insurance investments as regards equity (common stock) investments. Further the *deposit administration plan* has been developed by life insurance companies to make insured plans more flexible. These will be discussed later in the chapter.

It should be mentioned here that only registered and licensed life insurance companies (with the provincial or federal government) may guarantee the amount of annuity payable under any pension arrangement. Thus any individual or corporate trustee or investment firm wishing to guarantee any specific pension to a member of an employee pension plan on retirement must do so by purchasing an annuity from a life insurance company or the Government Annuities Branch, applying the necessary funds at the time of retirement.

THE TRUSTEED OR SELF-ADMINISTERED PENSION PLAN

Historically, self-administered pension funds or trusteed plans were in operation many years before life insurance companies in Canada extended their services to pension funds which they did through group annuities in the 1920s. It would be expected that firms with tens of thousands of employees would operate their own pension fund for such a pension fund would compare in the size of its operations with a life insurance company. Here is the criterion regarding self-administered plans: it is a life insurance company confining its operations to annuities exclusively and, as has been pointed out, the business of annuities is a difficult one and historically has been one of frustration and loss.

With a large self-administered pension fund as that referred to, there is all the security of experienced management, trained investment counsel, consultation with or the employment of qualified actuaries, and the other responsible specialists which go to make up an established life insurance company. Further, and above all, there is the well-established firm behind it which can draw on its resources and profits to replenish or strengthen the pension fund if this should prove necessary. The statements of accounts of industrial and financial organizations published each year have indicated that this has evidently been found necessary quite often in recent years. When consideration is being given to whether a pension fund should be self-administered rather than insured these points should be considered. The main consideration should be the security of the employee who attains pension age after a lifetime of service.

Pension Funds Insured with Life Insurance Companies

We refer below to four methods whereby life insurance companies in Canada have extended their services to pension funds. They are: (1) individual policies; (2) group annuity contracts; (3) deposit administration plan; (4) segregated investment funds.

INDIVIDUAL POLICIES

In the previous chapter we referred to the large number of very small *pension trusts* in force in Canada. Here the pension fund or plan consists of a number of individual policies on the lives of the individual employees and assigned under the terms of a trust agreement for the purpose of carrying out the conditions of the pension plan. They developed originally from the desire of an employer to guarantee a certain pension on retirement of an employee and the simplest method was to use the regular deferred annuity policies issued by the life insurance companies. These insured pension trusts (not to be confused with trusteed pension funds) were relatively costly as bearing the overhead of individual policies.

Considerable ingenuity has been exercised by the life insurance companies in adapting these individual policies as the field for pension plans developed, with the object of reducing overhead and hence making them more attractive. The advantage to an employee, on the termination of his employment, of being able to take over the policy effected in his name is clear. The simplicity of the arrangement was another advantage; for the very small firm it has considerable merit.

GROUP ANNUITY CONTRACTS

The first mention of group annuities in the reports of the federal Superintendent of Insurance is in that for the year 1928 and related to a plan written by the Sun Life; the credit for this development should go to the Metropolitan Life who placed the first such plan in operation in the U.S. in 1921.[2] This is the most important form of insured pension plan in Canada.

The basic feature of the plan is that each unit of pension is purchased by a single premium. As a result all credited pensions are fully paid and at any time a list can be prepared of the accrued fully paid pensions for each individual in the plan. A master policy is issued to the employer outlining all the conditions of the arrangement and a certificate of participation is issed to the employee. A booklet is generally issued by the employer outlining the various benefits and contributions to be made under the plan.

In a typical group annuity policy the employees' contributions are used to purchase a deferred annuity with return of the contributions on death prior to the pension age, generally with interest. The employer's contributions, however, are used to purchase an annuity without the return of the contributions on death before the pension age for it is not intended that the employee's estate should receive the employer's contributions.

It is important to note the relative amounts of annuity obtained for a fixed amount of premium according to whether or not the premiums are returnable, on the death of the employee before pension age. The following figures are for illustration purposes only and relate to a male life age 40, the pension to commence at age 65 being purchased by a single premium. The pension would be for life with five years guaranteed.

	Return with interest	Without return
Amount of annuity	$100	$111

The ratio of one benefit to the other varies with the age at entry and as would be expected the differences would be greater at the younger ages with a longer period to the pension age.

Where a specific pension is promised, the employer takes the responsibility of paying for the excess over what the employees' contributions provide. The older the employee the greater the cost to the employer per unit of pension. At the younger ages the employees' own contributions

[2]See Reinhard A. Hohaus, "Group Annuities," *Record*, American Institute of Actuaries, vol. 18 (1929).

may pay the whole or more of the pension accruing for current service thus reducing the cost for the employee in question when at older ages the cost to the employer per unit of pension is relatively heavy.

COSTING A GROUP ANNUITY

Table 27.1 illustrates the relative cost at the various ages of employees in a firm, assuming that the current earnings are $10,000 a year and the pension at 65 is 2 per cent of average career earnings which means $200 a year pension (payable monthly in advance) on account of the year's service. Contributions by the employees are 5 per cent, i.e., $500 a year each, the employer paying the balance of the cost.

TABLE 27.1
Costing of a Group Annuity
Period: One Year
Yearly Earnings $10,000; Employee's Contribution $500
Pension Formula: At 65, 2 per cent of Career Earnings
(i.e., $200 p.a. payable monthly in advance)
Death Benefit: Employee's Contribution Returned with Interest; Employer's Contribution Not Returned

Attained age of employee	Pension purchased by employee's contribution	Balance of pension	Cost to employer
30	$379.32	—	—
40	247.20	—	—
50	147.12	$ 52.88	$159.26
60	75.48	124.52	762.15

The successive reductions in group annuity premium rates made possible by rising interest rates have normally not been accompanied by reductions in the accepted rate of employee contributions and/or a significant increase in the level of the benefits. A disproportionate sharing of cost of the benefits between employees and employer has become evident. In fact, for those who enter the plan while young, it may become virtually a device for inducing the employee to save for old age on his own without any employer contribution being made toward the cost of the benefits. Such plans cannot give satisfaction to the employees if premium rates remain at their current level and therefore they have been restructured on a combination money-purchase and unit benefit basis. Essentially a combination type plan would apply, the employee contributions being used on a money-purchase basis to buy an amount of pension to which will be added a unit benefit, based on a career average earnings, purchased solely by employer contributions. For example, the employee may contribute 5 per cent of earnings on a money-purchase basis and to the amount of pension purchased by such employee contributions there will be added a unit of pension equal to one per cent of earnings which will be purchased by employer contributions.

Thus instead of Table 27.1 we would have Table 27.2. It will be seen that the total pension for the year exceeds $200 (cf. Table 27.1) except at age 60, and that the employer's contribution is greater than under Table 27.1 except at that age.

TABLE 27.2

Employee's Contribution $500: Money Purchase Basis
Employer buys Pension of 1 per cent of Salary

Attained age of employees	Pension purchased by employee's contribution	Total Pension for year	Cost to employer
	$	$	$
30	379.32	479.32	121.16
40	247.20	347.20	183.23
50	147.12	247.12	301.17
60	75.48	175.48	612.07

The criterion in working out a cost table as shown in Table 27.1 or 27.2 is the over-all cost to the employer. In practice, deaths, withdrawals, and retirements tend to stabilize the age composition of the employees and hence the cost to the employer. Originally the minimum number of employees accepted under a group annuity was 50 for this reason but much smaller groups are now accepted. Employer costs may fluctuate widely in small cases.

Past Service Benefits. Past service benefits are also purchased by single premiums, but as already stated it is desirable in practice amd there are taxation advantages in spreading the cost over a number of years. A customary practice is to allocate contributions for past services to the purchase of individual annuities in the order of nearness to retirement. This ensures that on retirement each employee will have the full amount of annuity due to him fully paid for. A modification is whereby payments on account of past services are accumulated at interest in a separate fund and not allocated to individuals until they retire or until the entire past service liability in full has been covered. Care should be taken to limit any right to full past service benefits on early retirement or for employer to guarantee any rights to past service benefits as these may involve substantial sums.

Rate Guarantees. Group annuity business is very long-term. Calculating the single premium for the cost of a pension benefit for an employee age 20 means a benefit which will not be finally determined for some 60 years: 45 years to pension age and then an average expectancy of some 15 years. A realization of half of one per cent *less* in interest earnings than assumed, can mean a loss of 30 per cent in relation to the cost of the pension benefit commencing at age 65 for an employee age 20; 18 per cent at age 40 and 6 per cent at age 60 (i.e., of the single premium). These figures are based on the assumption of 4 per cent and the realization of $3^1/_2$ per cent per annum interest earnings, but if the difference were between 6 and $5^1/_2$ per cent per annum the percentage losses would be little different.

Another adverse factor in guaranteeing group annuity rates is that the possibility of a reversal of trends benefiting the insurance company is limited by the employer having the right to discontinue premium payments without penalty, leaving benefits already bought fully secured. As a rule, guarantees of rates are for a five-year period, but insurers are often prepared to quote more competitive rates provided they are guaranteed for a shorter period. Competition between life insurance companies for group annuity business is keen, and as a result margins for contingencies are kept to a minimum to produce competitive rates.

With or Without Profits. Experience with individual policies suggests that it would be advantageous for a definitely higher premium rate to be guaranteed that would be sufficient for the business to be self-supporting in any contingency and, in reasonable circumstances, to pay a significant dividend each year. Sometimes dividends are applied to secure additional pensions for members of the pension plan, but more frequently employers favour the pension to be determined by a definite formula. Speaking very generally, where business is described as non-participating in profits, the distribution has been by way of reducing rates and sometimes these are made retroactive.

Controlled Funding. We referred above in the disposition of credits for past services to the possibility of concentrating on employees nearing retirement age rather than purchasing annuities for all employees in accordance with the pension formula. Any variation whereby benefits are not purchased until a specific age is attained or whereby the employer varies the payment he makes deliberately is called *controlled funding*. From this the next development in insured pension plans followed.

With controlled funding plans it is necessary to review the contribution rates periodically to ensure that the pace of build-up of funds is in line with the build-up of liability. The reviews are generally carried out every three years, or more frequently particularly when there is any change in the plan. The complex actuarial techniques used are beyond the scope of this text. Reports are made to the employer on the sufficiency of the premiums paid; should the premiums be insufficient, the deficiency must be made good in the future if the plan is to continue and should they be more than sufficient the surplus may be used by the employer to improve benefits or to reduce future contributions. Neither deficit nor surplus belongs to the insurance company.

DEPOSIT ADMINISTRATION PLANS

The Deposit Administration method of funding insured pension plans was developed in the United States and became an active form of negotiation for business about 1950. It allows for a greater degree of flexibility than under group annuity plans. The main difference is that under a group annuity, allocations to individual employees are made on account of future service pensions (and often on account of past service pensions). Under deposit administration plans no allocation to individual employees is made until retirement actually takes place.

The contributions by employers and employees (if it is a contributory plan) are accumulated in a separate deposit fund to which the life insurance company credits a rate of interest based on its earnings on its entire portfolio and a minimum rate of interest and a maximum administration charge are guaranteed for, say, the first five years. The higher the guaranteed rate of interest, the shorter is the period of the guarantee. The life insurance company also guarantees the single premium rate for immediate annuities. These guarantees are attached permanently to each dollar of contributions as they are paid. Therefore the interest rate and single premium rates guaranteed initially are applicable to all contributions paid during say the first five years from date of commencement until the last dollar of such contributions is applied to purchase an annuity.

A definite procedure must be provided in the event of the discontinuance of the plan for allocating the fund equitably among the employees.

On account of the interest guarantees the life insurance company will generally reserve the right to limit the amount which can be paid in or withdrawn from the fund in any year. A life insurance company prefers long-term investments and mortgages to stabilize its interest earnings and capital position as much as possible. It should not jeopardize this by allowing a large employer to dump funds with the insurance company when outside investment opportunities are poor and have the privilege of withdrawing large sums when the reverse holds true.

The chief advantage of the plan is its greater flexibility, but it should be noted that the insurance company does not guarantee that the accumulated deposits to the credit of the employer will cover the accrued pension liability. It is usual for the insurance company to require that any actuary's reports on the pension fund in question be made available to it for, if the employer or trustee should be unable to keep the fund in a state of solvency or any other adverse developments arise, the name of the insurance company would inevitably be associated with the plan by the public. Although the life insurance company does not guarantee the fulfilment of the employer's promises it has a definite responsibility particularly when the function of the actuarial consultant is filled by its own actuarial staff as is sometimes the case and for which an appropriate charge is made by the life insurance company.

SEGREGATED FUNDS

In Chapter 30 we deal with the effects of inflation and the means taken to attempt to modify those effects as regards pensions. In March 1961 the federal insurance laws were modified to remove any doubts whether federally registered life insurance companies in Canada could issue contracts, the policy-reserves of which would vary with the market value of a specified group of assets as common stocks and other equity investments. Under the revised laws the insurance company was required to maintain a separate fund or funds for these policies so as to segregate them from its regular life insurance and annuity business; hence the expression *segregated funds*. The policy-reserves covered by the segregated fund are expressed in *units* of the fund, the currency value of each unit varying with the market value of the assets in the fund. Where a pension benefit is expressed in currency, the insurance company may be most successful in its investment policy and distribute part of the increased market value of its assets to policyholders. However, it is always faced with the possibility of losses and must set aside part of the profits to cover this. When the pension benefit is expressed in units, the policyholder takes the risk of a fall in value and hence is entitled to the full increase in market value less a charge for administration.

The purpose of the change in the federal laws was to enable the life insurance companies to compete more effectively with trust companies for pension business. The fear of inflation and the belief that equities will increase in value corresponding to increased inflation is widespread. Managers in industry and finance who have the responsibility of setting up employees' pension plans assume that employers must adjust pensions with living costs as the latter increase and hence their interest in equity investments, as the basis for the funding of pension plans. The importance of segregated funds to life insurance companies is that it enables them to offer unrestricted investment in equities for pension funds should the employer desire it.

The companies who have entered the business vary in their procedures. Some companies have several funds: (i) bonds, (ii) common stocks, (iii) mortgages, etc. and the employer decides on the distribution of his contributions between the funds and can change that at any time. Other companies have only one segregated fund but contributions can be divided between that and its Deposit Administration Plan where they share in the general investment policy of the company whereas the segregated fund is confined to equity investments. With many companies the contributions by the employees are excluded from the segregated fund, for it is considered advisable that they be on a guaranteed accumulation basis. For very large plans an entirely separate fund may be set up.

There are two methods of procedure in the payment of pensions under segregated funds. In one case the procedure is: on the retirement of an individual the dollar value of the assets representing the accumulations on behalf of the person in question, in the segregated fund and elsewhere, are used to purchase an immediate annuity for a fixed dollar amount. The pension and the corresponding policy-reserve then form part of the regular business of the company and not of the segregated fund.

In the second method the policy-reserve of the pension from the segregated fund continues to form part of the segregated fund. The amount of the pension may be fixed or may vary from year to year with the value of the assets in the segregated fund. Such annuities are called "variable annuities" and will be dealt with in Chapter 30.

CHAPTER TWENTY-EIGHT

Government Supervision and Company Statements

As at the end of 1974 there were 389 insurance companies registered with the Department of Insurance at Ottawa. Of these 247 transacted property and casualty business only; 142 transacted life insurance business (120 actively). Of the 142, 28 were registered for life insurance only, 100 for life accident and sickness only, and 14 for life property and casualty; 56 were Canadian companies, 12 British, and 72 foreign (66 from the U.S.A.). There were also 26 provincially registered companies.

The life insurance in force is divided approximately as follows:

Canadian companies, federally registered	68%
Canadian companies, provincially registered	6%
British companies	5%
Foreign companies	21%

In addition to the business written by insurance companies a relatively small amount is written by fraternal insurance societies, both federal and provincial. There were about 3 billions of insurance in force in these societies at the end of 1974, i.e., less than 2 per cent of the amount in force in insurance companies; 42 fraternal societies were federally registered.

The total assets of the Canadian life insurance companies at the end of 1974 amounted to over $21,100 millions and the deposits and trusteed funds in Canada of British and foreign companies covering their Canadian life business amounted to $4,660 millions. The assets of the provincial life companies at the same date were about $1,100 millions; thus the total assets of life insurance companies in Canada subject to government supervision in Canada were about 27 billions of dollars.

WHY GOVERNMENT SUPERVISION?

No other line of business in Canada is so rigorously regulated and so closely supervised as the life insurance business and the first point is to enquire the reason for this. The magnitude of their assets, as just indicated, might be one factor, but the banks with their large aggregations of assets are not so closely supervised or regulated.

Life insurance and annuity policies may have a period of existence of forty years and in some cases far longer. To ensure payment of the amounts due during and at the end of such long periods, the company has to set aside certain amounts, actuarially calculated, namely policy-reserves and accumulate them in order to meet these liabilities. No individual policyholder can be expected to be in a position to ascertain that the proper policy-reserves are being accumulated. Policy contracts are technical documents and as the business of life insurance became an everyday concern of the average "man of the street" it became necessary for the government to supervise the business. Such supervision ensures that adequate policy-reserves are being held and regulates the type of contracts offered and the conditions under which the business is sold; this includes not only policy conditions but the licensing of agents also. The beneficent nature of a business in which the rights of the aged, the widow, and the orphan have to be safeguarded is another factor justifying close government supervision.

Supervision in Canada has undoubtedly been beneficial to the business for the ratio of life insurance in force to the national income in Canada (150 per cent) is third highest in the world. In the United States, where supervision is in many ways more strict, the ratio is 168 per cent. Japan leads with 193 per cent.

UNDER WHOSE JURISDICTION?

The relative powers and spheres of jurisdiction between the federal government at Ottawa and the provinces were laid down by the British North America Act in 1867. This is the instrument of confederation. Insurance is not mentioned in this Act, although it has been stated that in an early draft of the Act the right to control insurance was given to the federal government. At the time of confederation, there were a large number of purely parish or county municipal fire insurance companies formed under the legislation of Lower Canada in 1834 and of Upper Canada in 1836. It was undoubtedly owing to the negligible importance of insurance in Canada at that time that no reference to insurance was made in the British North America Act. At the time of confederation, apart from these local fire insurance companies, there were also other established insurance corporations (Canada Life was founded in 1847) and insurance laws had been passed respecting fire and fraternal insurance by some of the provinces.

Until 1949 all matters of dispute between the federal government and the provinces had to be settled through the Judicial Committee of the Privy Council in London, England; the Supreme Court of Canada at Ottawa fulfils this function now. On over one hundred occasions since 1867 the matter of interpreting Canada's constitution had been brought before the Privy Council. Insurance has not been the only bone of contention. However, time and again Ottawa passed laws governing insurance which were declared outside of its jurisdiction when challenged by one of the provinces.

It is most creditable to the officials at Ottawa and of the provincial governments that these legal contests were not allowed to interfere with the growth or practical operation of the business.

CANADIAN FEDERAL INSURANCE LAWS

The first federal Insurance Act was passed in 1868 and required every company transacting life insurance to be licensed by Ottawa (unless it had a provincial license). It also required a substantial deposit and the filing of an annual statement of operations. In 1910 an important federal Insurance Act was passed following the report of a Canadian Royal Commission along the lines of the New York Armstrong-Hughes investigation, referred to earlier in this text. The Insurance Act of 1910 set the pattern of Canadian federal insurance legislation as follows:

1. Restricted the investment powers of the life insurance companies;
2. Obligated companies with a capital stock to have policyholders' directors elected by the policyholders and numbering at least one-third of the total number of directors;
3. Required Canadian companies to keep separate accounts of participating and non-participating business, for Canadian companies, whether stock or mutual, issue both classes of business;
4. Fixed the respective rights of shareholders and policyholders in the distribution of profits.

The next great change in the insurance laws in Canada was the federal Insurance Acts of 1932, one relating to Canadian and British companies, and the other to foreign companies. It followed a decision of the Judicial Committee of the Privy Council, and the federal government removed from the insurance laws all references to policy conditions and concentrated its functions of supervision and regulation on the solvency of the companies. In particular, it established the principle that British and foreign companies may not transact business in Canada unless they are registered at Ottawa and have given satisfactory proof of their solvency, etc. Registration at Ottawa by the federal government is a privilege valued by Canadian, British, and foreign life insurance companies, and 94 per cent of the business in force with companies operating in Canada is with companies registered at Ottawa.

Another aspect of control of insurance in Canada is the large amount of deposits held by the Canadian government and by Canadian trustees for the protection of policyholders of insurance companies registered at Ottawa. British and foreign insurance companies are required at all times to maintain assets in Canada at least equal to their liabilities to Canadian policyholders. These assets, on deposit with the Canadian government and approved trustees, have to be in approved securities and, as regards life insurance business alone, at the end of 1968 amounted to $4,660 millions as stated earlier in the chapter.

Changes in the federal insurance laws have been made periodically and in particular we would refer to changes made in 1950, '61 and '65 affecting the investment powers of life insurance companies and in 1957 regarding mutualization which are covered in this text in Chapters 29 and 9 respectively. However, the 1932 revision has remained the foundation of federal insurance legislation in Canada.

THE DEPARTMENT OF INSURANCE AT OTTAWA

In 1875, in the early days of confederation, a Department of Insurance was established by the federal government and at a time when there were very few actuaries on this continent it chose as its first Superintendent of Insurance Professor J. B. Cherriman who was professor of mathematics at the University of Toronto and a fully qualified actuary. The same high standard of personnel has been continued. There have been only six incumbents of the position of Superintendent of Insurance and the present incumbent, Mr. Richard Humphrys, holds the rank of deputy minister, the highest in the federal Canadian civil service. Of the six, five were actuaries and one a lawyer who was also a trained mathematician.

The supervision of the federal Department of Insurance covers the business outside Canada of Canadian insurance companies and for life insurance this is quite substantial (27 per cent of the business in force).

We referred in a previous chapter to the duties of the Department in checking the valuation of the policy-reserves which should be held by the companies. The checking and supervision of more than $21,100 millions of assets of the life insurance companies alone is itself a major task.

The supervisory work of the Department of Insurance includes trust, loan, and finance companies, but not banks. There are thirteen fully qualified actuaries on the staff, undoubtedly one of the strongest actuarial teams serving any government in the world. Their duties extend beyond the Department of Insurance in serving the government of Canada. Reference will be made later in the chapter to the published reports of the federal Department of Insurance.

PROVINCIAL INSURANCE SUPERVISION

Provincial insurance supervision in Canada has developed concurrently with federal supervision. The first Inspector (later called Superintendent) of Insurance and Registrar of Friendly Societies for Ontario was appointed in 1879, only four years after the first federal Superintendent was appointed. While the uncertainty regarding jurisdiction has resulted in much legislation, the results may be said to have been beneficial. Provincial legislatures are naturally closer to the people and there seems to be much in favour of the present subdivision of powers as follows:

1. The provincial legislature has exclusive jurisdiction to prescribe the statutory conditions of insurance contracts and exclusive jurisdiction to license insurance agents, brokers, and adjusters.
2. The federal government has exclusive jurisdiction for registering all insurance companies incorporated or organized outside Canada who do business in Canada. Further, it takes the responsibility of supervising the financial solvency of these companies, requiring deposits from them. It is understood that such registration at Ottawa gives the right to these companies to do business anywhere in Canada subject to such conditions as provinces may require from all insurance companies doing business within their borders.

It will be noted from the above that there is no duplication of functions and, so long as the interested parties adhere to this understanding, the so-called "conflict of jurisdiction" should present no difficulties in practice, as has been evidenced by experience in the last thirty years and more.

As regards companies operating under a provincial charter the provincial Superintendent has all the responsibilities assumed by the federal Superintendent of Insurance with regard to federally licensed companies. These have been outlined above, and include verification of assets and policy-reserves. These details or a summary of them are published in the individual annual reports of the provincial superintendents.

ASSOCIATION OF SUPERVISORY OFFICIALS

The association of the provincial Superintendents of Insurance in Canada which concerns itself with supervisory matters under provincial jurisdiction is called the *Association of Superintendents of Insurance of the Provinces of Canada.* In Chapter 16 we outlined the Uniform Life Insurance Act which applies to all the provinces except Quebec, where much of the legislation is similar. The revision and continuing uniformity of provincial legislation in Canada is one of the outstanding achievements of this Association.

Company Statements

The statements required to be filed with the supervisory authorities by a life insurance company operating in Canada are of three kinds:

1. To the federal Superintendent of Insurance. This applies to all federally registered insurance companies. They have to be submitted annually and semi-annually, the latter being confined to the changes in the investments and loans of the company in the preceding half-year.
2. To the provincial Superintendent of Insurance of any province by all insurance companies doing business in that province.
3. To the shareholders and public including policyholders.

As previously stated, the main responsibility of the federal Superintendent is with the solvency of the companies. The licensing of agents and policy conditions are regulated by the provincial Superintendents of the ten provinces. This explains the technical and actuarial nature of the work of the federal Department of Insurance of which further details will be given below.

ANNUAL STATEMENT OF FEDERAL DEPARTMENT OF INSURANCE

WARNING: *It is probable that substantial changes will be made in the form of the Federal Statement during 1977 or 1978. Thus much of what follows may soon become outdated.*

The work of the federal Superintendent regarding the life insurance companies registered at Ottawa is accomplished by personal contact, by audits by his staff, and through the completion of official statements by the companies giving extensive material detail of their activities. The annual statement required from federally registered life insurance companies is undoubtedly the most important document relating to the business of life insurance in Canada. The current form of annual statement was introduced in 1954. It consists of at least fifty detailed schedules, tables, exhibits, analyses, and a number of explanatory statements. In one schedule, every bond or debenture owned by the company has to be named and described with its maturity date, rate of interest, when due, the par value, book value, market value, and the interest accrued to the end of the financial year. Thus the Annual Statement of the larger life insurance company is a huge document with a hundred and more large pages of detailed figures of tens of thousands of items relating to the business of the company both in and out of Canada.

The statement of a non-Canadian life insurance company is in the same form but refers only to its business in Canada. Certified copies of its official statement, as made to the government of the country of its domicile, and relating to its entire business, have to be filed with Ottawa.

The federal Superintendent or a qualified member of his staff is required by law to visit the head office of each company in Canada at least once in every year to "examine the statements of the condition and affairs of each company and report thereon to the Minister," i.e., the Minister of Finance, unless the Superintendent decides he can do this less frequently, but he must do it as least once in every three years. Further, once in every five years or oftener if the Minister so decides, the federal Superintendent computes the policy-reserves included in the company's Annual Statement. He may satisfy himself by checking the company's own figures, but the important point is that practically every material figure in the detailed statements of the companies is checked by the government.

Probably the most technical part of the Annual Statement is the "Valuation Summary" where the "in-force" and the "policy-reserves" must be given according to each basis used for calculating the company's policy-reserves, i.e., every variation of mortality, interest, or net premium. As outlined earlier all these bases are either established by law or approved by the Superintendent. Descriptions of the methods used to compute dividends to policyholders and the apportionment of surplus between policyholders and shareholders (where they exist) also have to be outlined. A certificate signed by the actuary of the company has to be attached to this statement to the effect that the policy-reserves shown are not less than those required by the federal insurance act and further that, in his opinion, they make "a good and sufficient provision for all unmatured obligations of the company guaranteed under the terms of its policies."

The annual statement has to be verified under oath by certain specified officers, if a Canadian company, and by the chief agent for Canada, if a non-Canadian company.

PROVINCIAL STATEMENTS

Companies operating under provincial registration submit to the Superintendent of the province of registration an Annual Statement giving details similar to those mentioned above regarding federal companies. In addition all companies must submit to provinces where they operate an annaul statement devised by the provincial Superintendents of Insurance. The statement shows for each province the premiums, claims, policy payments, dividends, policies issued and terminated and in force, separated into Ordinary, Industrial, and Group. The same statement is sent to each provincial Superintendent. Provinces are interested in the business done within their boundaries and the statements are used to compute the premium taxes due to the provinces.

Each provincial Superintendent of Insurance issues an annual report covering the business done in his province with the appropriate summaries.

THE FEDERAL SUPERINTENDENT'S ANNUAL REPORTS

In April, each year, the federal Superintendent makes his personal report to the Minister of Finance, attaching to it his "Abstract of Statements," which is Volume I of the final report. This relates to all forms of insurance transacted in Canada in the previous year. The life insurance summaries form only part of the 500-page volume. The printed volume is, as a rule, available to the public in August at a small cost. Tables of life insurance operation in Canada since 1875 are given. Other tables give the Canadian business, both new and in force, of every federally registered life insurance company, whether Canadian, British, U.S. or other, doing business in Canada. As regards Canadian life insurance companies the summaries give the new business and business in force in Canada and out of Canada, as well as the total business. There are summaries of the assets, liabilities, surplus and many other details of the company's operations. The statements made by federally registered Fraternal Benefit Societies doing business in Canada are given in summary form in the same volume.

These summary tables are followed by details of legislation passed in the year by the Parliament of Canada and the ten provincial legislatures relating to any branch of insurance or which has any bearing on insurance. Then follow brief notices of all the legal decisions of any importance made by Canadian courts of law relating to the various forms of insurance.

About a year after the federal Superintendent's Report appears, two volumes containing the detailed returns of each company according to its Annual and Half-Yearly Statements are published; one is devoted to life insurance and fraternal organizations and the other to the non-life branches of insurance.

The volume dealing with life and fraternal insurance consists of some 1700 pages of accounts and schedules following closely the pattern of the Annual Statement to the federal government excepting that investments are given in summary form only.

There are in these government "blue books," which are given a wide circulation, some 1500 pages giving details of the operations of the life insurance business in Canada in any calendar year. This bears out the statement made earlier that no other business in Canada is subjected to the detailed supervision, regulation, and publication of its most intimate operations as is the case with life insurance. But the real security is that provided by the federal Superintendent and his technical staff of actuaries and auditors. The insurance laws of Canada give the federal Superintendent very wide powers to see that the laws are obeyed.

ANNUAL REPORT TO THE PUBLIC BY A LIFE INSURANCE COMPANY

In the remainder of this chapter we deal with the annual report of a Canadian life insurance company as would be published for the information of its policyholders and its shareholders (if any). The first point is its relationship to the government annaul statement as rendered to the federal Superintendent of Insurance. We referred to the enormous detail of the latter statement and its technical background and resulting bulk. Apart from the cost, the distribution to policyholders of this statement would serve no purpose. However, there is no reason why the report to policyholders and shareholders should not follow the lines of that rendered to the government and convey the same picture of its status and progress.

In preparing their reports, companies generally follow closely the first few pages of the government statement which is a summary of the detailed schedules in the statement. In our illustrative accounts which follow we have assumed that this has been done and thus our references may be taken as either to the published report of the company or to the government annual statement.

A life insurance company differs from, say, a manufacturing company in that it is not concerned with raw materials, partly manufactured goods, or stocks of its manufactured goods in its own hands or in those of dealers. It is the value placed on these which is of such importance to a manufacturing concern. A life insurance company deals in promises to pay certain amounts on the happening of certain events, which may not happen for fifty years or more. Hence the importance of the necessary policy-reserves which have to be covered by investments. Thus the two main parts of a life insurance company's annual statement deal with (1) the investments and cash owned by the company and other amounts due (the assets), and (2) the policy-reserves and other amounts owing to the policyholders and others (the liabilities).

ASSETS AND LIABILITIES: THE BALANCE SHEET

Assets. The things of value a life insurance company owns are called its assets. They are of three kinds:

1. Invested assets such as real estate, bonds, stock and mortgages and cash;
2. Furniture and equipment;
3. Amounts owing to the company including investment income and premiums due.

A life insurance company is not permitted to include in its assets in its government statement the value of its furniture and equipment.[1] Further any invested assets which are not acceptable investments for life insurance companies according to the insurance laws may not be included in its statements of assets. These are referred to by accountants as "non-admitted assets," the phrase being self-explanatory. Bonds and mortgages have a fixed interest rate and at the end of the financial year the proportionate amount of interest owing is calculated and treated as an asset. The same applies to any other interest due but not received but

[1]An exception has been made in recent years. To encourage the larger companies to obtain electronic computers which involve expenditures of hundreds of thousands of dollars, the federal Superintendent has allowed them to insert such equipment as an admitted asset provided it is written off in instalments within a few years.

expected to be received. It also applies to premiums due but not received from which an allowance for commissions and costs is deducted before they are treated as an asset.

Liabilities. What the company owes to its policyholders and others—in other words, its obligations—are called its liabilities. Other ways of expressing this are that all claims against the assets are liabilities, or that the assets are the property held to ensure the fulfilment of the liabilities.

The excess of the assets over the liabilities is the surplus or free surplus as we have called it. If by chance the liabilities were greater than the total of the assets then the "capital would be impaired" and the shareholders would be called upon to meet the deficiency. In default of this the company would be declared to be insolvent. It is the job of the Superintendents of Insurance to endeavour to make sure that this position is never reached. *The Balance Sheet* is the statement of the financial condition of the company at a given date and for a life insurance company this is, as a rule, December 31. The balance sheet indicates the assets and liabilities as described above with the surplus or the deficit as the balancing item.

REVENUE ACCOUNT

In layman's language "revenue" means "income," but in accounting the phrase "Revenue Account" means income and outgo reckoned in a special way. It means the theoretical earned income and the expenditure incurred. The phrases "earned income" and "expenditure incurred" are intended to make it clear that something more is meant than the income received in cash or the cash which may have been spent.

Take as an example the interest earnings referred to above. Interest on bonds and mortgages falls due on specific dates, but in presenting a true figure of the interest earnings in a calendar year one should allow for the proportionate interest earnings on bonds and mortgages from their due dates to the end of the year. Thus the "revenue account" for interest earnings should be the actual interest which was paid during the year plus the proportionate interest from due dates to the end of the year (accrued interest) plus any interest which fell due and was not paid (outstanding) less the items of accrued and outstanding interest as at the end of the preceding year.

Outgo, including expenses, has to be dealt with in a similar fashion. Thus interest on deposits by policyholders with the company would be that actually allotted during the year added to that accrued by the end of the year less that accrued as at the end of the previous year.

All items in the revenue account are expressed in this way in the annual statement of life insurance companies to Ottawa.

A HYPOTHETICAL COMPANY

To illustrate the principles underlying the published statements of Canadian life insurance companies we are giving figures of a hypothetical company. We shall call this company the "Sea to Sea Life Insurance Company," which name is inspired by the biblical quotation, Psalm 72, v. 8, "He shall have dominion also from sea to sea," from which Canada's national motto is taken. This hypothetical company has its head office in Canada.

The figures in the accounts shown of the Sea to Sea company are illustrative only but do represent, in a general way, the operations of a typical Canadian life insurance company. It was decided to make the Sea to Sea a stock company. In recent years as outlined in Chapter 9 some of Canada's largest life companies have been mutualized, but whether mutual or stock makes no difference in the presentation of accounts. If items as capital stock and dividends to shareholders be omitted these accounts might as well represent those of a mutual company.

Sea to Sea Life Insurance Company
Head Office: Canada

ASSETS OF SEA TO SEA COMPANY

Table 28.1 gives the Balance Sheet of the Sea to Sea Life Insurance Company as at December 31. All items are given to the nearest thousand dollars. The total assets are shown as $211,690,000. The distribution of assets by type of investment, liabilities etc., is approximately that for Canadian companies as a whole in 1974. In Table 29.1 in the next chapter the division of assets as the end of various years is shown for Canadian life insurance companies, but excluding segregated funds.

In the summary of assets in the government statement, preferred and common stocks are lumped together, but of course in the attached

TABLE 28.1

Sea to Sea Life Insurance Company
BALANCE SHEET
as at December 31

Assets	
Bonds	$ 67,030,000
Preferred stocks	1,890,000
Common stocks	15,040,000
Mortgage loans on real estate	76,850,000
Real estate owned by the Company	13,100,000
Policy loans	15,140,000
Cash	1,780,000
Investment income earned but not received	2,410,000
Premiums due but not received	1,330,000
Other assets	1,200,000
Segregated Investment Fund	15,920,000
	$211,690,000
Liabilities	
Actuarial reserve for policies in force	$152,860,000
Policyholders' deposits with the Company	12,630,000
Staff benefit funds	2,630,000
Policy benefits in process of payment	2,240,000
Provision for dividends to policyholders	4,160,000
Other contract liabilities	270,000
Other liabilities	3,010,000
Segregated investment fund liabilities	15,780,000
Investment and contingency reserves	5,200,000
Capital stock	400,000
Surplus	12,510,000
	$211,690,000

schedules they are given separately. The differences between the two classes of stocks are so fundamental that in any statement for the public the items should be given separately as is here done for the Sea to Sea company.

LIABILITIES OF SEA TO SEA COMPANY

We give below further explanations of each item given in Table 28.1 under "Liabilities."

Actuarial reserve for policies in force. Throughout this text for reasons given in Chapter 7 we have used the phrase "policy-reserve" to describe this item. The $152,860,000 is the total of the "policy-reserves" for all policies in force as certified by the actuary of the company. It covers insurance and annuities, both individual and group. It also includes settlement annuities.

Policyholders' deposits with the Company. The $12,630,000 are the proceeds of policies which have become payable and left with the company at interest. The amount also includes dividends similarly left at interest and prepaid future premiums.

Staff benefit funds. The amount of $2,630,000 represents the liability accrued under pension plans for salaried employees, branch managers and agents. Liability for other benefits might also be included. Some companies do not include a liability under this item but instead issue a group annuity policy to provide the benefits in which case the liability appears under *actuarial reserves.* Group life insurance benefits are usually arranged by means of a policy.

Policy benefits in process of payment. The amount of $2,240,000 is the total of claims waiting completion of forms. In accordance with the idea of "Revenue Account" it includes an amount for possible claims which may have accrued before December 31, but of which the company has not been advised at the time it closed its books.

Provision for dividends to policyholders. As the dividends payable in "the year following," are the result of the operations for the current year of account, it is only proper in determining the surplus for that year to set aside the amount of policyholders' dividends which should be paid as a result of the current year's operations. Also, when dividends are not payable annually, the company is expected to apportion them annually (and accumulate them until they are paid), and the dividends apportioned are included in the $4,160,000 stated.

Other contract liabilities. This small item of $270,000 is made up mainly of premiums paid in advance. Premiums paid for some years in advance would be included in deposits above; this item covers small amounts paid, say, in December, for premiums due in January.

Other liabilities. This amount of $3,010,000 includes taxes, commissions and expenses due and accrued. The object is to include every item owing by the company, actual and proportionate to the date of the closing of the books. Taxes payable in the following year on the earnings of the year just past must be included. Also under this heading are a number of miscellaneous items.

INVESTMENT AND CONTINGENCY RESERVES

Nearly all Canadian life insurance companies have these special reserves apart from their surplus funds. The amount of these reserves is a question of management practice or circumstances varying with each company. The investments of a company are under continuous survey; a company does not wait until a bond or other investment defaults before taking action but will set up an amount out of its surplus earnings to cover all or part of the depreciation in the value of the security. There are two ways to do this: one by "writing down" the "book value" of the security in its books. The "book value" is the value the company places on the security according to the amount shown in listing its assets for balance sheet purposes, at the end of the year.

Instead of writing down the "book value" the company may prefer to place the amount in a separate fund called *investment reserve fund*. One advantage of this is that this reserve is not tied to specific investments. Both of these procedures may be followed, namely, writing down book values of some securities and creating an investment reserve fund for others.

A company doing business abroad may be faced with a trend in foreign exchange which may make it advisable to set up special additional reserves for a period of years, to meet a situation which, if the worst happened, might mean a substantial loss in a single year. Since the Second World War (1939–45) such occasions have arisen. Such an additional reserve could be called a *foreign exchange reserve fund* or a *contingency reserve*.

The trend of mortality under a part of its pension business may indicate lighter mortality than assumed in its policy-reserves for that business. The company may decide to strengthen or increase the policy-reserves but if the amount required is too large to absorb in any one year the company might plan to set aside a sum each year over a period. These amounts would go into this special reserve fund until the transfer could be made when it would be added to the "policy-reserves" and taken out of this special reserve without affecting the surplus of the company.

We have not exhausted by any means the circumstances under which special reserves are created. The point we wish to stress is that in some cases the additional reserves are not "surplus" and so must be kept out of the free surplus which is the balancing item as between assets and liabilities.

The Balance Sheet of the Sea to Sea Life Insurance Company shows that it has $5,200,000 in this special reserve which it calls "Investment and contingency reserves." The depreciation in the values of bonds and the fall in values in the stock market which have accompanied the inflation of the 1970s have shown the necessity of maintaining special reserves to cover fluctuations and losses.

Capital Stock. The Sea to Sea is evidently a stock company and the $400,000 shown is the capital paid in by the stockholders and hence is an amount owing to them and is shown accordingly.

Surplus. The surplus totals $12,510,000 of which $11,710,000 is in insurance funds, $140,000 in segregated funds and $660,000 in the shareholders' fund. In the insurance funds, $6,810,000 is in the participating fund and $4,900,000 in the non-participating fund.

REVENUE ACCOUNT OF THE SEA TO SEA COMPANY

Table 28.2 gives the Revenue Account covering the income and outgo of the Sea to Sea Life Insurance Company for the year. As some very large items, such as the increase in policy-reserves are internal transfers, the

TABLE 28.2

Sea to Sea Life Insurance Company
REVENUE ACCOUNT
for the year ended December 31

Income	
Premiums	$29,900,000
Consideration for settlement annuities	340,000
Net investment income	12,880,000
Net investment gain–segregated funds	(2,300,000)
Contributions to staff benefit funds	270,000
Other income	60,000
	$41,150,000
Disposition of Income	
Claims	$14,850,000
Settlement annuity payments	340,000
Increase in actuarial reserves	11,580,000
Increase in segregated funds	350,000
Increase in staff benefit funds	240,000
Interest paid on deposits	700,000
Taxes licences and fees	1,080,000
Commission and general expenses	7,310,000
Other payments	310,000
Dividends to policyholders	3,250,000
Increase in provision for dividends	410,000
Transfer to statement of surplus	730,000
	$41,150,000

term "outgo" is not an exact description and in Table 28.2 the term "Disposition of Income" is used. We comment on each item in the order in which it occurs in the Revenue Account.

Dealing with items of *income*, firstly:

Premiums. This includes premiums for insurance and annuities both individual policies and group. The total is $29,900,000.

Consideration for settlement annuities. The amount is $340,000. When an insured or beneficiary decides to take the proceeds of his policy as an annuity, the amount of the policy proceeds is shown here as "income." As payments are made, they go under the corresponding item of "disposition of income." The values of the amounts so left with the company as of the end of the year are included in the corresponding items under "liabilities."

Net Investment income. The total for the year is $12,880,000. Whether it is interest on loans or bonds or dividends on equities or rents on properties, the total is included here. The term "net" is used because investment expenses are deducted.

Net investment gain—segregated funds. This represents the investment income on segregated funds *plus* the *capital gain* on sales and the appreciation on investments held at the year end; capital gain or appreciation is measured from the value at the previous year end or from cost on acquisitions during the year. *Capital loss* or *depreciation* is deducted. The figure is net of investment expenses. The amount was negative ($2,300,000) reflecting considerable declines in market values.

Contributions to staff benefit funds. It has already been explained that such contributions may be paid into a separate fund, or, if benefits are provided through a group insurance or annuity policy, will be recorded as premiums.

Other income. This is a miscellaneous item. The largest amount recorded is refunds received under reinsurance agreements. Reinsurers often make such refunds when mortality experience is favourable.

The various items of outgo or *disposition of income* are commented upon next.

Claims. The $14,850,000 shown under claims is made up of the following items and arise from its regular (individual) and group business, both insurance and annuities.

Death claims	$6,100,000
Accidental death claims	100,000
Disability claims	150,000
Matured endowments	1,110,000
Annuity payments	2,400,000
Surrender values	4,990,000

Settlement annuity payments. The item shows that $340,000 was paid out. It is a coincidence that this amount is identical with the "consideration for settlement annuities" shown under income.

Increase in actuarial reserves. The amount of $11,580,000 is the difference between the actuarial reserve in the liabilities at the year-end and the corresponding figure at the previous year-end. As premiums are paid, reserves increase; as policies terminate, reserves are released. The net increase in the liability is recorded here.

Increase in segregated funds. The actuarial reserves apply only to liability in the participating and non-participating funds. Increases in the liability under segregated fund policies are included here. Obviously amounts paid into (or withdrawn from) segregated funds increase (or decrease) this item. It is also increased (or decreased) by the net investment gain which by the nature of the policies directly affects the liability to the policyholders.

Increase in staff benefit funds. In the same way as the increase in the actuarial liabilities for policies is reflected above, the increase in liability in staff benefit funds is reflected here.

Interest paid on deposits. This refers to interest on dividends and policy proceeds as well as on amounts deposited to pay premiums for several years in advance.

Taxes, licences and fees. This item includes premium tax, income tax, assessments of the federal Superintendent for supervision, and other payments to governments. Real estate taxes are charged against investment income and do not appear here.

Commission and general expenses. This item includes commissions on premiums, salaries, fringe benefits, legal fees, medical fees, rent, travelling expenses, printing and stationery, and all other expenses of doing business.

Other payments. Examples of items included under this heading are interest on borrowed money and payments out of staff benefit funds.

Dividends to policyholders. The amount of $3,250,000 includes all dividends allotted to policyholders whether taken in cash, used to reduce premiums, used to provide additional insurance, or left on deposit with the company. If used to reduce premiums or to provide additional insurance, they are also included under premiums in the income statement.

Increase in provision for dividends. This is the difference between the provision in the liabilities at the year-end and the corresponding figure for the previous year. As the company grows, this provision is normally increased.

Transfer to statement of surplus. The Revenue Account shows total income of $41,150,000. The total of outgo and the increase in policy-reserves, etc., amounted to $40,420,000, giving a balancing item of $730,000, or the excess which may be said to be the surplus earnings for the year after all payments and liabilities to policyholders (including dividends) have been met.

SURPLUS ACCOUNT

The surplus at the end of the previous year in the Sea to Sea company was $12,640,000. From the Revenue Account (Table 28.2) we note that after making provision for dividends to policyholders and the necessary increase in actuarial policy-reserves, etc., the surplus earnings for the year were $730,000. After this amount was ascertained various adjustments of capital values of assets were made with transfers to investment and contingency reserves and the balance added to the surplus of the

TABLE 28.3
Sea to Sea Life Insurance Company
STATEMENT OF SURPLUS
for the year ended December 31

Source of Surplus		
Surplus for year after allocating dividends to policyholders	$730,000	
Add capital gains on investments	750,000	
Other increase	640,000	
		$ 2,120,000
Surplus as at December 31 previous year		12,640,000
		$14,760,000
Allocation of Surplus		
Assets written down and capital losses	$1,350,000	
Dividends to shareholders	120,000	
Increase in investments and contingency reserves	780,000	
		$ 2,250,000
Surplus as at December 31 as in Balance Sheet for current year		12,510,000
		$14,760,000

preceding year to show the surplus at the end of the year as $12,510,000 as in the Balance Sheet (Table 28.1). The details of what was done is shown in Table 28.3, "Statement of Surplus" of the Sea to Sea company. Comments on the individual items follow.

Capital gains and losses. The item of $750,000 under "capital gains on investments" arises from a number of "capital" transactions of which the following are typical:

1. When bonds, stocks or real estate are sold at a higher value than the "book value" in the company's books, the difference is a capital gain;
2. When bonds, stocks, mortgages, and other securities are written down or written off in value and their value is recovered, the increase in "book value" is a capital gain.

Corresponding to this $750,000 item there is another amount shown on the other side of the account. This is the $1,350,000 under "assets written down and capital losses." This would include any amounts in the previous paragraph of bonds bought at a premium. In a period of falling bond prices companies would write down the values of their bonds as an alternative or in addition to making transfers to investment reserves.

Writing up of "book values" is less frequent than writing down, but is done occasionally. It is a common practice, when bonds are purchased at a premium, i.e., above their final redemption value, for the value to be written down to that value at the outset.

In the government statement summary of the surplus and its disposition the net amount of the two items is shown. However, the breakdown into its component parts is shown in an attached schedule. We have deliberately shown the "gains" and "losses" separately and some companies in their statement to the public make a point of separating them as we have done.

Other increases. This may include payments into surplus by shareholders, or reductions in actuarial reserves on certain blocks of business. The normal annual increase in actuarial reserves is shown in the Revenue Account, but if a decision is made to change the actuarial basis of the reserves, the resulting change goes through the surplus account.

Dividends to shareholders. The Sea to Sea is a stock company and the $120,000 represents the dividends to shareholders.

Increase in investment and contingency reserves. We have explained the circumstances relating to this fund and its object. The amount is $780,000.

Surplus at the end-of-year. The surplus at the end of the year is $12,510,000 or $130,000 less than at the end of the previous year. The main reason for the reduction is the loss on and writing down of investments, reflecting adverse market conditions.

SUMMARY OF FINANCIAL STATEMENT

Another way of showing the figures would have been to put both the Revenue Account and the Statement of Surplus into one statement as in Table 28.4 where various items are lumped together for convenience.

AUDITORS' REPORT

We emphasized above that the annual statement to policyholders and shareholders is a distinct and separate statement from the government statement although their relationship is very close. The invariable prac-

TABLE 28.4

Sea to Sea Life Insurance Company
SUMMARY OF FINANCIAL STATEMENT FOR YEAR

Income for year		$41,150,000
Special increases in surplus		640,000
		$41,790,000
Amounts paid out or set aside:		
Claims and settlement annuities	$15,190,000	
Normal increases in actuarial reserves, etc.	12,170,000	
Interest on deposits	700,000	
Commisions, expenses, taxes	8,700,000	
Dividends to policyholders including increase in provision	3,660,000	
Dividends to shareholders	120,000	
Added to special reserves	780,000	
		$41,320,000
Balance		470,000
less Investment adjustment		−600,000
Reduction in surplus		−130,000
Surplus at beginning of year		12,640,000
Surplus at end of year		$12,510,000

tice of Canadian life insurance companies is to employ a firm of independent auditors and their report is attached to the annual statement distributed to their policyholders, etc.

The independent auditors accept the certificate of the company's actuary as to the adequacy of the policy-reserves but apart from this acknowledgment their report is similar to that which they attach to the balance sheets and revenue accounts of other financial institutions.

SEGREGATED FUNDS: SECTION 81 (5)

By the end of 1974 the total amount of such funds with federally registered life insurance companies in Canada was $1,578 millions with 48 companies. This compares with funds of $5 millions with 7 companies at the end of 1962. This is a most important development of life insurance in Canada, and it will be discussed in Chapter 30. As already mentioned, the amounts payable under the policies issued are based on the market value of a specified group of assets. Although the payments in and out of such funds are included with those arising from the regular business in the main returns on the company, further details concerning them are required to be given in a supplementary statement.

CHAPTER TWENTY-NINE

Investments of Life Insurance Companies

THE NEED FOR INVESTMENT EARNINGS

Life insurance companies differ from other industrial enterprises. The investments of most industrial enterprises are in the nature of a surplus fund to meet fluctuations in business conditions and earnings. These investments are part of their working capital and any interest or dividends earned on such investments will, as a rule, be of minor importance compared with the profits of the enterprise. The earnings of a life insurance company on its investments are essential to its existence.

We have referred very frequently to the fundamental principle of level premium life insurance that, owing to the increase of mortality with advancing age, policy-reserves must be accumulated, which, with incoming premiums and interest, will provide for death claims and other benefits payable, as they fall due.

In the calculation of the premium rates charged and the policy-reserves held, it is assumed that specific rates of interest will be earned. Without earning at least the rate of interest assumed for calculating policy-reserves the requisite policy-reserves could not be accumulated unless the money was supplied from some other source. Canadian federal insurance legislation did not permit the assumption of a higher rate of interest that $3^1/_2$ per cent for insurances or 4 per cent for life annuities in the calculation of policy-reserves, but as noted in Chapter 17 the Superintendent of Insurance is authorized to permit higher rates of interest; authority has been given for rates as high as 9 per cent for certain classes of annuities. It follows that where companies assume these maximum rates in calculating their policy-reserves they must earn at least those rates on their funds.

The higher the rate of interest earnings, other factors being unchanged, the larger is the "asset share." Also the larger should be the surplus earnings which on participating policies would mean larger policy dividends. Having assumed a certain minimum rate of interest in calculating premiums to be charged and policy-reserves to be set up, the higher the rate of interest which can actually be earned the more prosperous the life insurance company will be. This is provided the security of the capital invested is not thereby prejudiced.

The assets of federally registered Canadian life insurance companies on behalf of their policyholders were about $21,100 millions at December 31, 1974, including assets in segregated funds. Apart from some 9 per cent of this amount, which is in the nature of surplus, special reserves, and shareholders' capital, etc., the rest represents the necessary policy-reserves and amounts owing to policyholders, etc. These obligations are as real as if the policyholders held I.O.U. notes for that amount. Thus the preservation of the capital value of its investments and the earning of a certain minimum rate of interest on them is of vital concern to the life insurance company.

LIFE INSURANCE AND PERSONAL SAVINGS

In Figure 1, Chapter 2, the premiums paid to life insurance companies in Canada from 1925 to 1974 are shown and at the beginning of Chapter 3 the volume of new business and the life insurance in force are given from which the importance of the life insurance business in the Canadian economy can be judged. Here we wish to stress the importance of the premiums paid to the life insurance companies as "savings." For the vast majority of life insurance policyholders in Canadian life insurance companies their life insurance represents the major part if not the sole form of long-term investment by them. In Chapter 3 we gave figures illustrating the important part played by life insurance savings in the economy of Canada. This is of particular importance in Canada, a country under the necessity of importing huge amounts of capital for the development of its natural resources and industries.

The broad pattern of Canadian life insurance company investments can be seen from Table 29.1 giving the investments of Canadian life insurance companies as at December 31 of various years from 1920 to 1974. We are here dealing with the investments of companies several of which do a world-wide business, and the pattern of investment out of Canada may be different from that in Canada. For example, some Canadian companies which confine their business to Canada may show a higher percentage of their assets in mortgages. One such large company, the London Life, as at the end of 1974 had nearly 70 per cent of its

TABLE 29.1

Classification of Assets* of Federally Registered Canadian Life Insurance Companies, Per Cent of Total Assets at End of Year

Class of assets	Year 1920	1945	1955	1965	1974
Mortgage loans	24.5	7.7	30.4	41.5	39.3
Bonds	47.8	75.9	54.1	41.6	34.2
Government	*20.0*	*57.0*	*19.0*	*13.4*	*8.1*
Local authority	*13.9*	*4.6*	*5.3*	*5.9*	*2.3*
Other	*13.9*	*14.3*	*29.8*	*22.3*	*23.8*
Preferred stocks	3.2	1.7	1.9	1.3	1.0
Common stocks	2.8	4.2	3.3	4.7	7.7
Real estate and sale agreements	4.1	1.8	2.6	3.2	6.0
Policy loans	11.7	5.1	4.8	4.6	7.7
Cash	0.7	1.1	1.0	0.9	0.9
Other assets	5.2	2.5	1.9	2.2	3.2
Total assets	100.0 $423 millions	100.0 $3,450 millions	100.0 $6,278 millions	100.0 $12,002 millions	100.0 $19,577 millions

*Does not include assets in respect of accident and sickness business or assets in segregated funds.

assets in mortgage loans compared with some 39 per cent for all companies as shown.

The footnote to Table 29.1 states that the segregated assets are not included in the ratios given, for the investment policy for those funds is necessarily and intentionally different to that for other assets of the companies, as has been explained in Chapter 27 and will be further dealt with in Chapter 30.

Before discussing the trends shown in Table 29.1 some explanation of the classes of investments shown in that table is necessary.

CLASSES OF INVESTMENT

In Table 29.1 the types of investment may be classed in two broad divisions: loans and equities. *Loans* include all types of *bonds* and *mortgages* as well as *policy loans*. The life insurance company lends the money, represented by the bond or mortgage, to a concern which may pledge its entire physical assets and earning power as a going concern, as security for the repayment of the debt. A mortgage is generally a loan on the security of land, house, or other property, but in practice the distinction between a bond and a mortgage may be a fine one. The mortgage on a large office building may well be expressed in bonds; a railway bond may often be a specific pledge of certain equipment or part of its property. Under these loans a specific rate of interest is agreed to be paid with repayment of the principal amount on a specific date or dates. Legally, if default occurs, either in payment of the interest or principal, the lender is entitled to take possession of the property pledged and take over the concern if that were part of the collateral security and by realizing same obtain repayment of loan and interest due.

Under *equities* the purchaser is an owner not just a lender. Equities are represented in the remainder of the portfolio as *common stocks* and *real estate*. There is no promise of a fixed rate of interest in equities or repayment of the purchase money in any amount at any fixed date.

Legally the owner of an equity participates in the ownership of the concern and has no remedy, other than what he shares with the other owners, for changing the management, if the profits or returns on his investment are unsatisfactory.

In this distinction between loans and equities lies much of the policy and practice of life insurance company investment.

A *debenture bond* is a contractual obligation not secured by a mortgage. It would permit the corporation to issue *mortgage bonds* which would rank ahead of the debentures if it found this necessary. In the division in Table 29.1, the word "Other" refers to bonds and debentures of business corporations as distinct from governments: national, provincial (and state), and municipal.

Preferred Stocks. Dividends on preferred stocks are limited to a fixed annual amount and are not a contractual obligation of the corporation as is the interest on a bond issue. However, such dividends must be paid and usually on a cumulative basis before dividends can be paid on the common stock. Some very outstanding Canadian corporations have issues of preferred stock, but they are relatively a minor class of security in the Canadian investment field and as indicated have played a negligible part in Canadian life insurance investments in recent years.

Common Stocks. The common stock is the main equity security. As a rule there is only one class of security in a corporation called *common stock* although in some cases there may be two or more classes. Dividends on common stock rank last after all other obligations are met which explains the wide fluctuations in the market value of common stocks, not only with the profitable operation or otherwise of the corporation in question but with economic conditions generally. The subject of common stock investments will receive further attention both in this chapter and the next.

In the government statement summaries, preferred and common stocks are lumped together. However, not only in the legal aspect but in many other ways, they are essentially different types of security. It was interesting to note that in the June 1962 submission of the Canadian Life Insurance Officers Association to the Royal Commission on Banking and Finance, presumably drawn up by the investment experts of the companies, preferred stocks were grouped with bonds in the summaries of classes of securities.

THE PATTERN OF CANADIAN LIFE INSURANCE COMPANIES' INVESTMENTS

We now consider the trends indicated by Table 29.1. Note the high proportion of government bonds in 1945, namely 57 per cent of assets. It shows the effect of the Second World War during which most of the new money invested or reinvested by Canadian life insurance companies went to the various governments for war needs, to which practically all other needs were subordinated. Government of Canada bonds accounted for 11.4 per cent in 1939, the year war was declared, and increased to 33.6 per cent of total assets in 1946 when the war was over. In 1974 the proportion was only 1.3 per cent.

After the War, as the deferred and pent-up demands arose from industry for capital, and money was required for building residences, apartments, and office buildings, the companies switched over to supplying these needs. The increase in mortgages and industrial bonds is shown. Mortgage loans which had fallen from 24.5 per cent of assets in 1920 to 7.7. in 1945 rose to 30.4 per cent in 1955, an increase of over $1,600 millions in ten years. Note the increase still continued, the amount reaching the figure of five billion dollars by 1965 and seven billion dollars by 1973. Although the absolute amount has continued to increase, the proportion invested in mortgages has declined a little in recent years.

An increasing interest in real estate investment will be noted from the table. This has followed liberalization of the law regarding such investments as is mentioned below.

The percentage of policy loans had fallen to less than 5 per cent because consumer credit at moderate interest rates had become available. The increase in recent years is due to the margin between the 6 per cent maximum rate of interest applicable to loans in many life insurance policies in force and rates well over 10 per cent charged by other lenders in recent years; many policyholders have borrowed large sums at 6 per cent to reinvest them at higher rates.

Corresponding to the building boom between 1945 and 1955 was the demand for funds by industry; the increase from 14.3 to 29.8 per cent in the ten year period in "Other" bonds represents an increase of over $1,300 millions.

The interest of Canadian life insurance companies generally in common stocks has until recently been negligible. From Table 29.1 an increased interest in recent years is noticeable. Of the 7.7 per cent of assets in common stocks noted at the end of 1974, 3.8 per cent was in Canadian corporations, 3.0 per cent in U.S. corporations, and 0.4 per cent in other corporations.

General Principles of Investment

The object in this part of the chapter is to discuss the investment policy of life insurance companies rather than to give details of the various types of investment, each of which can well be the lifetime study of a specialist. We discuss why some life insurance companies favour one type of investment rather than another.

There are eight tests to which any type of security can be submitted to determine its suitability for investment purposes and in particular for a life insurance company. They are:

1. security of capital	5. stability of value
2. interest yield	6. economic purpose
3. marketability	7. currency
4. diversification	8. legality

These are closely related and each must be considered in relation to the others.

1. SECURITY OF CAPITAL

This is the first and most important consideration in an investment. There is no such thing as absolute security, for even governments have been known to be overthrown and their bonds repudiated. Government bonds are secured by the power of taxation. As the Government of

Canada has the broadest power to tax, as well as control of the banking system, its bonds are considered to provide the greatest security. Provincial bonds rate next. The security of municipal bonds and of corporate bonds varies greatly depending on the size and reputation of the borrower. Mortgages are considered as offering excellent security because the amount advanced is usually well within the value of the property. The security of real estate depends on location and use. Common stocks are, by their nature, less secure than bonds.

2. INTEREST YIELD

We have outlined how important it is for a specified minimum rate of interest to be earned by a life insurance company and how the higher the rate of interest, the greater the advantage to the company. It is thus always a matter to choose between lower interest and higher security or *vice versa*, indicating how tests (1) and (2) cannot be separated. Of course, part of the interest earnings on a higher-yielding security can be set aside to write down gradually the capital value of the security. In this way the possibility of default can be insured against, so to speak. Another way—and some companies practise both methods—is to accumulate from such excess interest earnings a special fund, and we referred in a previous chapter to the "investment reserve fund" of many life insurance companies.

A further point is that some securities involve a greater measure of supervision and overhead costs than others. A case in point is that of mortgages on family residences which have a higher overhead of supervisory costs and commission paid to the broker who introduces the mortgage than, say, on government bonds where the purchase commission is a relatively trivial proportion of the cost and the interest is automatically paid on the due date. Hence it is not the *gross rate of interest* which should be considered but the interest after expenses involved in obtaining and supervising the investment. This is called the *net rate of interest*.

The difference between the gross and net rates of interest would depend on the distribution of the assets as stated above and also on the size of the company. An approximate figure used in practice is $^1/_4$ per cent or $^1/_2$ per cent, the larger amount applying to a smaller company with a large proportion of its assets in residential mortgages. The submission to the Royal Commission on Banking and Finance referred to above and based on a few representative companies indicated a difference between gross and net yields of 0.33 per cent.

Record and Trend of Interest Earnings. The net rates of interest earned by Canadian life insurance companies as a whole are not available for the period prior to 1954 when the current government statement form was adopted. Prior to that year the gross rates of interest earned are on record. Thus in Table 29.2 the record is divided into two parts. The first gives the *gross* rate of interest earned in decennial years from 1881 to 1951 with intervening values given where there has been a change of trend in interest earnings. The second part gives the *net* rates for selected years from 1945 to 1974.

TABLE 29.2
Average Rate of Interest Earned by Canadian Life Insurance Companies
Federally Registered Companies—World Wide Business

Year	Gross Rate	Year	Net rate
1881	6.99%	1945	3.60%
1891	5.74	1955	4.18
1901	4.80	1960	4.98
1911	5.90	1965	5.65
1921	6.42	1970	6.20
1929	6.48	1974	7.11
1931	5.59		
1941	4.24		
1947	3.57		
1951	3.90		

Note that from 1881 to 1901 there was a steady fall in the rate of interest. About the turn of the century Canadian government bonds were selling to yield less than 3 per cent, but mortgages have always been the mainstay of high Canadian life insurance earnings so that the rate earned on all investments in 1901 was 4.80 per cent. From 1901 to 1921 there was a rise in interest rates greatly accelerated by the First World War (1914–18), the rise continuing until the stock market crash of 1929. After this the rate of interest fell continuously and even continued to do so during the Second World War (1939–45). The rate continued to fall thereafter until 1947 when it was at 3.57 per cent, which was the all-time low for Canadian life insurance company earnings. The rate for 1948 was the same as for 1947 after which the interest rate turned upwards as shown and has continued upwards to the present time as shown in the table.

All rates quoted are before deduction of any federal income taxes. This matter of federal income taxes on interest earnings of life insurance companies in Canada was dealt with in Chapter 18.

Interest Earnings and Policyholders' Dividends. The world-wide invested assets of Canadian life insurance companies averaged $19,000 millions during 1968. The provision for dividends to policyholders at the end of that year amounted to $416 millions. Thus an increase of $^1/_4$ per cent in the net yield would have meant increased investment earnings of $47 millions, say, making possible something like an 11 per cent increase in dividends to policyholders. This illustrates the importance of interest earnings to a life insurance company.

3. MARKETABILITY

The ready sale of securities is of the utmost importance to a bank or an industrial corporation where securities are their alternative to "cash" or part of their working capital. This is particularly important in times of crisis or economic distress. With life insurance companies, history has shown that income will generally exceed outgo and that so long as the banking system is functioning there should rarely, if ever, be any need to sell securities just for the sake of getting the equivalent cash. Marketability, convertibility, or liquidity (the various phrases used) are essential for some investors, and government securities, which form the first line of reserve for banks, have this in the highest measure and give a correspondingly low interest yield. The exact reverse holds with mortgages, for example, for the lender cannot demand the repayment of the mortgage other than on the mortgage expiry date.

We have referred to the danger of a "run" on life insurance companies, in times of panic, in connection with the guaranteed cash surrender and loan values in policies. There is also the danger of a calamity requiring a large amount of cash for the payment of death claims. Therefore it used to follow that as companies increased their proportion of mortgages the necessity for reviewing their other assets on the score of liquidity would receive attention. However, as mortgages are generally repaid by equal monthly instalments comprising interest and principal, they do provide a *cash-flow*, as it is technically described.

Life insurance contracts are essentially long-term contracts and ordinarily the longer the period before the bond matures the better. However, when bond interest rates are moving upwards it would be good policy to switch to bonds of as long duration as possible, and when the trend of bond interest yields is downwards new bonds should be of short duration with the hope that when the bond matures there will be an opportunity to reinvest it at a higher rate. The point of time for change, and anticipation of trends, makes the practice of bond investment of great importance. This means that there is a fair amount of switching between securities in the average life insurance company and bonds are not bought to be held in every case of maturity.

These points are made to stress the importance of marketability. As a rule a life insurance company has its bonds maturing over a long period of maturity dates and when substantial bond maturities fall due each year liquidity is obtained. Further, so long as the banking system is functioning no life insurance company operating on a sound basis should be in difficulties in obtaining any unexpected amount of cash.

4. DIVERSIFICATION 5. STABILITY OF VALUE

The old saying of not having all the eggs in one basket was never more true than in investment policy. With so many uncertainties a large degree of *diversification* is essential. Diversification may be attained by spreading investments between classes of assets, as well as, within classes, by spreading geographically, by type of industry, and by avoiding very large loans to or investments in any one firm.

The test of *legality* could have been stated as the first in importance. Life insurance is a business of a trustee character in which the government has special responsibilities to the public. No law can make a bad investment into a good one, but life insurance companies doing business in Canada are subject to the insurance laws of Canada which restrict and govern the investment of life insurance company assets. Thus the principles advocated above are all subject to these laws.

LAWS GOVERNING CANADIAN LIFE INSURANCE COMPANY INVESTMENTS

Canadian companies which are federally registered may invest their funds only in certain classes of assets, as described below. Provincially registered companies are subject to somewhat similar requirements in the jurisdictions in which they are incorporated. British and foreign companies are required to maintain in Canada assets of a value not less than their liabilities in Canada and of the same classes as apply to federally registered Canadian companies.

Segregated Funds. Reference has been made to policies the benefits under which are determined by the market value of a specified group of assets. The investments covering these policies require to be segregated from the rest of the assets of the company hence the phrase "segregated fund." It should be noted that the regulations regarding the proportion to total assets of common stocks and real estate for the production of income which apply to the investments of a life insurance company as noted below, do not apply to these segregated funds.

Life Insurance Funds. We outline briefly below the authorized investments according to the federal Insurance Act. The main classes of securities only are noted and the actual Act should be referred to for a more detailed account. The necessity for authorized investments to cover a world-wide business should be noted.

(i) *Government bonds*. Bonds of or guaranteed by the Government of:

(*a*) Canada, the United Kingdom and specified countries of, or formerly of the British Commonwealth; the United States of America;

(*b*) Any province or state of the countries described in (*a*);

(*c*) Any colony of the United Kingdom;

(*d*) Any country in which the company is carrying on business or a province or state thereof;

(*e*) Any colony of a country if the company is carrying on business in that colony.

(ii) *Municipal or school corporation securities* of a country where the company is carrying on business.

(iii) *Subsidized bonds fully* secured by a subsidy from the Government of Canada or a province of Canada.

(iv) *Revenue bonds of a public authority* (harbour, highway, electricity, water, etc.) of a country in which the company is doing business or a province or a state thereof or of a colony thereof in which the company is doing business.

(v) *Bonds of a corporation* fully secured by mortgages on real estate, plant, or by equipment used in the transaction of its business, or securities which would qualify for a life insurance company's investments.

(vi) *Debentures of a corporation* subject to certain tests based on the earnings record of the corporation or its guarantor.

(vii) *Preferred shares* of a corporation that has paid the full dividends on its preferred shares for at least the previous five years or the common shares of which are authorized investments.

(viii) *The fully paid common shares* of a corporation that has paid a dividend in each year or had earnings in each year available for the payment of a dividend of at least 4 per cent on its capital stock for at least the previous five years. Subject to various provisos which will be dealt with later in the chapter, a company (*a*) shall not purchase more than 30 per cent of the common shares of any corporation; or (*b*) purchase its own shares; or (*c*) purchase the shares of a corporation incorporated in Canada transacting the business of life insurance; or (*d*) invest more than 25 per cent of its total assets (book value) in common shares (common stocks).

(ix) *Real estate mortgages* in Canada or elsewhere where it is carrying on business up to three quarters of the value of the real estate; this was 60 per cent until 1961, then $66^2/_3$ per cent until 1964. The proportion of three quarters may be exceeded in certain cases when there is a government guarantee or a policy of mortgage insurance. There is no restriction on the proportion of assets which may be invested in mortgages on real estate.

(x) *Real estate for the production of income* in any country in which the company is doing business if: (*a*) a lease of the real estate is made to or guaranteed by a corporation whose preferred or common shares would be an eligible investment as outlined above, and (*b*) 85 per cent of the amount invested is to be repaid within 30 years or the period of the lease if less. The amount of the investment in any one parcel of real estate is limited to 2 per cent of the total assets of the company. Some further reference to this section will be made later on in this chapter.

(xi) *National Housing Act* investments on loans. Further reference to this will be made.

(xii) *Real estate needed for its own use or occupancy*, present and prospective.

(xiii) *Policy loans.*

(xiv) *Basket clause.* Up to 7 per cent of total assets permitted in investments and loans not otherwise permissible; but no so as to exceed the limits in (viii) above as regards common shares. Further details are given below.

No Investment in Securities in Default. Section 63 (10) of the Act states "A company shall not invest any of its funds in bonds, debentures or other evidences of indebtedness on which payment of principal or interest is in default."

SOME ADDITIONAL DETAILS RE INVESTMENT CLASSES

Basket Clause. In 1948 the federal insurance laws were changed to permit Canadian life insurance companies to acquire investments not falling within the classes previously permitted by law, but the total of such investments was limited first to 3, then to 5 and now to 7 per cent of the company's total assets. The purpose of the 1948 amendment was to enable the companies to invest within a narrow limit in income-producing real estate and in bonds and stocks which were considered desirable by the companies and yet were not previously permitted by law. The division of securities under this basket clause is shown in the following table.

TABLE 29.3

Year	Bonds	Stocks	Real Estate & Other	Total	% of Total Assets
		Millions of dollars			
1952	$ 5.2	$ 8.5	$ 16.0	$ 29.7	0.59
1957	70.9	10.8	38.4	120.1	1.72
1961	33.5	20.0	42.7	96.2	1.05
1968	115.0	49.8	130.8	295.6	2.09
1974	120.0	80.4	503.4	703.8	3.60

The fall in the amount of bonds from 1957 to 1961 indicates how securities which are ineligible under other sections of the law may become eligible investments and hence are transferred to regularly prescribed classes. The basket clause permits Canadian life insurance companies to undertake to a limited extent new classes of investment which may be suggested by changing economic conditions. It recognizes that there are acceptable investments which do not meet the restrictions of the Insurance Act. Under this clause, the upper limit on any one parcel of real estate is 1 per cent of the total assets of the life company.

Income-Producing Real Estate. A Canadian life insurance company was until 1948 only permitted to own real estate for its own use and occupancy, current and prospective. The change in law, first in the basket clause and later as a specified class of authorized investment, now permits it to own incoming-producing real estate on a "lease back" or "net lease" basis. Operators of department stores, shopping centres, food and variety chain stores, factories, and warehouses prefer to lease rather than own their property. The property is owned by the life insurance company, but the lessee pays all maintenance costs, taxes, and insurance and a rental which returns the life insurance company's total investment plus interest over the period of the lease which may run as long as thirty years. The life insurance company owns the property at the end of the period of the lease although its whole investment has been repaid. There are generally guarantees to the lessee as to renewal at reduced rent.

Investments in income-producing real estate have grown rapidly. The amount was about $100 millions in 1955, $300 millions in 1967, and in 1974, $866 millions. Two large companies which have specialised in this field have over $500 millions between them so invested.

National Housing Act. In recent years a considerable volume of lending on residential property in Canada has been done under the provisions of the National Housing Act, through the Central Mortgage and Housing Corporation (C.M.H.C.), a government institution. The main features are that the C.M.H.C. sets up standards of construction and value with a maximum interest charge on such loans and insures against default mortgages approved under the National Housing Act. The current maximum loan in large metropolitan centres is $45,096, obtained by taking 95 per cent of a value of $47,000, i.e. $44,650 and adding 1 per cent for insurance. In smaller cities, lower maxima apply.

A main feature is that the loan and interest and insurance fee are all repaid in equal monthly instalments over a period of up to 40 years. The main purpose of the scheme is to stimulate the erection of houses for home ownership. These N.H.A. loans also cover apartment houses. Under the Act life insurance companies have found a fertile field for all the money they wish to invest in mortgages. The mortgage loans of Canadian life insurance companies amounted to $7,685 millions at the end of 1974. This figure includes conventional mortgages in houses, apartment buildings, commercial and industrial property.

COMMON STOCK INVESTMENTS

The suitability of common stocks for the investments of life insurance companies to cover their guaranteed dollar liabilities has been a subject of debate for many years. As stated above, the federal insurance laws of Canada restrict the percentage of assets which a life insurance company may invest in common stocks, but the restriction in Canada to 25 per cent of assets does not explain why the percentage is only 7.7 as shown in Table 29.1.

The main deterrent to substantial investments in common stocks is that they must be taken into the company's statement at market value and the wide fluctuations in market values, which occur frequently, may jeopardize the theoretical standing of a company according to its statement. Further it is quite possible for interest rates to be moving up sharply at the time of a severe fall in common stock market values and hence heavy depreciation of the bonds and debentures might be experienced to depress its surplus even further.

It is agreed that this may represent a theoretical slump only as the value behind the common stocks, bonds, and debentures may be quite unimpaired. However, no life insurance company official would wish to publish a statement showing the surplus of his company had been halved or practically wiped out in the past year, however theoretical such a position might be. One answer, of course, is the holding of far larger surpluses than is common in Canada and this is the position of the life insurance companies in Great Britain. The whole aspect in Canada and the U.S. is different and the public in those countries would challenge unusually large holdings of surplus on the grounds that policyholders' dividends were thereby reduced and the cost of life insurance unduly increased. The insurance laws of the State of New York definitely restrict the free surplus which a life insurance company can hold.

However, the inflation of recent years with the serious depreciation in the purchasing value of the dollars on which life insurance and annuity contracts are based has given a new direction to investment philosophy in Canada and the United States. Inflation and the development of equity linked contracts are dealt with in the next chapter, but the principle of common stock investments to cover the guaranteed dollar liabilities of a life insurance company is a subject of major interest.

We give briefly the points against common stocks as investments to cover the guaranteed dollar liabilities of a life insurance company with some contrary arguments.

1. The wide fluctuation in market values make then unsuitable. With policy-reserve and other liabilities fixed there is a conflict when the value of the assets to balance the liabilities vary considerably. The preservation of the capital in life insurance investments is traditional. The possibility of using an averaging formula for the values included in the published statement will be referred to later.

2. Holding common stocks would give the companies an undesirable degree of control of industry. One insurance company would be unlikely to hold a substantial proportion of the shares of a large corporation, although as a group the life insurance companies might have power to influence management if they acted together. One can only visualize them acting in unison when the public interest demanded intervention. One might say that this is a point in favour of, not against, life insurance companies holding common stocks of outstanding corporations.

3. Life insurance company contracts in Canada (except under segregated funds) call for payment in fixed amounts of Canadian dollars, hence the securities they should hold should guarantee repayment in fixed amounts of dollars, which common stocks do not do.

4. Historically, common stocks have been considered as unsuitable

investments for trustees. This is why they were prohibited after the Armstrong-Hughes investigation in 1905 in the State of New York. The record of interlocking directorships and abuse of trust which led to this investigation resulted in the prohibition of all investments in preferred and common stocks in New York State by life insurance companies subject to its laws. The complete ban was raised in 1951 as regards common stocks but to a limited degree as outlined earlier. Business and industry have changed considerably in the past sixty years. The huge organizations whose common stocks are available represent the economic life of the country and their true value is independent of the vagaries of the stock market. Many pension funds hold substantial percentages of their assets in common stocks.

Subsidiaries. Although the general rule is that a life insurance company may not hold more than 30 per cent of the common shares of a corporation, there are some specific exceptions intended to permit life insurance companies to establish subsidiaries. Thus a company may purchase more than 30 per cent of the shares of

(*a*) a life insurance company outside Canada;
(*b*) a corporation to provide advisory management or sales distribution services in respect of its segregated funds;
(*c*) a general insurance company in Canada;
(*d*) a corporation to acquire or manage real estate;
(*e*) a corporation to offer participation in an investment portfolio;
(*f*) a corporation to provide such investment company with advisory, management or sales distribution services;
(*g*) with the approval of the Minister, a corporation to carry on a business ancillary to the business of insurance.

Examples of businesses under the last section are computer service companies, and clinics to provide medical examinations.

The Valuation of Assets

WARNING. *The reader should be aware that legislation will probably be introduced in 1977 which will change considerably the laws concerning the valuation of assets.*

MARKET VALUES AND AUTHORIZED VALUES

The financial position of a life insurance company is determined by its balance sheet. On the one side is stated its liabilities (what it owes) of which the main item is its policy-reserves. On the other side it gives the value of its assets, that is, its investments, cash, and amounts owing to it. The differences of the two determines the free surplus available, indicative of its financial strength. As the policy-reserves are valued by an inflexible formula, largely determined by the cash surrender values guaranteed in the policies it has issued, it can be seen that the values placed on its assets determine the whole picture. Hence, the strict laws regarding the values of securities owned which are entered in the company's balance sheet. The significance of what has been said earlier regarding wide fluctuations in the value of securities held by life insurance companies will now be more apparent.

The strictest formula to apply to the value of assets is the market value: what it would fetch if sold. But this is, in a way, theoretical for if any attempt were made to realize on millions of dollars of any securities on any particular day, they might well prove unsaleable except at a sacrifice. There is a limit to what the market can absorb; a buyer has to be found for each security offered for sale.

Bond dealers have their lists indicating market values of the various types of bonds, debentures and preferred stocks, and the stock market lists give the market values of common stocks day by day. The federal Superintendent publishes a book at the end of the year based on these sources which gives the authorized value of every security held by the insurance companies doing business in Canada. To be in the hands of the companies in time for the completion of their annual statements the values at a date sometime before December 31 may have to be taken and the law provides for that by allowing a margin of 60 days prior to the date of the statement. When the market values are unduly depressed, the Minister of Finance, under whose jurisdiction the federal Superintendent operates, is permitted to authorize values in excess of the market values but not greater than those used in the last preceding financial statement or the book values for securities acquired in the interim. Thus the test of market values is not inflexible but has been changed when circumstances so require.

AMORTIZED VALUES

For redeemable securities issued or guaranteed by the Government of Canada, a province thereof, by the governments of the U.K. or the U.S., a Canadian life insurance company may use the amortized value instead of the market value stated in the list of authorized values published by the federal Superintendent. This was permitted in 1950 for the first time.

Amortization is best explained by an actual example. Assume the company buys a 5 per cent, 20-year bond at the price of $95.14 for each $100 bond and that the interest is payable yearly. The company receives $5 interest each year and $100, the principal, at the end of 20 years.

The actual yield on the bond is more than 5 per cent per annum for it was bought at a discount, namely, $95.14 and will be redeemed at $100. If worked out actuarially the actual yield can be shown to be 5.40 per cent per annum. By amortization a table is worked out showing the result of accumulating $95.14 and deducting $5.00 each year as interest due. If the balance is accumulated at 5.40 per cent per annum it will come to exactly $100 at the end of 20 years.

If bond yields rose the market values of existing bonds would fall. If bond yields fell the market value of existing bonds would rise. However, such movements would have no effect on the amortized bonds as valued in the books of the insurance company. The amortized values of such bonds year by year are determined by the tables worked out when each bond is first bought. Note that by amortization you place a value on a bond which is independent of market values once it has been purchased.

Many life insurance officials favour an extension of the amortization principle to bonds outside the narrow field of government and provincial bonds provided they are not in default as to interest payments, which is the practice in the United States. The result would be to stabilize the bond values appearing in life insurance company statements.

The arguments against amortization when applied generally to all bonds are that it can so readily provide a "cover-up" for bonds which possibly should never have been purchased in the first place. Should such bonds be carried on the books at a high artificial value with the plea that they are "amortized" when the market places a truer and much lower value on them?

STATEMENT VALUES OF SECURITIES

It was to be expected that, as long as the surplus position of a Canadian life insurance company had to be shown with the values of common stocks at market values, so long would the proportion of such investments be kept to a relatively small figure. We have referred to the changing philosophy of investment towards a greater proportion of common stock securities. The possibility of some system of averaging to reduce the wider swings of stock market fluctuations has been debated for years and was suggested in the 1964 edition of this text. This was done by a 1965 amendment to the federal insurance acts. Apart from certain government and government guaranteed securities which as stated above could be amortized, all other securities formerly had to be carried at values not greater than the market values. The amendment in effect permits a company to spread the impact of a drop in market values over a three-year period rather than absorb it all in one year as formerly.

POSITION OF A COMPANY: BOOK VALUES AND MARKET VALUES

In the government statement submitted by the life insurance companies to the Superintendent of Insurance at Ottawa the market value of every security must be shown so that the standing of each company on a market value basis is indicated: a Canadian company as regards its total business and other companies as regards their business in Canada.

As mentioned previously, several Canadian life companies do a substantial business in the U.S.A. and do a world-wide business so that the rates of exchange are important and may affect a life company's standing appreciably as regards its free surplus as indicated by the government statement.

One of the schedules in the government statement shows the free surplus on two bases: one using the book values of the securities and the book rates of exchange (this is the one shown in the Balance Sheet) and the other using market values for the securities and the current rates of exchange.

If the free surplus using market values and current rates of exchange (C dollars) is less than that shown using book values and book rates of exchange (A dollars) then the free surplus in the Balance Sheet could be said to have been overstated by ($A - C$) dollars. So long as the investment reserve fund (or any other name by which the fund is called) is greater than $A - C$ then no change is made in the Balance Sheet but it is recorded that the investment reserve fund covers the deficiency with both amounts shown. This is the purpose of the investment reserve fund and it frees the company from changing the values of individual securities and liabilities due to fluctuating market values and rates of exchange from year to year in its books, the summary in the government statement indicating the actual position.

SECURITIES TO BE HELD IN CANADA

Section 85(1) of the Insurance Act requires that a Canadian life insurance company retain in Canada under its own control assets at least equal to its liabilities to policyholders in Canada and that at least two-thirds of those liabilities be covered by investments in or loans upon Canadian securities.

CHAPTER THIRTY

Inflation and Life Insurance

There is no subtler, no surer means of overturning the existing basis of Society than to debauch the currency. The process engages all the hidden forces of economic law on the side of destruction, and does it in a manner which not one man in a million is able to diagnose.

LORD KEYNES[1]

There is no denying that the political and social ideas on which the structure of our modern society is based have implicit in them a bias towards inflation.

GRAHAM TOWERS
Former Governor, Bank of Canada[2]

Inflation, of course, was destructive of saving.

SIR ROY HARROD[3]

The general opinion that Lord Keynes' views favoured inflation is based on his writings during the great depression of the 1930s, but it is as well to have his considered views on the dangers of inflation as expressed in 1919. The importance to our economy of the large assets of the life insurance companies representing the long-term savings of the public and necessitated by the nature of level premium life insurance has been stressed repeatedly. Sir Roy Harrod's matter of fact statement cuts at the root of the danger. Must we accept inflation as inevitable? This chapter gives some recent illustrations of the destructive effects of inflation and discusses some investment and insurance plans which have been devised to attempt to cover the hazards of inflation.

Definition of Inflation. Inflation means a fall in the purchasing power of the currency. Before the Second World War a package of cigarettes cost

[1]*Essays in Persuasion* (New York, 1931).
[2]Address to Life Underwriters Association, Toronto (1957).
[3]"Savings and Inflation," *Journal of the Institute of Actuaries*, London, vol. 78 (1951). Sir Roy Harrod is an outstanding economist, author of a biography of Lord Keynes.

a quarter, a chocolate bar a nickel; a good shirt could be bought for less than $5.00. Compare these with today's prices and you see what inflation can do.

Obviously those whose incomes are largely fixed in terms of dollars are those who suffer most from inflation. Numbered among such people are pensioners, widows and orphans. Thus, inflation attacks those least able to help themselves.

In inflationary times it is sometimes said that there are too many dollars chasing too few goods; an excess of dollars can come about by a government printing currency. In recent times, inflation has rather been due to changes in distribution of purchasing power through expansion of employment in government at all levels and transfer payments (unemployment insurance, government pensions, etc.). Too few goods can result from destruction, as in war, poor crops as a few years ago in Russia, or by embargo, or the threat of exhaustion of resources as in the recent case of oil.

DOLLARS FOR FUTURE DELIVERY

Life insurance provides protection for dependents in the event of premature death and for one's self on retirement and is a means of long-term savings. The purchase is based on needs expressed in terms of money and also in terms of the current value of money. The needs are expressed in thousands of dollars of sums insured or in income of so many dollars a month. The life insurance business has been called the "sale of dollars for future delivery." The fact of the variation in the purchasing power of the units of money had not until comparatively recently been seriously considered in Canada. We have heard about the galloping inflation in Germany after the First World War and we give some facts concerning this below.

Figure 18 gives the Wholesale Price Index in the United States from 1760 to 1960. The chart indicates four main points: (1) prices vary from year to year; (2) prices rise in war-time; (3) prices fall after the war; and (4) there have been long periods when prices, although fluctuating, remain relatively stable. The nineteenth century was a period of disturbance for the U.S. for not only did it engage in two wars but economically the cycle of over-expansion and resulting depression occurred repeatedly. The chart for Canada, Figure 19, covering 100 years is more representative of world conditions and indicates a remarkably stable period during the first half of the period up to the First World War.

Ignoring the trend after the Second World War it can with reason be

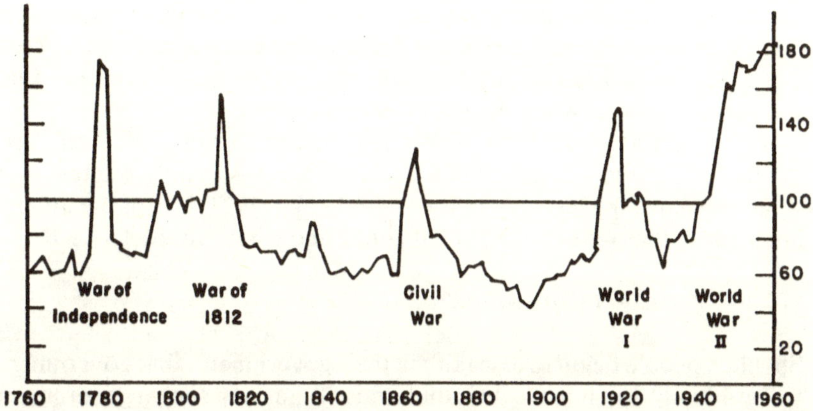

FIGURE 18. United States Wholesale Price Index, All Commodities, Yearly Average 1926 = 100

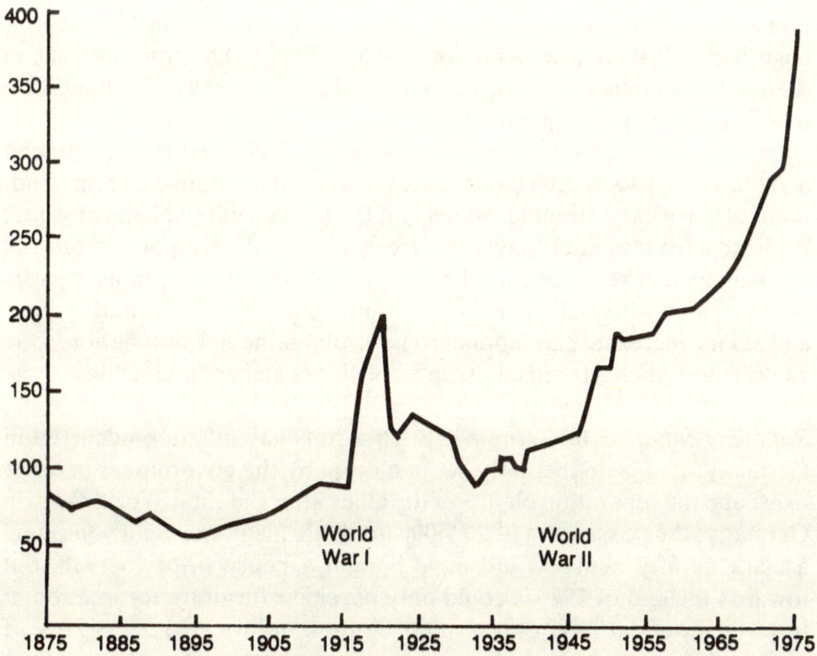

FIGURE 19. Canadian Wholesale Price Index, 1935–39 = 100

stated that except for periods of active war and immediately thereafter there was some assurance that the dollars received when the policy fell due would purchase roughly the economic "goods and services" that were contemplated when the policy was taken out.

It was only after the First World War that the terms "inflation" and "deflation" came into every-day use and this was mainly the result of what happened in Germany in the years 1920 to 1923. It is of the utmost importance that we know what happened and what caused it.

THE VICIOUS CIRCLE OF INFLATION

Should a people begin to lose faith in their government, that government will gradually find it more difficult to raise funds and such a government generally fears to incur increased opposition by raising taxes. Firstly, the government has to pay higher interest rates to attract purchasers for its bonds. As uncertainty develops these interest rates become higher and as they increase, the price of the existing bond obligations of the country decreases and this depreciation results in even greater lack of confidence in the government. Through the banking system the government can raise all the money it requires by just printing the bills; it costs just as little to print a bill for $1,000 as for $1. The government can then spend as much as it likes making up for any excess of expenditure over income by printing more bills.

It does not take long for business people to realize what is happening and there begins a flight from currency into goods. A house, a farm, land, food, clothes have tangible values, but the printed bills, tokens of value, begin to buy less each day they are held. Goods disappear from the markets as it is realized that the longer they are held the more "paper money" they will fetch. There is, of course, a progressive round of wage and salary increases, all tending to pour oil on the fire of inflation. One can see how such a trend can stop all business and economic life.

Runaway Inflation in Germany. Such a runaway inflation occurred in Germany. It was deliberately set in motion by the government in order to escape the reparation claims of the allies after the First World War. In Germany, the possession of a 25,000 mark life insurance policy (assume a mark as fifty cents) could have bought a house prior to 1918, but towards the end of 1920 it could only purchase furniture for one room; towards the end of 1922 only a suit of clothes; in July 1923 only 45 lbs. of coal; and, finally, the cost of the postage stamps for mailing the premium notice exceeded the face value of the policy.

All sorts of devices were tried by the German life insurance companies to continue in business. Some of these were to allow premiums to accumulate as a debt without interest and making premiums and sum insured payable in gold or U.S. dollars. However, in spite of all efforts the business of the life insurance companies in Germany was practically wiped out. With the establishment of a new currency the business had to start all over again.

The greatest danger of inflation is not the economic chaos it creates, but the legacy of class hatred and bitterness it engenders. In the struggle to keep up with runaway prices each class accuses the other of profiteering and the fixed income class—the middle group—is ruined irretrievably. This happened in Germany and was one of the principal causes of the Second World War.

Uncontrolled Inflation Can Still Happen. The disturbances due to war must be accepted and in the present age another world war would entail disasters compared with which those of inflation would be minor indeed. However, uncontrolled inflation has occurred in recent years in a number of countries solely due to the lack of restraint in spending by governments and their use of the printing press to pay for it. In the upper part of Table 30.1 we show what has been happening in several quite important countries in the period 1965 to 1975. The fall in value of the purchasing power of the currency from 100 to less than 1 in Argentina and Chile and from 100 to 11 in Brazil in a period of ten years recently and in our own hemisphere, indicates the reality of the danger of inflation. The unrest, the suffering, and distress caused by this destruction of the value of the currency can be imagined.

CREEPING INFLATION

Above we referred to certain South American countries. The lower part of Table 30.1 shows what has been happening in Canada, the U.S., Britain and other countries of the Commonwealth and Western Europe. Canada, over the ten-year period 1965 to 1975 has done better than Britain and India, and about the same as most other countries. West Germany's performance has been the best.

There are those who maintain that so long as inflation can be kept at a figure of 2 per cent per annum or less, the advantages of full employment and the boom conditions should these be the result, are not only tolerable but a preferable alternative to a recession. However, once inflation is accepted as inevitable there is no reason why it should stop at 1 or 2 per

TABLE 30.1

Depreciation of Money*
1965–1975

	Indexes of value of money			Annual depreciation	
	1965	1970	1975	'65–70†	'70–75†
		Uncontrolled inflation			
Argentina	100	41	††	16.2%	39.2%
Brazil	100	30	11	21.5	17.4
Chile	100	31	††	20.9	67.5
		Creeping inflation			
Canada	100	83	58	3.7%	6.8%
United States	100	81	59	4.1	6.3
United Kingdom	100	80	43	4.4	11.5
France	100	81	53	4.2	8.1
West Germany	100	88	65	2.8	5.8
Switzerland	100	85	58	3.3	7.1
Australia	100	86	53	3.0	9.3
India	100	72	42	6.4	10.4

**Monthly Economic Letter*, Citibank, N.Y., Sept., 1976.
†Compounded annually. ††Less than one.

cent a year for the same forces which caused this amount of inflation, unless checked, will cause more and more inflation. In the five years from 1965–1970 there was concern because the rate of inflation averaged 3.7 per cent; this is equivalent to money losing half its value in 19 years. For the next five years the rate averaged 6.8 per cent, equivalent to a loss of half the value of money in only 10 years. We have lived through a short period of double-digit inflation, and while there has been some indication of a slowing down in the rate of inflation, no one is sure that it will not speed up again.

Creeping inflation is like "addiction to dope." A "little" of it might be helpful, but how can one keep to the "little" when we know that more of the drug is continually needed to get the same effect? The very determination of a government to prevent the continuous erosion of its currency—deeds not words—might be expected to set in force trends to counteract inflation.

However, it may be noted that the anti-inflation programme adopted in Canada in 1975, did not set out to reduce inflation to zero, but, effectively, to 4 per cent per annum over a three-year period, a rate double that accepted as a maximum for increases in the Canada Pension Plan when it was adopted in 1965.

THE INFLATIONARY PROCESS

As stated in *The Way Ahead*, a study made by a group of deputy ministers of the Canadian government in 1975, "Inflation is a complex economic, social and political phenomenon, both in its origins and in its effects." It points out that "the debilitating effects of inflation extend beyond economic considerations to threaten the very nature of our institutions and traditions" and quotes from the Budget Speech of 23 June 1975: ". . . inflation ultimately inflicts grievous damage to the fabric of society. It lowers the living standards of those on fixed incomes, including pensioners. It leaves people without reliable, understandable guideposts by which to arrange their economic affairs. It injects grave uncertainty into decisions on family budgets, housing, savings and provision for old age. It provokes deep frustration, social tension and mistrust of private and public institutions. Collective bargaining is embittered. Industrial relations are damaged. We in Canada are already beginning to live some of these experiences."

The section entitled "The Inflationary Process" concludes: "It is therefore imperative that inflation be controlled if governments are to be free, in responding to and serving social and economic objectives, to opt for less rather than more intervention in the economy."

Taking money out of circulation and investing it to expand manufacturing plants and to develop the resources of a country tends to fight inflation. The first reduces the money in circulation, and the other tends to increase the volume of goods available. Hence the tremendous importance of savings and in particular the work of the life insurance companies.

INFLATION AND LIFE INSURANCE

Life insurance as an industry can exist whatever be the value of the currency, but not as the important medium for long-term savings which has made it the great business it has become. In Canada the assets representing life insurance and annuities in force with life insurance companies amounted to over $20 billion at the end of 1974; these are the dollars with which we are concerned.

The average rate of premium on new business in Canada is about $13 per thousand sum insured. By no other means than life insurance can one provide for an immediate estate with a down payment of 1.3% and an equal payment each year thereafter if one lives! On this basis consider

TABLE 30.2

Return on Life Insurance
Ratio of Sum Insured to Premiums Paid
Annual Premium $13 per $1,000 Sum Insured

Death takes place in year	Ratio	Death takes place in year	Ratio
1	76.92	10	7.69
2	38.46	15	5.13
3	25.64	20	3.85
4	19.23	25	3.08
5	15.38	30	2.56

the relation of the premium paid to the sum insured or the estate created. If death takes place in the first year, the premiums paid total $13 and the sum insured payable is $1,000. The sum insured is thus over seventy-six times the premiums paid. If death takes place in the second year the premiums paid total $26 so that the sum insured is over 38 times the premiums paid. Table 30.2 gives the ratios in various years of death.

Term Insurance and Consumer Price Index. It might appear a simple matter to counter "creeping inflation" in life insurance if one were concerned only with the amount payable on death. Thus, a yearly renewable term policy as outlined in Chapter 6 could have the sum insured and premium adjusted proportionately each year to meet the rate of inflation of the past year. Provided limitations were made to the total increase in sum insured permitted without evidence of insurability and allowing for the practical difficulty of a variable premium, year by year, which can only be known some time after the period to which it relates, the plan is feasible. It could meet a degree of creeping inflation. If the total increase in sum insured allowed were as much as the original sum insured or double that amount it would cover a period of years, such as to a pension age of 65. However, the premium rate per thousand sum insured begins to climb quite steeply after age 45. At 55, it is more than double the rate at 45; at 60, over four times. Increases in premium based on both an increase in age and an increase in inflation, year by year, would in practice deter most people.

Term Rider and Consumer Price Index. The idea of adding a variable amount of term insurance, determined by the consumer price index, to a basic plan on a fixed dollar permanent plan of life insurance would follow from the above. It would be possible to allow for a constant annual increase each year in the sum insured such as 2 or 3 per cent per annum with an increasing premium or a level annual premium determined in advance.

A similar system has been tried for life annuities; that is, instead of paying a lump sum for an annuity of say $100.00 a month for life, the purchaser would pay more and receive (using 3 per cent) $100.00 monthly in the first year, $103.00 monthly in the second, $106.09 monthly in the third and so on. The plan has not been popular because annual inflation rates recently have been much more than 3 per cent.

In Chapter 12 we dealt with the additional benefit which can be attached to a life insurance policy enabling the life insured, no matter his health and insurability, to increase his insurance at specified intervals. This *guaranteed insurability benefit* could be looked upon as a means of meeting the depreciation of the purchasing power of the sum insured, but is not regarded as practicable at attained age beyond about 40.

Paid-up Additions. In Chapter 15 we referred to the British system of allotting dividends in the form of paid-up additions to the sum insured; with Canadian companies this system is available in the form of a dividend option. It follows that a $15 or $20 per thousand paid-up addition to the sum insured each year covers an inflation of $1\frac{1}{2}$ or 2 per cent per annum, and when the bonuses are compounded the analogy is exact. Where the fear of inflation is a factor, the paid-up addition method of taking dividends could be encouraged with advantage. Again current inflation rates have outstripped rates at which paid-up additions have been allotted.

It should be noted that the above methods do not safeguard the savings element in the existing policy; they are merely methods to obtain additional insurance at additional cost. If a life insurance company held assets to cover policy-reserves the value of which varied directly with the consumer price index and the premiums to be paid were also adjusted accordingly, the company could similarly adjust all benefits under the policy, not only the sum insured payable on death, but cash surrender and loan values. This has been followed as indicated below in certain countries of Continental Europe which have been plagued by continuing inflation. These methods are also of interest as indicating what inflation leads to:

1. Bonds and mortgages are available where both capital and interest are tied to a consumer price index or to a foreign currency exchange rate.

2. Public utilities issue bonds repayable in terms of their own product. For example, if the bonds were issued by a power company, as the price per kilowatt hour increased so the amount of the bonds as expressed in terms of the local currency would increase.
3. In one country the government co-operates with the life insurance companies by issuing bonds linked to the consumer price index of the country. The life insurance companies thus issue life policies where the premium, sum insured, and cash values are all linked in value to the consumer price index, the companies investing the policy-reserves in these special bonds. Illustrating one factor of these special issues, the yield on these special bonds is $4^1/_2$ per cent whereas regular government bonds in this country yield about 10 per cent. The premiums as they fall due would be increased to cover the current degree of inflation, but no payment would be made on account of back premiums.

MUTUAL FUNDS

The Foreign and Colonial Government Trust, founded in London, England in 1868 may be considered to be the original *investment trust*. Its original prospectus stated that its purpose was to provide "the investor of moderate means the same advantages as the large capitalist, in diminishing the risk of investing in foreign and colonial government stocks." This company would now be called a *closed-end investment trust*, for it had a fixed capital. The shares of this type of investment trust can only be purchased from other holders and its price is quoted on the stock exchange. To obtain additional funds it could issue bonds or preferred stock or increase its common share capitalization as could any other incorporated body.

The *mutual fund* is a later development and may be described as an *open-end investment trust*; its shares or *units* can only be bought from or sold to the management of the fund. It has two functions: the investment of the money received from the purchasers of its units and the sale of more units. The plan of a purchaser undertaking to pay a fixed amount each month for the purchase of units and an organized sales force to promote such sales explains a tremendous increase in the 1960s in the numbers and size of mutual funds. Investment firms and brokers also handle purchases and sales for their clients. The total assets of mutual funds incorporated in Canada amounted in 1968 to over two and a half billion dollars.

The great development of mutual funds stemmed from the same incentives:

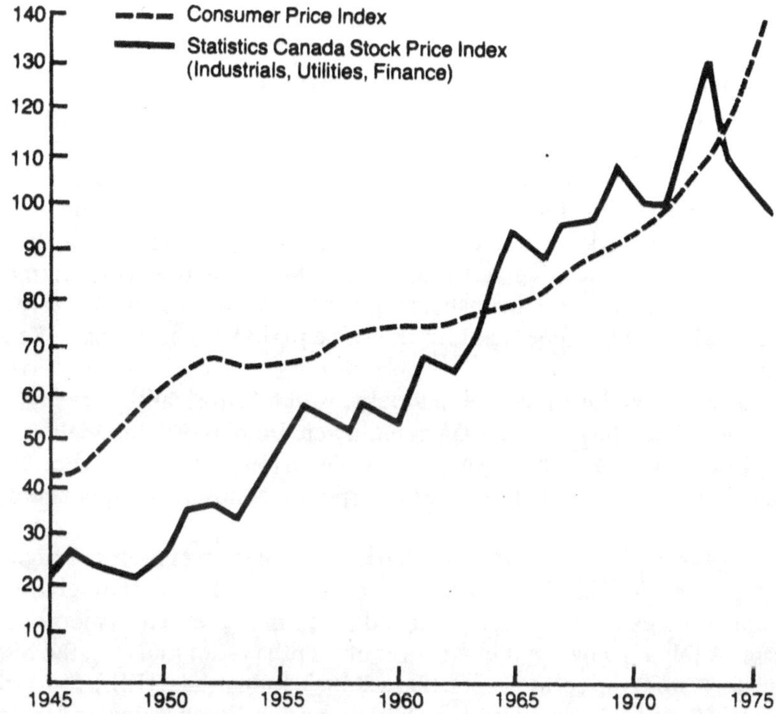

FIGURE 20. Consumer and Common Stock Price Indexes, Consumer Prices and Stock Prices 1971 = 100 Annual Averages

1. A phenomenal increase in the market price of common stocks—most if not all of the fund is invested in common stocks (see Figure 20).
2. Some twenty years of a boom economy.
3. Increasing public interest in investments. The increased standard of living of recent history means increased margins for saving and investment by a larger proportion of the population.
4. Vigorous promotion by a large sales force.
5 Finally and most important of all is the spread of *inflation psychology*; the realization by a large part of the population of the effects of inflation and the apparent inability of governments to control it and so a belief in its continuance.

However, the poor performance of the stock market since 1969, during a period of sharply rising prices, has led to disenchantment and, as a result the total assets of mutual funds were less at the end of 1974, than at the end of 1968.

COMMON STOCKS AS AN INFLATION HEDGE

The chart in Figure 20 shows the cost of living or consumer price index relative to the index of common stock prices in Canada from 1945 to 1975.

The continuing upward movement of both cost of living and stock prices from 1945 to 1969 with an occasional hesitation led to the belief that common stocks are an infallible hedge against inflation. But experience since that time has given a rude jolt to those who relied on common stocks to protect them against rising prices. From 1969 to 1975, stock prices fell by about 3 per cent; in the same period prices rose by 47 per cent.

Moreover, yields on common stocks, which historically were higher than on bonds, have since 1955 been lower. In mid-1977 the yield on a stock portfolio was about 5 per cent, while on long-term federal bonds it was near 9 per cent and on long-term corporate bonds over $9^1/_2$ per cent.

Stock Market Fluctuations. The charts of stock market prices in Figure 20 indicate the wide fluctuations in those prices, but as they give the average prices for the whole year indicated they are in a "smoothed" form. A fall of 20 per cent in a matter of months is not unusual; the high and low stock-price averages (Dow-Jones Industrials U.S.) for 1969 were 969 and 790 respectively. Following the Stock Price Index for Canada in Figure 20, the fall in the average price from November 1965 to October 1966 was from 449 to 378. From the 1937 high to the wartime low in 1942 the U.S. market was off 60 per cent.

The degree of fluctuation in stock prices indicated above does explain the historically restricted basis of Canadian life insurance companies' investment in common stocks. Although the three-year smoothing for entering the market values of its common stock investments in its balance sheet, made up as on a specific date, does assist a company, the illustrations given do explain the limitations in common stock investments. The necessity of holding substantial reserves or margins between book values and market values of common stocks results in limited benefits being passed on to participating policyholders when a company does increase its proportion of common stock investments. Hence the idea developed that, if the policyholder were prepared under certain policies to assume the risk of market fluctuations, the company could invest the greater part or the whole of the assets covering such policies in common stocks and pass on the whole of the benefits of such investments to the policyholder.

It would be expected that this idea would develop firstly with pension funds where the employee's contributions were fixed and the employer assumed the cost of the balance of the plan. Also in dealing with employers a more sophisticated approach can be made. In Chapter 27 and elsewhere we have shown how the development of segregated funds enabled life insurance companies to continue to offer their services for employee pension plans where the employer wanted to base his funding on common stocks to a greater degree than the life insurance companies considered desirable and, prior to 1961, were permitted by law to do. We will return to this aspect later in the chapter and now deal with its application to life insurance plans.

EQUITY-LINKED LIFE INSURANCE CONTRACTS

We have referred to the changes made in the Canadian and British Insurance Companies Act in March 1961, section 81(5), permitting federally licensed life insurance companies to issue policies, the policy-reserves of which would vary with the market value of a specified group of assets such as common stocks provided these assets were segregated from its regular life and annuity business. We outline below some of the plans of this type which have been issued in Canada.

1. *Level-Term Insurance plus Equity Units.* The first life insurance policy of this type was issued by a British life insurance company in Canada in April 1966. The life insurance part may be regarded as level-premium fixed dollar term insurance to age 65. Twenty per cent of the gross premium paid in the first year and 75 per cent in other years are used to obtain credits for units in a segregated fund invested wholly in Canadian common stocks or other Canadian securities. The balance of the premium pays for the term insurance, commissions, and administrative expenses. The values of the units are determined monthly and are dependent on the market values of the investments in the segregated fund. The income of the segregated fund forms part of the fund and increases the values of the units.

At five-year intervals, but not beyond age 49, the value of the units standing to the credit of the policy may be used to secure paid-up whole life insurance for an amount dependent on the attained age of the life insured and the value of the units and without evidence of insurability. If this option is elected the insured may continue premium payments, the insurance continues and 75 per cent of the gross premium continues to be used to obtain additional units in the fund. At age 65 all premium payments cease and all units standing to the credit of the policy must be converted to paid-up whole life insurance. At or after age 65 the policyholder may surrender his paid-up insurance if he so wishes.

2. *Decreasing Term plus Equity Units.* One Canadian company which was a pioneer in the adoption of equity-linked contracts issues four types of policies, two with life insurance and two without life insurance but with annuity benefits. Of the life insurance plans one provides a decreasing term insurance of five dollars a month per unit to age 65 and the other level $1,000 term insurance to age 70, both of the fixed dollar type; of the premium paid $30 per unit in the first year and $60 per unit in subsequent years are used to obtain units in the company's segregated fund. Of course, on death the value of the units credited to the policy is added to the fixed dollar sum insured. Under the second type of policy the level premium for the insurance increases every fifteen years. Conversion of the term insurance on a permanent plan of insurance prior to age 60 without evidence of insurability may be made but on such conversion the equity investment cannot be continued. Both plans provide that the equity investment portion of the premium may be discontinued at any time and the fixed dollar life insurance continued. The value of the equity investment at age 65 may be used to purchase paid-up whole life insurance at guaranteed rates without evidence of insurability.

3. *Policy-reserve in Equity Units.* Another idea used by some companies is the issue of a participating straight life policy at its regular rates. Part or all of the policy-reserve (the proportion is chosen by the policyholder) is invested in an equity fund. Year by year the difference between the performance of the equity fund and the interest earnings on the company's general fund is reflected in the adjustment (positive or negative) to the regular fixed dollar dividend allotted in the form of a paid-up addition.

4. *Policy Dividends and Equity Units.* Another development is where all the features of a fixed dollar contract are preserved, but the dividends allotted may be used to purchase units in the segregated fund of the company. This does introduce an equity-linked benefit and may be regarded as an additional dividend option to the five outlined in Chapter 15.

5. *Dividends and Consumer Price Index.* Another development by a Canadian company is a policy on the straight life plan but at a higher

premium than its regular plan so as to earn a larger dividend. The dividend is allotted annually as a paid-up addition to the sum insured. Should the increase in the paid-up insurance thus added not equal the amount necessary to offset the annual increase in the consumer price index at a point three months earlier than the renewal date, a part of the paid-up addition is surrendered to give the requisite amount of one-year term insurance without evidence of insurability. There is no limit to the amount of term insurance thus granted in any year, but the total amount of term insurance is limited to an amount equal to the original basic sum insured.

6. *Guarantees.* There has been some controversy as to whether a life insurance company should, under equity-linked contracts, guarantee a minimum return on death as the premiums paid up to the date of death; also on maturity of an endowment insurance the return of premiums paid to the date of maturity. The fundamental principle of an equity-linked contract is that the insured frees the life insurance company from all risk of a fall in the value of the assets covering the equity-linked part of the contract. The argument is that death and maturity are not controlled by the insured and, just as it is possible to calculate the death risk under a policy and charge the appropriate premium therefor, so it should be possible to calculate the value of the risk of death or maturity occurring during a period of depressed stock market values which would involve the payment of an amount exceeding the market value of the units held. It has been calculated that based on the fluctuation of stock market prices in the past a charge of one per cent of the gross premium would cover the risk. Supervisory authorities in Canada are insisting that an additional reserve be held when such a guarantee is given. Some guarantee is required under individual (as opposed to group) contracts if the contracts are not to fall under the jurisdiction of provincial securities commissions.

7. *Dual Licensing and Mutual Funds.* The factor behind the planning of the first two types of policies described above is the relation of the premium payable for the death benefit, which is a minimum amount of fixed dollars, and the amount of premium which can be invested in units of the segregated fund. For a specific premium, the lower the first the higher the second. It could be asked "why this intricacy?" Why not keep the two policies separate on a regular basis, either straight life, paid-up at 65, or endowment insurance at 65 with an additional premium to be invested in equity units?

This is now permitted under an amendment to Section 65 of the Canadian and British Insurance Companies Act; a life insurance company may own control of a mutual fund company. Moreover, many provinces permit agents to sell both life insurance and mutual funds provided there is an arrangement between the life insurance company and the mutual fund company for the supervision of their activities. This is called *dual licensing*.

VARIABLE ANNUITIES

Life insurance companies seeking to meet the competition of mutual funds for long-term savings have sought to develop contracts where death benefits are not desired or feasible. A ruling by the federal Superintendent of Insurance requires that all contracts issued by federally licensed life insurance companies in Canada must contain some element of insurance and the companies have met this be developing their deferred annuity and immediate annuity contracts which have survivorship benefits. Where the premiums paid, less an expense charge, are invested in units of a segregated fund, and the cash value based on the market value of units of that fund, or the amount of annuity paid, depends on the value of units of such a fund, the contract is called a *variable annuity*. There is no object in giving details of the plans and annuity options available or of the many forms in which premiums may be paid: there can be a single premium, level premiums, or the policyholder can, within limits, vary the premium payable. We outline below the development of CREF which illustrates the procedures followed.

THE ORIGIN OF VARIABLE ANNUITIES

Teachers Insurance and Annuity Association was founded in 1918 by the Carnegie foundations as a non-profit organization headquartered in New York City; it restricts its operations to college and university staffs and similar non-profit educational bodies in Canada and the United States; it employs no agents. The main business of TIAA is the issue of fixed-dollar individually owned deferred annuities to fund retirement benefits for staff members of colleges and universities. As with all legal reserve life insurance companies subject to the requirements of New York State insurance law, TIAA was, prior to 1951, prohibited from investing annuity funds in common stocks.

An analysis of the endowment funds of 29 colleges and universities made as of June 30, 1951, totalling $1,600 millions indicated that 40.7 per cent of their new funds were going into common stocks and their holdings of common stocks were 30 per cent of their total assets. The point was made by institutions which entrusted their pension funds to TIAA that they were obtaining higher yields on their endowment funds than those generally obtained by TIAA's fixed-dollar investments. We mentioned above that yields on common stocks prior to 1955 were higher than those on high grade corporation bonds and government bonds which has not been the case since.

Having conducted extensive economic studies on the feasibility of investing retirement funds in common stocks, TIAA in 1952 incorporated the first variable annuity, College Retirement Equities Fund by a special act of the New York State legislature. CREF is subject to certain provisions of the New York Insurance Law but is not subject to the investment requirements applicable to life insurance companies operating in New York State. CREF is financially separate from TIAA with its own portfolio of investments and although sharing the same officers and staff does have a separate Board of Trustees from TIAA. Neither TIAA nor CREF regular annuity contracts provide for cash surrender or loan values.

CREF issues *variable annuities* only. As the meaning of the word *annuity* is the payment of a stated amount or amounts, the term "variable annuity" may appear a misnomer and the expression "unit annuity" is a more suitable description. However, the term "variable annuity" has been widely accepted and both terms will be used here. The main idea behind a variable annuity is that it is expressed in units of a fund invested in common stocks, although other equity type investments are not ruled out. Each applicant has to choose as to what part of his or her contributions has to be in a fixed dollar deferred annuity with TIAA or a unit annuity with CREF. Originally not more than half the contributions made on the participants' behalf could be placed in unit annuities. Today participants may allocate their premiums to TIAA and CREF in any proportion, including 100 per cent to either.

Accumulation Units. CREF deferred "variable" annuity or unit annuity works in this way. Each deposit less expense charge purchases a number of "accumulation units" based on the current market value of the CREF common stock fund. Accumulation unit values are determined once a month. Dividend earnings on accumulation units already held are apportioned to participants in the form of additional accumulation units. There is no dollar guarantee and hence no need to even out fluctuations on common stock prices or yields and thus there is no need to accumulate surplus or maintain contingency funds. Each participant is periodically informed of the number of units he or she holds and of the current dollar value of the units.

Annuity Units. At the time of retirement the number of accumulation units held by the participant are exchanged for a contract promising to pay him (or her) each month the dollar value of a specified number of annuity units. The number of annuity units will vary with the sex and the age of the annuitant when the annuity commences to be payable, the type of annuity (whether straight life, with a guaranteed period and the number of guaranteed payments), or whether it is a joint and survivorship annuity. The number of annuity units is fixed once it has been determined, although the dollar value of each annuity unit varies from year to year, reflecting the investment experience of CREF's common stocks as well as mortality and expense experience. The dollar value decided upon at a fixed date each year holds for the following twelve months.

The formation of CREF marked an epoch in life insurance development. Its assets at year-end 1976 totalled over four billion dollars and it had some 475,000 participants.

Segregated Funds and Annuities in Canada. Although *variable annuities* have not become of importance in Canada, *segregated funds* have become a major factor in the accumulation of money to pay pensions, with the actual pensions being provided either by the purchase of a *level* life annuity, or paid out of the fund. Many employers have endeavoured to assist pensioners to meet the rising cost of living by granting increases in existing pensions. As has been mentioned above, annuities linked to stock values have, in recent years, frequently declined in amount while the cost of living was rising.

The growth of segregated funds has been described in Chapter 2. These are invested not only in common stocks, but also in bonds and mortgages. They have been used for group annuities and for individual life insurance and annuity policies. Supervisory authorities are particularly concerned that individual purchasers understand the variable nature of the contracts; copies of policy forms and of illustrative material are required to be approved by provincial insurance departments.

THE NEW MONEY CONCEPT

When variable contracts were first issued, they seemed to many to be an excellent hedge against inflation. Present events have proved that they are not, for the stock market has fallen or been stagnant during periods of double-digit inflation. The current public attitude to common stock investments is generally cynical.

Much investment is now for a relatively short term and at historically high interest rates. Many savers are more interested in taking advantage of such rates, even though reinvestment may be at lower rates. Thus many companies are now issuing policies, particularly deferred annuities under registered pension plans, which provide a guaranteed rate of interest at current levels, usually for five years, on each premium, after an expense charge. There is no undertaking as to the rate which will be allowed after the period has expired or on premiums to be paid in future, or, if there is an undertaking, it is for a modest minimum rate, with a higher rate to apply if justified by the company's practice at the time of payment of the premium.

This practice is another response of the industry to inflation and has been very successful in the annuity field; it has so far had little impact on life insurance although some plans are available.

CHAPTER THIRTY-ONE

Industrial Life Insurance

DEFINITION AND INTRODUCTION

Industrial life insurance was originally developed in order that the lowest paid wage earner could make some provision for meeting the expenses which inevitably follow a death in the family. Broadly speaking, industrial life insurance is issued for small sums and paid for by weekly premiums collected at the homes of the policyholders.

In the Ontario Insurance Act the definition of industrial life insurance is as follows; it is not uniform throughout the provinces. (1) The policy must not exceed $2,000 face value. (2) The policy must provide for payment of premiums fortnightly or more frequently, but, if premiums are usually collected at the home of the insured, the premium may be payable monthly.

No further reference to industrial life insurance of any significance is made in the Ontario Act and apart from the calculation of policy-reserves it is not referred to in the Canadian federal insurance acts being included with other forms of life insurance. Different companies apply the label "Industrial Life Insurance" in different ways as a matter of administrative convenience.

In Great Britain, where industrial life insurance originated, the companies transacting this form of business have given it the name "Home Service Life Insurance" to emphasize the service given by the collection of premiums at the home of the insured and the personal service given by the agent on his weekly, fortnightly, or monthly rounds.

A notable feature of industrial life insurance is the issue of a receipt book kept by the insured, or head of the family, in which a record of all premiums paid is kept. One receipt book usually covers all the industrial policies of an insured or all the policies on members of the same family: father, mother, and children. The record of individual premium payments is confined to the receipt book and the record kept by the agent. As a rule, once a policy is issued, entries are made in the company records only when and if it is terminated. This is most economical in reducing overhead costs. An agent is thus "debited" with a certain amount of premiums which he has to collect each week or month as the case may be and he has to account for this amount debited to him. To economize effort, an agent's collections are confined to a specific area and no other agent of the same company is permitted to collect premiums or service business in that area. Hence the area serviced by a particular agent has become known as his "debit" or "district," and the arrangement is known as the "block system."

Although industrial life insurance is no longer sold in Canada the method of marketing and servicing insurance by the concentration of the efforts of an agent on a specific part of a company's business in a particular area has become an important part of the organization of those companies which used to sell industrial life insurance. They, of course, still sell ordinary life insurance.

Abbreviations to distinguish between the two branches of business, Industrial Branch and Ordinary Branch, when transacted by one company are I.B. and O.B. and these abbreviations will be used when convenient. Life insurance companies which transact both I.B. and O.B. business are referred to as "Industrial-Ordinary" companies or "Combination" companies.

ORIGINS OF INDUSTRIAL LIFE INSURANCE

In Britain. Industrial life insurance originated in England with The Prudential Assurance Company Limited which is by far the largest insurance organization in Britain. It was founded in 1848 to write regular life insurance and made very little progress in its early years. By 1854 its total premium income was only £3,075 (say $15,000). A committee of the British Parliament reporting on Assurance Associations in 1853 drew attention to the relative inactivity of the life insurance business in Great Britain, and the possibilities of its expansion "not only in the higher and middle classes of society, but also among the humbler classes."

In 1854 the English Prudential decided to transact life insurance among the "humbler classes" mainly as a result of the report referred to above. At the time of the committee's report in 1853 the working classes could only satisfy their need for life insurance through Burial Clubs and Friendly Societies. The chequered careers of the early friendly societies will be referred to in the next chapter; life insurance benefits were a minor part of their activities. The burial clubs were in the main just "rackets" preying on the ignorance and helplessness of working class people. Small sums were collected by house to house collection and on the first claim arising the "collector" would disappear to continue his work in another neighbourhood. The difficulties of I.B. business in 1850 can be seen from Table 21.1 where the rate of mortality up to age 40 is shown to be about five times what it was in 1961. Also, in the artisan class to whom I.B. insurance was directed the mortality would be heavier than for the population as a whole. These people would be weekly wage earners and at that time all, with few exceptions, would be hard put to maintain a minimum standard of living. The birth rate was high and the death rate among children proportionately high. Premiums would have to be collected weekly at the homes of the insured and often with as little interval as possible after the pay envelope had been opened. Yet there was no other means available to meet the cost of burial when a death occurred in the family. From 1854 to 1864 the premium income of the English Prudential increased twenty-fold and by 1879 it had increased twenty-fold again.

In the U.S. In February, 1875, there was organized in Newark, New Jersey, the Prudential Friendly Society with the intention of transacting working class insurance along the lines of the English Prudential. Actual business operations commenced in November 1875. By the end of 1876 expenses had exceeded income and the outlook seemed black when the directors voted two hundred and fifty dollars for the Secretary, John F. Dryden, to go to London, England, to see how the English Prudential operated. Dryden was only two weeks in London, but he got the information he sought. He was advised to give up the sickness insurance he was transacting. He also learned the English way of remunerating agents writing industrial business; in particular the deduction for lapses from new business. In the three years 1876 to 1879 business increased almost ten-fold. This was the origin of the Prudential Insurance Company of America to which the name was changed later.

In New York City in March, 1868, a re-organization of a life insurance company took place under a new charter. The company was called the Metropolitan Life Insurance Company. It found the competition of the big life insurance companies operating in New York quite severe and during the hard times of the 1870s it made little progress. The company had transacted insurance on the lives of artisans through workers' organizations, and so Joseph F. Knapp, the President, watched the progress of the Prudential Friendly Society across the Hudson with some interest. In 1879 Mr. Knapp sailed to England to visit the English

Prudential and on his return decided to go into industrial life insurance in a big way. Records are in existence in the Metropolitan relating to the bringing over from England of 544 experienced industrial life insurance agents and superintendents with 757 dependants, although tradition places the total number at two thousand. Mr. Knapp had evidently learned one thing from the English Prudential: that success in I.B. depended on volume and concentration of effort. In 1880, the first full year of operation in I.B., the Metropolitan had become the leading industrial life insurance company in the U.S. The Metropolitan and the Prudential of America are now the two largest life insurance companies in the world.

In Canada. In 1874 there was organized by a group of local men in London, Ontario, the London Life Insurance Company. The story here is the same as the others mentioned. Its first years were rather difficult and it found competition severe. In 1883, J. G. Richter was appointed manager and a new era began. As at December 31, 1886 its assets totalled $175,543 and apart from its capital of $33,650 its surplus was $4,884. Under Richter's direction, the London Life started writing weekly premium industrial life insurance in 1887 and in his report for that year the president, Joseph Jeffery, referred to the English Prudential as having over seven million policies in force. In the early years of the London Life its premium income from industrial business far exceeded that from ordinary business. At that time the London Life was the only Canadian company transacting industrial business.

Five companies were actively transacting I.B. business in Canada in the 1950s. The dates of their commencement to write such business in Canada were: Metropolitan 1885, London Life 1887, Industrial Life 1905, Prudential of America 1909, and Toronto Mutual 1929. It is an interesting reflection that the four combination companies (one British, two U.S., and one Canadian), whose histories we have referred to above, include the largest life insurance company in Great Britain, the two largest in the U.S., and the Canadian company doing the largest business in Canada. Thus the high degree of concentration which industrial life insurance requires has fostered organizations which have dominated life insurance in their countries of origin.

TREND OF INDUSTRIAL LIFE INSURANCE

In Canada. As from January 1, 1960 the London Life reported all its new business under individual life policies as O.B. business and a substantial part of its industrial business (for $500 and over) was transferred to and recorded as ordinary business. The Metropolitan similarly reported all its new business on individual lives in Canada as O.B. business in 1966.

No company now reports new Industrial business but at the end of 1974, there were still 900,000 policies in force with a sum assured of $450 millions.

Collections of premiums at the houses of policyholders is still an important feature of life insurance in Canada with combination companies. This justifies the importance given to it in this text, although statistically I.B. business is disappearing gradually from the published records of Canadian life insurance business. Even much of the weekly premium business is collected at the houses of the policyholders at monthly intervals. This trend should be borne in mind in examining figures of recent years given in the tables in this chapter and explains why in some cases no effort has been made to bring up-to-date ratios illustrating certain points: recent figures would not be illustrative.

The figures in Table 31.1 give the new sums insured and business in force reported as I.B. business in Canada for both federally registered companies and those with provincial charters.[1] The change made by the London Life in 1960 is indicated in these figures.

TABLE 31.1

Year	New	In force
1959	$88 millions	$1,664 millions
1960	40 millions	1,112 millions
1967	16 millions	816 millions
1968	5 millions	774 millions
1975	—	434 millions

I.B. VERSUS O.B. AND GROUP

Among the reasons for the cessation of writing new industrial business are:

1. The improvement in the standard of living of the industrial or hourly paid workers in recent years has been such that the need for weekly premium collection at the home of the insured has lost much of its importance. These workers can now affort to purchase life insurance for larger amounts and thus obtain the benefit of a substantially lower rate of premium.

2. A considerable volume of monthly premium life insurance is

[1]*Canadian Life Insurance Facts, 1976*, and other years (Toronto, C.L.I.A.).

classed by some companies as "ordinary" although premiums are collected on the "debit" at the home of the insured. A proportion of the increase in O.B. in recent years is due to the increased purchases of ordinary policies by the hourly paid workers or "industrial workers" who gave the original name to "Industrial Life Insurance."

3. A part of the tremendous increase in group life insurance has undoubtedly filled a need for life insurance among industrial workers which would otherwise have resulted in greater I.B. sales. Under group the employer pays part or all the premium.

4. The development of the Family Insurance Plan which covers particularly "industrial class" needs.

It follows that the changes which have occurred are to the advantage of the industrial worker.

NOTE: *Because industrial insurance is no longer written in Canada, the remainder of the chapter may be of little interest to the reader concerned only with the current situation. It is reprinted from the previous edition for the benefit of readers interested in historical aspects.*

AVERAGE POLICY I.B. VERSUS O.B.

In Table 31.2 we show the average I.B. policy purchased in Canada and the corresponding average O.B. policy together with the average policy in force, for a period back to 1945. The overlapping of the two classes of

TABLE 31.2
Size of Average Policy
Canada, Federally Registered Companies

	New business		Business in force	
Year	I.B.	O.B.	I.B.	O.B.
1945	$437	$ 2,158	$317	$2,004
1955	656	4,350	439	2,913
1965	579	8,883	419	4,880
1967	576	10,069	436	5,475
1968	592	10,902	443	5,783

business should be borne in mind as well as the continuous trend of transfers from I.B. to O.B. The change in the recording of the London Life and Metropolitan business has influenced Canadian I.B. figures after 1960.

MONTHLY DEBIT BUSINESS

For the first fifty years or so of its history industrial business in Canada and the U.S. meant weekly premium business. We have referred frequently to the improved standard of living among working-class people over the past century. By the 1920s this improvement was indicated by a demand for life insurance which while not ordinary business with its annual, semi-annual or quarterly premiums yet was more akin to that type of business. There was also a desire on the part of the combination companies to provide life insurance at a lower cost than was possible when premiums were collected weekly. This demand was met by "monthly debit premiums." The premiums were still collected at the home of the insured, but on a monthly rather than weekly basis, with resulting lower cost. Figures published by one of the leading U.S. companies indicates the growth of monthly debit insurance. In 1933 monthly debit business comprised 38 per cent of the total debit insurance, in 1943 it was 62 per cent, and in 1953 it had increased to 77 per cent. It is reported that agents no longer find it necessary to call weekly at homes where there is weekly industrial business, the insured being able to pay two or more weekly premiums at a time with much saving of time to the agent.

With improved standards of living and with the inflationary trends since the Second World War, there has been a demand for larger life insurance policies by the artisan class. This has been met in Canada by monthly debit policies to the advantage of the insured for the insurance is thereby obtained at a lower cost.

It is of little consequence whether the label "ordinary" or "industrial" is attached to a policy. It is the mode of collection which is the important factor for it determines the overhead cost. Monthly debit ordinarily referred to as M.D.O. has become of considerable significance in the development of combination companies. The business is classed as "ordinary" for government statement purposes but is still "on the debit." The regular monthly call at the home of the insured to collect the monthly premium is the present variation of the original I.B. business and undoubtedly dominates the picture of the sales organization of present-day combination companies. The association of monthly collections with the monthly budgeting for instalment purchases is a clear one. The distinction between monthly debit ordinary and the other forms of paying life insurance premiums by monthly instalments should be recognized clearly. Under M.D.O. the premiums are collected by a personal call by an agent at the policyholder's home.

I.B. PLANS AND LIMITS

Originally I.B. sums insured were quoted for multiples of premiums of five cents a week. Nowadays weekly premiums for specific sums insured are quoted as for sums insured of $250, $500, ... $1,000.

To keep the business as simple as possible the number of plans available under weekly I.B. policies are usually restricted and for M.D.O. the range is wider but still restricted. As the bulk of insurance, even ordinary business, is sold under two or three plans where a range of, say, thirty plans is available, it is no hardship for industrial policyholders to be limited to a narrow range of plans. In particular the tendency is to restrict them to plans which will be paid up, or mature as endowments within the working lifetime as at age 65 or 70. The 20-payment life is a popular plan as this class of insured considers a premium-paying period of twenty years as long enough! The desire for policies with a high investment element by industrial policyholders and the necessarily high expense of collection are problems of I.B. business. It does emphasize the keen desire by the public for a form of long-term savings.

Owing to the changing practice in I.B. business in Canada it is difficult to cover phases of the business without referring to the practice of a particular company. The practice of the leading Canadian combination company varies somewhat from what has been outlined in the previous paragraph. The company issues I.B. policies for exactly $500, $1,000, and $1,500 on a wide range of plans. It now has a minimum policy of $500. These policies may be paid for by weekly and monthly premiums "on the debit." This company also issues a $2,000 I.B. policy which can be paid by weekly or monthly premiums "on the debit." The rates of these I.B. policies decrease as the sum insured increases giving the insured the advantage of the policy being for a larger amount.

The method of payment of premiums under these I.B. policies can be changed from weekly to monthly or from either to annual. The lower the frequency of premium payment, the lower is the rate of premium due to the saving in overhead cost by the company.

WIVES AND CHILDREN

One phase of I.B. life insurance is the popularity of insurance on wives and children. The companies make a great effort to restrict the proportion of insurance premiums spent on insurance on the wife and children. One figure quoted gives the proportion of life insurance on men under

O.B. policies as 80 per cent and under group policies as 88 per cent. Under I.B. the proportions on the women are given as 50 per cent and on children as 20 per cent. To meet this situation one of the U.S. companies restricts the total weekly I.B. insurance it will accept on a wife or a dependent child unless proportionately substantial insurance is held by the family head; it also restricts the amount of insurance on a child under five years of age to what twenty-five cents a week will purchase. This company has restrictions in the issue of its O.B. policies with the same intention, namely, to keep the insurance on the head of the family relatively as high as possible.

I.B. MORTALITY

Due to environment, heredity, education, medical attention, and occupational hazards the class from which the lives insured under industrial life insurance policies are drawn would be at a disadvantage as far as mortality is concerned compared with those insured under ordinary policies. The improvement in living standards and industrial hygiene is narrowing the disadvantage as the years pass. Further the imperative need to keep costs down when small sums insured are involved requires broad underwriting standards and simple home office underwriting procedures. Medical examination on I.B. business is required only rarely and even then is not as detailed as and hence is less expensive than for O.B. policies. The class for standard risks is also wider under I.B. policies. All this explains why mortality under I.B. business has been definitely higher than under O.B. business, as one would expect.

However, it is not so obvious why I.B. mortality should be higher than the corresponding population mortality. This is due to (1) the exclusion of those in the higher social classes who are included in the general population; (2) the preponderance of urban dwellers in I.B. business: mortality in rural areas is less than in urban areas; (3) the adverse influence of withdrawals.

It is important to note that these three mortality classes (I.B., O.B. and general population) are drawing closer together with each investigation indicating the effect on mortality of improving living standards among the industrial classes. We refer here to the business as a whole and not to the experience of any one company.

The reference to the adverse influence of withdrawals may appear to contradict what was said in an earlier chapter. I.B. insureds are subject to fluctuating economic conditions to a far greater extent than O.B. When expenses have to be curtailed and as is usual there are policies on every member of the family, it is to be expected that anti-selection will be exercised as to which policy is surrendered.

FREQUENCY OF PREMIUM PAYMENT: EXTRA CHARGES

It is instructive to indicate the extra charges involved in the different systems of premium payment by one company. In Table 31.3 we show the premiums corresponding to an annual premium of $25 and also, in

TABLE 31.3

Regular Ordinary	Annual	$25.00	
	Semi-annual	12.88	(3%)
	Quarterly	6.56	(5%)
	Monthly*	2.21	(6%)
On the debit	Monthly	2.29	(10%)
	Weekly	0.57	(16%)

*Minimum premium $7.50 a month.

brackets, the additional amount expressed as a percentage. Fifty-one weeks' payment is assumed in the weekly premium because an additional "dividend" of one week's premium is given on weekly premium business on an agent's debit by this company.

All premiums are "true" premiums so that on death there is no amount deducted for the balance of premiums due in the year of death. The increased premiums payable not only cover loss of interest to the company and the loss of part of the premium in the year of death but also the additional overhead cost when premiums are payable in instalments. For premiums "on the debit" the extra charge has to cover the additional cost of collection by a personal call at the home of the insured.

The 16 per cent for weekly premiums means an additional 8 cents a week on a 57 cents a week premium. A discount may be obtained by paying the premium direct to the head office of the company. Some companies allow a 10 per cent discount for payment to the local office and this would mean a saving of 5 cents on a 57 cent a week premium.

I.B. EXPENSE

The problem of I.B. business is to provide "Home Service" at a reasonable cost. The following figures were given in a paper published some years ago to show the ratio of the total expenses and taxes to premiums in I.B. business of three companies who have the largest volume of I.B. business in force in Canada.

1936—24.5% 1940—25.2% 1945—25.2%

If the trend of expenses in Canada in the inflation following the Second World War in I.B. business is similar to that in O.B. business, these ratios, if available for later years, would undoubtedly be closer to 30 per cent than 25. The emphasis placed on the high cost of "service" when we considered O.B. expense ratios and in particular on the cost of servicing a unit of insurance irrespective of its size would make one wonder how business would be possible with an average weekly premium of 30 cents per policy. Another way of looking at it is that an agent may have to call at a house fifty-two times to collect $16.00 in a year.[2]

It is from this angle that the charges noted previously for weekly premiums should be considered and compared with the over-all cost. It is also worthy of note that the English Prudential, the pioneer industrial life insurance company, has very recently withdrawn its weekly premium table so that all future business for home collection will be on a four-weeks' basis.

The policy-reserves under I.B. business have become a great economic reservoir of investment for the benefit of the country, on which substantial interest is earned, which would not be so if the funds had not been used to purchase life insurance. It would be a fair proposition to offset the interest earned on the I.B. policy-reserves which is credited to the I.B. policyholders, against the expenses. One of the prominent I.B. companies calculated that if this were done the total net expenses charged to its I.B. insured, would be only 5 per cent of the premiums paid.

I.B. POLICY PROVISIONS

When industrial life insurance was first introduced in Canada the contracts differed widely from those designated as ordinary life insurance policies. Through the years such differences have largely disappeared.

[2]Undoubtedly the introduction of the "block system" in 1912 made possible the continuation of industrial life insurance. This was the work of the late Sir Joseph Burn (1871–1950) who served the English Prudential for 64 years occupying the positions of Actuary, General Manager, and President. Another of his achievements in reducing costs was the introduction of punch cards for accounts, records, and valuation—the forerunner of present-day electronic computers. He also gained a reputation as an investment authority.

Canadian Company. The leading Canadian combination company now uses its regular O.B. policy forms for its I.B. business and took a major step in this direction as long ago as 1940. Its I.B. policies have guaranteed cash and loan values after two years in force; the non-forfeiture provision is the automatic premium loan which applies after two years; reduced paid-up values are guaranteed after two years and these have cash values. The I.B. policies up to $1,500 have a waiver of premium benefit included automatically. In children's policies, the waiver of premium to age 21, on the death of the parent, is also included. These are without separate charge. The $2,000 I.B. plan is, however, similar to a regular ordinary plan and can have the usual disability benefits, waiver on death of parent, double indemnity accident benefits, all added at the regular rates.

This company allots dividends to I.B. policies on an annual basis paying the same annual dividend as on corresponding ordinary policies. In addition weekly premium policies receive a "holiday" dividend of one week's premium except in the calendar year of issue.

U.S. Companies. As a substantial volume of I.B. business is sold in Canada by U.S. companies and classified as I.B., it is of interest to note the following characteristics of these policies with emphasis on the points where they may differ from policies issued in the ordinary branch of the companies.

1. *Facility of payments clause.* The policy provides for a named beneficiary, but if such beneficiary does not make a claim, or cannot give a valid release (a minor, etc.), it permits the company to pay any relative of the insured who seems equitably entitled to receive payment. It is of considerable help in effecting settlement under small policies.

2. *Dismemberment benefit.* The following benefit is included without separate charge: For "irrecoverable loss of sight of both eyes, or loss by severance of both feet or hands, or one hand and one foot," the company pays the full face amount immediately and in addition the policy becomes paid-up for the full face amount paid again on death. On loss of one hand or one foot, half the face value is paid immediately and also the policy becomes paid-up. The benefits are not payable if disability is due to service in the Armed Forces.

3. *Double indemnity accident benefit.* This is included without separate charge. It is not applicable if death is due to suicide, inhalation of gas, aviation (except as a passenger), war, or service in the Armed Forces.

4. *Dividends and cash surrender values.* Normally, dividends and cash surrender values do not become available until the policy has been three years in force. Dividends are allotted in the form of paid-up additions to the sum insured. The cash surrender values are guaranteed and set out in the policy as with O.B. policies.

5. *Reduced paid-up values.* These are available as an option after premiums have been paid for three full years. The amounts are guaranteed and are set out in the policy and such paid-up policies have cash values.

6. *Non-forfeiture provision.* This is extended term insurance and applies after premiums have been paid for thirteen weeks. The periods are guaranteed in the policy.

7. *Assignments.* The policy is, as a rule, not assignable except to a bank.

8. *Change of premium payments.* The policy provides for changing the basis of premium payment to one with less frequency.

9. *Omissions.* There are no settlement options as being of limited value in such small policies. There are no options to take the dividends in various forms on account of the cost. There is no provision for policy loans which would necessarily be small and the cost of servicing them would be disproportionately great.

PERSISTENCY

The agents' commissions for selling I.B. business are designed to discourage the writing of business that does not stay on the books; part or all of the first year's commission is charged back if the insurance lapses within a stated period. The industrial class is much exposed to the hazards of economic fluctuations with less ability to meet that hazard. In the circumstances the record is a good one.

Taking the statistics available for business in Canada as given in the report of the federal Superintendent of Insurance for 1961 we show below in Table 31.4 the ratio of terminations to the business in force at the beginning of the year for the three leading combination companies.

TABLE 31.4

	I.B.	O.B.
Company *A*	4.82%	5.73%
Company *B*	5.53%	5.54%
Company *C*	6.73%	7.28%

We compare the ratios for I.B. and O.B. business and base the ratios on the number of policies. The terminations are those due to expiry, surrender, and lapse less revivals, that is, all terminations excluding those due to death or maturity of endowment insurances.

Considering the narrow financial margins of so many of the insureds covered by I.B. policies and the attraction of any sums payable on surrender, it must be agreed that the record of I.B. terminations compares very favourably with O.B. It does indicate able and efficient control by the management, and services as a tribute to the agents serving in this field.

APPRAISAL OF INDUSTRIAL LIFE INSURANCE

The need for weekly premium insurance is evidently diminishing, and it is being replaced by monthly debit business which has grown tremendously in volume.

It is easy to point out that a minor adjustment in social security benefits would remove the need for the smaller industrial insurance policy. But something precious to human development is lost if everything is provided "automatically" and no personal choice is available in providing for death benefits, for small endowments, for education or retirement, or just long-term savings.

There is another point. As our modern society develops, a greater proportion of the spendable income of the country falls to the wage-earning classes. The personal savings or lack of it of this section of the population becomes of increasing importance to the economy of the country. A government scheme means merely a redistribution of taxes gathered. Through level premium life insurance large policy-reserves representing long-term savings of hundreds of millions of dollars can be obtained from this class which otherwise would have to be attracted from abroad. These savings are invested in wealth-producing assets or in public services for the common good.

In the debit system, combination companies have a powerful merchandising force which has been increasing in importance and sales effectiveness, notwithstanding the decline of weekly premium industrial life insurance.

CHAPTER THIRTY-TWO

Fraternal Life Insurance

THE ORIGIN OF FRATERNAL ASSOCIATIONS

In fraternal insurance we touch directly on one of the oldest instincts of mankind: to associate for mutual advantage and protection. Throughout history this was evident long before there was any thought of actuarial science or vital statistics. Although this text deals with life insurance and hence that form of protection is emphasized, we must acknowledge that elemental family needs in event of sickness of the breadwinner are at least as important as death benefits. Hence sickness benefits have played a prominent part in these associations for mutual protection. It is only in recent years that, due to the introduction of social security measures by governments and group health insurance by insurance companies, widespread sickness benefits for workers have become available. During the development of the industrial age in Britain, in the eighteenth and nineteenth centuries, sickness insurance was only available through fraternal associations called "friendly societies" and organized by the working people themselves. In Old English the word "friendly" inferred a high degree of affection or regard.

Much as existing fraternal associations like to use the phrase "ancient" there is no continuity between them and the distant past. One can refer to associations of Greeks, many centuries before the Christian era, formed to celebrate the feast days of their divinities. On the death of a member there were elaborate ceremonies "to propitiate the gods," which was part of their religion and these were paid for by the celebrants.

The Romans had similar gatherings. But these had no relation to the fraternal orders which grew up in Britain and spread to Canada and the U.S., and which are in existence today. The joining together for fellowship and mutual assistance in "death, sickness and sorrow" is the basis of fraternalism. That explains the expansion of their benefits to embrace a vast variety of seemingly unrelated activities, in addition to the love of pageantry with passwords and initiation ceremonies. Among these are the provision of sanitaria, orphanages, and old people's homes. Fraternalism has been governed to a large extent by national and religious ties, as in Canada: the Croatian Fraternal Union, Sons of Scotland, Lutheran Life Insurance Society, and so on. In some cases the ties are occupational such as Commercial Travelers and Railwaymen.

It can be understood why associations of this kind for mutual aid and benevolent purposes were left free from taxation. With the exception of Ontario and Quebec, they are free from provincial and state premium taxes both in Canada and the United States. In the 1969 amendments to the Canadian Income Tax Act fraternal societies as well as life insurance companies in Canada became subject to a business income tax and investment tax; fraternal societies are still exempt in the United States. One regrets to see this exemption from taxation being eroded in Canada.

MANCHESTER UNITY

Friendly societies, as fraternal associations are called in Britain, developed in the 1700s mainly in the industrial areas. By the end of that century there were thousands in existence in Britain with over a thousand in each of the areas comprising metropolitan London and Manchester. Their great numbers led to their recognition through legislation by the British Parliament in 1793. One of the outstanding British Friendly Societies was the Manchester Unity of Odd Fellows. This particular friendly society was founded in 1812 and by 1845 had about 400,000 members increasing at the rate of 25,000 a year and with an annual income of £250,000 and funds of £700,000. In 1845 the Society was charging an initiation fee varying with age at entry and then, for a few pence a week granted benefits which might best be expressed today as follows. For a contribution of twenty cents a week benefits of $6.00 a week were paid for sickness, with $120.00 on the death of a member and $72.00 on the death of a member's wife.

We single out the Manchester Unity for two reasons. Firstly commencing in 1845 its actuarial officers began to publish periodically figures of its mortality and sickness experience, which played a part in the development of actuarial science. A set of tables giving its sickness experience in great detail over the years 1893–97, called the Manchester Unity Tables, were outstanding and are still used in Canada and Britain.

The word "Unity" refers to the organization of the Manchester Unity as an association of "lodges" which were independent financially, with a central administrative body. In 1848 some 138 lodges were closed as insolvent and not one of the lodges then in existence had been organized before 1827. The Society as a whole flourished, but due to inadequate premiums and the fallacy of charging the same premium for all, irrespective of age, individual lodges found their funds exhausted in course of time. In 1853 the Manchester Unity adopted new rates advancing with age and made other changes and ceased to be an *assessment organization*. The significance of this last sentence will be made apparent later on.

ANCIENT ORDER OF UNITED WORKMEN

The foundation of the fraternal insurance system on the North American continent, is credited to J. J. Upchurch who established the first lodge of the Ancient Order of United Workmen in Meadville, Pennsylvania, in 1868. The object was "the elevation of labor to that standard it is justly entitled to." Fraternal benefits were a secondary consideration, but the death benefit was quite substantial and was paid for as follows. One dollar was paid by each member into the insurance fund and when a member died the proceeds of this assessment, to the limit of $2,000, were paid over to the member's widow or dependant, and another dollar was collected from each member to prepare for the next death. The movement was a great success at first: claims were paid as they arose and the cost was moderate.

ASSESSMENT LIFE INSURANCE

The A.O.U.W. became not only popular but served as an inspiration for the creation of a host of imitators. The gregarious nature of Americans delighted in the fraternal idea. A more practical form of levies by *flat assessments* at regular intervals took the place of assessments at each death and the next change was to vary the assessment with age at entry. Thus, a man entering at age 20 would pay an assessment of $1 a month and it would be presumed that this would remain unaltered throughout the member's life; the assessment increased with age at entry so that a member age 35 at entry would pay $1.75 a month. This was called the *graded assessment plan*. The fundamental idea was that premiums should be just sufficient to pay current claims, and the right to levy "extra assessments" constituted the reserve for emergencies. There was no intention of charging a level annual premium which would cover the death risk however long the member lived.

The fundamental fact is that, as the average age of the members increases, the yearly cost of the death claims also increases. It is astonishing that this fact, which was learnt so soon in Britain, and was the reason for failures among the early lodges of the Manchester Unity, took a long time to be appreciated in the U.S. The numbers of failures among the fraternals did not stop the growth of these assessment organizations. They competed bitterly with the regular life insurance companies, and could offer much lower premiums in the early years of their organization when the members were young and the claims were few. The phrase *old line* came into use in the U.S. to distinguish the regular life insurance companies with level annual premiums and policy-reserves from the assessment fraternals and assessment life insurance companies.

We referred to the severe economic conditions in the U.S. in the 1870s following the American Civil War. The failure of numerous "old line" companies in that period spurred even further the formation of assessment companies in the U.S. The growth of assessment life insurance in the period 1875 to 1895 was prodigious and at one time the business in force exceeded that of the ordinary business of the life insurance companies in the United States.

A Demonstration. In Table 32.1 we demonstrate the principle that unless there is a considerable influx of new young members in an assessment organization the cost of insurance must increase. As the cost increases so assessments increase. As this occurs, the younger men and healthier members tend to withdraw, which increases the average age and the cost still further. This vicious circle means the eventual break-up of the scheme; vigorous and honest management may delay it, but eventually it happens.

Let us assume that a fraternal assessment association has 225,000 members: 100,000 at exact ages 25 and 40 and 25,000 at age 55. We work out the net cost of $1,000 insurance payable on each death in the first year of operation and on the survivors for the second year of operation using the CAA 58-64 Ultimate Table of mortality. The first year's cost is $2.34 per $1,000 sum insured and the second year's cost is $2.52 per $1,000 sum insured. As the sum insured is payable at the end of the year all these amounts would be discounted for one year.

To keep the cost in the second year down to $2.34 would require an additional 29,186 new entrants at exact age 25. This means a 13 per cent increase in membership. To keep the premium constant for the third year would have required another substantial increase in young new members. Can this be carried on year after year? We have kept the figures simple but a more complex distribution would still show the same

TABLE 32.1

Illustration of Assessment Life Insurance
Number of New Entrants Required in a Fraternal Association to Keep Net Cost Constant,
Mortality Assumed: CAA 58–64 Ultimate Male

First Year				Second Year			
Age	Number	Deaths rate $1{,}000q_x$	No. of deaths in year	Age	No. of survivors	Death rate $1{,}000q_x$	No of deaths in year
25	100,000	1.012	101	26	99,899	.960	96
40	100,000	1.913	191	41	99,809	2.122	212
55	25,000	9.350	234	56	24,766	10.316	255
Total	225,000		526		224,474		563
Cost to each entrant: $2.34 (discounted for one year) per $1,000 sum insured				Cost to each person entering second year $2.51 (discounted for one year) per $1,000 sum insured.			
				New entrants			
				25	29,186	1.012	30
				Total	253,660		593
				Cost reduced to $2.34 (discounted for one year) per $1,000 sum insured.			

result. Increasing mortality with increasing age is a fact which cannot be avoided.

The actual record of one assessment company is of interest. In the first year the death rate was 2.76 per thousand and thus apart from expenses an assessment of $2.76 would be levied. For the second year it was 4.64, the third year 5.33 and the rate increased slowly year by year. In the fifth year it was 6.71, in the tenth year 10.70; in the fifteenth year it was 16.00 and in the twentieth year 28.90. An entrant at the time the cost was between $5 and $6 per thousand would be disillusioned by the time it rose to $15 and $25.

Group life insurance is a form of assessment insurance of the flat assessment type, but the employer not only pays part of the assessment, but bears the risk of the increasing cost. The significance of the comments made regarding "association group life insurance" in Chapter 25 and the grave doubts expressed as to its permanence should be considered in the light of the experience of fraternal assessment insurance described in this chapter.

N.F.C. TABLE AND THE DECLINE OF ASSESSMENTISM

We have dealt with assessment insurance in some detail as it refers to a fundamental principle of life insurance and its history covers an important phase in the development of life insurance. In due course the weaknesses of assessment life insurance and the failures of companies operating on that basis drew the attention of legislatures who sought to regulate it.

In 1886 a number of representatives of the fraternal benefit societies operating in the U.S. and Canada met to exchange ideas and discuss legislative activities. This body adopted officially a mortality table based on the mortality tables in use in the U.S. at that time and in 1906 this National Fraternal Congress constructed its own mortality table based on the experience of 43 fraternal societies. This is referred to as the N.F.C. Table, and was used extensively for many years for the calculation of rates and policy-reserves, by U.S. fraternals. The N.F.C. Table indicated definitely higher mortality than the AM (5) Table at the younger ages up to age 50.

The State of Massachusetts was the first state in the U.S. to legislate regarding assessment life insurance, and in 1899 it was banned in that state. The National Fraternal Congress took a prominent part in the movement away from assessment life insurance towards level premium life insurance with the corresponding policy-reserves which is often referred to in the U.S. as the *legal reserve* basis.

At the end of 1975, the amount of assessment life insurance in force in the U.S.A. was negligible compared with the $2,000,000 millions of life insurance in force with old line companies and $37,000 millions in force with fraternal societies. With the possible exception of some quite small and local bodies the fraternal societies in the U.S. operate on the legal reserve basis.

In Canada assessment life insurance has been outlawed by the federal government for a number of years, but there is still some stated to be in force in Western Canada operating under provincial licences.

Fraternal Life Insurance in Canada

STATISTICS

As outlined in Chapter 28 there are two levels of insurance supervisory bodies in Canada, federal and provincial, and their spheres of operation as outlined for life insurance, apply also to fraternal insurance. Statistics for the combined provinces are not published officially.

As at the end of 1975 the life insurance in force in Canada with fraternal societies represented less than 2% of the total life insurance in force as here indicated.

Life companies, federally registered	$206,505 millions	92.6%
Life companies, provincial charters	13,075 millions	5.9%
Fraternal benefit societies	3,309 millions	1.5%
	$222,889 millions	100.0%

Although the volume of life insurance in force in Canada with fraternals has increased in recent years its percentage of the total has decreased. In 1925 it was 6.7 per cent; in 1956 it was 2.4 per cent, and in 1975 as shown above it was 1.5 per cent. The great growth of group life insurance in recent years is one explanation. The trend in the U.S.A. has been similar.

As at the end of 1975 there were 41 fraternal benefit societies under federal registration in Canada: 15 Canadian and 26 foreign (U.S.) with total life insurance in force in Canada of $1,959 millions. The life insurance premium income of these federally registered fraternals in Canada was over $34 millions. One of the Canadian societies operates outside Canada as well.

FRATERNAL SOCIETIES AND MUTUAL BENEFIT SOCIETIES

Undoubtedly fraternal societies existing in Britain and Europe were introduced into Canada and the U.S. by immigrants from those countries. The Grand Orange Lodge of British North America with its head office in Toronto was organized in 1832. The Ancient Order of Foresters was organized in 1881 and in 1934 the members of its mortuary fund (i.e., covering death benefits) were incorporated as a mutual life insurance company, now known as the Toronto Mutual Life Insurance Company. La Société des Artisans which was organized in 1876 was converted from a fraternal to a cooperative society in 1972. The Independent Order of Foresters was organized in 1877.

In Ontario, fraternal societies in which the insurance benefits are nominal or severely limited are exempted from the regulations regarding fraternal benefit societies particularly the actuarial valuation of the benefits granted. They are called in Ontario *mutual benefit societies* and the limitation on benefits is a maximum sick benefit of $30 per week and a funeral benefit of $800. As at the end of 1968 there were 57 of these mutual benefit societies in operation in Ontario with 41,107 members.

The numbers are declining: they were 102 with 129,452 members at the end of 1958. The great majority originate with ethnic groups and apparently the members of the younger generation tend to break away from the associations of their parents. They are a negligible factor in the insurance field and no further reference will be made to them in this text.

In considering the other aspects of fraternal benefit societies in Canada and the legislation concerning them it will be adequate to consider only those registered with the Canadian federal government and those provincially incorporated and doing business in Ontario.

FRATERNAL INSURANCE LEGISLATION IN CANADA

Before 1875 there were few, if any, incorporated fraternal societies in Canada, but in the period 1875–80 a number were incorporated mostly under provincial charters—a development undoubtedly influenced by the great expansion of fraternalism in the U.S. The first legislative reference to fraternals was made by amendments to the federal Insurance Act in 1885 and this specifically exempted fraternal and benevolent associations from the laws requiring actuarially calculated policy-reserves and from the $50,000 deposit with the Receiver General. In 1897 Ontario decided to register new societies only if they adopted premium rates prepared by the Ontario Registrar of Friendly Societies.

Following the disclosures of the Armstrong-Hughes investigation into life insurance in the state of New York in 1905 the Canadian goverment appointed a Royal Commission to investigate the life insurance business in Canada, but although the Canadian investigation followed similar lines, there was one important difference: it also made an exhaustive investigation of fraternal insurance in Canada. The Royal Commission made recommendations respecting fraternal societies to the effect, that although it would be inexpedient to alter contractual rights, actuarial policy-reserves should be set up for all new business and the policy-reserves of all adequately rated business were to be kept separate and distinct for the benefit of the policyholders under such business. It also made suggestions whereby adjustments of existing business could be made to place it on a satisfactory basis.

By 1917 all Canadian federally registered benefit societies had voluntarily put their business on an adequate policy-reserve basis. In 1919 the federal Insurance Act was changed to make it apply to fraternal benefit societies. The provisions regarding assessment insurance companies were repealed as there were no more assessment companies operating under Canadian federal registration. One result of the 1919 amendment was to require foreign fraternals operating in Canada to become actuarially solvent. Federal legislation, although it could not be enforced regarding provincially licensed Canadian fraternals was effective regarding foreign fraternals operating up to then under provincial registration. However in 1921 the Ontario Act was amended to require adequate policy-reserves and four years was given each society to reach actuarial solvency.

FEDERALLY REGISTERED FRATERNALS IN CANADA

Definition. Under the federal insurance laws a "Fraternal Benefit Society" means a corporation (1) having a representative form of government, and (2) incorporated for fraternal, benevolent or religious purposes, and having (3) among its purposes the insuring of the members and the children and spouses of the members exclusively, against accident, sickness, disability or death. The phrase "having a representative form of government" means that the board of directors, executive council or governing body (however called) must be elected by the members.

Canadian Federal Fraternal Law. The main current provisions of the federal Insurance Act relating to federally registered fraternal benefit societies are outlined below.

1. The mutual principle is fundamental. The societies must not operate as trading or mercantile ventures or for purposes of commercial gain. A society must not be the property of its officers or collectors or belong to any private proprietary.

2. Before registration the society must present a report by an actuary, showing a valuation of the assets and liabilities of each of its benefit funds and establishing the solvency of each fund based on the scale of contributions in force and the adequacy of the latter. The assets have to be taken at values acceptable to the federal Superintendent of Insurance.

3. Annual statements in prescribed form are required and must contain an actuarial valuation of the liabilities under the contracts issued by the fraternal. The valuation must establish the solvency of each benefit fund based on the scale of contributions in force. Solvency means, of course, that the value of assets in each fund must exceed the policy-reserves for the benefits granted by that fund.

4. Where it appears that the assets of any fraternal or of any benefit fund are insufficient to cover the liabilities without reducing benefits or

increasing premiums, the fraternal is given a specified period in which to make good the deficiency. In default of this the certificate of registration is withdrawn.

5. Separate funds must be maintained for (*a*) accident and sickness benefits; (*b*) life, endowment and term insurance benefits.

6. The actuary of the society must certify to the reasonableness of the rates of benefit and indemnity and amounts of insurance, conditions of issue, cash and loan values, etc.

7. A foreign fraternal must keep deposited with Ottawa assets to cover its liabilities under its contracts issued in Canada.

8. Every fraternal benefit society has to make a deposit of $10,000 before being registered.

The Actuary and Fraternals. One is impressed by the power and responsibility place upon the actuary in fraternal benefit societies registered with Ottawa. The Act requires the actuary to be a Fellow of the Canadian Institute of Actuaries.

There are no specified bases set out for the actuarial valuation of the contracts issued by fraternals registered at Ottawa. The actuary is allowed considerable leeway, but with the great variety of benefits issued by fraternals it is perhaps simpler and more practicable for the federal Superintendent of Insurance to challenge any basis considered inadequate rather than specify rigid bases for a multitude of benefits.

Policy Provisions. It will be noted that all the above items of federal law, refer to matters of solvency and deposits, as is the case with insurance companies. The question of details of policy contracts and beneficiary clauses are left to the provinces, as explained in Chapter 28.

ONTARIO FRATERNAL SOCIETY LAWS

In Ontario fraternal benefit societies are called simply fraternal societies. The definition of a *fraternal society* and the conditions it has to fulfil to obtain a licence and continue to be licensed by the Province of Ontario are basically the same as those already outlined as required for a federally registered fraternal benefit society.

With a few exceptions the bulk of fraternal insurance in Ontario is transacted through federally licensed societies. There were only six provincially incorporated fraternal societies operating in Ontario in 1974, and several of these were limited to firemen, police, civil servants, and secondary school teachers.

There is one specific provision relating to the contracts issued by fraternals which should be noted here. The constitution, by-laws, and rules (and amendments from time to time of them) of the fraternals are part of the contract as well as the application and medical statement of the applicant. This differs from the contract issued by a life insurance company as outlined in Chapter 16.

Provincial laws regarding provincially incorporated fraternal societies tend to be more specific regarding procedures in the event of an impairment of funds, or as described in the Ontario law: "in the event of an epidemic or other unforseen contingency." This is desirable for relatively small organizations might look to the provincial authorities for guidance in such an emergency.

THE FUTURE OF FRATERNALISM

As was indicated earlier, in recent years the increase of life insurance in force under fraternal benefit societies has been far less than among life insurance companies. The development of group life insurance and group sickness plans as part of negotiations between employers and employees and otherwise; the increase in social security measures covering widows, orphans, and the aged needy, may have reduced the appeal of association for fraternal purposes. There has also been a change in social habits and the appeal of the monthly lodge meetings has waned.

At its best fraternal life insurance is represented by one of the major Canadian fraternal organizations with $7,296 millions of sums insured in force whose individual lodges maintain the spirit of fraternalism in fellowship and mutual assistance in "death, sickness and sorrow." Its policies covering life insurance and disability benefits differ little from those of the large life insurance companies. A very substantial part of its business is done in the U.S.A. and in Britain.

Fraternalism has played an important part in the history of life insurance. The spirit of fraternalism is a valuable one. It is to the good of a country, especially a growing country like Canada, that the spirit of fraternalism should be encouraged. It is the inborn instinct of men to combine in groups for mutual advantage and protection and this is the essence of life insurance, pensions, and annuities to which this text is devoted. It is this spirit which has created both the fraternal insurance societies and the life insurance companies.

Index

E

J

K

L

S

www.ingramcontent.com/pod-product-compliance
Lightning Source LLC
LaVergne TN
LVHW100247210926
848480LV00003B/854
* 9 7 8 1 4 8 7 5 8 7 3 0 7 *